North-East Biodiversity and Sustainable Economic Development

ABOUT THE EDITORS

Dr. Atul Kumar Gupta, IFS (1982 batch) is MBA, Postgraduate in Zoology, Sociology, Forestry, Wildlife Management, and PhD from Cambridge University, U. K. Dr. Gupta is currently serving as PCCF & Chief Wildlife Warden, Forest Department, Government of Tripura, and also working as CEO & PD, Indo-German Project; MS, Tripura Biodiversity Board and VC, State Medicinal Plants Board. Dr. Gupta has about 30 years of field-based experience in planning, formulation, implementation and monitoring of several uni- and multi-disciplinary projects. Dr. Gupta has to his credits many peer reviewed and popular articles, edited books, book chapters, Abstracts to National and International seminars/ workshops, project reports, etc. on varied topics.

Er Dhiman Daschaudhuri an Agricultural Engineer from Marathawada Agricultual University, Parbhani, Maharashtra is now working as Technical Officer in Agro-meteorological Advisory Services of ICAR Research Complex for NEH Region, Tripura Centre. He has 15 years of working experience in Agro-meteorological Research. He has published 9 full length papers in different national scientific journals, 5 short communication, 11 book chapters, 1 research bulletin and 3 edited books, besides being involved in conducting many seminars, training programme and review meetings.

Biswendu Bhattacharjee is post graduate in Journalism and Mass Communication. He has authored several books on environment science for secondary students of Tripura besides practicing professional journalism over past one and half decades in nationally and internationally renowned media organisations. He has been trained in environmental journalism in United States under prestigious IV Programme of the State department. Mr. Bhattacharjee has also been the recipient of number of fellowships and awards for professional excellence and environmental activism.

Dr Mrinmoy Datta had Ph.D. in Soil Science & Agricultural Chemistry from the University of Calcutta and is currently Joint Director in Tripura Centre of ICAR Research Complex for NEH Region. Dr. Datta has 34 years of research experience in the domain of Soil Chemistry and Soil Fertility, Agroforestry, Farming System Research and Agrometeorology He has published 55 research papers in Indian and International Journal, 14 popular articles, 40 abstracts in National Symposium, 11 book chapters, 4 Books, 2 edited books and 11 nos. Research/ Extension Bulletin. He is also recipient of Bharat Excellence award by the Friendship Forum of India, New Delhi in 2009.

North-East Biodiversity and Sustainable Economic Development

Issues and Challenges

Editors

Atul Kumar Gupta

Dhiman Daschaudhuri

Biswendu Bhattacharjee

M. Datta

CONCEPT PUBLISHING COMPANY PVT. LTD.

NEW DELHI-110059

ISBN-13 : 978-93-5125-030-2

First Published 2014

Published and Printed by

Concept
Since 1974

Concept Publishing Company Pvt. Ltd.
A/15-16, Commercial Block, Mohan Garden
New Delhi-110059 (India)
T: 25351460, 25351794, *F*: 091-11-25357109
E: publishing@conceptpub.com, W: www.conceptpub.com
Editorial Office: H-13, Bali Nagar, New Delhi-110 015, India.

Cataloging in Publication Data--*Courtesy:* D.K. Agencies (P) Ltd. <docinfo@dkagencies.com>

National Seminar on Biodiversity (2010 : Agartala, India)

North-east biodiversity and sustainable economic development : issues and challenges/ editors, Atul Kumar Gupta ... [et al.].
p. cm.
Includes bibliographical references and index.
ISBN 9789351250302

1. Biodiversity conservation--India--Tripura--Congresses. 2. Biodiversity--India, Northeastern--Congresses. 3. Sustainable development--India--Tripura--Congresses. 4. Sustainable development--India, Northeastern--Congresses. I. Gupta, Atul Kumar. II. Title.

DDC 333.95160954 23

This Edited Volume is dedicated
to
Late Professor Amitabh Sinha

Foreword

Tripura, a hilly State in North-East India with nearly 60 per cent forest cover can be a great location for biodiversity conservation. The factors that operate against biodiversity conservation in this State are its high population density (350/sq. km) and their dependency on the natural resources for survival. Agriculture and allied activities are the mainstay of the economy and provide employment to about 64 per cent of the population. Food crop production dominates the agricultural sector (62%) followed by cash crops such as tea and rubber. In the context of understanding the biodiversity values crucial for the well-being of the people of Tripura and North-East India, and the threats these values face, the workshop convened on the Environment Day on 5th June, 2010 by ARPAN, Tripura has become extremely relevant. It is notable that 61 per cent of the authors of the 18 abstracts that were submitted for the workshop were from Tripura.

The topics presented were varied but important. Some covered broader topics like biodiversity and its values, biodiversity conservation in North-East India with reference to Tripura, and fresh water biodiversity in North-East India with reference to Tripura. Their findings seem to suggest that high income countries are not technically more efficient in maintaining biodiversity and the diverse climatic regime of Tripura could be the basis for its rich biodiversity. Since Tripura is largely an agricultural State, knowledge on experiments on bacterial wilt disease affecting tomato and information on seed protein variability in diverse indigenous rice varieties become exceedingly important. Methods for conservation agriculture in North-Eastern Hill regions have been suggested and it appears that indigenous conservation practices in Nagaland have increased economic returns from the field by three-fold.

The people of North-East India, live close to nature and have great faith in the curative properties of medicinal plants, and this is evident in some of the abstracts presented. More than 270 species of medicinal plants have been identified in Tripura which give the State a unique position in traditional systems of medicine. Another Chapter discusses 28 edible fruit plants in Cachar district in Assam which have medicinal properties against dysentery, jaundice, diabetes, stomach disorders, cough, and fever. Some of these plant products also have anti-septic properties, can cure skin diseases and purify blood. Over the past few decades, an increasing prevalence of antibiotic resistant strains of bacteria has underscored the need for alternatives. It has been reported that several members of the Rubiaceae family, 48 genera out of 611, have anti-bacterial properties which would be vital for strengthening the health of mankind. When the world faces increasing incidents of cancer affecting people of all age classes it is comforting to know that anthocyanins isolated from the corms of taro (*Colocasia* sp.) are reported to have anti-inflammatory and anti-oxidant properties which could protect the intestine from carcinogens.

During the workshop, suggestions emerged from a number of other topics which were discussed. Fish conservation in North-East India's rivers, and for that matter in any river system in India, may need modern tools like GIS and remote sensing but for the fish populations to thrive there should be controlled over unregulated fishing particularly in the spawning grounds. Besides, habitats should be protected from over-exploitation, especially excessive sand collection, garbage disposal and pollution. Exotic harmful weeds such as *Ipmoea carnea* and *Eichornia crassipes* should be eradicated from aquatic systems. If there are species like mahseer, cat fishes and murrel, the concerned agencies could think about promoting sport fishing which can bring in benefits to the local population and paving the way for the protection of fishes and their habitats. The problem of E-waste, which is hazardous to the environment, was highlighted and needs to be addressed. It has also been suggested during the workshop that the media which reports on environmental issues could be much more effective if it were united in fighting for the cause of biodiversity conservation.

I admire and wish best wishes to the organizers of the Workshop for taking pains to organize this workshop which has led to this volume containing valuable information for strengthening conservation in North-East India. I congratulate the entire Editorial team led by Dr. A. K. Gupta, a forester, wildlife biologist and conservationist for bringing together this volume of valuable and informative Chapters that wil not only be useful to the scientists but also would make an interesting and informative reading to the general public for raising awareness towards conservation of biodiversity.

Dr. A.J.T. Johnsingh
Naturalist
Ex Dean, Wildlife Institute of India, Dehradun
Nature Conservation Foundation
Mysore and WWF (India)

Preface

North-East India (2,62,040 km^2) comprising of the States of Arunachal Pradesh, Assam, Meghalaya, Manipur, Tripura, Mizoram, Nagaland and Sikkim can be physiographically categorized into the Eastern Himalayas, North-east hills, the Brahmaputra and Barak valley plains. The region has a wide diversity of zonation, viz., agro-climatic zones, Alpine Zone, Temperate Zone, Sub-tropical Hill Zone, Sub-Tropical Plain Zone, Mild Tropical Humid Hill Zone and Mild Tropical Humid Plain Zone. The region is also the abode of approximately 225 out of total 450 recorded tribes in the country. The cultural and customary variations and differentiations have an important role in understanding biodiversity conservation and management issues. The region is rich in medicinal plants and many other rare and endangered taxa. Its high endemism in higher plants, vertebrates and avian diversity has qualified it to be a biodiversity hotspot. A total of 51 Forest types have been identified in the region that are broadly classified into six major forest types, viz., tropical moist, deciduous forests, tropical semi-evergreen forests, tropical wet evergreen forests, subtropical forests, temperate forests and alpine forests. Out of the 9 important vegetation types of India, 6 are found in the North-Eastern region. These forests harbour 40 out of 54 species of gymnosperms, 500 out of 1,012 species of Pteridophytes, 825 out of 1,145 species of orchids, 80 out of 90 species of rhododendrons, 60 out of 110 species of bamboo, 25 out of 56 species of canes. In terms of floral species richness, the highest diversity is reported from the States of Arunachal Pradesh (5,000) and Sikkim (4,000) amongst the North Eastern States belonging to about 200 families out of 315 recorded from North-East India. Some of the families such as *Nepanthaceae, Illiciaceae* and *Clethraceae* are unique in the world. These families are reported from the South-East Asian countries and are represented by a limited number of species like *Clethra* sp. and *Nepenthus khasiana* in North-East India. It is pertinent to mention that 10 per cent of the total flowering plants in the country are endangered. Of the 1500 endangered floral species, 800 alone are reported from North-East India. The faunal diversity is also varied in nature. However, the recent discovery of new faunal species across the North-Eastern regions [such as the *Tawang, Macaque* (*Macaca* spp.), extended range the Chinese goral (*Nemorhaedatus caudatus*), and leaf deer (*Mentiacus putaoensis*)] calls for immediate actions for more extensive research and systematic documentation of biodiversity of the North-East.

The main stay of economy in the entire North-East India is agrarian in nature and, therefore, agriculture has been one main source of livelihood amongst the hills and the plain tribes. About 63.3 per cent of the total geographical area in the North-East is under forest cover, 5.38 per cent of the area is being used for non-agricultural purposes, 9.06 per cent is reportedly barren land, 6.64 per cent is the uncultivated land excluding fallow and only 15.31 per cent is the net sown area in the region. The settled agriculture is supplemented, rather overshadowed at places by the shifting cultivation, locally called *jhuming*, which is practiced by many tribal groups. *Jhuming*, wherein as many as 35 varieties of crop is raised on single plot, may be ranked as one of the most ancient systems of farming believed to have originated around 7000 BC in the Neolithic period. That the *jhuming* has survived so long is an indication of its intimate and intricate linkages with the ethos of the social and cultural values of the tribal communities.

This edited volume *North-East Biodiversity and Sustainable Economic Development* is a collection of papers from across the region presented and discussed in a National Symposium organized to observe the Environment Day. The chapters describe and explore wide range of topics in the domain of biodiversity highlighting issues and challenges, threats to biodiversity, role of media in conservation of biodiversity, biodiversity and human interference and finally socio-economic issues and biodiversity. The sustainable development of the region mainly depends upon agriculture and allied activities, of which rich biodiversity of the region provides much needed food security to the people who are away from mainstream development. Agriculture sector in North-

Eastern region (NER) provides livelihood to almost 84 per cent population but it accounts for only 30 per cent of Net State Domestic Product (NSDP). Contribution of this region to national foodgrain production is hardly 1.5 per cent, which is insufficient to sustain 3.8 per cent of country's population. Though agriculture in NER grew at a much higher rate (3.8%) than the average for the country but still the region has to import foodgrains for its consumption. As the region hosts species-rich tropical rainforests and supports diverse flora and fauna and several crop species, the present volume is an attempt to present the readers a treasure in this direction, would definitely help the readers to enrich the horizon of knowledge and unravel a roadmap to utilise the available diversity for the sustainable development in the region to address the issue of poverty alleviation thus helping fulfiliing one of the major goals of Millennium Development Goals in the region and overall across the South-East Asia.

Editors

Acknowledgements

It gives us the immense pleasure to express our deep gratitude to Sri Jitendra Chaudhury, Hon'ble Minister for Forest, Government of Tripura, Shri Pabitra Kar, Hon'ble Member, Tripura Legislative Assembly, Tripura & Chairman, Tripura Industries Development Corporation, and Sri R.P. Tangwan, IFS, the then Principal Chief Conservator of Forest, Government of Tripura for kindly consenting to be the Patrons of the Organizing Committee for National Seminar on Biodiversity held at Agartala, Tripura during June 5-7, 2010. The seminar was organized to address the issues of implications of forestry in economy with rising societal demands on a sustainable basis. The deliberations were also made on topics addressing how to minimize the gaps between the demand and supply for the forest based products linked very intimately with the livelihoods of the forest dependent communities, with special focus on Tripura.

We express our deep sense of gratitude to the members of the Advisory Board, namely, Dr A K Gupta, IFS, PCCF & CWLW; Dr M Datta, Joint Director, ICAR, Tripura Centre; Dr S N Sen, Director, Department of Agriculture; Dr C Bandopadhayay, Director, Department of Horticulture; Shri P Biswas, IFS, Conservator of Forest; Dr J R Dhanze, Dean, College of Fisheries; Dr K Sasikumar, IFS, CEO, Medicinal Plant Board; Sri Pranab Sarkar, Secretary, Agartala Press Club for their valuable suggestions and guidance for successful organization of the event.

Our heartfelt thanks are also due to ONGC, Tripura Asset; Tripura State Pollution Control Board; NEEPCO; TIDC Ltd.; and Tripura Biodiversity Board for their financial contributions and technical and administrative support for organizing the event.

We are equally indebted to every member of Organizing

Committee and the member of ARPAN Society for their untiring efforts in making the event a great success and also bringing out this publication.

Editorial Team

Contents

Part 4
BIODIVERSITY AND HUMAN INTERFACE

Part 5
SOCIO-ECONOMIC ISSUES AND BIODIVERSITY

List of Contributors

Barbhuiya, Anjam Hussain, Research Scholar, Department of Life Science, Assam University Silchar-11
E-mail anjam.barbhuiya@gmail.com

Baruah, M.K., Department of Botany, Cachar College, Silchar-788001, Assam, India
E-mail: mkb_taxonomy@rediffmail.com

Bhattacharjee, Biswendu, Correspondent, United News of India, Agartala Bureau, Tripura, Regular Contributor, Times of India
E-mail: biswendu.tripura@gmail.com

Biswas, P.

Biswas, Swati, Research Associate, NAIP Comp-III, Division of Agronomy, ICAR Research Complex for NEH Region, Umroi Road, Umiam-793103, Meghalaya
E-mail: swati0biswas@gmail.com.

Chakraborty, G., Department of Botany, Cachar College, Silchar-788001, Assam, India.

Chattopadhyay, Krishnendu, Crop Improvement Division, Central Rice Research Institute, Cuttack, Orissa-753006
E-mail: krishnendu_c@sify.com

Chaudhury, Jitendra, Ministry for Forest, Rural Development, Industries & Commerce, Government of Tripura
E-mail: chaudhuryj@hotmail.com

Choudhury, K.D., Department of Life Sciences, Assam University, Silchar-788011.

Choudhury, Katyayani Dutta, Ethnobotany and Medicinal Plant Research Laboratory, Department of Life Science and

Bioinformatics, Assam University. Silchar-788011
E-mail: katyayanidc@gmail.com

Choudhury, M. Dutta, Ethnobotany and Medicinal Plant Research Laboratory, Department of Life Science and Bioinformatics, Assam University, Silchar-788011.

Choudhury, P.D., Department of Botany, Cachar College, Silchar-788001, Assam, India.

Chowdhury, P., Technical Officer, Division of Agricultural Engineering, ICAR Research Complex for NEH Region, Umroi Road, Umiam-793103, Meghalaya.

Das, Avijit, ICAR Research Complex for NEH Region, Tripura Centre, Lembucherra.

Das, S.P., Sr. Scientist, ICAR Research Complex for NEH Region, Lembucherra, Tripura-799210.

Das, Sukhen Chandra, Assistant Professor, College of Agriculture, Lembucherra, Tripura-799210, Tripura, India
E-mail: sukhenchandra@rediffmail.com

Daschaudhuri, D., Technical Officer (Agromet), ICAR Research Complex for NEH Region, Tripura Centre, Lembucherra-799210, Tripura
E-mail: dhiman.neh@gmail.com.

Datta, M., Joint Director, ICAR Research Complex for NEH Region, Lembucherra, Tripura-799210
E-mail : mdatta2@rediffmail.com.

De, L.C., NRC for Orchids, Pakyong-737106, Sikkim.

Deb, A.K., Medicinal plants Board of Tripura, Forest Research Division, Gandhigram, Agartala-12, Tripura, India.

Debbarma, Bijit, Lecturer, Department of Management, Tripura University, Suryamanninagar-799130 E-mail: bijitdb@yahoo.com.

Debnath, Sajal, Faculty of Information Technology, Department of Management, Tripura University.

Dutta, P., Programme Coordinator, Divyodaya KVK-West Tripura, Chebri-799207.

Dutta, Pranab, Programme Coordinator,

Ghosh, A.K., Centre for Environment and Development, 329, Jodhpur Park, Kolkata 700068
E-mail: cedkolkata@yahoo.com.

Gupta, Atul Kumar, PCCF, Forest Department of Govt. of Tripura, Agartala.

Islam, N., SMS-Animal Science
E-mail: nurul1977@gmail.com

Malik, S., Senior Scientist-Poultry Division, ICAR RC for NEH Region, Tripura Centre.

Medhi, R.P., NRC for Orchids, Pakyong-737106, Sikkim.

Misra, Anupam, Principal Scientist and Head, Division of Agriculture Extension, ICAR Research Complex for NEH Region, Umroi Road, Umiam-793103, Meghalaya.

Munda, G.C., Principal Scientist and PI, NAIP Comp-III, Division of Agronomy, ICAR Research Complex for NEH Region, Umroi Road, Umiam-793103, Meghalaya.

Nagaraj, K.V., Head, Department of Mass Communication, Assam University, Silchar.

Nath, Rumki, Ethnobotany and Medicinal Plants Research Laboratory, Department of Life Science, Assam University, Silchar-788011
E-mail: rumki_nath2000@yahoo.com

Ngachan, S.V., Director, ICAR Research Complex for NEH Region, Lembucherra, Tripura-799210.

Ngachan, S.V., Director, ICAR Research Complex for NEH Region, Umiam, Meghalaya, Umroi Road, Umiam-793103, Meghalaya.

Rahman, Britan, SMS, Krishi Vigyan Kendra, Chebri-799207, West Tripura.

Roy, Saswati, Ethnobotany and Medicinal Plants Research Laboratory, Department of Life Science, Assam University, Silchar-788011
E-mail: roysaswati97@gmail.com.

Saha, Ratan K., Department of Fish Health and Environment, College of Fisheries, Central Agricultural University, Lembucherra, Post Box No. 60, Agartala.
E-mail: ratankumarsaha123@rediffmail.com

Sharma, Jai Prakash, ICAR Research Complex for Eastern Region, Research Centre, Plandu, Ranchi, Jharkhand-834010.
E-mail: jaibina_05@yahoo.co.in,
dr.jai.prakash.sharma@gmail.com

Singh, R.K., Senior Scientist (SWCE) and Head I/c, Division of Agricultural Engineering, ICAR Research Complex for NEH Region, Umroi Road, Umiam-793103, Meghalaya.

Singha, A.K., Senior Scientist, Zonal Project Directorate, Zone-III, ICAR RC for NEH Region, Umium (Barapani), Meghalaya-793103.

Singha, A.K., Sr. Scientist, ZPD, Zone-III, ICAR, Umium (Barapani), Meghalaya-793103.

Sinha, Amitabha, Reader, Department of Analytical Applied Economics, Tripura University, Agartala
E-mail: omitabha@gmail.com

Upadhyaya, Deepak, Assistant Professor, Department of Journalism and Mass Communication, Tripura University, Agartala-799130
E-mail: deepakupadhyaya81@gmail.com

A 20 Point Recommendations for Sustainable Biodiversity in Tripura

1. Detail documentation of aquatic biodiversity resources and issue based intervention.
2. Measures to contain the habitat loss of aquatic resources and conservation of natural wetlands.
3. Strict implementation of laws related to conservation of biodiversity.
4. Set Up Biodiversity Management Committee (BMC) at Block level on priority basis.
5. Beneficiary-wise, location-wise Register has to be made mandatory biodiversity resources.
6. Apposite steps to be taken for soil conservation especially to soil eco-system, soil health, checking soil and mapping of soil microbial diversity.
7. Steps to be taken for conservation of Rudrasagar and other wetlands with a comprehensive approach to strengthen Wetland Board.
8. Wetland conservation has to be incorporated in all development plans.
9. Agartala City urgently need of a Master Plan.
10. Agartala needs a practical approach for mobility plan.
11. Integrated plan for conservation of urban biodiversity.
12. A comprehensive training programme has to be framed on biodiversity and environmental issues for the working journalists.
13. Use micro media in awareness campaign.
14. Emphasis to be given on media sensitization.
15. *In situ* and *ex situ* preservation of Germplasm with special reference to rice.
16. Steps need to be taken for preservation of local *jhum* varieties of rice and vegetables.

17. Enhancement of sustainable medicinal plant research and ensure the codification under the provisions of Intellectual Property Right Act.
18. Promotion of Clean Development Mechanism (CDM) in Tripura for environmental sustainability.
19. Kerala model has to be replicated for promotion of eco-tourism in Tripura.
20. Develop and practice the mechanism of real value assessment of natural resources for the benefit of the local people.

Part 1
Biodiversity: Issues and Challenges

1
Biodiversity for Prosperity: Unique Assemblage of Biodiversity and Conservation Challenges in Northeast India, with Special Reference to Tripura

A.K. Gupta

Introduction

Northeast India (lying between 22-30 degree N latitude and 89-97 degree E longitude) is one of the richest in biological values and is considered as the geographical 'gateway' for much of India's flora and fauna, owing, mainly to its location at the confluence of Indian, Indo-Malayan and Indo-Chinese biogeographic regions and has been a meeting place of the Himalayan Mountains and peninsular India. The immense variety of the climatic, edaphic and altitudinal variations in Northeast India have resulted in a great range of ecological habitats, lowland-highland transition zone supporting the highest diversity of biomass or ecological communities where species diversities within these communities are also extremely high. Northeast India is considered a part of the [northward migrating] 'Deccan Peninsula' that first touched the Asian landmass after the breakup of Gondwanaland in the early Tertiary Period.

Northeast India is blessed with a wide range of physiography and eco-climatic conditions. The State of Assam has extensive flood plains, while Khangchendzonga in Sikkim stands 8586 m tall. Cherrapunjee in the State of Meghalaya holds the record for the highest rainfall in a single month (9300 mm) as well as the most in a year (26461 mm) in India, while the nearby Mawsynram has the world's highest average rainfall (11873 mm). The forests in the region are extremely diverse in structure and composition and combine tropical and temperate forest types, alpine meadows and cold deserts. There are regions, for example, in the State of Sikkim, where the faunal assemblages also change rapidly from tropical to subtropical, temperate, alpine and finally to cold desert forms.

After the Andaman and Nicobar Islands and the Western Ghats, Northeast India forms the main region of tropical forests in India, especially the species—rich tropical rain forests. The tropical semi-evergreen and moist deciduous forests in the lowlands of this region extend south and west into the subcontinent, and east into Southern China and Southeast Asia. The subtropical forests extend from northern Pakistan and adjacent Afgahanistan through Northeast India to Southwest China. Each of the eight States of the region namely Arunachal Pradesh, Assam, Meghalaya, Manipur, Mizoram, Nagaland, Sikkim and Tripura, boast of several endemics in flora as well as fauna. This region represents an important part of the Indo-Myanmar biodiversity hotspot, one of the 25 global biodiversity hotspots recognized currently (Ramakantha, Gupta & Ajith, 2003).

The Floral Diversity in Northeast India and Tripura

This region accounts for nearly 50 per cent of the total number of plant species in India as a whole, and about one third of total northeastern flora is endemic. However, this region also exhibits close affinity and resemblance with Indo-Malayan and other neighbouring and far off countries. In over 1.7 lakh sq. km of forest area in the northeast, more than 200 families (about 7500 species) out of a total of 315 families of angiosperms are represented in this region, and Sikkim support about 5000 species of flowering plants. It is considered that the northeastern region has been the originator of gene pools of citrus, banana, mango and rice. The pitcher plant (*Nepenthes Khasiana)* is endemic to Meghalaya and Siroy Lily (*Lilium mackiniae)* is endemic in the eastern border area of Manipur.

Presence of many primitive flowering plants (*Magnolia pealiana, M. qustavii, Manglietia sp., Myrica esculenta, Corylopsis himalayana,* etc. and families, such as, Coriariaceae, Nepenthaceae, Tumeraceae, llliciaceae, Rupiaceae, Siphonodontaceae and Tetracentraceae and monogeneric are unique features of flowering plants in the northeast India. Among the species representing the tropical forests (located at Indo-Myanmar border), such as, *Dipterocarpus tuberculatus, D. turbinatus and Melanorrhea usiṭata,* are few unique species *vis-à-vis* found in India elsewhere. Some of the northeastern states (Sikkim) exhibit floristic elements of Sino-Japanese near and far-off lands. Certain areas in the northeast region have also been responsible for Isolation of certain species. Northeast India has presence of about 700 species of orchids (34 of these are listed among the threatened plants of India) out of a total of 1300 in India (158 genera). Arunachal Pradesh alone has about 530 species of orchids, of which many are of medicinal importance, being used as aphrodisiac, analgesic and for longevity. The regions also abounds in species for human consumption, be it medicinal plants, species yielding Non-Timber Forest Products (NTFP), and bamboo. Tripura has about 65 such species yielding NTFPs and 266 species producing medicinal value. Sikkim contribute for human consumption from about 180 species; 430 medicinal plants from Manipur.

Out of 82 species of rhododendrons recorded from Himalaya, 70 species are confined to eastern Himalaya, including 45 new species alone from Sikkim. Most of these are now highly rare and endangered facing extinction pressure.

Northeast is heaven for bamboo species, which found their uses among the people of the northeast from proverbial 'cradle to coffin'. Of the total about 140 reported species on bamboo in India, 64 species (from 22 genera) are found in northeast, of which about 26 species are considered rare and endangered. There is a definite distribution pattern among the species based on the altitude; *Bambusa, Dendrocalamus, Dinochloa, Cephalostachyum* and *Neohouzeoua* are mostly confined to the lower altitude upto 800 m and *Arundinaria, Chimonobambusa, Semiarundinaria, Sinobambusa, Thamnocalamus* and *Phyllostachys* beyond that altitude. The largest contribution to the growing stock is from *Dendrocalamus strictus (45%), followed by Melocanna baccifera (20%), Bambusa bambos (13%), D. hamittonii (7%)* and B. *tulda (5%),* with the rest sharing 6 per cent. In Northeast India, conifers are represented by 28 species. *Pinus Kesia* and *Gnetum gnemon* from Khasi, Jaintia and the Naga hills, *Cycas pectinata* in *Kamrup, Podocarpus nerifolia,* a broad-leaved gymnosperm is reported from the Khasi hills, but also occurs in the tropical forests of Barak Valley in Manipur State and in Assam. Northeast India is also known for a variety of saprophytic and high diversity of non- flowering plants. Of about 1000 species of ferns found in India, nearly half are represented in Northeastern India. *Dipteris wallichii, Aspienium nidus. Osmunda cinnamomea, O. claytoniana. O. regalis, Helminthostachys zeylanica, Botrychium lanuginusam, Angiopteris evecta, Cyathea gigantean, C. spinulosa, Psilotum nudum, phagopteres auriculata* etc., are some of the rare non-flowering vascular plants. Of these, Platycerium wallichii (Staghorn Fern) from Manipur appears to be the first report of its occurrence within India. This epiphytic fern grows in the moist deciduous forests in the Indo-Myanmar border areas in great profusion. Fern-allies such as Lycopodium and Selaginella are also diverse in this region. The region is exceedingly rich in lichens, mosses and liverworts. These seemingly unimportant plants need to be investigated, studied, appreciated and above all, protected, as they serve vital ecological roles as soil protectors; contribute to the recycling of nutrients and water, offer food and shelter to an assemblage of invertebrates and take a part in purification and carbon sequestration (Ramakantha, Gupta & Ajith, 2003).

Floral Biodiversity of Tripura

The research on status of flora identifying 379 species of trees, 320 shrubs, 581 herbs, 165 climbers, 16 climbing shrubs, 35 ferns, 45 epiphytes and 4 parasites (Total 1,545 taxa) reveal that there are 50 plants species restricted to Tripura and its neighbouring States. Out of them 7 are endemic and 18 are rare plants. *Angiopteris evecta*, a fern and *Gnetum montanum*, a giant climber belonging to Gymnosperm are two rare species but occur in profusely in Trishna Sanctuary. Tree ferns (*Cyathia* spp.), which are also primitive and endangered, are found in South Tripura. There are 24 species of orchids of which and *Dendrobium* has the highest species diversity (14 species). Endangered orchids like Blue vanda (*Vanda caerulea*) and Red vanda (*Renunthera imschootiana*) are found in the state. There are 266 species of medicinal plants in the State (68 trees, 39 shrubs, 71 herbs and 88 climbers). Maximum value of *Plant-Diversity Index (Shannon-Weiner)* reported is 5.23, which generally ranges from 3-4, indicating presence of a variety of species uniformly.

The floral diversity of Trishna WLS is unique all over its area. A total of about 230 tree species, 400 species of herbs, 110 species of shrubs and about 150 species of climbers have been recorded in the sanctuary. Besides, large numbers of orchid species have also been noted in the sanctuary. Of the total vegetation diversity, many plant species are rich in medicinal values. Some of the major tree species are (local name): Dipterocarpus turbinatus (garjan), Schima wallichi (kanak), Terminalia belerica (bahera), Artocarpus chaplasha (chamal), Terminalia chebula (harr), Syzygium cumini (jamun), Ficus species (butt), Dillenia pentagyna (hargaza), Careya arborea (kumira), Sterculia villosa (udal), Shorea robusta (sal), Albizzia procera (koroi), etc. The tree density is about 111 trees/ha. The tree volume varies between 21 to 28 m^3. The non-clump forming bamboos have 1252 culms/ha. The heterogeneous mixture of ground flora is indicated in the agglomeration of various monocots and dicots, herbs, shrubs, climbers, lichens, ferns, fern allies, underground rhizomes and regeneration of species.

Medicinal Plants Resource

Tripura has one of the oldest, richest and most diverse cultural traditions associated with use of medical plants. There are large number of village based herbal medicines practitioners who have traditional knowledge of herbal home remedies of ailments & nutrition. Besídes the above, registered medical practitioners of modified system of Indian Medicine (such as Ayurveda) use medical plants. The herbal medicines used by rural people including tribal have not yet been documented. Compiling an exhaustive inventory of medicinal plants in the State is the need of the hour. So far about 266 species of medicinal plants (68 trees, 39 shrubs, 71 herbs and 88 climbers) have been identified and documented.

Bamboo and Cane Resource

Bamboo plays a very vital role in the economy of the State as it serves the artisan and non-artisan users of the state. The bamboo forests of Tripura may be fitted into the following types and sub-types as per Champion and Seth classification.

(i) Moist mixed Deciduous Forest – 1/3/3C/C3
(ii) Secondary moist Bamboo Brakers – 1/2/2B/2Si

Species of bamboo found in Tripura

A total of 19 species of bamboo are reported in the State; Barak (*Bambusa balcooa*), Bari (*Bambusa polymorpha*), Mritinga (*Bambusa tulda*), Muli (Melocanna baccifera), Kai (*Bambusa nutans*), Paora (*Bambusa teres*), Rupai (*Dendrocalamus longispathus*), Dolu (*Neohuzeaua dullooa*), Makal (*Bambusa pallida*), Pecha (*Dendrocalamus hamiltonii*), Kailyai (*Oxytenanthera nigrociliata*), Kanak kaich (*Bambusa offinis*), Lanthi bans (*Dendrocalamus strictus*), Tetua (*Bambusa spp.*), Ish (*Bambusa spp.*), Jai (*Bambusa spp.*), Bombash (*Bambusa spp.*), Sairil/Wadu bamboo (*Melocalamus compactiflorus*), Bosai (*bambusa spp.*).

The Faunal Diversity in Northeast India and Tripura

There is a paucity of exploration and research concerning the fauna of Northeast India. Mammals are often considered the best-known groups, especially the ungulates. However, a new species of barking deer,' Leaf Deer (*Muntiacus putaoensis*), which was recently discovered in Myanmar, is reported from the forests of Arunachal Pradesh in the year 2003 as a new record for India, and this amply justifies the above observation that much is yet to be identified, named and studied in Northeast India. The remoteness of the region, difficult terrain as well as the severe hunting pressures exerted by the people around their immediate surroundings in many parts of the region a make it extremely difficult to document the fauna of the region (Ramakantha, Gupta & Ajith, 2003).

Primates

Of the total sixteen species of primates in India, 11 are reported from the Northeast India as per the revised taxonomy description. However, excepting three species, all are facing severe threat of extinction due to various anthropogenic reasons. Hoolock gibbon (*Bunopithecus hoolock*) is the only ape in India, has been reported from 6 of the 8 northeastern states, with uncertain distribution in Nagaland and no reporting from Sikkim. The eastern limit for this lesser ape is Salween River in Myanmar and its range extends to Southern China. In spite of extensive distribution range, this species faces severe extinction pressure due to its own specific habitat requirements and specialized behvioural traits and ecological needs, such as frugivory, brachiation for movement, monogamy, small family size, etc. Moreover, hunting is another major cause of its disappearance, mainly linked with superstition that its body possesses medicinal properties. Among langur, there are three species, namely, Phayre's (*Trachypithecus phayeri*), capped (*Trachypithecus pileatus*) and golden (*Trachpithecus geel*). While the Phayre's langur is restricted in its distribution in Tripura mainly, with splinter populations reported from Cachar of Assam and some part of Mizoram, the golden is confined between Manas and Sankosh Rivers in the Himalayan foothills along the Assam – Bhutan border areas. This narrow endemic was discovered in Chakrashilla Hills Reserve in the Dhubri District of Assam. The capped langur, though widely distributed across the region, yet population is very thinly distributed. Another langur species, namely, Semnopethicus schistaceus (*Nepal Langur*) is endemic to the higher elevations in Sikkim and Nepal.

The Rhesus, macaque (Macaca mulatta), pig-tailed macaque (Macaca nemestrina), Assamese macaque (M. assamensis), Stump-tailed macaque (*Macaca arctoides*), Northern pigtailed macaque (*M. leonine*), and recently reported Arunachal macaque (Macaca munzala) are found in different sympatric combination, and except rhesus macaque, all other species are in severe extinction crisis. The Slow Loris (*Nycticebus bengalensis*), is another highly endangered primate species has its distribution in northeast south of the Brahmaputra River.

Of the six large cat species in India, 4 species, namely, tiger (*Panthera tigris*), leopard (*Panthera pardus*), snow leopard (*Uncia uncial*) and the clouded leopard (*Neofelis nebulosa*) are reported from northeast India. Of these, the clouded leopard is restricted to northeastern regions. Arunachal Pradesh has a unique distinction of supporting all four large cats, while other state have combination of 2 to 3 species of large cats. While, many know extinction pressure on tigers, one main concern is now felt for the survival of clouded leopard, whose habitat is shrinking fast.

Northeast region is perhaps the richest region for small carnivores having their diverse assemblages of small cats, martens, badgers, viverrids, otter etc. The marbled cat (*Pardofelis marmorata*), golden cat (*Catopuma temmincki*), leopard cat (*Prionailurus bengalensis*), fishing cat (*Prionailurus viverrinus*), jungle cat (*Felis chaus*), yellow-throated marten (*Martes flavigula*), ferret badger (*melogale sp.*), hog badger (*Arctoyx collaris*), Eurasian otter (*Lutra lutra*), smooth-coated otter (*Lutrogale perspicillata*), small Indian civet (*Viverricula indica*), large Indian civet (*Viverra zibetha*), common palm civet (*Paradoxurus hermaphrodites*), Himalayan palm civet (*Paguma larvata*), binturong (*Arctictis binturong*) and spotted linsang (*Prionodon paradicolor*), etc. are the main species inhabiting many states of northeastern region.

The red Panda (*Aliurus fulgens*) is yet another flagship species of this region, restricted to the higher altitudes. The rich assemblage of small carnivores and other biota in the northeastern states could be attributed to the wide ranging altitudinal variations that one comes across in the region and also to the heavy rainfall and humidity that support luxurious plant growth especially in the lower elevations. It needs to be emphasized that all these rare animals occupy narrow bands of forests in the hills and valleys of the region, and, living in small populations, they are extremely susceptible to habitat degradation and hunting pressures. Many of the species in lowland forests are already on the brink of extinction as these forests were the first to be occupied, altered and degraded by man (Ramakantha, Gupta & Ajith, 2003, Gupta 2000). All the bear species that occur in India are recorded from the northeastern region. Besides, Northeast India forms the western end of the range for Malayan Sun Bear (*Helarctos malayanus*). Bears of the lower elevations are under especially serious threats owing to habitat degradation as well as persecution by man, as the bile of the animal is considered highly medicinal. Wild dog or dhole, is yet another rarity in the wilderness of Northeast India. Wild dog found in Sikkim (*Cuon alpinus primaevus*) is considered as same subspecies of *Cuon alpinus adjustus* found in eastern Arunachal Pradesh. Although lacking in systematic inventory on bats and rodents, yet, sparse documentation indicate that bats dominate the mammalian fauna of Northeast India. The Wroughton's free-tailed bat (*Otomops wroughtonii*), Namdapha flying squirrel (*Biswamayopterus biswas*), hairy-footed flying squirrel (*Belomys pearsoni*) and parti-coloured flying squirrel (*Hylopetes alboniger*), Orange-bellied Himalayan squirrel (*Dremomys lokriah*), Malayan giant squirrel (*Ratufa bicolor*), Hoary-bellied squirrel (*Callosciurus pygerythrus*) and Himalayan striped squirrel (*Callosciurus macclellandi*), hispid hare (*Caprolagus hispidus*), etc. are few habitat specialists present in northeastern region and facing the threat of elimination from the region. In northeastern region, the elephants make up for about 32 per cent of the total population in India of about 27500. Assam alone accounts for more elephants than Myanmar, Thailand, Indonesia or any other country in Asia. However, elephant population is dwindling sharply, especially in central Assam whereas those in the southern parts have virtually vanished. Only a few left in Manipur and Mizoram and probably none in Nagaland, almost constant in Tripura. Heavy loss of prime elephant habitat is an issue of great concern as loss of elephant habitats heralds doom for smaller creatures as well. Great Indian Rhinoceros (*Rhinoceros unicornis*) is restricted to Kaziranga, Pabitora and Orang in Assam. Historical records suggest that both the one – horned javan rhinoceros (*Rhinoceros sondaicus*) and the two-horned Surmatran rhinoceros (*Didermocerus sumatrensis*) were once found in parts of Northeast India. Both the species are now extinct from the region. The water buffalo (*Bubalus bubalis*) found in Northeastern India has a rather alarming genetic problem due to breeding with the domestic buffalo. The banteng (*Bos javanicus*), was earlier reported from the hills of Manipur till as late as 1990s is now reported extinct from the State. The brow- antlered deer (*Cervus eldi eldi*) is endemic to the State of Manipur. The Swamp Deer (*Cervus duvauceli*) found in Assam is yet another cervid of great conservation significance. The serow (*Capricornis sumatraensis*), goral (*Naemorhedus foral*) and red goral (*Naemorhedus baileyi*) are three other species that are of great conservation significance in this region. The pygmy hog (*Sus salavanius*) is the smallest and the rarest wild suid in the world, and only a few isolated wild population survive in Northeast India. Among other mammals in the northeast India, yak (*Bos grunniens*), Tibetan wild ass (*Equus hemionus kiang*), markhor (*Capra falconeri*), Ibex (*Capra ibex*), great Tibetan sheep (*Ovis ammon hodgsoni*), blue sheep (*Pseudois nayaur*), Chinese Pangolin (*Manis pentadactyla*), Indian Pangolin (*Manis crassicaudata*), Ganges river dolphin (*Platanista gangetica*) are few unique fauna recorded in the northeastern region.

Northeast India supports some of the rare most, least known and most sought after birds of the Oriental region. This region perhaps supports the highest diversity of bird species in the Orient. More than 400 species of birds are recorded from Kaziranga National Park alone in Assam and although not thoroughly explored, the State of Arunachal Pradesh has a record of 665 species of birds and Tripura more than 350 species. Through avifauna is one of the most studied group, there is acute paucity of information concerning the avian fauna of the region and at the same time new species are continuously being added to the regions list. The Assam Plains and the Eastern Himalaya have been identified as endemic Bird Areas by Bird Life International. The Eastern Himalayan part of Northeast India supports 22 restricted range bird species and with the exception of Manipur bush quail (*Perdicula manipurensis*), which is considered to be extinct, other remaining 21 bird species holds one of the largest concentrations of globally zones in the region. White-winged wood duck (*Cairina scutulata*) is perhaps the rare most duck in the world today and this bird occupied the pride of place among the avifauna of the region. However, extensive destruction of its natural habitat ranging from Assam and Arunachal Pradesh to Java has pushed this species into isolated groups of small populations. The Sclater's Monal (*Lophophorus sclateri*) and Vlyth's Tragopan (*Tragopan blythii*) are among the rare and beautiful pheasants that live in a limited range of the eastern Himalaya. All the pheasant species that occur in this region are to be considered endangered. Ward's Trogon (*Harpactes ward*) is yet another beautiful resident bird reported from Arunachal Pradesh and Sikkim. The bird is sighted in the State of Manipur also. Buff-throated Partridge (*Tetraophasis szechenyii*) is a rare resident of rocky ravines and Rhododendron thickets in the subalpine zone of central Arunachal Pradesh. Though there is less information about the migration routes of birds in Northeast India, the Brahmaputra River and her tributaries are thought to form a flyway for birds from Northeast Asia.

The reptilian fauna of northeast India has the greatest affinity to the Oriental, Indo-Malayan and Indo-Chinese regions. According to existing records, there are 137 species of reptiles in Northeast India, but in reality there could be many more species that are yet to be identified. With better sampling and studies on the herpetofauna, the number of species is expected to change considerably for each of the states and for the region as a whole. Among the component of reptilian fauna, the gharial (*Gabialis gangeticus*) found in Brahmaputra River is of great conservation significance. Northeast India has the highest diversity of turtles. Of the 26 species of non-marine chelonians reported from India, 19 are found in this region. However, the information on this group of reptiles is also quite inadequate as most of the available records concerning the known species available are from the Brahmaputra Plain and adjoining areas in lower Eastern Himalaya. The hill states, especially south of Brahmaputra basin, viz., Nagaland, Manipur, Tripura, Meghalaya and Mizoram, remain poorly studied. As recently as 2000, a chelonian species- *Amyda cartilaginaea,* was reported from Mizoram as first record for India, the previous range for this species being from southern Myanmar to central Vietnam, Laos, Cambodia, and Thailand. This species was not found to be particularly rare in the study area but was not reported. *Kachuga sythetensis* is endemic to the region. The elongated tortoise (*Indotestudo elongate*), Asian brown tortoise (*Manouria emys*), narrow-headed soft-shell turtle (*Chitra indica*) and Indian flap-shell turtle (*Lissemys punctata*) are very rare among the recorded species.

The Lizard fauna of Northeast India is profoundly influenced by the Indo- Chinese connection. Published records indicate 20 lizard species from the State of Assam, and 18 species from the tiny state of Manipur. The tokay gecko (*Gekko gekko*) is the largest gecko alive today and is found in northeast India. The Burmese glass snake (*Ophisaurus gracilis*) is yet another interesting reptile of Northeast India. Fifty eight species of snakes have been recorded in Assam and 34 from Manipur. *Python reticulates,* the largest snake in India, is found in northeast India and *Python molurus bivittatus* is known from a single specimen from the Arunachal Pradesh, which was a first record for India. One can expect to sight both the snakes in 'Mouling National Park' in the Upper Siang District of Arunachal Pradesh. King Cobra (*Ophiophagus Hannah*) is the most awe –inspiring reptile of the region. *Typhlops jerdoni, T. tenuicollis, Stoliczkia khasiensis, Elaphe mandarina, Oligiopan melazonotus, Xenochrophis punctulatus, Bungarus bungaroides, Trimeresurus jerdoni* are just a few examples of very elusive and rare snakes of Northeast India.

Due to inadequate systematic studies, presence of only 64 species of amphibians could be too less representation than the actual number. A survey of amphibians conducted in the State of Nagaland from 1998 to 2002 has resulted in 19 species as new records for the State and 5 species (*Megophtys wuliangshanensis, M. glandulosa, Amolops viridimaculatus, Rana humeralis and Rhacophorus gongshanensis*) as new records for India. Only four species of caecilians, *Ichthyophis gareonsis, Ichthyophis hussaini, Ichthyophis sikkimensis and Gegeneophis fuller* are known from Northeast India. The Himalayan newt (*Tylototiton verrucosus*) deserves a special mention, as it is the only species of Salamander known from India, occurring in Manipur, Khasi Hills and Sikkim in Northeast India. Hitherto, they were little affected by man, but use of the pesticides in paddy cultivation is posing a threat to the species.

Fishes are the most ancient and numerous of vertebrates. Northeast India is exceptionally rich in freshwater fishes, and it is heartening to note that the region has been extensively surveyed, and accounts for 236 species from the State of Manipur alone, 167 species of freshwater species belonging to 11 orders, 31 families and 84 genera are recorded. The fish fauna of Loktak Lake in Manipur comprises 64 species. Sona Lake (1.5 km long and 3.0 km. wide), is one of the biggest tectonic lakes in Assam. It sustains 75 species of fishes under 24 families and 49 genra and of which, 20 species are widely distributed while 8 species are native to Northeast India. Despite a very high diversity of fresh-water fishes, Northeast India does not have many endemic species (the fish fauna of India contains 2 endemic families, both of which are absent from the region).

Invertebrates

The biodiversity strategy and Action Plan for Northeast Eco-region suggests that 3624 species of insects and 50 mollusks are recorded from the region. Butterflies and moths are by far the best studied invertebrates in Northeast India, and the region contributes the maximum number of species for the group in the country. A decade ago, 689 species of butterflies were recorded from the State of Sikkim. Honey-bees, render very valuable ecological services like pollinating wild and cultivated plant species apart from producing honey, and their advanced social behaviour has always been a source of fascination for man. Four indigenous species of honey-bees are recognized from India: *Apis cerana, A. dorsata, A. florae and A. andreniformes.* Of these, *Apis andreniformis* is only known from a few specimens collected from Northeast India where the species is exceedingly uncommon. It is an unfortunate practice that people in certain parts of Northeast India not only consume the honey and larvae of this insect, but also fry and eat the honey bees themselves.

THE FAUNAL DIVERSITY: TRIPURA

Introduction

Tripura is a small (10,490km^2) State located in the Northeastern part of India. It is located between 2256′-2432′N and 9010′ – 9221′E. It has a common international border with Bangladesh for about 839 kms towards its West, South and North. It also shares boundary with Assam and Mizoram in the East. The geographical continuity with the Indian mainland is maintained only in the NE with Karimganj sub-division in Cachar district of Assam. In British political parlance Tripura was known as Hill Tipperah and true to its name about 70 per cent of the total geographical area in Tripura is hilly. The small geographical area, however, does not deprive Tripura is being one of the richest areas with regards to the bio-diversity and biological resources. Tripura owes this rich biodiversity and copious wealth of biological resources to her unique bio-geographical [Tripura falls under "North East Hills Province (9B)" of the "North East (9) Biogeographic Zone (Rodgers, *el al.,* 2002)] and zoogeographical (Indian sub-region of Oriental Zoogeographical Regions) location and position. Although by virtue of her location in Assam Hills, Tripura is a part of Indian sub-region of Oriental Zoogeographical Region, yet, the flora and fauna in Tripura bear a very close affinity and resemblances with the floral and faunal components of Indo-Malayan and Indo-Chinese sub-regions of Oriental Region. In addition to this, the flora and fauna in Tripura also has a close affinity with Ethiopian and Palaearctic Zoogeographical Regions.

Physiography and Climate

Physiography

The physiography of the entire state can be divided into three distinct physiographic zones, namely, Hill Ranges, Highland &

Plateau, and Alluvial Valleys. The Hill Ranges Zone includes five major hill ranges with North-South orientation, each separated by narrow valleys (20 kms). The Highland and Plateau zone forms the western limit of the hilly region. The plateau gradually rises from West to East with an elevation ranging from 3m to 37 meters and finally merges with the eastern hilly tract. This zone is dissected by valleys, streams and gullies and is severely eroded. The Alluvial Valleys are below 7 meters in height above mean sea level. Low lands interspersed by hillocks and swamps are locally called 'loongas'.

Climate

The State has typical warm and humid tropical climate with four distinct seasons, i.e. winter (December to February), summers (March to May), South West monsoon (June to September) and post monsoon (October to November). The average rainfall is 2100 mm. (82.7"). Mean maximum temperature is 10.4°C. Humidity is generally high throughout the year ranging from 70 per cent to 80 per cent.

Ecosystem

Tripura has diverse ecosystems ranging from forests and grasslands to freshwater wetlands. There are six types of 408 wetlands, of which, water logged (seasonal) are most numerous followed by oxbow lakes and lakes/ponds.

Watershed/Catchments Areas: The State has 10 major rivers running over a total length of 903 km across the State. All these rivers have watershed/catchments areas of over 9400 ha covering 6 major hill range.

Ecological Hot Spots

A total of 30 (thirty) Conservation Hot Spots (CHS) were identified and assessed based on their performance against four major Values, namely, Biodiversity Values, Taxa-based Values, Socio-economic Values, and Conservation Feasibility Values (Gupta 2000). All CHS were further assessed for their ranking based on their score-types for each of the Sub-values under above mentioned 4 major Values, Of these 30 CHS, 11 are from South District, 5 from West District,

6 from Dhalai District, and remaining 8 from North District. The area of hot spots ranged between 2 to 15 km^2, majority of these CHS (22) were above 10 km^2 in size.

Biodiversity

Faunal Biodiversity

Unfortunately, there is no authentic or scientific record of wildlife resources in Tripura. Whatever little information of wildlife wealth in the state is available, it is based either on personal casual observations by different scientists or available in the literary works by contemporary writers.

Sterndale (1884) provides the first scientific report about the wildlife species in Tripura, and in his book entitled 'Mammalia of India', has described the presence of Javan rhinoceros, capped langurs, brush tailed porcupines, Tipperah langurs, etc. Stray records are, however, available on mammalian fauna in Tipperah (the old name of Tripura) from the reports of Blyth (1844,1847), Sclatter (1891), Khajuria (1954-55) and others, based on the collections made by F. Skipwith, A. Grobe and J. Barbe during the middle of 19th century. Rajamala, the famous literary work by Sh. Kailash Chandra Singha (1897), mentions the abundance of different species of wild mammals all over the State such as rhinoceros, tigers, wild dogs, wild goats, slow loris, etc. These descriptions are mostly on large mammalian species, e.g., large population of Rhinoceros (Rhinoceros unicornis) a place in Dhalai District in Tripura is called'Gandachhara', because large population of Rhinos (locally called as 'Ganda') existed there in the past. The mixture of facts and myths and above all the absence of any corroborative accounts and evidence in want of any detailed studies, has made it difficult to project the true picture of wildlife resources in Tripura. However, on the basis of the trophies still left with the local inhabitants, there are sufficient indications to prove that three Schedule-I wildlife species, wild buffalo, rhinoceros and tiger had once existed in plenty. About 35 tigers were killed in and around Fatikroy in the North district of Tripura in one single year (Datta Roy, 1986)

Pocock (1939) reported the presence of the leaf monkey [(*Prebyits (Trachypithecus) phayrei*, Blyth (1847)], capped langur [P

(*Trachypithecus*) pileatus] and slow loris (*Nycticebus coucang*), from Tipperah region. In 1970, a report on wildlife of Tripura by the Forest Department recorded presence of 6 Tigers in the State. The census report on Manu Forest Division in 1972 confirms the presence of many wildlife species including Elephant, Sloth Bear, Indian Bison, Leopard, Hoolock Gibbon, Sambar, Hog Deer, Barking Deer, Wild Dog, etc (Table No.1). In 1974, the Tiger census report of Tripura confirmed presence of 7 Tigers in Longtharai RF (North Tripura). Menon (1975) has noted in the Tripura District Gazetteers that "Fauna of Tripura bear a close resemblance to that of Chittagong Hill Tracts of Bangladesh and Hills of Southern Assam in India, thus, exhibiting a mixture of fauna peculiar to these two regions". Many species have been listed in the Gazetteers which were once abundant in Tripura.

Agarwal and Bhattacharjee (1977) described 31 species and sub-species of mammalian fauna based on the survey in Tripura conducted during 1969-73. This includes one species of bat (*Rousettus amplexi candatus*) and one sub-species of mongoose (*Herpestes auropunctatus birmanicus*) new to the Indian region. They have noted that several species, e.g. the short nosed fruit bat (*Cynopterus sphinx*), the rhesus macaque (*Macaca mulatta*) and the Irrawaddi squirrel (*Callosciurus pygerythrus*), etc. are widely distributed throughout the state, whereas, some other species e.g. the slow loris (*Nyciticebus coucang*), the leopard cat (*Felis begalensis*), the golden cat (*Felis temmincki*), elephants (*Elephas maximus*) etc. which were quite common in this area in the last century, have now become scarce and are now confined/localized in the south-eastern portion (foothills of Longtharai, Salkhan and Atharamura-Kalajhari belt) of the State (Gupta (1998). Kali Prasanna Sen in his Rajmala has also dealt at length with elephants and elephant resources of Tripura. The large populations of Elephants have reportedly shifted to the adjoining Bangladesh area.

In 1984, Bhattacharjee and Chakraborty further updated this list of mammalian fauna to 56 Mammalian species belonging to 9 Orders and 20 Families. In 1989-90, based on a thorough survey all over the State, this list was further updated and 90 land-mammal species from 65 Genera and 10 Orders were identified by Gupta and Mukherjee (1994), which make up for about 19 per cent, 48 per cent and 100 per cent of total land-mammal species, genera, and orders, respectively, in India. Main extant land-mammal species include Elephant (*Elephas maximus*), Bear (*Melursus ursinus*), Binturong (*Arctitis binturong*), Wild Dog (*Cuon alphinus*), Porcupine (*Artherurus assamensis*), Barking Deer (*Muntiacus muntajak*), Sambar (*Cervus unicolor*), Wild Boar (*Sus scrofa*), Gaur (*Bos gaurus*), Leopard (*Panthera pardus*), Clouded Leopard (*Neofelis nebulosa*), and many species of small Cats and Primates.

Gupta (1999) has described presence of rich diversity of mustelids, viverids and herpestids. Based on the published information and surveys conducted in the state, a total of 6 species of mutelids (Eurasian otterm *Lutra lutra*; small clawed otter *Aonyx cinerea*; Yellow throated martin *Martis flavigula*; Burmese ferret badger *Melogale personata*; Hog badger *Arctonyx collaris*; Yellow bellied weasel *Mustela kathiah*), 5 species of viverids (large civet *Viverra zibetha*; small civet *Viverricula indica*; palm civet *Paradoxurus hermaphroditus*; spotted linsang *Prionodon pardicolor*; and binturong *Arctitis binturong*) and 3 species of herpestids (common mongoose *Herpestes edwardsii*; crab-eating mongoose *H. urva*, and small Indian mongoose *H. javanicus*). Recently, in the year 2003, a tigress with two cubs was sighted in Trishna Wildlife Sanctuary.

Primates: Tripura has amazingly high density of primates all over the State, including some highly endangered species. Different survey teams from Zoological Survey of India, Eastern Region, Calcutta had conducted primate surveys in the State in the past. Their reports have confirmed that out of a total of 15 free-ranging primate species in India, 7 (46.7%) species are found in Tripura, which is highest recording in any one Indian State. In 1988, one more primate species was added to the list of 7 free ranging primates in the State, when two groups of golden langur (*Trachypithecus geei*) were released in the wild at Sepahijala and Trishna Wildlife Sanctuary (one group in each area). Of these two groups, the one in Sepahijala has survived well and with suitable increase in its population size has further split into two sub-groups (Gupta and Mukherjee, 1994). In 1989, based on the primate survey conducted by the author all over the State, a total of 287 groups of all 7-primate species were located in Tripura (Gupta, 1994). In 1994, primate survey in Sepahijala Wildlife Sanctuary revealed presence of 5 species in very high density (17 groups of Phayre's langur, 18 groups of Capped langur, 11 of Pig-tailed macaque, 30-35 groups of Rhesus macaque and 3-4 individuals of slow loris) (Gupta, 1996).

Avifauna: Ornithofauna comprises 342 reported species in the State, of which about 58 are migratory species one near threatened species – the darter. There is high diversity of birds of prey, frugivorous birds, marsh birds and flower peckers. In the aquatic ecosystem 14 (fourteen) species of fish have been recorded, of which 2 are endangered (*Anguilla bengalensis* and *Psuedeatroptus alterinoides*) and 12 vulnerable. Due to silting of river-beds and filling up of wetlands, different species of marsh birds and fishes are on decline.

Tripura is also very rich in its avifauna. According to various estimates and also as per the mid-winter waterfowl census results (Gupta, 1989, 1990) about 400 different species of both land and water birds are identified in Tripura. These also include many migratory species (e.g., Large and Small Whistling Teals) that occupy many water bodies across the State in large numbers all over the State for wintering. A preliminary list of avifauna was documented from the Sepahijala Wildlife Sanctuary (Gupta and Gupta, 1994).

Reptiles, Amphibians and Fish fauna: Definite information on various reptilian and amphibian species and their population status is also not known in Tripura. Based on the available habitat conditions, however, it can safely be concluded that Tripura must be rich in those. This is very well reflected in presence of 21 species of aquatic terrapines and soft-shelled turtles [including 7 endangered species according to Wildlife (Protection) Act, 1972], and other endangered poisonous (pit viper, viper, krait, cobra, etc.) and non-poisonous (python) snakes. Among the amphibian fauna noticeable are the skipping frog, Indian Bull frog, tree frog, toad, etc. *Heteropneustes fossillis* (singhis), *Cirrhina mrigala* (Mrigal), *Pautius sophole* (Ptui), *Labeo rohita* (rohu), *Catla catla* (Katal), Kal, Maka, carps, Durkina, etc. are the major fish fauna in the State.

Endangered Status of Wild Fauna of Tripura

In current habitat conditions, most of the wildlife species are facing extinction pressure in the State. Of the total 65 genera and 90 species of mammalian fauna in the State, about 14 genera and 18 species are included in Schedule I of Wildlife (Protection) Amendment Act, 2002 as highly 'endangered' species. Similarly, 10 genera and 14 species are included in the Appendix I of CITES (Convention in International Trade in Endangered Species of Flora and Fauna).

Three land mammal species, namely, tiger (*Panthera tigris*), rhinoceros (*Rhinoceros unicornis*), and wild buffalo (*Bubalus bubalis*) have already become extinct from Tripura. Some highly endangered wildlife species are as follows:

(a) *In Part I of Schedule I of WL(P) Act* : Phayre's Langur (*Trachypithecus phayrei*), Capped Langur (*T.pileatus*), Gibbon (*Bunopithecus hoolock*), Slow Loris (*Nycticebus coucang*), Leopard (*Panthera pardus*), Clouded Leopard (*Neofelis nebulosa*), Gaur (*Bos gaurus*), Serow (*Capricornis sumtraensis*), Giant Squirrel (*Petaurista petaurista*), Chinese Pangolin (*Manis pentadactyla*), Mouse Deer (*Tragulus meminna*), Common Otter (*Lutra lutra*), Elephant (*Elephas maximum*), Binturong (*Arctitis binturong*), Caracal (*Felis caracal*), Fishing Cat (*Felis viverrina*), Golden Cat (*Felis temmincki*), Leopard cat (*Felis bengalensis*), Sloth Bear (*Melursus ursinus*).

(b) *In Part II of Schedule I of WL (P) Act* : Python and 7 species of turtles and Tortoises (*Lissamus punctata, Kechuga tecta tecta, Trionyx gangeticus, Trinyx hurum, Kechuga kechuga, Geoclemys hamiltoni, Betagus baska.*

(c) *Part III of Schedule I of WL(P) Act* : Bamboo Partridge, Black Necked Crane, Great Indian Hornbill, Indian Pied Hornbill, Hawks, Large Whistling Teals, etc.

(d) *In Part I of Schedule II of WL(P) Act*: Pig tailed Macaque (*Macaca nemestrina*), Stumptailed Macaque (*M. arctoides*), Rhesus Macaque (*M. mulatta*), Wild Dog (*Cuon alpinus*), etc.

(e) *In Part II of the Schedule II of WL (P) Act*: Black Himalayan Bear (*Selenarctos thibetanus*), civets (Viverridae), Jackel (*Canis aureus*), jungle cat (*Felis chaus*), yellow throated marten (*Martes flovigule*), Eurasian otters (*Lutra lutra*), giant squirrel (*Ratufa indica*).

(f) *In Appendix I of CITES*: species included in Appendix I of CITES are already covered under different Schedules of WL(P) Act as noted above.

History of Wildlife/Biodiversity Management in Tripura

The history of wildlife management in Tripura is not very old. In 1939 A.D. in which year for the first time rules were framed for the first time to organize the Forest Department followed by the constitution of some Reserved Forests that could actually be demarcated only during the years 1954-55 A.D. The first ever attention towards wildlife matters related with the assessment of the provisions of the Indian Forest Act 1927 and the Wildlife Elephant Preservation Act, 1879,which were found inadequate for the purpose of management and protection of wildlife in the State. The first ever wildlife sanctuary covering the central catchment area in the North District was notified in 1979. However, it could not remain operational for long and had to be de-notified. Later, after a gap of about seven years in 1986 Trishna Wildlife Sanctuary was declared covering an area of 173 km^2 to provide protection to the only surviving population of Indian bison (Bos gaurus) Tripura. In the year 1989, three more wildlife sanctuaries were notified, namely, Gumti, Roa, and Sepahijala Wildlife Sanctuary:

Name of the sanctuary	Area in Km^2	Important flora and fauna found
1. Sepahijala Wildlife Sanctuary (West district)	18.540	Birds and primates, migratory birds in the winter
2. Gumti Wildlife Sanctuary (South district)	389.540	Elephant, samber, barking deer, wild goats, serrow etc.
3. Trishna Wildlife Sanctuary (South district)	194.710	Bison, leopard, barking deer, wild dog, capped langur, king cobra, spectacled monkey, slow lorries, etc.
4. Bison National Park	31.63	Bison, Hoolock, barking deer, wild dog
5. Clouded National Park	5.08	Clouded leopard, barking deer, Phayre's langur
4. Roa Wildlife Sanctuary (North district)	0.860	Many species of birds and primates
TOTAL (4 WL Sanctuaries)	**603.650**	

In addition to *in-situ* conservation efforts, *ex-situ* conservation measures are being fulfilled in the State through Sepahijala zoo. The zoo houses 532 animals belonging to 56 different species. Conservation breeding programme on clouded leopard, binturong, pig-tailed macaque and Phayre's langur is strongly contributing to ex-situ conservation, education and awareness promotion efforts.

Problems in Management and Protection of Biodiversity

While the forests of northeastern states have been under systematic management for past century or so, this fragile resource base has been shrinking due to various anthropogenic disturbances resulting in degradation which is directly affecting the ecological stability, biological diversity, economic viability & environmental security of the states. The impact has been so severe that even species like wild buffalo, rhinoceros and tiger are now extinct in Tripura state and few other faunal and floral species are struggling hard under extremities for their viable survival in many other northeastern states. The factors responsible for the deterioration in the environment quality leading to the neglect and decimation of the biodiversity could broadly be ranked either as direct and indirect factors. These are briefly discussed in the following paragraphs.

Direct Factors

Forest Degradation

Almost entire area of forests of the northeastern states has been subjected to severe degradation. During survey of forest resources in the state by FSI in 1989, it is shown that majority of forest areas (up to 72.73%) are heavily to moderately degrade. During the past few years there has been a reversal trend in degradation. Although, the area of dense cover has increased, yet the area under open forests has also increased reflecting degradation. The primary vegetation in extensive areas of the Northeast India has been disturbed and modified and in some places destroyed by seismic activities, frequent landslides and resultant soil erosion. While these natural causes have contributed only marginally to the change in vegetation type, it is the activity of man has led to the irreversible transformation in the landscapes and has resulted in colossal loss of biodiversity in the entire region. Human influences have pushed many species to the brink of extinction and have caused havoc to natural fragile ecosystems. Such devastations to natural ecosystems are witnessed almost everywhere in the region and is a cause of great concern.

Northeast India has 64 per cent of the total geographical area under forest cover and it is often quoted that it continues to be a forest surplus region. However, the forest cover is rapidly disappearing from the entire region. There has been a decrease of about 1800 sq km forest cover between 1991 and 1999 including the quality resulting into conversion of the dense forests (canopy closure of 40% or more) into open forests or scrubs. Though there is a succession of several edaphic formations, a vast area of land has already been transformed into barren and unproductive wastelands. For example though the forest cover in Manipur extends to 75 per cent of the total geographic area, only 22 per cent of forest area is under dense forest cover and has been converted to open forests.

Though Northeast India is predominantly mountainous, the region is very rich in aquatic ecosystem diversity. A large number of bheels, ponds and marshlands in the low-lying and floodplain areas of Assam, Arunachal Pradesh and Tripura represent the diversity in lentic ecosystems. However, deforestation and the resultant loss of soil, especially in the hill areas, are leading to increased siltation of rivers and streams. The deep pools that are the favoured habitats of many species, are rapidly becoming shallow and choked with silt, leading to a decline in habitat. At the same time, swamps, marshes, and other wetlands are increasingly being reclaimed for urban and agricultural expansion. The forests of Assam once acted as sponge, absorbing the tremendous impact of the monsoons. The natural drainage of the vast northeastern Himalaya is channelled through Assam. However, with the loss of thick forest cover, Brahmaputra, one of the largest and fastest flowing rivers of the subcontinent is the main cause of floods with devastating effects. A decline in primary forests in the northeastern regions, specially in Assam and Meghalaya, has been very fast and irrecoverable (Balakrishnan, 1981). Referring to the colossal losses to the biodiversity with reference to the Arunachal Pradesh, Agarwal (1986) has remarked that more than 700 species of plants from the Northeast India are facing the threat of survival in the wild.

Influx of People from Across the Border

There has been large influx of people in Tripura from the neighbouring country, the erstwhile East Pakistan (now

Bangladesh). The fast growth in population (density 304 per square km., 2001 Census) in the State, coupled with poor infrastructure and lack of alternative livelihood options resulted in mounting pressure on forest and forestland. This has also led to in reduction in per capita forest area from 0.97 ha to a present level of 0.18 ha. and encroachments and over exploitation of forest resources. Smuggling of forest produce through 856 km long porous border with Bangladesh has posed most serious conservation problem in the State. The enormity and extent of such illegal fellings can be judged from the annual revenue earned from intercepted illicitly extracted forest produce (1.85 crores) which is only a small portion (around 10%) of produce stolen/ and smuggled across the border. This is a big challenge and need be tackled head on through creation of infrastructure and other assets including capacity-building and networking with active cooperation of the local people.

Shifting Cultivation

This form of primitive agricultural practice is well rooted in cultural ethos of the tribal and is major cause of deforestation, land degradation and soil impoverishment. From the survey conducted by Tribal Welfare Department (1990), it is estimated that this form of cultivation is presently practiced by around 55,049 tribal households over 35,000-40,000 ha annually, equivalent to 6 per cent of the forestland in the State. Systematic efforts are being made through different schemes for in-situ rehabilitation of these tribal along with rehabilitation of degraded forests, but the problem still persists. Many forest bird species, especially those with ranges restricted to Northeast India declined in abundance or disappeared in successional fallows of less than 10 years of regeneration in secondary successional and mature tropical rain forests in shifting cultivation mosaic habitat in Dampa Tiger Reserve, Mizoram (Raman, 2001). Gupta and Kumar (1994) revealed that the Phayrer's langur (*T.phayrei*) could survive in secondary forests, provided that regeneration is allowed to continue for at least 15 years and degradation of forests poses a threat even for such adaptive animals. Similarly, studies conducted by Raman, (1997) reveal that arboreal mammal species such as Malayan Giant Squirrel (*Ratufa bicolor*), Pallas's Squirrel (*Callosciurus erythraeus*) and gibbon are dependent on tall, undisturbed primary forests or at least, late successional vegetation (25 years old, or more). However, it is a stark reality that in most parts of Northeast India, fallow periods have declined to 5-10 years and in some places may be as short as 3-5 years. With sharp decline in their population, the role of birds, bats, ungulates and primates as seed dispersers is decreasing, leading to further impoverishment of the primary as well as the secondary forests. Choudhury, (2003) described that though there are good populations of Hoolock (*Bunopithecus hoolock*) in the forests of West Khasi Hills, but those are on private and community lands and there long-term survival may be a great cause of concern.

Forest Encroachments

Encroachment of forestland is a serious threat to forests and its conservation. As per record maintained by the Forest Department, the position is alarming and needs special attention to tackle this problem. The category-wise position of encroachment of forest land in Tripura is as given below:

Period	*R.F. (ha)*	*P.R.F. (ha)*	*P.F. (ha)*	*Total (ha)*
Before 1980	3209.50	752.61	1343.19	5305.30
After 1980	4981.34	1374.93	2264.14	8620.41
Total	**8190.84**	**2127.54**	**3607.33**	**13,925.71**

The position of encroachment has further aggravated. The latest survey conducted by Revenue Department of Tripura to assess the actual encroachment in forestland, has shown encroachment to the extent of 593.11 km^2. This has not only caused loss of forest area but has also created perpetual site of degradation of forest. This is true in almost all the northeastern states resulting into habitat loss for the key indicator species, losses of which create a cascading effect resulting into decimation of other subsidiary species as well.

Forest Fire

Forest fires are common and frequent in the plains (around 20% of the total forest area of the State) as the villagers, at the end of winter, set fire to get flush of new grass for their cattle. Forest Survey of India has estimated that forest fire has led to heavy to moderate degradation of around 6.16 per cent of the forests. The forests atop all the hills get burnt due to *Jhum* fire, which spreads to nearby forest areas. This causes immense harm by completely wiping out regeneration (natural as well as artificial). It also adversely affect already threatened many a wildlife species. The main constraints in control of forest fires are lack of communication facility for early detection of forest fire and also the lack of effective fire fighting equipment.

Grazing

In Tripura alone, the estimate indicate presence of more than 22 lakhs of domestic animals (cattle, sheep and goat) in the State with 2.9 per cent annual rate of increase, against the human population of about 35 lakhs. It is estimated that 60 per cent of this animal population graze in the forest area and cause soil compaction and heavy damage to the forest plantations and natural regeneration areas. The intensity of such disturbances, especially near the habitation, is far beyond the carrying capacity of the forests. There are no grazing grounds. The community lands for grazing purpose in villages have either been encroached upon or diverted to other land uses. Thus grazing constitutes a threat to conservation of biodiversity in all the northeastern states. Enforcement of strict control or imposition of restrictions on such disturbance under present socio-economic condition is practically impossible. A well designed interface with the department of Animal Resource for a rational livestock planning and augmenting fodder availability is urgently required.

Overburdening Rights and Concessions

Forests of the State are presently overburdened with rights and concessions. The adverse effect on forests of unregulated removal of forest produce on this account is steadily increasing with increase in population, without corresponding increase in biodiversity rich areas. Taking a case in point from Tripura, it is seen that there is immense pressure on forests from fringe dwellers for basic requirements, as well as from miscreants involved in illegal felling and smuggling of forest resources across the border. This has lead to severe degradation of existing forest resources in the State. Simultaneously, the forests are viewed as a source of livelihood by the millions living below poverty line, leading to unsustainable utilization of biodiversity resource well beyond the recuperating capabilities. This is common in practically all other northeastern states who share almost same geo graphical, demographical and ecological parameters.

Forestry as a Source of Livelihood

Forestry is one of the most important sectors to support the tribal and rural poor for subsistence, employment and household income. Enhanced outlay for development works have resulted in creation of more man-days during last decade or so. The people get gainful employment in collection of bamboo and minor forest produce and selling them in the market and other ancillary activities such as value additions. Many people are earning their livelihood through forest-based industries (saw mills, wood based industries, etc.). This dependency has most often taken a heavy toll on the biodiversity resources whenever their exploitation crosses the sustainable limits. More man-days shall be generated from the forest-based industries. The Department has already issued licenses to 57 saw mills and about 600 furniture shops and other wood-based establishments/units. The forest based industries using bamboos and timber products shall be encouraged as a permanent source of income and employment.

Indirect Factors

Population Explosion

It is one of the most striking among the indirect factors. The unprecedented increase in population by 143.5 per cent from the period 1952-1971 clearly shows that Tripura was severely affected by the political upheveals, which took place in the Indian sub-continent just after Independence. The spurt in population in Tripura is mainly due to the influx of migrants from Bangladesh that started in 1942 and was most alarming during the years 1950,

1952 and 1955-56. The high percentage of increase in population by 78-79 per cent from 1951-61 is clearly indicative of this phenomenon. It had a direct and severe impact on the forest cover, which got chiseled out from the administrative control of the Forest Department. The per capita forest cover in Tripura comes to 0.12 hac only as against 1.40 hac that was available in 1951. The shrinkage in forest cover thus had been to the extent of about 90 per cent in about six decades.

Encroachment Over Forest Lands

In Tripura, there are hardly any protected forest, proposed reserved forest and reserved forests land, which are totally free from any kind of encroachment. The influx of thousand of destitute families after partition started making inroads into forests as a result of which the legality of the reserves constituted by Maharajas were questioned in the later part of the 1950s. In compliance with the verdict of Supreme Court in 1961 a new process of reservation had to be started under section 4 of the Indian Forest Act, 1927. The finalization of this took many years and the encroachments increased. It was more so for land having rich forest cover due to the sale value of standing trees therein.

Amendment of Land Rules

In the year 1984, the amendment in the Land Rules (TLR and LR Rules, 1961) in Tripura gave full property rights over trees standing on Government land to the applicants as soon as the land in question has been allotted to them. It has led to the rapid depletion of the forest cover, first of valuable timber species and then of non-timber value species. The beneficiaries who are mostly the tribal sell those trees to the forest contractors for petty sum of money. The contractors in turn reap a rich harvest by further selling them in the open market. The depletion of the forest cover from such private lands has adversely affected the biodiversity status therein.

Unawareness and Apathy Towards Biodiversity

Even though, the entire northeastern regions is rich in biodiversity, the apathy and unawareness of its role and importance in the conservation and preservation of ecology prevails amongst the people. It was only during the yearly celebration of Van Mahotsava and Wildlife Week that the importance of biodiversity is highlighted as a routine matter without seriousness. This attitude has caused irreparable damage to the rich habitat of wild flora and fauna, which in turn has led to the depletion of the biodiversity. With the enactment of the Biodiversity Act 2002 and constitution of the State Biodiversity Boards in practically all the northeastern states, there has been much better awareness on the conservation of biodiversity in its different formats. The BD Act has also provided scope for biodiversity conservation linked with economic gains through Access and Benefit Sharing provisions at the ground level with the provision of Biodiversity Management Committees at the village level.

Hunting

Tripura is primarily a tribal state. The tribal population in Tripura stands about 30 per cent of the total population. There are 19 different tribes. Though hunting is basically resorted to for meeting food requirements, it is also resorted to in a small scale for protecting crop fields from animal damage. There are instances to suggest that the guns provided to the tribal for crop protection had also been used for shooting the wildlife thronging their paddy fields. There were no rules and regulations to control hunting till 1952, when the rules to regulate hunting/shooting, etc. were enacted and enforced in the state. As a consequence of this, these interior areas, which incidentally also form rich wildlife refuge, were left unprotected and poachers had a free hunting ground. It is primarily due to the severe hunting pressure that some of the wildlife species have now become endangered, such as slow loris, hoolock gibbon, few poisonous snakes, etc. and some species such as rhinoceros, tiger and wild buffalo, have become extinct from Tripura. Moreover, similar to jhooming, hunting is also an inherent cultural trend in the life style of most of the tribal communities, which they find quite difficult to shun.

Similarly, a vast majority of the indigenous inhabitants of northeastern region are meat-eating in their food habits and almost all communities have expert hunters, trappers and fishermen. One can find bones, skulls and hides of large and small mammals in tribal huts. It should be noted that though the traditional practices of trapping, snaring etc. of animals are carried out in very remote areas, in most parts of Northeast India shooting wild animals with guns is prevalent. Besides, certain meat is valued as medicinal and such animals are persecuted as great efforts are made by a few individuals to seek such animals and bring home their body parts. In the past, the hunting/trapping was done with considerable prudence with many taboos and restrictions. For example, the Anaal Naga in Manipur did not consume turtle or tortoise meat. The Maram Naga did not eat pork and the Thangkhul Naga did not eat any member of the cat family. Unfortunately, such taboos no more hold any sway among the people now. It is great tragedy that in many parts of Northeast India some people poison the rivers, streams and other water bodies to get good catches of fish. Apart from using plant poisons, lime, DDT, copper sulphate ($Cu SO_4$) and other synthetic chemicals are being used for fishing. Some are even using dynamite and gelatin sticks for the same purpose. This has serious ill effects on the entire aquatic ecosystem. Fish stocks are being entirely wiped out; several species of amphibians, birds and other fish predators are also being affected in the process; and nothing is known as to what happens to human beings on consuming such poisoned fishes. Northeastern India is often called India's forgotten corner and it was perceived that the remoteness of the place has helped preserve its biodiversity. However, the penetration of roads into interior areas has already exposed the local populace to market economy, unscrupulous urban traders and middlemen in most parts of the region. A series of proposed dams across Northeastern region may lead to submergence of vast tracts of rainforests. Comprehensive environmental impact assessments, which are mandatory as per the law of the land, reveal the possible danger that these projects pose to the biodiversity of the region (Ramakantha, Gupta & Ajith, 2003).

Disappearance of Wetlands

Practically no records are available regarding draining of 'jala' areas (wetlands) for cultivation and with that, few prime habitats for different life forms (plants and animals) have been lost forever. Tripura is still rich in its bird population which includes about 300 species; but loss of habitat is the prime cause for decimation of avi-fauna, amphibians and reptiles.

Low Financing of Forestry Sector

Current investment in Forestry Sector is very low. The allocation to the sector under State Plan has actually declined steadily as a proportion of total plan outlay of the States, which stand at roughly 1 per cent of the total State outlays. It is also seen that total budgetary allocation to the sector (Plan+Non-Plan+CSS) is inadequate in comparison to minimum requirement of the sector as per working plan prescriptions for sustainable management of the forests. The gap between the budgetary requirement and the flow to the sector is a cause of concern. In view of low and declining investment in the sector under State Plan, there has been hardly any scope for investment in essential infrastructure, while even modest facilities created earlier have withered due to inadequate financial allocation.

Conclusion: The Way Ahead

Realizing that the long term economic security of the people is contingent upon the ecological security of the natural resources, it is considered essential to jealously augment forestry and biodiversity resources for generating sustained tangible and intangible benefits. Taking advantage of the unique juxtaposition of the geographic and demographic features in the region consisting of large tracts of watershed/catchments, it is proposed by the forest department to undertake an integrated approach for the enhancement of forestry resources on one hand (ecological stability and biodiversity conservation) and sustained flow of tangible and intangible benefits (socio-economic security) to the human society at large, on the other hand. The aim is to link all biodiversity conservation and management related activities with the poverty reduction mechanisms. This could be achieved broadly in two ways: (1) through indirect and intangible sustained benefits flowing as a result of ecological restoration of forestry and biodiversity resources, and (2) direct economic benefits emanating through various existing and proposed beneficiary oriented forestry and non-forestry schemes. The traditional ethno-botanical knowledge among the people of Northeast India is praiseworthy and need be linked with the technological advanced techniques for enhanced economic benefits on the one hand and ecologically sustainable use of the natural resources without adversely affecting the biodiversity, on the other.

However, colossal deforestation and the loss of species on the region is a matter of serious concern. It is recommended that the mandatory provision of having at least 10 per cent of the total geographical area under the protected area cover should be ceremoniously followed by the states through the applicability of Wildlife (Protection) Act, 1972. With the provision of constitution of Conservation and Community Protected Areas under the Act, enough scope exists to address the economic and social issues of the local population sharing the wildlife habitat, thus bringing in the participatory approach into play to avoid conflict between the conservation and people's needs. Surveys all across the region has also revealed in no uncertain terms presence of more biodiversity outside the protected areas. This mandates putting into practice the provisions of forestry management for biodiversity conservation as well in areas of unusually rich in biodiversity. The provisions as in existence in the new Working Plan Code necessitating vetting of the Working Plan by the Chief Wildlife Warden ensuring the Wildlife Circles are constituted wherever necessary for wildlife and biodiversity rich habitats.

The Biodiversity Act, 2002, is a very progressive legislation, which not only talks of conservation of biodiversity, but also facilitates economic gains to communities who have been engaged in the protection and conservation of the biodiversity. This Act further provides scope for economic benefits to the local communities out of the commercial benefits accruing following commercial use of biodiversity components from a given area. The provisions of patenting of traditional knowledge being possessed by the local communities can also be used for augmenting conservation values.

The provision of Forest Rights Act, 2005 that provides right to cultivate over forest lands that had been occupied by the local people for past many years for their sustenance, can be very judiciously used for settling the shifting cultivators, which in turn shall help in restoration of degraded forests, thus adding to the biodiversity richness. The sustainable use of lands under forest rights to the forest dwellers shall in long run help in providing alternative livelihood options to the forest dwellers thus reducing their dependency on the forestry and wildlife resources.

The scope of carbon trading under the REDD and REDD Plus provisions may also be used for ensuring economic benefits to the forest dwellers and reducing their dependency on the forestry resources, which will help in building up of the lost biodiversity.

The northeastern regions have immense potential for eco-tourism development as the entire region is endowed with vast natural resources. The eco-tourism in all the states has the potential to provide income opportunities to the local people in the service sector coupled with the recreation and education awareness. To realize this potential, enabling policies have to be framed for integrated development of (eco)tourism sector in the state as livelihood provider to the local people.

The main issue addressing the biodiversity conservation may revolve around the need for improved and sustained flow of goods and services to the entire population with maximum livelihood opportunities consistent with conservation and enhancement of ecology and environment of the State. The Economics of Ecosystem and Biodiversity approach need be taken to actually work out the price tags on various components of the biodiversity that do not form the part of the gross domestic products due to their intangible nature as benefit provider.

The Afforestation policy of the Forest Departments must favour active and meaningful participation and support of local communities and their grass-root representatives for protection and development of forests. Joint Forest Management has been taken in all the States in large scale benefiting the people and the forests on equal footing and adding to the biodiversity status of the given area of operation.

All above efforts are bound to lift the status of biodiversity in the region and also enhance the economic and social status of all. The policies and practices being followed in this direction would also help raise the economic standard of the dependent people by way of providing them alternative sustainable livelihood options.

REFERENCES

Agarwal, V.C. and T. A. Bhattacharya. (1977). Report on a collection of mammals from Tripura. Record Zoological Survey of India. 73:135-137.

Blyth, E. (1844). Report of the zoological curator (Museum of the Asiatic Society of Bengal). *J. Asiatic Soc. Bengal*. 42:766-782.

Blyth, E. (1847). Supplementary report of the curator of the zoological department. *J. Asiatic Soc. Bengal*. 16:728-737.

Gupta, A.K. & Mukherjee, S.K. (1989). Study on impact of settlements in Gumti Wildlife Sanctuary, Tripura, *Van Vigyan*. Vol. 27, No. 4 : 195-202.

Gupta, A. K. (1989). Mid-winter waterfowl counts in Southern and Eastern Asia – contribution through counts made in Gumti Reservoir, Tripura in 1989. Asian Waterfowl Census, IWRB, The Asian Wetland Bureau, UK.

Gupta, A. K. & S. K. Mukherjee.(1989). Study on impact of settlements in Gumti Wildlife Sanctuary, Tripura, *Van Vigyan*. Vol. 27, No. 4: 195-202.

Gupta, A. K. (1990). Mid-winter waterfowl counts in Southern and Eastern Asia – contribution through counts made in Gumti Reservoir, Tripura in 1990. Asian Waterfowl Census, IWRB, The Asian Wetland Bureau, UK.

Gupta, A.K. (1994). Status and conservation of non-human primates in Tripura, India. In *Current Primatology*, Vol. I: Ecology and Evolution (Eds. B. Thierry; J.R. Anderson; J.J. Roeder; N. Herrenschmidt). Strasbourg, Univ. Louis Pasteur.

Gupta, A.K., & Kumar, A (1994). Feeding ecology of Phayre's leaf monkey *(Presbytis phayrei*, Blyth 1847) in Tripura, *Biological Conservation* 69. 301-306.

Gupta, Gunjan and Gupta, A.K. (1994). A Check-list of birds around the research camp in Sepahijala Wildlife Sanctuary, Tripura. *Cheetal*. Vol. 33 (2), pp 34-41.

Gupta, A. K. and A. Kumar. (1994). Feeding ecology and conservation of the phayre's leaf monkey (*Presbytis phayrei*) in northeast India. *Biological Conservation*. 69:301-306.

Gupta, A. K. and S. K. Mukherjee. (1994). A note on the release of golden langur (*Presbytis geei*, Khajuria) into the wild in Tripura, India. *Indian Forester*. 120(10): 915-919.

Gupta, A. K. and S. K. Mukherjee. (1994). Status of Wildlife in Tripura: Problems in its Management. *Environ*, Vol. 2(1): 34-49.

Gupta, A. K. (1996). Conservation Ecology of Non-human Primates and Human Impact in Northeast India. PhD dissertation. University of Cambridge, Cambridge, United Kingdom.

Gupta, A.K. (1997). Importance of forestry plantations of exotic and native plant species for conservation of Phayre's langur (*Trachypithecus phayrei*) in North-east India. *Tropical Biodiversity*, 4(2): 187-195.

Gupta, A. K. (1998). A note on a review of the taxonomic status of the Phayre's langur (*Trachypithecus phayrei*) in Tripura, Northeast India. *Folia Primatol*, 69 (1): 22-27.

Gupta, A. K. (1999). Mustelids, Viverids and Herpestids of Tripura. In ENVIS: Wildlife and Protected Areas, Mustelids, Viverrids and Herpestids of India. S. A. Hussain (editor), Vol 2, No. 2, 54-58.

Gupta, A. K. (2000). Prioritisation of Biodiversity Rich Sites in the State of Tripura. In "Setting Biodiversity Conservation Priorities for India", Singh, S., A. R. K. Sastry, R. Mehta and V. Uppal (eds.), Pp. 267-280. WWF-India, New Delhi, India.

Gupta, A. K. (2000): "Survey of binturong (*Arctitis binturong*) in Trishna Wildlife Sanctuary, Tripura, India" – a preliminary report prepared for Wildlife Conservation Society, USA.

Khajuria, H. (1954). Catalogue of mammals in the Indian museum (Zool. Survey). III. Primates : Colobidae. *Rec. Ind. Mus.*. 52:195-220.

Khajuria, H. (1956). A new langur (Primates: Colobidae) from Goalpara District, Assam. *Ann. Mag. Nat. Hist.*, Ser. 12, 9: 86-88.

Menon, K. D. (1975). *Tripura District Gazetteers*. Calcutta, India.

Pocock, R.I. (1939). *The fauna of British India, including Ceylon and Burma. Mammalia*. Vol. II.Taylor and Francis, London.

Prater, S. H. (1948). *The Book of Indian Animals*. Bombay Natural History Society, Bombay, India.

Ramakantha, V., A. K. Gupta, and Ajith Kumar (2003). Biodiversity of Northeast India: An Overview. In ENVIS Bulletin: Wildlife & Protected Areas, Conservation of Rainforests in India, A. K. Gupta, Ajith Kumar, and V. Ramakantha (eds.), Vol. 4, No. 1, 1-24.

Singh, K. C. (1896). *Rajmala*, Comilla.

Sterndale, R. A. (1884). *Natural History of the Mammalia of India and Ceylon*.

2
Biodiversity Conservation : North-East India with Focus on Tripura

A.K. Ghosh

Introduction

Eastern Himalaya, as a part of Biogeographic division of Indian Himalayas, include Arunachal Pradesh, Assam (17%), Manipur (100%), Meghalaya (100%), Mizoram (100%), Nagaland (100%) and Tripura (100%). It is a transition zone between Indo-Malayan, Indo-Chinese and typically Indian biogeographic region (Alfred, *et al.*, 2002). It is well known for heavy rainfall, flood and landslide with a wide diversity of ecosystems ranging from Forests, Grasslands, Wetlands, Rivers and Streams of mountains and agro-system.

Species diversity in flora include 700 of 1,000 Orchid species known from India (Jain and Mehrotra, 1984), 70 of the total of 90 species of *Rhododendron*, 35 species of bamboo besides 37 species of timber trees; diversity in medicinal plants, primitive flowering plants (e.g., *Magnolia*), fern and fern allies are other striking features. In summary, more than 50 per cent of the flowering plants known from India occur in the region. A number of monotypic genera also occur in the region. The range of endemicity is significant (Ghosh, A K, 1987; Bhagabat, 2006).

Noted Russian Botanist Vavilov considered the region as "Hindusthan Centre of Origin of Cultivated Plants"; it is regarded as the centre of origin of *Musa, Citrus,* Cucurbits and various temperate fruits. Likewise diversity in legume crops is also well documented (e.g., *Cajanus, Vigna, Glycine, Lathyrus*), including 200 non-conventional legumes. It is also one of the well known centres of origin of wild tea plants (Arora, *et al.*, 1983).

Faunatically, the area is rich in hill stream fishes, with a total of nearly 200 species (16% of Indian freshwater fish fauna) more than 100 species of Amphibia, including 30 endemic species. Reptilian fauna include more than 100 species, representing 30 per cent of Indian reptile fauna. A rich avifauna, including endemic form and nearly 45 per cent of Indian mammals, including endemic genus and species, inhabit the area. Invertebrate fauna of NE India has been well investigated and Butterflies and Moths indicative of rich biodiversity, (along with birds and flowering plants), represent a significant Figure; out of 1,500 species of butterflies of India, more than 50 per cent and out of 13,000 species of Moths nearly 30 per cent occur in the region (Alfred, *et al.* (ed.) 1998; Ghosh, A. K. 2001).

The state of Tripura occupies a unique position in the NE Indian scenario.

Tripura Scenario

The State of Tripura with 0.3 per cent of land area of the country shows four major ecosystem, viz., Mountain ecosystem, Forest ecosystem, Freshwater ecosystem, Agricultural ecosystem. A synoptic account of biodiversity in Tripura has been provided by Ghosh (2001) in the Report on "The Status of Environment in Tripura" prepared under 'Tripura State Pollution Control Board.

The richness of flora can be seen from the Table 2.1. With less than one per cent of the land area, the State has 20 per cent species of Gymnosperms besides 5–10 per cent of other plant groups.

Table 2.1: Flora of Tripura

•	Flowering plants	: 1463 species (8.6% of Indian species)
•	Gymnosperms	: 13 species (20% of Indian species)
•	Pteridophytes	: 70 species (5.8% of Indian species)

An analysis of uses of plant biodiversity shows that a rich bioresource base offers opportunities for sustaining rural livelihoods. These include, timber producing trees, 10 species of bamboos and 6 species of canes, medicinal plants and varieties of crop plants (Table 2.2).

Table 2.2: Biodiversity Uses : Flora

- Timber producing : 24 species
- Bamboo : 10 species
- Cane : 6 species
- Medicinal plants : 266 species
- Crop plants
  - Rice: 119 wild varieties
  - Millets: 5 varieties
  - Maize: 5 bio-types
  - Pulses: 5 varieties
  - Cucurbits: 17 species and many varieties
  - Beans: 10 species with large number of bio-types
  - Sweet potato: 4 bio-types
  - Amaranth: 6 varieties
  - Arecaceae: 6 species and 20 bio-types
  - Sesames : 5 varieties
  - Cotton : 3 varieties
  - Jute and Mesta : 6 varieties
  - Spices : 27 species
  - Fruits : Guava, Jackfruit, Mango, Pineapple, Papaya.

Faunistically, the vertebrate fauna shows a rich species diversity in all the groups except in the case of Amphibia (Table 2.3).

Table 2.3: Fauna

Group	*Number of Species*	*Percentage of Indian species*	*Status*
Freshwater Fishes	134 species	10.75% of Indian species	11 vulnerable, 3 endangered and 3 rare species
Amphibia	6 species	Less than 1% of Indian species	—
Reptilia	32 species	7% of Indian species	6 endangered species
Birds	341 species	25% of Indian species	4 endangered species
Mammals	54 species	33% of Indian species	12 rare and endangered species

In terms of the domesticated crops and animal species, the State had a rich diversity of indigenous breeds and farmer's varieties. A total of 119 cultivars of local rice varieties were evaluated by ICAR. At least 20 biotypes of brinjal and 16 biotypes of chillies are also known from the State. However, due to promotion of high yielding varieties of crops and animal breeds, the indigenous varieties show an alarming rate of regression. The State government data shows the loss of indigenous breeds of domesticated animal from 25 per cent in cattle to 50 per cent in buffalo and pig population (Table 2.4).

Table 2.4 : Livestock: Decline of indigenous breeds (1992-1997)

• Cattle population	25%
• Buffalo and Pig population	50%
• Goat population	40%
• Duck population	30%

Source: Department of Animal Resources, Government of Tripura.

Loss of Biodiversity

There is no systematic study on the issue of loss of biodiversity (Table 2.5) or on the issue of invasive species from Tripura. Although the State did not witness large scale industrialization, in general the possible loss of biodiversity, though no quantified, can be ascribed largely to the shifting cultivation in the hills, pollution load in the freshwater bodies and land-use changes in the peri-urban areas.

Table 2.5 : Loss of Biodiversity : Causes

- Habitat destruction
- Grazing
- Forest fire
- Shifting cultivation
- Introduction of exotic species
- Illegal hunting

Conservation

The official data shows that less than 6 per cent of the land area has been put under "Protected area system". However, the notification under article 26(A) of Indian Wildlife Protection Act, was not issued till 2004; (the current position is not known to the author) (Table 2.6). The setting up of the State Biodiversity Board in June 2008, may lead to a better conservation strategy but, till

May 2010 information regarding formation of Biodiversity Management Committee, was not available. The assistance of external donor agency (JICA) may help in focusing the issues of conservation in future. The documentation of biodiversity both wild and domesticated, in and outside the forest area is an essential prerequisite condition for an effective conservation strategy. The State need to work on preparation of a "State Biodiversity Action Plan" following the guideline set up by the Ministry of Environment and Forests, Government of India (2008).

Table 2.6 : Conservation Efforts

In situ Conservation
• A total of 604 sq. km. Out of 10481 sq. km. Of land area (5.77%) of Tripura has been used for setting up four Sanctuaries, viz., Sepahijala, Gumti, Trishna and Roa.
• One more Sanctuary is proposed to be notified.
• Notification under Article 26 (A) of Wildlife Protection Act is yet to be issued for all the four declared sanctuaries.
Ex situ Conservation
Only one Zoological Gardens; No Aquarium, No Seed Bank for Germplasm collection.

REFERENCES

Alfred, J.R.B., *et al.* (ed.) 1998. *Faunal Diversity in India.* Zoological Survey of India.

Alfred, J.R.B., *et al.* (ed.) 2002. *Ecosystem of India.* Zoological Survey of India.

Arora, R.K., *et al.*, 1983. Conservation of wild relatives of crop plants in India. NBPGR *Science Monograph*, 6, New Delhi.

Bhagabat, A.K., *et al.*, 2006. *Biodiversity of Assam.* EHB Publishers, Gauhati.

Ghosh, A.K., 1987. *Qualitative Analysis of the Faunal Resources of Proposed Namdapha Biosphere Reserve,* Arunachal Pradesh, 1 – 29, Zoological Survey of India.

Ghosh, A.K., 2001. *Status of Environment in Tripura.* Chapter VII: Biodiversity, pp. 40-53. Tripura State Pollution Control Board, Government of Tripura

Jain, S.K. and Mehrotra, A., 1984. *A Preliminary Inventory of Orchidaceae in India.* Botanical Survey of India, Howrah.

Mani, M.S., (ed.), 1974. *Ecology and Biogeography in India.* Dr. N. Junk B.V. Publishers, The Hague.

MoEF, 2008. *National Biodiversity Action Plan,* Government of India.

Rao, R.R., 1994. *Biodiversity in India.* Bishan Singh Mahendra Pal Singh. Dehradun.

Rao, R.R. and Haridasan, K., 1991. An Ethno Botanical Survey of Medicinal and other useful plants of North East India. *J. Econ. Taxon. Bot.,* 15(2):423 – 435.

ZSI, 2000. *Fauna of Tripura.* Zoological Survey of India.

3

Freshwater Biodiversity of North-East India with Special Reference to Tripura Issues, Challenges and Conservation Strategies

Ratan K. Saha

Introduction

A recent research project has addressed the losses in freshwater biodiversity under probable climate change and water consumption scenarios. About half of the investigated rivers worldwide would experience reduced water availability due to both global warming and withdrawal of water for human needs. By 2070, in these drying rivers, loss in local fish species would range from less than 4 per cent to more than 22 per cent with a maximum of 75 per cent loss in the most affected rivers.

Over the past 30 years, freshwater species have declined faster as compared to terrestrial or marine species. Unfortunately, growing evidence indicate that this trend is likely to persist in the future. On the one hand, freshwater ecosystems will probably further suffer from invasive species and land-use changes. On the other hand, freshwater biota is likely to be impacted by the predicted reduction in water availability driven by increased water consumption for human uses and indirectly related to global climate change (Xenopoulos *et al.*, 2005).

According to Xenopoulos *et al.*, 2005, these forecasts are underestimates of fish losses because many other important causes were not included in the calculations (e.g., introduced species, reductions in channel-flood-plain connectivity).

However, the International Union for Conservation of Nature

(IUCN) is assessing India's freshwater biodiversity (which includes mollusks, plants and insects) after 13 years. Their assessment should prove to be an invaluable resource for freshwater biodiversity conservation and development planning should the government want to make use of the data. According to a preliminary IUCN report, only 13 species of freshwater fish found in India have been assessed using the Red List criteria. Four insect species, two species of freshwater mollusks, and one specie of freshwater plant have been assessed. Further, a report on the status of amphibians found that India has the most number of threatened amphibian species in Asia, with 67 (25%) species facing possible extinction. Of the 38 species of amphibians in Asia that are confirmed to be extinct by the Global Amphibian Assessment (GAA), one is from India. In addition, 13 species are listed as critically endangered, 31 as endangered, and 23 as vulnerable. A further 95 species are listed in the data deficient category, indicating the number of threatened species could be much higher once information becomes available. The IUCN has also sounded the alarm over the dwindling river dolphin population, which is down to 2,500.

Freshwater Resources of North-East India

The North-East India, (22°-30°N and 89°-97°E) spread over 2,62,379 sq.km., represents the transition zone between the Indian, Indo-Malayan and Indo-Chinese biogeographic regions and a meeting place of the Himalayan Mountains and Peninsular India. It was the part of the northward moving "Deccan Peninsula" that first touched the Asian landmass after the break up of Gondwana land in the early Tertiary Period.

North-East India is thus the geographical "gateway" for much of India's flora and fauna. It is in this lowland-highland transition zone that the highest diversity of biomes or ecological communities can be found, and species diversities within these communities are also extremely high.

The region is made up of eight States: Arunachal Pradesh, Assam, Meghalaya, Manipur, Mizoram, Nagaland, Sikkim and Tripura and is endowed with a wide range of physiography and eco-climatic conditions.

The State of Assam has extensive flood plains, while

Khangchendzonga in Sikkim stands 8,586 m tall. Cherrapunjee in the State of Meghalaya holds the record for the highest rainfall in a single month (9,300 mm) as well as the most in a year (26,461 mm) in India, while the nearby Mawsynram has the world's highest average rainfall (11,873 mm).

The forests in the region are extremely diverse in structure and composition and combine tropical and temperate forest types, alpine meadows and cold deserts. There are regions, for example, in the State of Sikkim, where the faunal assemblages also change rapidly from tropical to subtropical, temperate, alpine and finally to cold desert forms.

India is one of the eighteen mega-biodiversity countries of the world and one of the four in Asia. The country is divided into 3 mega-biodiversity hot spots namely Indo-Burma, the Western Ghats (WG), and the Eastern Himalayas (EH) with 10 bio-geographic regions. Further, India stands out as one of the few countries with high human populations as well as a high number of threatened species (IUCN, 2004).

Out of 54,711 identified vertebrates, fish contains 27,977 (51.14%) valid species (515 families, 4,494 genera) of which 11,952 (42.72%) freshwater species and 12,457 (44.53 %) species using freshwaters (Nelson, 2006). Fishes are the most ancient and numerous of vertebrates.

India is fortunate that out of this 2,500 valid species are known from our waterbodies (Jayaram, 2010) and 376 of them are economically important. Among the India's animal wealth fish genetic resources is the third richest one after insect (40,000) and mollusks (5,000) only out of total 49,778 (Agarwal, 1999). Out of the total ichthiofauna approximately 930 species inhabiting freshwaters of India (Jayaram, 2010), the North-Eastern region represents 267 species belonging to 112 genera under 38 families and 100 orders (Sen, 2000). This is approximately 28.71 per cent of total Indian freshwater fishes of recent data.

North-East India is exceptionally rich in freshwater fishes, and it is heartening to note that out of all the 8 States of the region, Manipur has been extensively surveyed, and the State alone accounts for 167 species of freshwater fish species belonging to 11 orders, 31 families and 84 genera are recorded. The fish fauna of Loktak Lake in Manipur comprises 64 species. Two of these species, *Monopterus albus* and *Osteobrama belangeri* are restricted in their distribution to the Yunan State of China, Myanmar, and in India only to the State of Manipur. The Loktak Lake also serves as the breeding ground for several species of migratory fishes *e.g.*, *Labeo dero, L. bata* and *Cirrhinus reba*.

Sone Lake (12.5 km. long and 3.0 km. wide), is one of the biggest tectonic lakes in Assam. It sustains 75 species of fishes under 24 families and 49 genera and of which, 20 species are widely distributed while 8 species are native to North-East India.

The major groups of fresh water fishes found in North-East India are Cyprinids (family: *Cyprinidae*), Live fish (family: *Anabantidae, Clariidae, Channidae, Heteropneustidae*), Cat fish (family: *Bagridae, Silurdae*), *Clupeids, Clupeidae*), featherbacks (family: *Notopteridae*), Loaches (family: *Cobitidae*), Eels (family: *Mastacembelidae*), Glass fishes (family: *Chandidae*) and Gobies (family: *Gobiidae*).

Cyprinidae is one of the largest families and is well represented in India with species ranging from few millimetres in length (minnows) to more than a metre (major carps).

A report says that despite a very high diversity of freshwater fishes, North-East India does not have many endemic species (the fish fauna of India contains 2 endemic families, both of which are absent from the region) (Ramakantha, *et al.*, 2008).

This chapter focuses on the diversity of freshwater species population and their conservation in an aquatic ecosystem and suggest conservation measures to preserve biodiversity of North-East India with special reference to Tripura.

The Indo-Burma Hotspot

The Indo-Burma hotspot encompasses 2,373,000 km^2 of tropical Asia. It contains the Lower Mekong catchment, and begins in eastern Bangladesh and then extends across north-eastern India, to encompass nearly all of Myanmar, part of southern and western Yunnan Province in China, all of the Lao People's Democratic Republic, Cambodia and Vietnam, the vast majority of Thailand, and a small part of Peninsular Malaysia. The hotspot also covers the coastal lowlands of southern China, and several offshore islands.

Some of the features of biodiversity richness in Indo-Burma include :

- Around 13,500 vascular plant species, of which about 7,000 (52%) are endemic.
- Over 1,260 bird species, more than 60 of which are endemic.
- 430 mammal species, of which more than 70 species and seven genera are endemic.
- 520 reptile species, of which 12 genera and over 200 species are endemic.
- Highest diversity of freshwater turtles in the world with 53 species, representing one-fifth of the world's species.
- More than 280 amphibian species, over 150 of which are endemic.
- More than 1,260 documented freshwater fish species, or about 10 per cent of the world's freshwater fishes. More than 560 of these species are endemic.

Geomorphology of Tripura

Tripura State falls in moist sub-humid climatic region and is characterized by tropical monsoon type of climate as mentioned in Table 3.1.

Table 3.1: Geomorphology of Tripura

Sl No	*Parameters*	*Characteristics*
1.	Climate	Moist sub-humid climate (Tropical monsoon type of climate)
2.	Season	Winter, Hot weather, South-West Monsoon, (Rainy season) and Retreating South-West Monsoon
3.	Annual Rainfall	2101 to 3047 mm (June–Wettest month)
4.	Temperature	Av. Max. Temp. 35 °C (24.8 °C Jan.) Av. Min. Temp. 10 °C (5.1 °C Jan.)
5.	Humidity	85 % (80–90 %) (During Rainy Season) 50–75 % (During Summer)
6.	Soil	Acidic to Slightly acidic (pH 4.5 to 6.5)
7.	Water Source	Rain fed Freshwater
8.	Areal Extent	22° 56?to 24° 32′ N latitude 91° 09′ to 92° 20′ E latitude
9.	Major Area	About 70 % hilly covered by Forest (57.8 %), Undulating terrain
10.	Soil colour	Red and Yellow soils
11.	Soil Texture	Sandy-loam and Laterite
12.	Geographical area	10,491.49 sq. km.

On the basis of monsoon's condition, a year can be divided

into four principal seasons, i.e. (i) Winter (December-February), (ii) Hot weather season (March-May), (iii) South-West monsoon, i.e., rainy season (June-September) and (iv) retreating South-West monsoon season (October-November). Average annual rainfall in the State is 2100 mm of which about 66 per cent is received from South-West monsoon. Pre-monsoon cyclonic thunder storms and occasional heavy showers are recorded during the month of April and May (Saha, 1989).

Freshwater Resources of Tripura

In total aqua-resources contribute only 2.02 per cent of the total geographical area of the State. Out of the total aqua-resources of 21,169.24 ha, 37.2 per cent belongs to the running water (lotic) and 62.5 per cent belongs to standing water (lentic) including one medium reservoir (Gumti) and wetlands. Among the different wetlands of Tripura, Rudrasagar has been identified by Ministry of Environment and Forest, Government of India as a national wetland having 100.46 ha water area. It is a floodplain wetland within Gumti River basin and has a rich aquatic resources including avifauna of resident type as well as migratory. It is periodically inundated leading to sustainable fisheries and agriculture development. In recent studies it has been observed that the surface water resources of Tripura are under tremendous stress.

As per remote sensing data during 2005, the water spread areas of Gumti reservoir and Rudrasagar lake is 3049.34 ha (32.24 % reduction) and 100.46 ha (58.14 % reduction), rivers, etc. 4728.96 ha (10.25 % reduction) whereas, previously these were 4,500 ha, 240 ha, and 5,269 ha respectively. Not only is that, all the rivers now become seasonal only with tremendous loss of local aquatic biodiversity. Among the reverine resources Manu, Khowai, Gumti, Deo, Dhalai, Fani Muhuri, Juri and Haora are important rivers (Table 3.2).

From the available literatures it has been observed that water quality (Table 3.3) of both lentic and lotic systems of Tripura are slightly acidic to moderately alkaline with low nutrients status.

Freshwater Biodiversity of Tripura

Among the North-Eastern region of India, Tripura (22°56′ –

Table 3.2: Important Reverine Resources of Tripura

Name of the River	*Flow length (km)*	*Remarks*
I. Northerly Flowing Rivers		
1. Longai	98	[Jampui range] Dharmsnagar ~ Assam.
2. Juri	79	[Jampui range] Dharmsnagar ~ river Kusiyara in Bangladesh.
3. Manu (Longest River)	167	[Longtharai] Kumarghat anc Kailashahar ~ Bangladesh.
4. Dhali	117	[Longtharai] Kamalpur ~ Bangladesh
5. Khowai	166	[Longtharai] Taliamura, Kalyanpur, Khowai ~ Bangladesh
II. Southward Flowing Rivers		
6. Muhuri	64	[Deotamura range] Belonia ~ Bangladesh
7. Fenni	—	[Border ofTripura and Bangladesh] ~ Bangladesh
III. Westward Flowing Rivers		
8. Gumti	133	[Longtharai and Atharamura] Gandacherra, Jatanbari, Amarpur, Udaipur, Sunamura ~Bangladesh
9. Haora (Smallest River)	53	[Baramura range] Champaknagar, Jirania, Agartala ~ Bangladesh
10. Deo	98	[Jampui range] Kanchanpur anc Pecharthal.

Note: All are seasonal nature, and All the hills extended in north-south direction.

Table 3.3 : Physico-chemical Properties of Surface Hydrology of Tripura

Sl. No.	*Parameter*	*Lentic*	*Lotic*
1.	pH	6.0 – 9.6	6.0 - 8.5
2.	Conductivity (μ mhos/cm)	57.0 – 716.0	62.7 – 244.0
3.	CO_2 (mg l^{-1})	0.0 – 23.6	1.0 – 72.9
4.	DO (mg l^{-1})	0.6 – 10.7	5.4 – 13.7
5.	$CO_3^{=}$ (mg l^{-1})	4.0 – 16.0	—
6.	HCO_3^- (mg l^{-1})	12.0 – 108.0	18.0 – 315.0
7.	NH_4-N (mg l^{-1})	0.04 – 7.7	0.02 – 1.0
8.	PO_4-P (mg l^{-1})	0.2 – 7.0	0.002 – 0.8
9.	K^+ (mg l^{-1})	0.4 – 5.0	0.9 – 4.9
10.	SiO_2 (mg l^{-1}	0.3 – 29.0	3.5 – 39.5
11.	Total Hardness (mg l^{-1})	4.0 – 110.0	9.0 – 64.0
12.	Ca^{++} (mg l^{-1})	2.8 – 18.8	—
13.	Mg^{++} (mg l^{-1})	0.3 – 102 .0	—
14.	Cl^- (mg l^{-1})	13.2 – 91.6	—
15.	Fe (mg l^{-1})	0.21 – 3.96	0.09 – 1.98
16.	BOD_5 (mg l^{-1})	1.5 – 80.0	0.4 – 7.5

24°32′N and 90°09′ – 32°20′ E) is the second smallest land locked State having 10,486 sq. km. Major areas (about 70%) of this State are hilly covered by forest (57.8%) and as such having undulating terrain. Tripura is endowed with tremendous natural wealth and belongs to the Indo-Burma mega-biodiversity hot spots of the country. The region, by and large, is characterized by fragility, marginality, inaccessibility, cultural heterogeneity, ethnicity and rich biodiversity.

Though the water resources are limited, even then well diversified aqua-bio resources enrich the State to a great extent (Table 3.4). In fact there are so many areas are still unexplored due to some reason or the other.

Fish genetic resources of the State revealed that a total of 134 species have been recorded from Tripura belonging to 82 genera under 32 families and 9 orders. Among the other aquatic resources, 42 species of shellfish, birds 33 species (aquatic and semi-aquatic), amphibians 6 species, reptiles 7 species, 45 species of macrophyton, 63 genera of phytoplankton, 239 species of zooplankton, 64 species of periphyton, 10 species of benthos, 17 species of aquatic insects and so on have been recorded.

Growing pressure resulting from human activities has adversely impacted many species and habitats around the country and Tripura in particular. Humans are changing the landscapes around them and in doing so they are damaging and eliminating the environmental resources necessary to sustain animal diversity. Living things face a constant barrage of external stresses or threats that challenges their ability to survive and reproduce.

However, very little work has been done systematically to explore the aquatic biodiversity as a whole in the State. The available potential can be exploited by way of adequate and appropriate scientific steps in this regard. The probable issues and challenges in relation to decline of the aquatic resources of the State, and the conservation strategies have been discussed in this chapter.

One of the richest biomes of the North-East India, high in endemism and rare species which is now under constant threat due to human pressure (having lost 70% of their original habitat). This region represents an important part of the Indo-Myanmar biodiversity hotspot.

Table 3.4: Freshwater Bio-resources of Tripura

Phytoplankton		
	1. Cyanophyceae-	12 genera
	2. Chlorophyceae-	24 genera
	3. Bacillariophyceae-	18 genera
	4. Euglenophyceae-	2 genera
	5. Dinophyceae-	2 genera
	6. Xanthophyceae-	2 genera
	7. Chrysophyceae-	3 genera
	Total	63 genera
Zooplankton		
	1. Protozoa-	5 species
	2. Rotifera-	112 species
	3. Gastrotricha-	1 species
	4. Conchostraca-	1 species
	5. Cladocera-	39 species
	6. Copepoda	8 species
	7. Ostracoda-	5 species
	Total	239 species
Macrophyton		
	1. Floating-	12 species
	2. Submerged-	8 species
	3. Emergent-	4 species
	4. Marginal-	8 species
	Total	45 species
Aqatic Insects		17 species
Benthos		10 species
Periphyton		64 species
Fin Fish		134 species 82 genera 32 families 09 orders
Shellfish		42 species
Aquatic and Semiaquatic Birds		33 species
Amphibians		6 species
Reptiles		7 species

As such, the aquatic resources of this region are not being inventoried fully in all respects and till date except few sporadic works there is no systematic initiative has been taken up by any agencies or individuals to work on them even their immense ecological and economical importance.

Only recently researchers are attracted and worked for the

fish germplasm of the State (Ghosh and Lipton 1982; Sen 1982; Barman, 1988; Anon, 1988; Sinha, 1992; Sinha, 1994; Kar 2000; Sen 2000; Saha, 2004).

According to Sinha (1994) fish genetic resources of the State revealed that a total of 115 species belonging to 75 genera and 31 families. Out of these 5 species viz. *Cyprinion Semiplotum, Neolissoclitus hexagonolepis (=Accrossocheilus hexagonolepis = Puntius dukai), Tor putitora, Tor tor, Nemacheilus elongates* belong to the threatened species (Sinha, 1992).

Presently, Sen (2000) did a comprehensive work on fish fauna of North-Eastern State and 134 species have been recorded from Tripura belonging to 82 genera under 32 families and 9 orders. But, current conservation status of individual fish germplasm as evaluated by conservation Assessment and Management Plan (CAMP) workshop held at National Bureau of Fish Genetic Resources (NBFGR) during 1997 is indicated as critically endangered (CR) extinct in the wild (EW) vulnerable (Vu), lower risk near threatened (LR-nt) Lower risk least concern (LR-lc) and data deficient (DD). Only recently, Sarkar and Ponniah (2000) depicted and categories the ichthiofauna of Tripura along with other North-Eastern States as 15 species Vu, 5 species LR-lc, 24 species LR-nt, and 9 species EN.

But according to Sen (2000) out of the total fish fauna 1 critically endangered (CR), 13 endangered (EN) and 24 vulnerable (Vu) species have so far been assessed from Tripura (Table 3.5). On the

Table 3.5: Status of Fish Fauna of Tripura

CR	= *Schismatorhynchus (Nukta) nukta*
EN	= *Chaca chaca, Tor puntitora, Tor tor, Ompok bimaculatus, Ompok pabda, Eutropichthys vacha, N. chitala, Rita rita, Pseudeutropius atherenoides, Pisodonophis bora, Bagarius bagarius. Neolissocheilus (Acrossocheilus) hexgonolepis.*
Vu	= *Puntius chola, Puntius conchonicus, Puntius sarana sarana, Aspidoparia jaya, Barilius barila, C. reba, Clupisoma garua, Anabas testudineus, H. fossilis, C. batrachus, Amphipnous cuchia, Channa orientalis, Mystus vittatus, Garra gotyla gotyla.*
LR-nt	= *A. morar, B. barna, B. shacra, X. caucila, B. lairoukensis, Cirrhinus mrigala, Danio acquipinnatus, D. (Danio) devario, Labeo bata, Labeo boga, L. calbasu, L. gonius, L. pangusia, Osteobrama cotio cotio, P. ticto, P. sophore, Eutropichthys murius, Wallago attu, Nemacheilus botia, Amblyceps mangois, Colisa faciata, N. notopterus, Tetraodon cutcutia.*
LR-lc	= *Channa striatus, Chanda bachulis, Salmostoma bacila, Esomus danricus, Chela laubuca.*

other hand, among 32 families Cyprinidae family is the largest one and having 53 species. Further, 10 exotic species (6 legal), 8 culturable species and 42 species of aqu-jewels, i.e., ornamental fishes are found in the State (Table 3.6).

Table 3.6: List of Aqua-Jewaels of Tripura

- BARBS: 1.Puntius conchonius (Rosy Barb), 2. P. chola (Swamp Barb), 3. P. ticto (Redfin two spot Barb), 4. P. sophore (Sophore's Barb), 5. Osteobrama cotio cotio (Diamond Barb).
- LOACHES: 1. *Botia dario* (Necktie loach), 2. *Botia rostrata* (Recticulated Loach), 3. *Lepidocephalus guntia* (Guntia loach), 4.*Noemacheilus botia botia* (Gutum).
- SNAKE HEADED FISHES: 1. *Channa punctatus* (Spotted snake head), 2. *C. marulius* (Gaint snake head), 3. *C. striatus* (Stiped snake head), 4. *C. (gachua) orientalis* (Asiatic snake head).
- CAT FISHES: 1. *Ailia coila* (GangeticAilia), 2. *Batasio batasio* 3. *Mystus tenggra* (Tengara mystus), 4. *M. cavasius* (Gangetic Mystus), 4. *Pseudouttopius aetherinoides* (Indian Potasi), 5.*Gangata cenia* (Indian ganan Gangata).
- FRESHWATER GARS: *Xenentodon cancila* (Long beak fish).
- MUD PERCHES: 1. *Nandus nandus* (Mottled nandus), 2.*Badis badis* (Dwarf chameleon fish).
- GOURAMI: 1.*Colisa fasciata* (Gaint Gourami/ Striped Gourami), 2. *C. lalia* (Dwarf Gourami), 3.*Colisa sota* (Honey Gourami /Sunset Gourami).
- PUFFER FISH: *Tetradon cutcutia* (Malayan Puffer/ Ocellated Puffer fish).
- GLASS FISH: 1. *Chanda nama* (Elongate glass perchlet), 2. *Pseudambassis (Chanda) ranga* (Jewel Glass Fish), 3.*P. (C.) baculis* (Black Spot Glass Fish).
- KNIFE FISHES: 1. *Notopterus notopterus* (GREY feather back), 2. *N. chitala* (Police fish).
- SWAMP EEL: *Monopterus cuchia* (Gangetic Mud Eel).
- SPINY EELS: 1. *Macrognathus (Mastacembalus) pancalus* (Striped spiny eel), 2. *M. aculeatus* (One-stripe spiny eel), 3. *Mastacembalus armatus* (Tire-tract spiny eel).
- FLYING BARB: 1. *Esomus danricus* (Flying barb), 2. *Rasbora daniconius daniconius* (Black line Rospora).
- ZEBRA FISHES: *Danio devario* (Devario danio).
- CHILWAS: *Chela laubuca* (Spot tailed hatchet fish).
- BRASS FISH: *Amblypharyngodon mola* (Pale carplt).
- HILL TROUTS: *Barrilius barila* (Brred baril).
- CALBASU: *Labeo calbasu* (Black rohu).

Causes of Declining

All the freshwater resources/bio-resources are in great threat and also suffocating in present day developing conditions of Tripura

State. Here, an attempt has been made as suggested by Saha (2004) to spell out different reasons of these conditions to take appropriate corrective measures to save the existing environment from further deterioration for future generation too.

- Construction of dam across the Gumti river reduces the adequate flow in the rivers and obstruct the breeding performance of indigenous fish species.
- Introduction of fast-growing exotic fish species (*Clarias gariepinus*, *Pangasius sutchi, O. niloticus, H. nobilis,* etc.) may cause existing natural ecological imbalance.
- Due to "Jhum cultivation" and deforestation in the upper catchments areas of the rivers, tributaries and reservoirs etc., for which ecology of all the natural waterbodies are badly disturbed.
- Due to indiscriminate use of pesticides/fertilizers, etc., in the agricultural field and also in the aquaculture system.
- Natural fish genetic resources are neglected because our full attentions are on the major carp aquaculture operations and their improvement.
- During culture operation one step is there "Eradication of Weed Fishes", i.e., *Puntius* spp., *Mastacembalus* spp., *Channa* spp., *Chanda nama, Chanda ranga,* etc., may be of another reason for declining.
- Repaid overall development of State and ever increasing demand of fish as food.
- Destruction of fish habitat by over fishing of important fishes.
- Land development.
- Domestication of fish species.
- Reclamation of shore line areas of lakes, rivers, etc.
- Over drawing of water for domestic and agricultural purposes have reduced the fish habitats.
- Epizootic ulcerative syndrome (EUS) may be another important reason for the declining trend of the fish genetic resources of the State.
- Release and dumping of domestic sewage and agricultural waste, etc., into the potential waterbodies.
- Flooding of natural waterbodies due to siltation.
- Indiscriminate and intentional use of plant origin toxicants

in the natural/open water systems.

- Unable to pay proper attention in the inaccessible or difficult areas where the potential rich ichthyological resources are there.

Conservation of Freshwater Habitats

In India, the idea of fish conservation is known from the time of king Ashoka (246 B.C) when catching of freshwater fish was prohibited based on their breeding periods, which peak from July to September (Menon, 1988).

On the other hand, in 1873, scientists like Francis Day and Sir Arthur Cotton drew the attention of the then Government of India to large scale slaughter of fish fry and fingerlings and pleaded urgent conservation measures (Paul, 1990).

After persistent pressure, the Indian Fisheries Act was enacted in 1897. Subsequently certain States, *viz.*, Pubjab, Haryana, Himachal Pradesh, Madhya Pradesh, Uttar Pradesh, etc., have promulgated and enforced rules successfully, whereas others have not.

Not only this, to conserve living resources, new Acts have been promulgated e.g., the Water (Prevention and Control of Pollution) Act, 1974 & Land Act, 1977; The Wildlife (Protection) Act, 1972, amended in 1983, 1986 and 1991; the Environment (Protection) Act, 1986 amended in 1989; the Insecticides Act, 1968 and the Forest (Conservation) Act, 1980.

Despite such enactments and rules, many problems remain, as because they are all in papers only. Freshwater resources are still declining in the natural as well as manmade habitat of the State and many fish species, particularly endemics, are greatly threatened and a few are on the verge of extinction. Following conservation strategies have been suggested by Saha (2004):

- Formulation of **"State Fisheries Act"** and its proper practical application.
- Revision of **"Fisheries Act of 1987"** of India should be done immediately by the Central Government and as far as possible, common rules should apply in State strictly (Dubey and Ahmad, 1995).
- **Auctioning of reservoir** and **lake** fishery rights should

be **abolished** if exist, because license owners could kill all the fish in waters for which they hold fishing rights (Dubey and Ahmad,1995).

- The rules should ban fishing with poisons, etc.
- The rules should ban the catching of certain important endangered fish species.
- Detailed **Environmental Impact Assessments** (EIA) should be carried out before implementing any project which might have negative impacts on fish and their habitats and management plan for ecologically sustainable development should be adopted (Afroz, 1988).
- Reservoir fisheries should be closed during breeding season **(Fishing holiday)** to safeguard pre-spawning and spent fishes and also the mesh size regulation should be implemented.
- **Fish sanctuaries** should be established in consultation with State Fisheries experts and local people wherever necessary.
- Rules should be formulated to **control the introduction of exotic species** quarantine and health certification approaches should be followed before imparting any aquatic organisms.
- Quarantine and health certification approaches should be followed before imparting any aquatic organisms.
- Regular **water quality monitoring** to assess the suitability of water for healthy fish and other aquatic resources.
- The **Forest (Conservation) Act 1980** should be strictly applied to prevent soil erosion by further deforestation close to river and their tributaries, on reservoir catchments and in other environmentally sensitive areas.
- To protect the natural ecological balance **large-scale scientific aforestation** of degraded catchment areas should be taken with first priority.
- Eco-friendly cultivation or **organic cultivation** should be discussed and encouraged among the actual users.
- If pesticides and inorganic fertilizers are used that should be properly treated before their release into the water system.
- Pollution due to power plants should be monitored and controlled.

- A comprehensive detailed in-depth scientific study should be conducted to know the real status of the individual fish germplasm of the State.
- Systematic breeding programme of endangered / rare and commercial species should be taken up by the Fisheries experts with topmost priority.
- **Sustained awareness** programmes (mass education through audio-visual aids) should be conducted to encourage conservation of genetic resources as well as the water resources.
- NGOs and other voluntary organizations should be involved to expedite the **mass awareness** programmes.
- Rules should be formulated to **stop the filling of water-bodies** for land development.
- Establishment of **gene bank** for ready availability of endangered fish germplasm (Dehadrai, *et al.*, 1994).
- Intensive fisheries **resource mapping** is essential through extensive field work in collaboration with different agencies.
- A hand book / booklet should be published periodically for the guidance of various departments by the appropriate authority, i.e., National Bureau of Fish Genetic Resources, etc.
- Rural stocking of natural waterbodies with advanced fingerlings of depleted species.
- A systematic categorization of the fish genetic resource like endangered, vulnerable, rare and threatened is required for long run careful planning in the State to save them.
- A serious step should be taken up to quantify the break up activities of human on the natural ecosystem towards cause of extinction of fish genetic resources and accordingly appropriate safety measures should be adopted in the State.
- The enforcement of rules and the protection of reservoir police force under the Fisheries Department of the State; provided with necessary equipment, including motor boats. (Dubey and Ahmad, 1995).
- We have a Wild Life Act 1972, provided for the protection of small and large mammals, birds, reptiles, etc., but the

question of conservation of our natural fish fauna has not yet received the desired attention of the policy makers. So, proper amendment has to be done with topmost priority.

- Last but not the least, the most important aspect is that the responsibility of conservation of fish genetic resource rests with fish breeder, geneticists, ecologists, law enforcing agencies and all other connected directly or indirectly with exploitation of fisheries. Development of water lands for aquaculture.
- Creation of water harvesting structure in the valley which in turn recharges the groundwater, etc.
- **Adoption of pen-culture** in the flood plain area / low lying area.
- Creation of water structure in the seasonal rivers / rivulets both for irrigation and aquaculture.

Conclusion

This chapter reveals that the freshwater habitats and species living in freshwater are less studied and needs immediate concern for thorough systematic investigation with dedicated expert groups in all the States of the North-East India.

Further, in order to promote the efficient management of freshwater biodiversity and eventually inverse its decline, there is an urgent need to provide solid estimations of fish species losses under plausible climate change and water consumption scenarios.

In any event, the scientists argue that along with the international efforts to minimize global warming, reducing water consumption could be an initial conservation strategy to prevent the predicted loss of fishes worldwide.

REFERENCES

Agarwal, K.C. (1999). *Environmental Biology*. Pub: Agro-Botanica, pp. 584.

Afroz, A. (1988) *Environmental Impact Assessment of Water Resources Projects in India*. Centre for Environmental Protection and Improvement, Berlin, Germany p. 98.

Anon. (1999) *Integrated Watershed Management of the Gumti River Valley: Final Report of the Himalayan Eco-development Project*. Tripura University, Agartala, 22-69.

Anon. (1996). *Handbook on Fisheries Statistics*, 1996, Ministry of Agriculture, Fisheries Division, Government of India, pp. 217.

Anon. (1998). *Conservation Assessment and Management Plan (CAMP) for Freshwater Fishes of India (1998)*. Zoo. Outreach Organization/ CBSG, India.

Anon. (2009). Conservation International (http://www.conservation.org/) and National Geographic News (news.nationalgrographic.com)

Barman, R.P. (1988). The fishes of the river Gumti, Tripura, North-Eastern India. *Rec. Zool. Surv. India*, Occ. Paper No. 119.

Datta, A.K. (1977). On a collection of Fishes from Tripura State. *Newsletter Zool. Surv. India*, 3(1) : 24-26.

Dehadrai, P.V., Das P. and Verma, S.R. (1994). *Threatened Fishes of India* (eds.), P.V. Dehadrai, P. Das and S.R. Verma, Pub: *Nature Conservations*, India, pp. 412.

Dubey, G.P. and Ahmad, A. (1995). Problems for the conservation of Freshwater Fish Genetic Resources in India, and some possible solutions. *Naga*, July: 21-25.

Ghosh, S.P. and Lipton, A.P. (1982). Ichthyofauna of NEH region with special reference to their economic importance. *ICAR Spl. Bull.* No.1, ICAR Complex for NEH Region, Shillong, pp. 126.

IUCN (2004). A Global Species Assessment. ISBN 2-8317-0826-5.

IUCN (2010). website, www.iucn.org, December 2010.

Jayaram, K.C. (2010). *The Freshwater Fishes of the Indian Region*. (Revised 2nd ed.). Pub: Narendra Pub. Housing, Delhi., pp. 616 + XXXIX.

Menon, A.G.K. (1988). *Conservation of Ichthyofauna of India, Conservation and Management of Inland Capture Fish Resources*. Bulletin No. **57**:25-33. Central Capture Fisheries Research Institute (CIFRI), Barrackpore, India.

Nelson, J. (2006) *Fishes of the World*. (4th ed.). Pub: John Wiley & Sons Inc., pp. 601+XIX.

Paul, S. (1990) *Riverine Environment Fisheries & Legislative Support, a Preliminary Report*. Central Fisheries Research Institute (CIFRI), Barrackpore, India.

Ramakantha, V., Gupta, A.K. and Kumar, A. (2008). Biodiversity of North-East India – An Overview. Biodiversity-mohanpai.blogspot.com/2008.

Saha, R.K. (1989). *An Ecological Study of Two Lentic Habitats of Agartala, India*, Ph.D. thesis, Calcutta University, p. 164 (18 Tables) + 20 Figures.

Saha, R.K. (2004). Aquatic Bio-resources of Tripura with Special Reference to Present Status and Future Conservation Strategy. *In*: Proc. Sem. Biodiversity, Jan. 10-11, 2004 (eds. R. C. Srivastava and B.K. Datta): 83-90.

Sen, T.K. (1985). The fish fauna of Assam and the neighbouring North-Eastern States of India. *Occ.Pap.* **64**. *Zool. Survey India*. pp. 216.

Sen, N. (2000). Overview of distribution and threatened status of North-East India fish fauna. Extended Abstract: A6:25-27. *Workshop on North East Fish Germplusm Inventory & Conservation*. 10-11 Feb. Shillong.

Sharkar, U.K. Ponniah, A.G. (2000). Evaluation of North-Eastern Indian fishes for their potential as cultivable, sport and ornamental fishes along with their conservation and endemic status, Base paper, 1-17: Workshop on North East India Fish Germplasm Invention and conservation, 10-11 February, Shillong.

Sharma, B.K. (2000). *Environmental Chemistry*, pub: Agro-Botanic, pp. 584.

Sinha, M. (1992). Threatened coldwater fishes of North-Eastern region of India. *Nat. Sem-Endangered Fishes of India*, Allahabad. April 25-26, 1992.

Sinha, M. (1994). Fish Genetics Resources of the North Eastern Region of India. *J. Inland Fish Soc. India*, **26** (1):1-19.

Talwar, P.K. and Jhingran, A.G. (1991). *Inland Fishes of India and Adjacent Countries*, **Vol. I & II**, Oxford & IBH Publishing Co., Calcutta, pp. 1158.

Xenopoulos, M.A., Lodge, D.M., Alcamo, J. Marker, M. Schulze, K. and Van Vuuren, D.P. (2005). Scenarios of freshwater fish extinctions from climate change and water withdrawal. *Global Change Biology*, 11 (10): 1557-1564.

4
Climatic Resources for Sustainable Biodiversity in Tripura

D. Daschaudhuri and *M. Datta*

Introduction

Climate maintains the forest and Forest mitigates the Climate Change. One is to take care of the other for the sustainability of both. It is the climate which influences the types of forest and at the same time, forest of that area also manipulates the dynamic of atmosphere. There are many evidences of effect of deforestation over climate but climate is not the singular aspects responsible for the deforestation, particularly in this part of the Globe. It is believed that man alter the climate, by changing of earth surface through change of land-use patterns. Out of several factors, most effective change in land-use pattern is done through deforestation or afforestation and agricultural practices. This change of land-use is correlated with the heat balance of the earth atmosphere. Deforestation is estimated to be responsible for 18 per cent of Greenhouse Gases (GHG) emission (WWF- www.worldlife.org). Among the entire suit of GHG, CO_2 is the major one which lasts for longest period, i.e., from decades to thousand years (James F. Casting, 1998). Though very modest work so far could be done to find out the long term consequences of increase in CO_2 in the atmosphere but among the likely physical factors being one of the worrisome factors, is the rise in sea level that would likely follow due to increase in surface temperature in high altitude regions. Now, forest could be better used in combating a change of physical composition of biosphere by new planting and replanting of deforested areas. Thus, for the best uses of atmospheric condition for maintenances of biodiversity resources, understanding of climate – biodiversity relationships in location specific level is needed. In this chapter it is tried to find out the climatic resources that might be helpful for sustainability of biodiversity resources in the State of Tripura particularly air temperature and rainfall, as these are the major components which maintains the growth of plant.

Material and Methods

The State of Tripura is located between 22° 57′ and 24° 32′N and 91° 10′ and 92° 20′E with tropic of cancer passing through it (Department of Economics and Statistics, Government of Tripura). The State is situated in the south-western part of North-East region of the country. In the context of climatic classification, the State of Tripura comes under Subtropical monsoon, mild dry winter, warm and humid summer with winter fog (Satapathy *et al.*, 2000) and according to the NARP Classification it is mild tropical plain zone. Sharma (1996), based on climatic features, topography, soil characteristics and agricultural practices, suggested 14 agro-climatic sub-regions of eight North-Eastern States including Sikkim. According to this the major part of the State, mostly West Tripura district and part of North, South and Dhalai comes under Humid Tropical zone and the rest comes under mild tropical sub-humid plain zone. A very small portion of centre of the State falls under mild tropical sub-humid zone. The general altitude of the State ranges from 10 m in the western part to 976 m in the North-Eastern part. The five principal hill ranges, the Jampui, the Sakhantang, the Longtarai, the Atharamura and the Baramura, running parallel in north-south direction which provides a good passage for the south-west monsoon to travel. Because of this unique geographical position the hill ranges which gradually increases in the south influence the monsoon activity in the State (Satapathy *et al.*, 2000). The vegetation in the State is mainly tropical, evergreen, semi-evergreen, and moist deciduous (Forest Department, Government of Tripura, 2007). About 60 per cent of total geographical area of the State is under forests out of which sizeable area is covered with bamboo brakes. As per Forest Survey of India, Ministry of Environment and Forests (MoEF) the net forest cover in the State has increased by 16 per cent considering the losses of 6 percent due to shifting cultivation and other reasons since 2001-03. According to classification of Champion and Seth, the forests of the State have been classified in six types out of which Low Alluvial Savannah Woodland and Moist Mixed Deciduous Forests and Dry Bamboo Brakes covers 60 per cent of total forest area. The State is located in the Biogeographic zone of 9B-North-East Hills and possesses extremely rich biodiversity. Out of more than 1,500 species of flora found in the State, 7 are endemic and 18 are rare. More than 250 species of medicinal plants are also found in the forest of Tripura.

The data of different parameters, air temperature, rainfall, and bright sunshine hour used in this study is collected from Agrometeorological Observatory of ICAR Research Complex for NEH Region, Tripura Centre, Lembucherra. Due to remoteness of the area, the numbers of Observatory approved by the India Meteorological Department (IMD) are very few. So availability of data length is also very less. Data period of 1992 to 2009 are considered for the study.

RESULTS & DISCUSSION

Data so collected are analysed in annual and monthly basis. The rainfall analyzed in annual, seasonal and monthly basis. Seasonal distribution defined as per following:

Summer or Pre-monsoon	:	April to May
Monsoon	:	June to September
Post-Monsoon	:	October to December
Winter	:	January to March

Air Temperature

Air temperature is the primary factor that controls the rate of plant development. The occurrence of different phonological events during plant growth period in relation to temperature can be estimated by using Accumulated heat units or growing degree days (GDD) (Gouri *et al.*, 2005). Heat use efficiency (HUE) i.e., efficiency of utilization of heat in terms of dry matter accumulation depends on plant type, genetic factors and sowing time which has great practical application. According to Das HP (2008) the normal growth of plant may be stopped with the variations of temperature just above or below the threshold value. Extreme temperature conditions during cold spell causes stress and frost; high temperature leads to heat stress, and both effect the growth of the plant.

Maximum Temperature

The yearly variation of maximum temperature is presented in Fig. 4.1. Yearly mean maximum temperature of the study area varied from 29° to 32°C. Yearly mean maximum temperature is showing a clear indication of increasing trend. The coolest year recorded was 2002 whereas 2009 was the hottest in respect to yearly

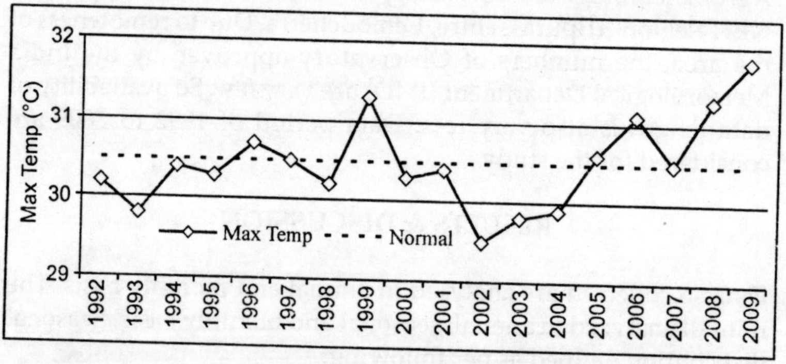

Fig. 4.1 : Yearly Mean Maximum Temperature (1992-2009).

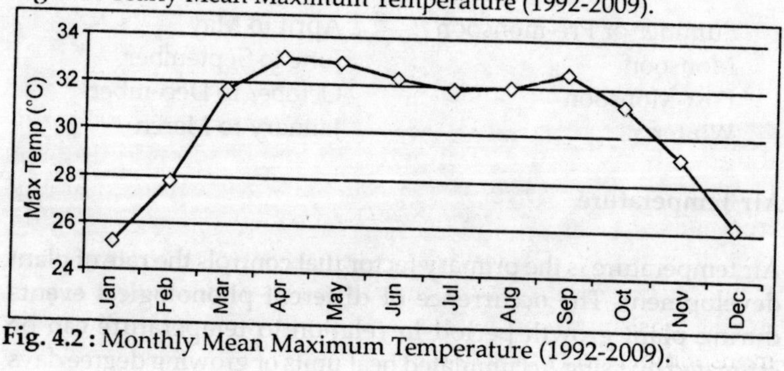

Fig. 4.2 : Monthly Mean Maximum Temperature (1992-2009).

mean maximum temperature. The yearly variations of temperature was mostly within ± 1°C except during the year 2002 and 2009. Monthly mean maximum temperature varied from 25.2°C during January to 33.1°C during April. April recorded the hottest month of the year and January coolest. During summer and monsoon season maximum temperature remains more than 30°C but for rest of the period it varies from 25 to 29°C.

Minimum Temperature

Yearly mean minimum temperature for the study period varied from 15.7°C in 1997 to 21.5°C during 2001. The yearly mean temperature was exceptionally below normal temperature during 1996 and 1997 by about 4°C. Other than this the variation ranged mostly below ± 1°C range of normal temperature. The coolest year recorded was 1997 and the hottest 2004 (Fig. 4.3).

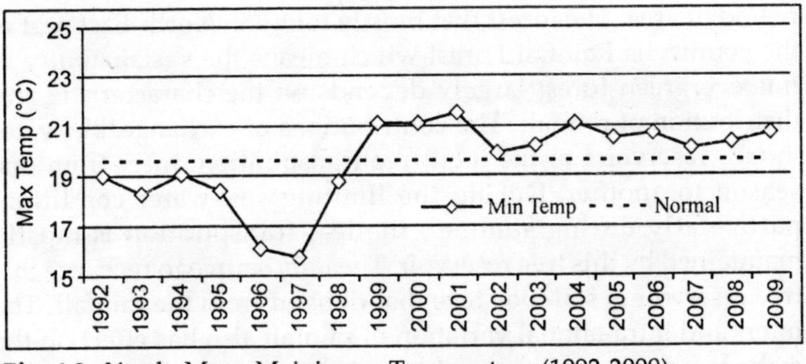

Fig. 4.3 : Yearly Mean Mainimum Temperature (1992-2009).

The plotted graphs of mean minimum temperature almost completed the cycle from where it starts and the variation is also found to be identical. Temperature found minimum during January which gradually increase and attains the peak in August from where it starts declining and came down almost its original position during December. Month to month variations of temperature remain maximum during September to April, i.e., during post-monsoon, winter and summer season, but during monsoon period (from June to September) this variation almost remain the same (Fig. 4.4).

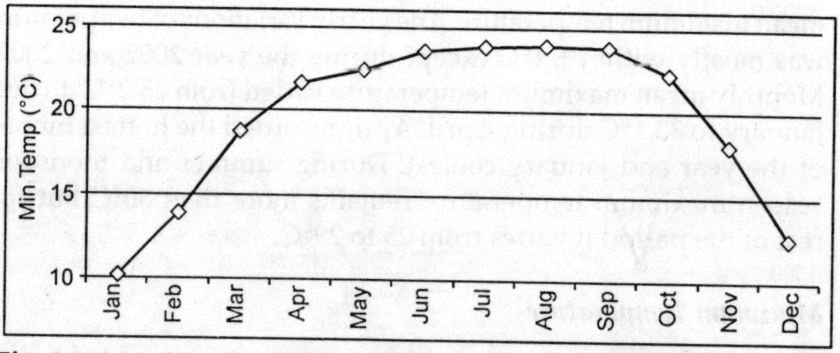

Fig. 4.4 : Monthly Mean Minimum Temperature (1992-2009).

Rainfall

The exceptional soil droughts which mostly occur due to the variation of distribution and amount of rainfall over a particular area or region has an effect over the forest cover of that particular region or area. The forest that mostly found in North-East part of the country is Rainfall Forest which means the sustainability of this evergreen forest largely depends on the characteristic and distribution of rainfall. The contributions of exchangeable water in tree reservoirs to the total tree transpiration differ from one season to another. During the limiting soil water condition, particularly during summer, the leaf transpiration is mostly maintained by this tree reservoir. The only source to recharge this tree reservoir is soil moisture that derived from the rainfall. The inter- and intra-annual variation of rainfall also has effect on the carbon and energy fluxes as both are associated with the change in soil water content. Thus, rainfall plays a vital role in maintaining and preserving forest eco-system.

The annual rainfall from 1992-2009 varied from 1457 mm in 1992 to 3421 mm in 2001 with annual average rainfall of 2288.9 mm (Fig 4.5). Annual total rainfall showed the alternate increasing and decreasing trend with exception from 1999 to 2003 where consecutive three years from 1999 to 2001 there were consecutive increasing trend followed by two consecutive decreasing trends (Daschaudhuri *et al.*). This is the period (2001) when the State received maximum amount of rainfall (almost 50% above average rainfall) in any single year. In three occasions during the study period the total annual rainfall crosses the 3,000 marks, *i.e.*, in 2001 (3,421 mm), 2004 (3,156 mm) and 2007 (3,321 mm).

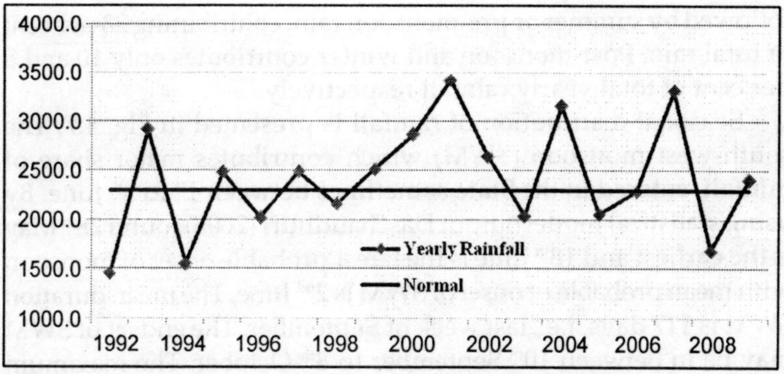

Fig. 4.5 : Yearly Variation of Total Rainfall over Yearly Normal Rainfall.

The variation of monthly average rainfall showing increasing trend from January to July and then starts declining till December (Fig. 4.6). Maximum rain occurred during the month of July, which contributes about 18 per cent of total yearly rainfall followed by June and May. Almost no rain occurs during November to February. Jointly these four months contribute only 3 per cent of total yearly rainfall. The highest rainfall in any single day recorded on June 6, 2001 which is about 286 mm. In every year there are at least one or two storm which recorded more than 100 mm rain in a single day except 1992 and 1997 when no storm measured 100 mm or more rain.

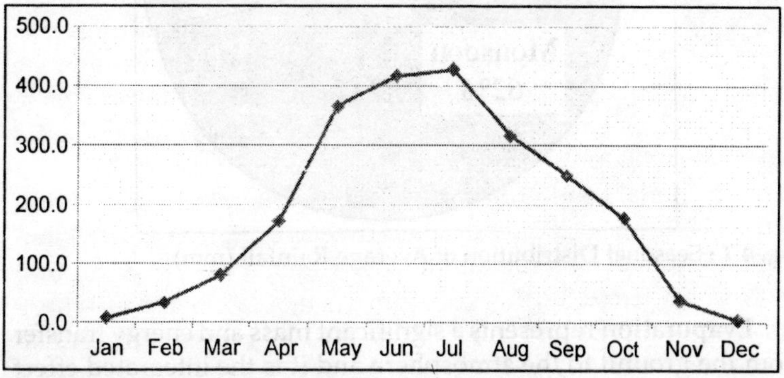

Fig. 4.6: Variation of Monthly Average Rainfall (mm).

The seasonal distribution of rainfall reveals that about 62 per cent rains occur during monsoon, i.e., from June to September followed by summer or pre-monsoon rain, contributing 23 per cent of total rain. Post-monsoon and winter contributes only 10 and 5 per cent of total yearly rainfall respectively.

Seasonal distribution of rainfall is presented in Fig. 4.7. The south-west monsoon (SWM) which contributes major share of rainfall, entered in the State sometimes between 1st to 5th June. By using statistical model output Daschaudhuri (2008) found 28th May is the earliest and 18th June is the latest probable onset of monsoon with mean probable of onset of SWM is 2nd June. The mean duration SWM is 117 days, i.e., last week of September. The endset of SWM may be in between 10th September to 8th October. The maximum and minimum duration of rainy season may be in between is 84 to 133 days (Daschaudhuri *et al.*).

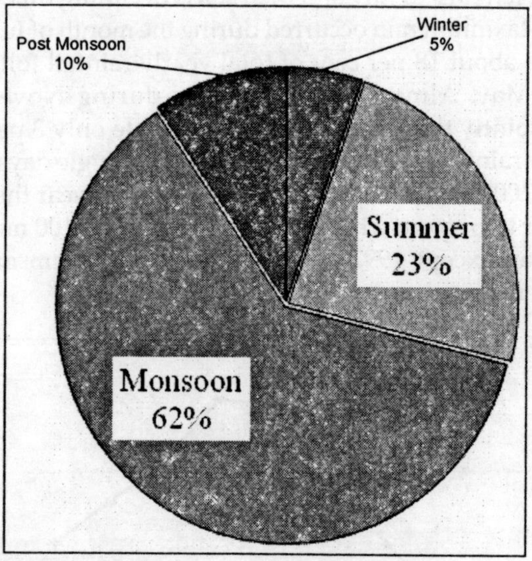

Fig. 4.7 : Seasonal Distribution of Average Rainfall (mm)

Evaporation represents a significant mass and energy transfer from the ground to the atmosphere and it is the integrated effect of several other elements including climatic factors of net radiation, wind velocity and humidity, etc. Thus, the natural evaporation is much more than the reverse of rainfall or the return of moisture to the atmosphere; it is also meant by which the downward flow of energy from the sun can be balanced. Natural evaporation proceeds only when the vapour pressure of the ambient air is less than the vapour pressure of the evaporating surface. There is a difference between total and net evaporation, for the former reflects the total movement of molecules of water away from the surface while the latter recognizes that there can be some downward movement of moisture to the surface, a recondensation of moisture.

The total evaporation during different year has been shown in Fig. 4.8. The total evaporation found maximum (1892 mm) in 2002 and minimum (959 mm) in 1992 with average yearly evaporation 1308 mm. In the comparative study with annual rainfall, it has been noticed that in an average 60 per cent of annual rainfall losses every year due to evaporation. The evaporation losses were maximum during 2008, when out of 1,683 mm of rain, 1,562 mm, i.e., 93 per cent was lost due to evaporation. The percentage of evaporation losses was lowest during 1997, 2000 and 2001; only 40 per cent loss was recorded.

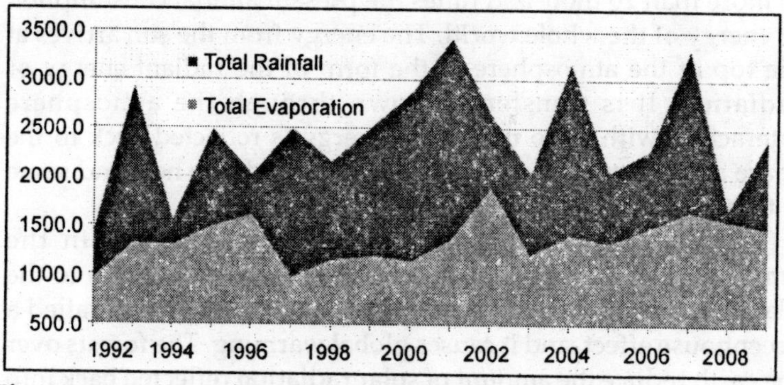

Fig. 4.8: Yearly Variation of Total Rainfall and Evaporation

The monthly distribution of evaporation as shown in Fig. 4.9 revealed that from the month of April to October there is a surplus of moisture as the evaporation is lesser than the rainfall. But, for the other months the evaporation is much higher than the rain, which indicates the stress in the available moisture. The rate of evaporation remains high, 4.0 mm/day during summer followed by post-monsoon season (3.5 mm/day) and lowest during monsoon (3.2 to 3.5 mm/day).

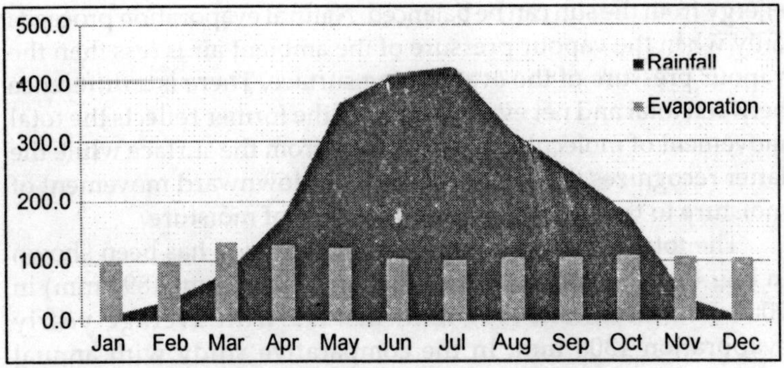

Fig. 4.9: Monthly variation of Total Rainfall and Evaporation

Sunshine Hour: All the energy for physical and biological processes at the earth's surface comes from the sun. The sun emits radiation in the entire electromagnetic spectrum. The earth receives annual energy of 1×10^{18} KwH from the sum, which is equivalent to more than 20 thousand times the present annual consumption of energy of the whole world. The energy from the sun arrives at the top of the atmosphere in the form of the radiant energy or radiation. It is transferred down through the atmosphere interacting with it, so that some energy is reflected back to the space and some is absorbed and transformed into heat and some is transmitted to the surface of the earth.

Some of the reflected radiation gets trapped in the atmosphere. This trapped radiation is re-reflected down to the planet and thus forces the temperature to rise. This is called a greenhouse effect, and it causes global warming. The forests over the earth reduce the amount of solar radiation reflected back into the atmosphere by absorption and, therefore, help to keep the temperatures stable.

The development of many solar energy devices and for estimates of their performances requires an accurate knowledge of solar radiation distribution at a particular geographical location. Unfortunately, solar radiation measurements still are not easily available for not being able to afford the measurement equipment and techniques involved. Therefore, it is rather important to elaborate methods to estimate the solar radiation on the basis of more readily meteorological data such as maximum bright sunshine hour or sunshine hours. Several empirical formulae have been developed to calculate the solar radiation using this meteorological parameter.

The number of sunshine hours amounts to almost 2,334 hr per year. The weather is most favourable for the utilisation of solar energy for diversified forest plantation. The yearly variation of yearly number of sunshine hours is presented in Fig. 4.10. The analysis shows a downward trend of the yearly possible sunshine hour. The amount varies from 1,898 hr per year in 2007 and 2,009 to 2,701 hr per year in 1996. The variation shows an alternate increasing and decreasing trend except from 1997 to 2000, when the values almost remain the same.

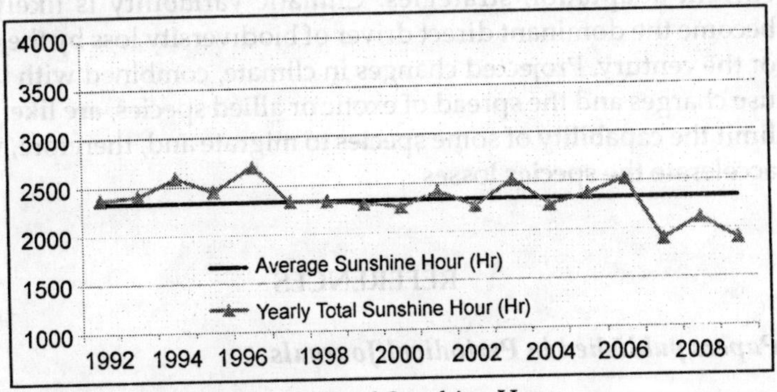

Fig. 4.10 : Yearly Variation of Total Sunshine Hour

The monthly variation of average sunshine hour presented in Fig. 4.8 which reveals that the sunshine hour remains lowest during

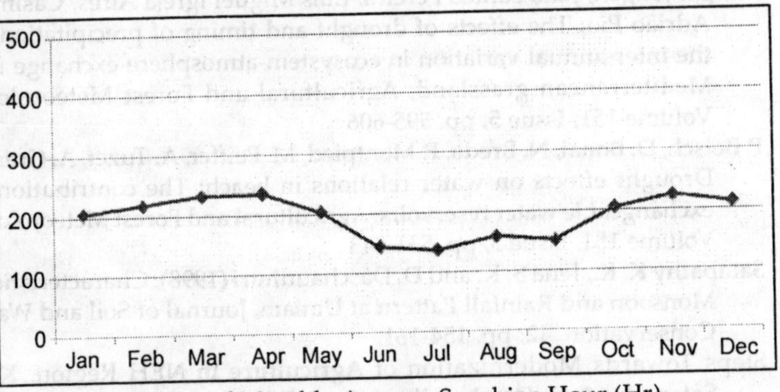

Fig. 4.11: Variation of Monthly Average Sunshine Hour (Hr)

monsoon period ranging from 140 to 150 hr per month. The sunshine ranges from 142 hr per month in June to 234 hr per year during April.

Conclusion

In Tripura, the climatic variability is mainly noted in the rainfall pattern and its distribution. A large variation in rainfall from one place to another in Tripura may lead to change in biodiversity as well as in the cropping pattern of the area. Policymakers seek ways to help the people to adopt to climate change priority particularly in the role of biodiversity, an element often neglected from the current adaptation strategies. Climatic variability is likely to become the dominant direct driver of biodiversity loss by the end of the century. Projected changes in climate, combined with land use charges and the spread of exotic or allied species, are likely to limit the capability of some species to migrate and, therefore, will accelerate the species losses.

REFERENCES

Papers published in Periodical/Journals

D. Daschaudhuri, M. Datta and N. P. Singh; Analysis of Rainfall Characteristics at Lembucherra (Tripura) in North East India, pp 199-213, *Climate Change and Food Security*, New India Publishing Agency, New Delhi.

Marjan Jongen, João Santos Pereira, Luis Miguel Igreja Aires, Casimiro Adrião Pio; The effects of drought and timing of precipitation on the inter-annual variation in ecosystem-atmosphere exchange in a Mediterranean grassland; Agricultural and Forest Meteorology, Volume 151, Issue 5, pp. 595-606.

P. Betsch, D. Bonal, N. Breda, P. Montpied, M. Peiffer, A. Tuzet, A. Granie; Drought effects on water relations in beach: The contribution of exchangeable water reservoirs; Agricultural and Forest Meteorology, Volume 151, Issue 5, pp. 531-543

Satapathy K. K., Jena S. K. and D. Daschaudhuri (1998), Characteristic of Monsoon and Rainfall Pattern at Umiam, Journal of Soil and Water Conservation, 42; pp. 154-161.

Steps Towards Modernization of Agriculture in NEH Region, K.K. Satapathy & D. Daschaudhuri, Book Edited by N.D. Verma & B.P.

Bhatt, Published by ICAR Research Complex for NEH Region, Umroi Road, Umiam, Chapter 1.2, pp. 25- 41.

Edited Books

Agriculture in Tripura: Its Problem and Prospects by Salim Shah.

Climate Change and Food Security by M. Datta, N. P. Singh and D. Daschaudhuri (2008) published by New India Publishing Agency, New Delhi.

Climate of Umiam by K. K. Satapathy, S. K. Jena and D. Daschaudhuri, published by ICAR Research Complex for NEH Region, Umiam – 793 103 (March, 2000).

Crop Micrometeorology by M. C. Varshneya and S. S. Salunke, Mahatma Phule Krishi Vidyapeeth, Rahuri, Maharashtra (M.P.K.V./Extn. Pub. No. 328/2001.

Solar Energy—Principles of Thermal Collection and Storage, 1991 by S. P. Sukhatme, Tata McGraw Hill Publishing Company Limited, New Delhi.

Steps Towards Modernization of Agriculture in NEH Region by N. D. Verma and B. P. Bhatt, Published by ICAR Research Complex for NEH Region, Umroi Road, Umiam, Chapter 1.2, pp. 25- 41.

Monographs/ Books

A. Compendium of Forests and Forestry in Tripura 2007, Forest Department, Government of Tripura.

Economic Review 2008-09, Directorate of Economics and Statistics, Planning Department, Government of Tripura.

Web-Site References

http://www.cder.dz/download/sipe_2.pdf
http://www.gcrio.org/CONSEQUENCES
http://www.sciencedirect. com
http://www.tropical-rainforest-animals.com

5
Diversity of Fishes of Barak Drainage using GIS and Remote Sensing as a Tool for their Conservation

Anjam Hussain Barbhuiya

Introduction

The North-Eastern Region of India lies between 22° 00′ N and 29° 05′ N latitude and 88° 00′ E and 97° 30′ E longitudes and shares international border with Bhutan, China, Myanmar and Bangladesh and contains more than one-third of the country's total biodiversity. This rich diversity of the region could be assigned to certain reasons, notably, the geomorphology and the tectonics of this zone. Assam is dominated by two river valley the Brahmaputra Valley (56,480 sq km), drained by the Brahmaputra river and its 43 tributaries; and the Barak valley (6,962 sq km) drained by the Barak river and its 11 major tributaries. The 11 major tributaries are Makru, Irang, Tuivai, Jiri, Chiri, Madhura, Jatinga, Ghagra, Sonai, Rukhni, Dhaleswari, etc. The other hill-stream tributaries are Bubankhal, Monkhal, Kotaikhal, Chotirkhal, Si-vadung, Lalmatikhal, Chandikhal, etc.

Study Sites of River Barak

River Barak is the biggest river in southern part of North-East (NE) India comprising the Barak valley region of Assam. Barak originates from Japvo peak in Nagaland (N 25° 28′ and E 94° 17′) at (approx 3000 m MSL) and flows through Karong village along the Manipur-Nagaland border, drains almost the entire Manipur valley before entering Assam. Then the river starts crawling eastward in the plains crossing Silchar city and receiving several other tributaries like Chiri, Jiri, Madhura, Sonai, etc. It then flows through the western part of Silchar where it is joined by the river Jatinga, Dhaleswari along with several other tributaries, bifurcates into Surma and Kushiara and enters Bangladesh before joining the Bay of Bengal.

Study Sites of River Jatinga

It is one of the major North bank tributaries of river Barak. The river originated from Barail Hill range in the village Jatinga (N 25° 7′29.0″ and E 93°1′36.0″) at North Cachar Hills district of Assam. The river Jatinga then flows all the way though the western boundary of the Barail Wildlife Sanctuary and after joining with several other tributaries like Chhotarekha, Bororekha, Daku, Chhota Lokha, Dimru, Ditokcherra, Kayang, Dolu, Badri, etc. merge with Barak river at a place called Jatingamukh below Barkhola village near Chandpur (N 24°53′ 3.2″ and E 92°44′34.8″) after travelling a distance of 71.5 Km.

Study Sites of Dhaleswari

One of the south bank tributaries of river Barak originated from the Mizo hills around Lunglei district of Mizoram at Zobawk (N 22°51′31.2″ and E 92°48′28.9″) in the name of river Tlawng at an altitude of 2500 m MSL. The river then enters its mid reach region around a place called Sairong, about 30 km from Aizwal city, the river flows thereafter mainly with riffle-pool and joins the tributaries like Thosibowk, Gutur, Meidum, Pakwa, etc., till it reaches the base level zone around the village Bhairabi along Assam-Mizoram border (N 24°10′25.2″ and E 92°32′20.5″). The river is called Dhaleswari from around the village Ramnathpur. A little ahead at village Rongpur-III (N 24°23′48.7″ and E 92°35′0.34″) the original course of the river is diverted and the main stream joined a canal called Katakhal that later falls in river Barak near village Katakhal (N 24°49′40.8″ and E 92°38′32.6″) traversing a total distance of 369.4 Km. However, the shallow original course of Dhaleswari joins Barak little downstream near Panchgram at Hailakandi District (N 24°51′35.2″ and E 92°36′48.2″) further travelling a distance of 101.5 km.

Among the different habitat inventory parameters (Table 5.1,

5.2 and 5.3) the valley segment is mostly alluvial. The flow rate of the river ranged from 2.01-0.27 m/s. The reach type is mostly regime. The river bottom mainly consists of sand and silt as substratum which is also the case with river bank. However, bedrocks are found on the bank in some places. Depth, turbulence and some amount of overhanging vegetations serve as moderate cover and protection of the fishes in Barak. Depending on the contact of soil with water, Barak is of mesoriparian type having grass, shrubs and evergreen trees as riparian vegetation. Bamboos form one of the most dominant types of riparian vegetations. The dominant texture of the riparian zone is mostly silt and fine grain sand stone with some amount of clay. The riparian land-use pattern includes mainly human habitation and agriculture. Signs of erosion are common along the river bank.

Critically, the surveys revealed very turbid river water mainly because of heavy rainfall during monsoon. High turbidity indicates bringing-in of eroded soil by the river. In spite of its high depth, the river depicted the existence of backwater type pools having dense vegetation cover at some spots. Interestingly, bedrocks are found even at some spots in the mid-stream and downstream regions of the river. There is variation in water temperature and transparency with seasons. Turbid water is less productive although it gives cover to fish. Barak also has undercut bank.

Significantly, Kar (2007) in his extensive studies on the systematics, distribution and ecology of rheophilic fishes of Assam, Mizoram, Manipur and Tripura and Dey (1973) in Assam and Meghalaya observed that the population of the fish species belonging to the genus *Tor* and *Neolissochilus* have been fast dwindling in the Barak and Brahmaputra drainages. The report of the National Commission on Agriculture (Anon., 1976) also accounts the observations maintained by Dey and Kar and considered most of the mahseer species as threatened. Angler Association of Assam has apprehended a more or less similar state of affairs in North-Eastern region in coming years (Anon., 1983). The tributaries of Barak and Brahmaputra once teeming with thousands of mahseer fishes have started presenting a dismal condition, with the fish fast vanishing due to indiscriminate hooking, massive netting, poisoning, dynamiting and above all, due to lack of a judicious harvesting and stocking policies.

Table 5.1: Habitat Inventory of the River Barak at Upstream and Downstream

Sl. No.	*Habitat parameters*	*Karong*	*Tamenlong*	*Panchgram*	*Katigarah*
1.	Stream order	2nd order	3rd order	Fifth order	Fifth order
2.	Position	N 25°18'16.5" E 94° 03'1.4"	N 24° 41'7.7" E 93° 20'29.8"	N 24° 51'45.5" E 92° 36'33.6"	N 24° 52'28.6" E 92° 33'52.8"
3.	Altitude m.s.l. (m)	1018	65	22	23
4.	Valley segment	Colluvial	Colluvial	Colluvial	Alluvial
5.	Microhabitat type	Fast water with much strong riffles with occasional pools.	Fast water with much strong riffles with occasional pools.	Mainly run-sheet and pool.	Mainly run-sheet and pool.
6.	Mean width (m)	110-40	150-45	200-50	300-90
7.	Mean depth (m)	7-0.5	5-0.5	20-6	25-2.5
8.	Cover type	Overhanging vegetation, turbulence, turbidity, undercut bank and depth cover.	Overhanging Vegetation, Bottom free boulders, undercut bank and turbulence.	Turbidity, depth and turbulence.	Turbidity, depth and turbulence.
9.	Substrate type	Gravels, cobbles, boulder and few bed rocks.	Cobbles, gravels, bedrocks and boulders.	Mostly fine and sand.	Mostly fine.
10.	Riparian land-use	Human habitation forests and agriculture	Human habitation and forests.	Human habitation and Industries.	Human habitation
11.	Signs of erosion	Visible	Visible.	Visible	Visible
12.	Water current (m/s)	2.01	1.51	0.33	0.27
13.	Gradient in degree	10°	17°	8°	10°

Table 5.2: Habitat Inventory of the River Jatinga at Different Study Sites

Sl. No.	*Habitat parameters*	*Maharajpur*	*Damcherra*	*Balacherra*	*Chandpur*
1.	Stream order	Fifth order	Fifth order	Fourth order	Fourth order
2.	Position	N 25° 07'3.9" E 92° 51'59 3"	N 25° 1'1.8" E 92° 45'37.0"	N 24° 57'55.3" E 92° 45'42.6"	N 24° 53' 20.1" E 92° 44' 39"
3.	Altitude above m.s.l. (m)	164.63	47.2	26.21	24.2
4.	Valley segment	Alluvial	Colluvial	Alluvial	Alluvial
5.	Microhabitat type	Mainly run-sheet and pool-riffle.	Mainly run-sheet and pool-riffle.	Mainly run-sheet with some pool-riffle.	Mainly run-sheet.
6.	Mean width (m)	300-90	150-80	130-55	300-150
7.	Mean depth (m)	25-2.5	5-0.6	10-1.2	24-3
8.	Cover type	Turbidity, depth turbulence, undercut banks and overhanging vegetation.	Turbidity, depth, turbulence, and overhanging vegetation.	Overhanging Vegetation, Depth and small woody Debris and turbidity.	Depth cover, overhanging vegetation, bottom free big boulders and undercut bank.
9.	Substrate type	Mostly fines along with cobbles gravels and boulders.	Mostly fine, sand cobbles and gravels.	Only fine, sand, cobbles.	Only fine, sand, silt and clay.
10.	Riparian land-use	Human habitation railways and forests.	Human habitation railways.	Mostly human habitation.	Human habitation
11.	Signs of erosion	Visible	Visible	Visible.	Much
12.	Water current (m/s)	0.46	0.77	0.17	0.07
13.	Gradient in degree	10°	8°	2°	1.5°

Table 5.3: Habitat Inventory of the River Dhaleswari at Different Study Sites

Sl. No.	Habitat parameters	Near Khawrihnim	Near Nghalchhun	Gharmura	Panchgram
1.	Stream order	Second order	Third order	Fourth order	Fourth order
2.	Position	N 23°37'50.7" E 92°39'0.6"	N 23°45'40.6" E 92° 37'37.9"	N 24°16' 39.2" E 92° 30' 57.9"	N 24°51'21.5" E 92°36'16.3"
3.	Altitude m.s.l. (m)	436	381	34.75	20.5
4.	Valley segment	Colluvial	Colluvial	Alluvial	Alluvial
5.	Microhabitat type	Mainly cascade and riffle-pools.	Mainly riffle-pool, with some cascade and run-sheet.	Pool riffle and run.	Run-sheet.
6.	Mean width (m)	10-4	50-8	110-50	50-17
7.	Mean depth (m)	7-1	15-1	20-13	15-4
8.	Cover type	Overhanging vegetation, bottom free big boulders and undercut bank.	Overhanging vegetation, bottom free big boulders and undercut bank.	Depth cover, Overhanging vegetation, turbulence and turbidity.	Overhanging Vegetation, Depth and small woody debris and turbidity.
9.	Substrate type	Mainly boulders with few bedrock, and cobbles.	Mainly boulders, bedrock, cobbles and gravels.	Mainly fines and sand.	Only fine, sand, silt and clay.
10.	Riparian land-use	Dense forest.	Dense forest.	Human habitation and market place.	Mostly human habitation and industries.
11.	Signs of erosion	Nil	Nil	Much	Visible.
12.	Water current (m/s)	0.12	0.96	0.10	0.07
13.	Gradient in degree	11.5°	9.5°	5°	4°

Methodology

Rivers were surveyed (June, 2007 to June, 09) and classified in to different habitat units based on morphology (Bisson *et al.*, 1982) and finally divided into different study sites after studying Survey of India topographic maps, satellite imageries, etc., for ease in further analysis with GIS and Remote Sensing. Sampling were done in the pre-monsoon and post-monsoon periods when the water level remains low, easy to travel remote areas to collect fish and other habitat inventory data. Habitat inventory parameters were recorded in a standard format (NBFGR, 2002) from each study spot in the field itself. Some of the physico-chemical parameters were measured on the field itself, and water samples were collected in the pre-cleaned bottles to study other parameters in the laboratory using instruments and titration methods after APHA (1998). Fishes were extensively sampled at each site on each occasion with the help of local fishermen through experimental fishing using different kinds nets and preserved in Aquaculture and Limnology laboratory of Assam University, morphometrically studied and identified from various authoritative sources including Day (1889), Jayaram (1999, 2003, 2010), Kar and Sen (2007), Menon (1999), and Talwar and Jhingran (1991). Some of the specimens were also identified from Zoological Survey of India (ZSI) Shillong. For the morphometrics and meristic characters the procedures of Dwivedi and Menezes (1974) was followed.

For habitat mapping Geomatica V 10.1 and ERDAS Imagine 9.1 software was used. Topographic maps (1965-73) have been georeferenced and mosaiced to depict the rivers Barak, Jatinga and Dhaleswari respectively from their origin to end. IRS-1D, LISS III satellite imageries have been used to register and georeferenced the topo maps concomitant to GPS field points. The vector layers of the above rivers have been digitized from the topo maps and updated with respect to georeferenced imageries. Finally, various habitat and water parameters were inserted in the vector layer as attribute data.

Results and Discussion

The total collection of the three rivers comprises of 101 species of

Table 5.4 : List of fishes in the three studied rivers

Sl. No.	*Ichthyospecies*	*Ba*	*Ja*	*Dh*
1.	*Notopterus notopterus* (Pallas).	+	–	+
2.	*Pisodonophis boro* (Hamilton).	+	–	–
3.	*Tenualosa ilisa* (Hamilton)	–	+	–
4.	*Gudusia chapra* (Hamilton)	+	+	–
5.	*Securicula gora* (Hamilton)	–	+	+
6.	*Salmophasia bacaila* (Hamilton)	+	+	+
7.	*Aspidoparia morar* (Hamilton)	+	+	+
8.	*Barilius bakeri* Day	+	–	–
9.	*Barilius barila* (Hamilton)	+	+	–
10.	*Barilius barna* (Hamilton)	+	+	+
11.	*Barilius barnoides* Vinciguerra	+	–	–
12.	*Barilius bendelisis* (Hamilton)	+	+	–
13.	*Barilius dogarsinghi* Hora	+	+	–
14.	*Barilius shacra* (Hamilton)	+	–	–
15.	*Barilius teleo* (Hamilton)	–	+	+
16.	*Barilius vagra* (Hamilton)	–	+	+
17.	*Chela cachius* (Hamilton)	+	–	–
18.	*Chela laubuca* (Hamilton)	+	–	+
19.	*Esomus danricus* (Hamilton)	+	–	+
20.	*Devario aequipinnatus* (McClelland)	+	+	–
21.	*Devario devario* (Hamilton)	–	+	–
22.	*Danio dangila* (Hamilton)	+	–	–
23.	*Devario naganensis* Chaudhuri	+	+	–
24.	*Rasbora daniconius* (Hamilton)	+	–	–
25.	*Amblypharyngodon mola* (Hamilton)	+	+	+
26.	*Tor mosal* (Hamilton)	+	–	–
27.	*Tor putitora* (Hamilton)	+	+	–
28.	*Tor tor* (Hamilton)	+	–	–
29.	*Tor progenius* (McClelland)	+	+	+
30.	*Neolissochilus heaxagonolepis* (McClelland)	+	–	–
31.	*Osteobrama cotio* (Hamilton)	+	–	+
32.	*Chagunius nicholsi* (Myers)	+	–	–
33.	*Puntius chola* (Hamilton)	+	+	–
34.	*Puntius conchonius* (Hamilton)	+	+	+
35.	*Puntius jerdoni* (Day)	+	–	–
36.	*Puntius puntio* (Hamilton)	+	+	+
37.	*Puntius sarana sarana* (Hamilton)	–	+	-
38.	*Puntius sophore* (Hamilton)	+	–	–
39.	*Puntius ticto* (Hamilton)	+	–	+
40.	*Cirrhinus cirrhosus* (Bloch)	+	+	+
41.	*Cirrhinus reba* (Hamilton)	+	–	+
42.	*Labeo boga* (Hamilton)	+	–	–
43.	*Labeo calbasu* (Hamilton)	+	+	+
44.	*Labeo gonius* (Hamilton)	+	+	–
45.	*Labeo pangusia* (Hamilton)	+	+	–
46.	*Labeo rohita* (Hamilton)	+	–	–
47.	*Crossocheilus latius* (Hamilton)	+	+	–
48.	*Garra gotyla* (Gray)	–	+	–
49.	*Garra gravelyi* (Annandale)	+	–	–
50.	*Garra nasuta* (McClelland)	+	+	–
51.	*Garra naganensis* Hora	+	–	–
52.	*Psilorhynchus balitora* (Hamilton)	+	+	–
53.	*Acanthocobitis botia* (Hamilton)	+	+	+

(Contd).

Table 5.4 : *(Contd).*

Sl. No.	*Ichthyospecies*	*Ba*	*Ja*	*Dh*
54.	*Neonemacheilus peguensis* (Hora)	+	–	–
55.	*Schistura multifasciatus* (Day)	+	–	–
56.	*Schistura rupecula* (McClelland)	+	–	–
57.	*Schistura vincigurrae* (Hora)	+	–	–
58.	*Botia Dario* (Hamilton)	+	+	+
59.	*Botia rostrata* Gunther	+	+	–
60.	*Lepidocephalichthys guntea* (Hamilton)	+	–	–
61.	*Rita rita* (Hamilton)	+	–	+
62.	*Mystus bleekeri* (Day)	+	–	+
63.	*Mystus cavasius* (Hamilton)	+	+	–
64.	*Mystus vittatus* (Bloch)	+	+	–
65.	*Sperata aor* (Hamilton)	–	–	+
66.	*Sperrata seenghala* (Sykes)	+	+	+
67..	*Ompock bimaculatus* (Bloch)	–	+	–
68.	*Wallago attu* (Bloch & Schnider)	+	–	+
69.	*Ailia coila* (Hamilton)	+	+	+
70.	*Clupisoma garua* (Hamilton)	+	–	+
71.	*Eutropiichthys murius* (Hamilton)	+	–	+
72.	*Eutropiichthys vacha* (Hamilton)	+	+	+
73.	*Amblyceps mangois* (Hamilton)	–	+	–
74.	*Bagarius bagarius* (Hamilton)	+	+	+
75.	*Gagata gagata* (Hamilton)	+	–	–
76.	*Nangra nangra* (Hamilton)	+	–	+
77.	*Gogangra viridescens* (Hamilton)	–	+	+
78.	*Erethistes pussilus* Muller & Troschel	+	–	+
79.	*Glyptothorax striatus* (McClelland)	–	+	–
80.	*Glyptothorax telchitta* (Hamilton)	+	+	+
81.	*Glyptothorax trilineatus* Blyth	+	–	–
82.	*Chaca chaca* (Hamilton)	+	–	–
83.	*Sicamugil cascasia* (Hamilton)	+	–	+
84.	*Xenentodon cancila* (Hamilton)	+	+	–
85.	*Aplocheilus panchax* (Hamilton)	+	–	+
86.	*Magrognathus aral* (Bloch & Schneider)	+	–	–
87.	*Macrognathus pancalus* Hamilton	+	+	–
88.	*Mastacembalus armatus* (Lacepede)	+	+	+
89.	*Chanda nama* Hamilton	+	+	+
90.	*Parambassis ranga* (Hamilton)	+	+	–
91.	*Johnius coitor* (Hamilton)	+	–	+
92.	*Badis badis* (Hamilton)	+	+	–
93.	*Nandus nandus* (Hamilton)	+	–	–
94.	*Glossogobius giuris* (Hamilton)	+	+	+
95.	*Anabas testudineus* (Bloch)	+	–	–
96.	*Colisa fasciatus* (Schneider)	+	–	–
97.	*Colisa lalia* (Hamilton)	+	–	–
98.	*Colisa sota* (Hamilton)	+	–	–
99.	*Channa gachua* (Hamilton)	+	–	–
100.	*Channa panctatus* (Bloch)	+	+	–
101.	*Channa striata* (Bloch)	–	+	–
		87	51	40

NB: '+' means Present, '—' means Absent.

'Bo'= Barak. 'Ja'= Jatinga and 'Dh'= Dhaleswari.

fishes including 5 species of mahseers under 57 genera belonging to 24 families and 10 orders (Table 5.4).

Out of the 101 species maximum number of ichthyospecies 87 species have been recorded from river Barak whereas minimum 40 species in river Dhaleswari. Mostly juveniles of the mahseer 6-10 cm size classes were abundant in all three rivers. The total length measured for mahseer varies from 5.35 cm to 30 cm. The river Barak along with its tributaries originated from the hills and consequently, these torrential hill streams has a rich diversity of mahseer fishes. Mahseer species recorded from main River Barak: *Tor putitora* (Ham.), *Tor tor* (Ham.), *Tor mosal* (Ham.), *Tor progenius* (McClelland), *Neolissochilus hexagonolepis* (McClelland); from river Jatinga: Tor putitora (Ham.), Tor progenius (McClelland), and from river Dhaleswari: Tor progenius (McClelland).

The Limnological parameters (Tables 5.5, 5.6 and 5.7) did not show much abrupt fluctuation with water temperature 19 to 32°C; turbidity 1.00 to 530.00 NTU; pH 5.60 to 8.40; DO 2.60 to 10.10 mg/*l*; FCO_2 1.50 to 150.00 mg/*l*; TA 17.00 to 305.00 mg/*l*; Conductivity 18.00 to 490.00 μmho/cm; PO_4 0.001 to 5.000 mg/*l*; NO_3 0.000 to 0.840 mg/*l*; Current velocity 0.04 to 2.40 m/s.

Unfortunately no breeding ground of mahseer was recorded in the main course of the river Barak, Jatinga and Dhaleswari. However, the breeding grounds were reported to be in the tributaries like Tuivai, Irang, Makru, Jiri (Singh, 2001), Jatinga (Kar, 2007).

Habitat destruction by construction of Dams and Barrages, Extraction of sand and stone from the river bed, Indiscriminate fishing and dynamiting, Poaching by destructive fishing method etc. were found to be the major causes of the decline of mahseer fisheries along with other hill stream fishes like *Garra* spp., *Glyptothorax* spp., *Schistura* spp., *Botia* spp., *Chela* spp., etc. But alarmingly, these lucrative fishes are feared to be in grave danger so much so that they are now practically on the threshold of extinction. This dismal state of affairs necessitated the present study, hitherto remained unattended, to undertake with utmost rigour and service.

For the protection of the game fishes over exploitation of fishery waters need be stopped including prevention of killing of brood fishes at the time of spawning and migration by implementation of laws and mass awareness. The possibility of

Table 5.5: Fluvial Dynamics and Physico-Chemical Characteristics of Water of the River Barak at Different Study Sites

Value	Temperature (°C)	Turbidity (NTU)	pH	Dissolved Oxygen (mg/l)	Free Carbon Dioxide (mg/l)	Total Alkalinity (mg/l)	Conductivity (µmho/cm)	Phosphate (mg/l)	Nitrate (mg/l)	Current Velocity (m/s)
					Karong					
Min	23.00	1.00	6.00	4.40	37.00	103.0	135.00	0.047	0.048	1.50
Max	29.00	35.00	7.00	7.50	49.00	305.0	192.00	0.090	0.099	2.40
Avg	25.8	13.0	6.5	6.2	42.8	206.3	164.25	0.064	0.067	2.01
					Tamenlong					
Min	22.0	4.5	6.3	5.0	7.0	80.5	143.0	0.100	0.048	1.3
Max	28.0	33.0	7.59	7.1	32.0	190.0	151.0	0.300	0.840	1.71
Avg	25.8	16.0	7.1	6.1	15.8	114.4	146.3	0.175	0.252	1.51
					Tipaimukh					
Min	22.0	2.5	5.95	4.35	6.0	102	134	0.03	0.03	0.55
Max	26.0	43.0	7.45	6.4	78.0	212	181	0.2	0.072	0.76
Avg	24.3	22.7	7.0	5.2	24.9	137.5	155.3	0.118	0.052	0.660
					Khangrendar					
Min	23.0	8.0	5.72	4.6	40.0	186.0	150.0	0.1	0.03	0.82
Max	28.0	150.0	6.32	7.0	150.0	218.0	158.0	5.0	0.084	0.9
Avg	26.0	45.3	6.1	5.8	73.5	199.0	154.0	1.425	0.050	0.87

(Contd.)

Table 5.5 : *(Contd.)*

Value	Temperature (^0C)	Turbidity (NTU)	pH	Dissolved Oxygen (mg/l)	Free Carbon-dioxide (mg/l)	Total Alkalinity (mg/l)	Conductivity (µmho/cm)	Phosphate (mg/l)	Nitrate (mg/l)	Current Velocity (m/s)
					Fulerlal					
Min	21.5	8.0	6.33	4.6	4.0	95.0	18.0	0.005	0.008	0.1
Max	30.0	24.0	6.92	7.9	35.0	143.0	187.0	1.12	0.04	0.91
Avg	26.25	16.5	6.66	6.65	17.25	121.8	99.75	0.367	0.021	0.50
					Tarapur					
Min	26.5	30.0	6.9	6.8	18.0	58.0	120.0	0.05	0.025	0.47
Max	29.0	63.0	7.5	8.8	25.0	80.0	180.0	0.099	0.083	0.62
Avg	27.63	51.5	7.21	7.83	21.0	66.75	150.25	0.072	0.046	0.55
					Panchgram					
Min	24.0	7.0	6.12	5.0	8.5	45.0	116.0	0.21	0.016	0.25
Max	28.0	140.0	7.2	7.5	24.0	75.0	390.0	1.04	0.036	0.41
Avg	26.25	66.25	6.72	6.125	15.88	56.5	218.75	0.64	0.023	0.33
					Near Katigarah					
Min	22.0	23.0	7.4	5.8	9.0	47.0	120.0	0.009	0.008	0.21
Max	28.0	89.0	7.86	7.0	25.0	101.0	190.0	0.11	0.07	0.31
Avg	25.63	55.25	7.65	6.30	16.75	73.5	151.25	0.055	0.046	0.27

Table 5.6: Fluvial Dynamics and Physico-Chemical Characteristics of Jatinga

Value	*Temp-erature (^0C)*	*Turbidity (NTU)*	*pH*	*Dissolved Oxygen (mg/l)*	*Free Carbon di-oxide (mg/l)*	*Total Alkalinity (mg/l)*	*Conductivity (μmho/cm)*	*Phosphate (mg/l)*	*Nitrate (mg/l)*	*Current Velocity (m/s)*
					Maharajpur					
Min	20.0	6.8	7.2	8.3	1.5	35.0	114.0	0.0125	0.022	0.39
Max	25.5	18.0	7.39	8.7	3.5	40.0	158.0	0.025	0.025	0.55
Avg	22.63	12.2	7.31	8.55	2.63	37.5	128.25	0.016	0.024	0.46
					Damcherra					
Min	20.0	3.0	6.5	6.6	4.0	30.0	96.0	0.204	0.016	0.69
Max	29.0	32.0	7.3	7.5	10.0	65.0	142.0	0.61	0.072	0.85
Avg	24.50	15.25	6.93	7.05	7.25	50.5	122.75	0.386	0.041	0.77
					Balacherra					
Min	24.0	3.0	6.3	6.3	7.0	19.0	65.0	0.001	0.000	0.11
Max	32.0	24.0	7.89	8.6	40.0	90.0	127.0	0.24	0.184	0.21
Avg	28.88	10.50	7.19	7.00	21.25	42.75	89.00	0.097	0.091	0.17
					Chandpur					
Min	19.0	9.0	6.7	6.9	9.0	40.0	65.0	0.12	0.023	0.04
Max	28.5	39.0	7.88	8.6	23.5	73.0	97.0	0.91	0.061	0.11
Avg	26.0	45.3	6.1	5.8	73.5	199.0	154.0	1.425	0.05	0.87

Table 5.7: Fluvial Dynamics and Physico-Chemical Characteristics Dhaleswari

Value	Temperature (°C)	Turbidity (NTU)	pH	Dissolved Oxygen (mg/l)	Free Carbon dioxide (mg/l)	Total Alkalinity (mg/l)	Conductivity (μmho/cm)	Phosphate (mg/l)	Nitrate (mg/l)	Current Velocity (m/s)
					Khawrihnim					
Min	21.0	5.0	6.34	7.9	16.0	20.0	87.0	0.38	0.036	0.06
Max	27.0	25.0	7.2	10.1	30.0	75.0	152.0	0.72	0.19	0.19
Avg	24.25	13.00	6.81	9.13	23.25	49.25	112.50	0.49	0.09	0.12
					Near Nghalchhun					
Min	23.0	7.0	6.02	6.5	4.0	48.0	89.0	0.1	0.036	0.8
Max	27.0	36.0	7.0	7.4	24.0	121.0	120.0	0.63	0.12	1.12
Avg	25.00	21.00	6.61	6.95	14.75	81.75	100.00	0.280	0.076	0.96
					Sairong					
Min	24.0	8.0	6.22	7.1	20.0	72.5	107.0	0.245	0.048	0.21
Max	28.0	530.0	8.4	9.96	45.0	128.0	162.0	0.58	0.18	0.35
Avg	26.25	269.50	7.41	8.14	30.00	105.88	125.25	0.381	0.096	0.29

(Contd.)

Table 5.7: *(Contd.)*

Value	Temperature (°C)	Turbidity (NTU)	pH	Dissolved Oxygen (mg/l)	Free Carbon dioxide (mg/l)	Total Alkalinity (mg/l)	Conductivity (µmho/cm)	Phosphate (mg/l)	Nitrate (mg/l)	Current Velocity (m/s)
					Bhairabi					
Min	23.0	31.0	7.2	6.9	2.0	63.0	60.0	0.4	0.48	0.43
Max	30.0	58.0	74.0	8.6	4.3	86.0	490.0	0.53	0.53	0.69
Avg	26.50	43.13	24.28	7.58	3.23	74.25	315.00	0.458	0.510	0.57
					Gharmura					
Min	20.0	23.0	6.3	2.6	9.0	80.0	101.0	0.150	0.020	0.06
Max	28.0	220.0	6.7	4.6	30.5	145.0	193.0	0.600	0.056	0.15
Avg	24.00	116.00	6.44	3.65	14.88	116.75	150.00	0.363	0.040	0.10
					Panchgram					
Min	24.0	40.0	5.60	5.0	8.5	17.0	126.0	0.31	0.017	0.04
Max	29.0	140.0	6.12	6.6	21.0	41.0	290.0	1.14	0.046	0.10
Avg	26.50	93.25	5.96	5.63	14.63	28.00	191.00	0.665	0.028	0.07

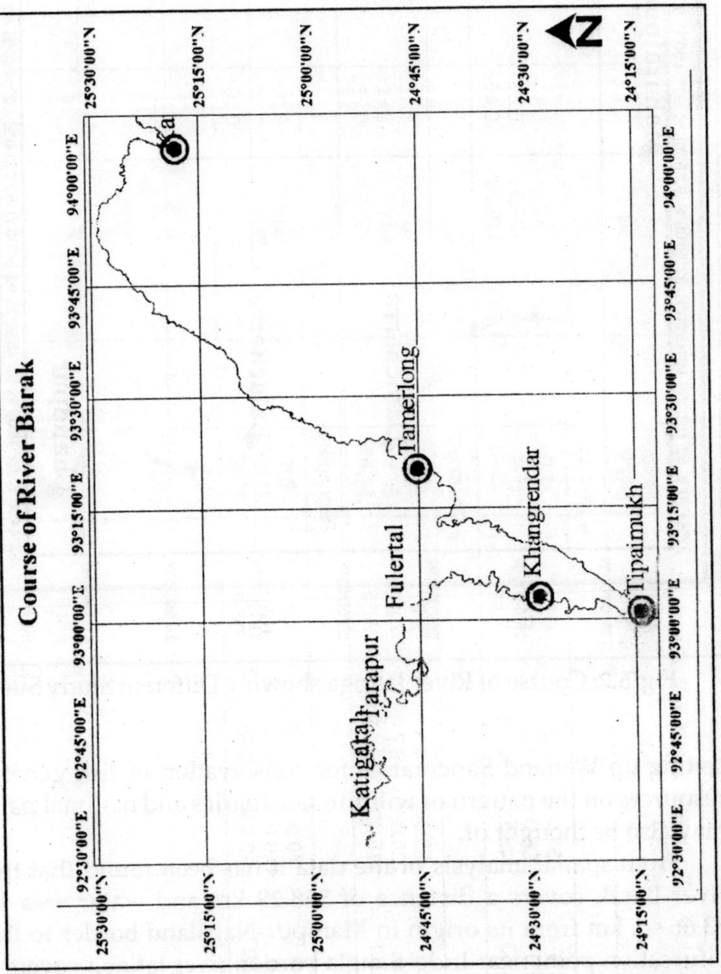

Fig. 5.1: Course of River Barak showing Different Study Sites

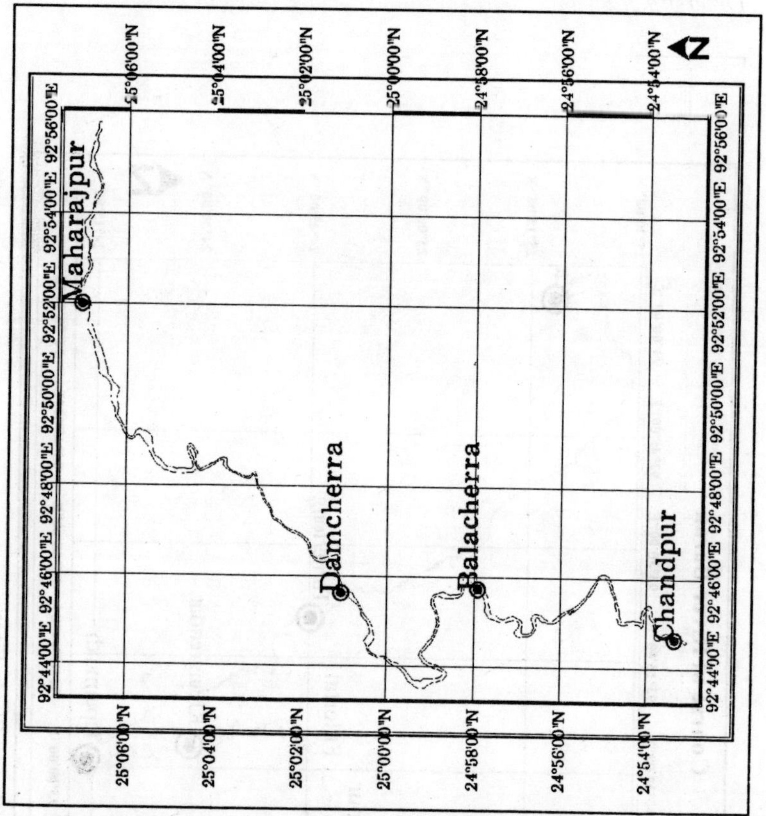

Fig. 5.2: Course of River Jatinga showing Different Study Sites.

setting up Wetland Sanctuaries for conservation of fish genetic resources on the pattern of wildlife sanctuaries and national park may also be thought of.

From spatial analysis of the data it has been found that the river Barak covers a distance of 568.29 km and water area of 73.66 sq. km from its origin in Manipur-Nagaland border to the bifurcation point near Indo-Bangla border, river Jatinga covers a distance of 71.5 km and water area of 7.74 sq. km and river Dhaleswari covers a distance of 369.4 km and water area of 26.86 sq. km.

However, in the present investigation considering the availability of mahseers, various habitat inventory, physico-

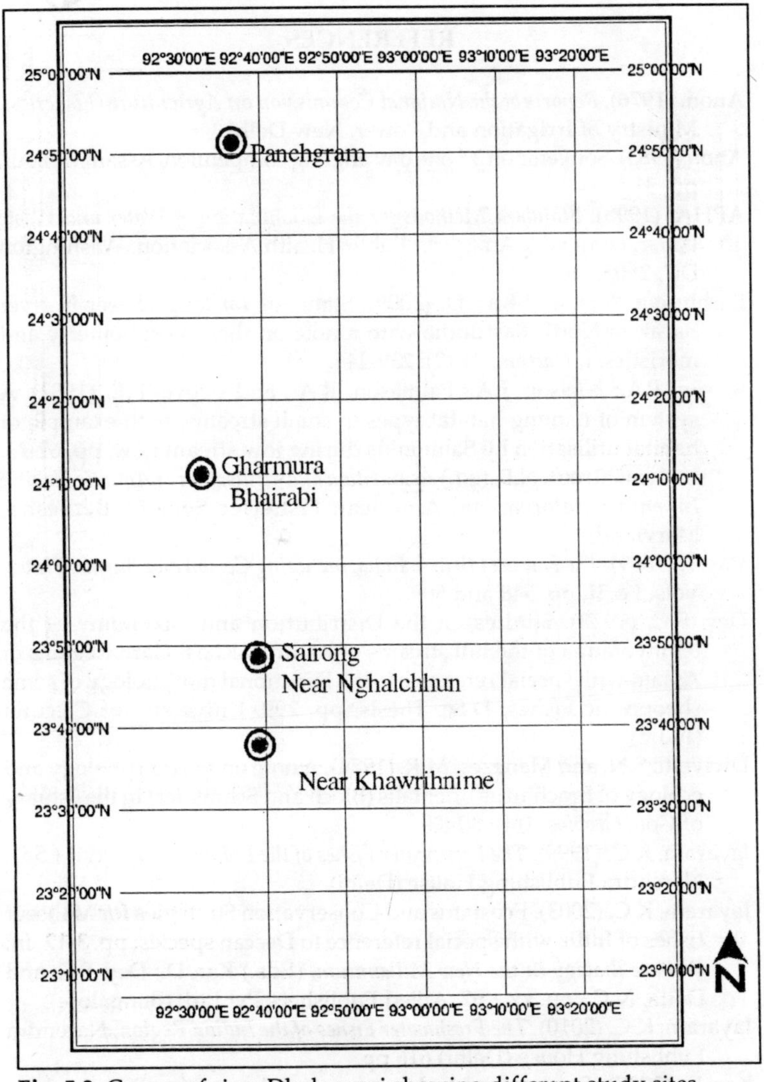

Fig. 5.3: Course of river Dhaleswari showing different study sites.

chemical parameters, breeding grounds in nearby tributaries and comparing them with that of the other rivers in India it is found that Tipaimukh site of river Barak, Damcherra of river Jatinga and Bhairabi site of river Dhaleswari are the most suitable places for the mahseer fishes.

REFERENCES

Anon. (1976). *Reports of the National Commission on Agriculture (Fisheries)*, Ministry of Irrigation and Power, New Delhi.

Anon (1983). Souvenir on 3rd one day angling competition, Assam, Tezpur, pp. 31.

APHA, (1998). *Standard Methods for the Examination of Water and Waste Water*. (20th ed.). American Public Health Association. Washington DC, 2605.

Barbhuiya, A.H. and Kar, D. (2009). Status of *Tor tor* mahseer in river Barak in North-East India with a note on their morphometry and meristics. *J. Natcon.*, 21 (2): 239-246.

Bisson, P.A.; Nielson, J.A.; Palmason, R.A.; and Grove, L.E. (1982). A system of naming habitat types in small streams, with example of habitat utilisation by Salmonids during low stream flow. pp. 62-73. In Armantrout, N.B. (ed.) *Acquisition and Utilisation of Aquatic Habitat Inventory Information*. American Fisheries Society, Bethesda, Maryland.

Day, F. (1889). *The Fauna of British India, including Ceylon and Burma: Fishes*, Vols. I & II: pp. 548 and 509.

Dey, S.C. (1973). Studies on the Distribution and Taxonomy of the Ichthyofauna of the hill streams of Kamrup-Khasi-Garo Regions of Assam with special reference to the Functional morphology of some rheophillic Fishes, D.Sc. Thesis, pp. 299, University of Calcutta (India).

Dwivedi, S.N. and Menezes, M.R. (1974). A note on the morphology and ecology of Brachiurus orientalis (Bloch and Schneider) in the estuary of Goa, *Geobios*, 1(4); 80-83.

Jayaram, K.C. (1999). *The Freshwater Fishes of the Indian Region*, xvii + 551, Narendra Publishing House (Delhi).

Jayaram, K.C. (2003). Ecostatus and Conservation Strategies for Mahseer fishes of India with special reference to Deccan species: pp. 3-12. In: *Welfare Biology in the New Millennium*, (Eds.) Kar, D.; Dey, S.C. and Datta, N.C., pp. xx + 97, Allied Publishers Pvt.Ltd. (Bangalore).

Jayaram, K.C. (2010). *The Freshwater Fishes of the Indian Region*. Narendra Publishing House (Delhi) 616 pp.

Kar, D. (2007). *Fundamentals of Limnology and Aquaculture Biotechnology*. Daya Publishing House (New Delhi), xiv+609 pp.

Kar, D. and Sen, N. (2007). Systematic List and Distribution of Fish Biodiversity in Mizoram, Tripura and Barak Drainage in North-East India. *ZOOs' Print Journal*, 22 (3) : 2599-2607.

Menon A.G.K. (1999). *Checklist: Freshwater Fishes of India*, xviii + 366, Occasional Paper No. 175, Zoological Survey of India (Calcutta).

Michael, R.G. and Sharma, B.K. (1988). *Indian Cladocera: Fauna of India and Adjacent Countries Series,* x + 261, Zoological Survey of India (Calcutta).

Mittermeier, R.A. and Mittemeier, C.G. (1997). Mega Diversity: Earth's Biologically Wealthiest Nation. In: *Global Freshwater Biodiversity* (Ed.) McAllister, D. E; Hamilton, A.L.; and, Harvery, B; Sea Wind, Cemex, Mexico City, 11: 1-140.

NBFGR (2000). Manual on Habitat Inventory. National Bureau of Fish Genetic Resources (ICAR) (Lucknow), 27 pp.

Singh, L.A. (2001). Ichthyofauna of Yu-river system and eco-biology of *Neolssochilus hexagonolepis* in Manipur, Ph.D. thesis, Department of Life Science, Manipur University. pp. 145.

Talwar, P.K. and Jhingran, A.G. (1991). *Inland Fishes of India and Adjacent Countries,* Vols. I & II, pp. 1158, Oxford and IBH Co. Pvt. Ltd. (New Delhi).

WCMC (1998). Freshwater Biodiversity: A Preliminary Global Assessment. *A Document prepared for the 4th Meeting of the Conference of the Practices to the Convention of Biological Diversity,* World Conservation Monitoring Centre.

6
Biodiversity Conservation Intended to Socio-Economic Development in Nagaland

Swati Biswas, G.C. Munda, Anupam Misra, S.V. Ngachan, P. Chowdhury, and *R.K. Singh*

Introduction

Nagaland is one of the seventh states in the North-Eastern region of India. The State of Nagaland extends between 25° 05′and 27° 10′ North latitude and 93° 28′ and 95° 05′ E longitudes (Singh, 2010). The capital of the State is Kohima 339 km distant from Guwahati. Sixty-seventy major ethnic groups of people are the inhabitants of the region (Hore, 2005). As per schedule, there are 16 number of major tribes in the State are *Angami, Ao, Chakesang, Sema, Chang, Khiamungan, Kuki, Konyak, Lotha, Phom, Pochury, Rengma, Sumi, Sangtam, Yimchungre, and Zeliang*. The area of the State is 16,527 km^2 with a population of 19,88,636. The population density is around 120 persons/km^2 with literacy rate of 67.11 per cent.

Nagaland is a hilly State with high mountains, deep gorges, lush valleys, and winding streams. The dominant geographic feature of the landscape is the Naga Hills, which run all the way through the State and contribute to the mountainous terrain (Singh, 2010). Nagaland comprises a part of the hill ranges which separates the basins of three major rivers, i.e., the Brahmaputra, the Chindwin and the Barak. The hills of Nagaland are in parallel folds running from north to south. The Saramati Peak (3,841 m) is the highest (Singh, 2010). There are around 1,317 villages in Nagaland. About

150 of these villages are located in the foothills, along the State's boundary with Assam in the west. The remaining villages are located on the top of ridges or on slopes, at altitudes of 500 to 2,500 metres above sea level. Nagaland has a total land area of 1,650,705 hectares of which about 1,450,000 hectares land is owned by the people in the villages (Fig **6.1**).

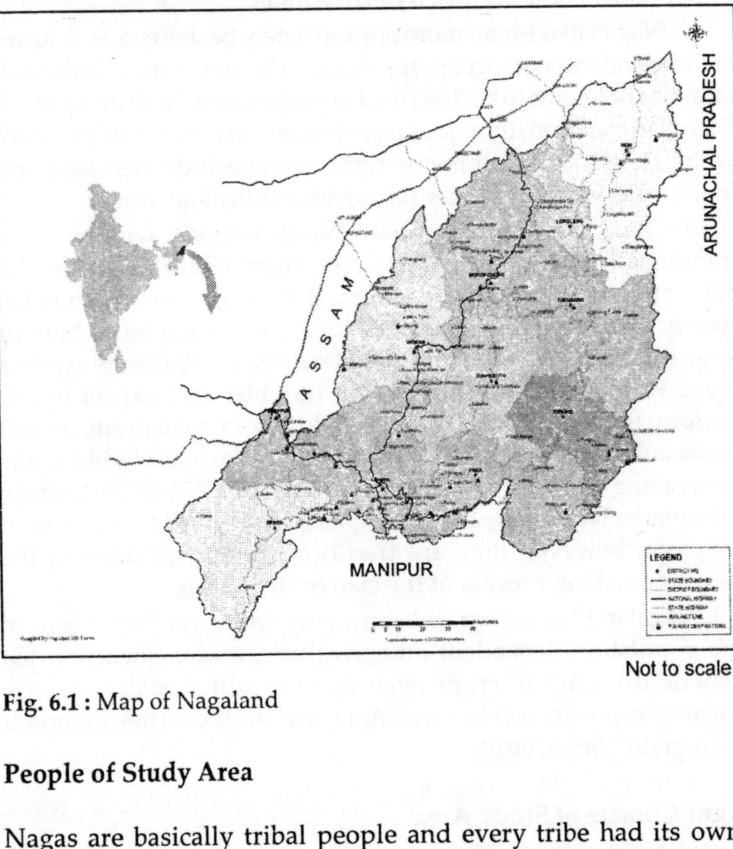

Not to scale

Fig. 6.1 : Map of Nagaland

People of Study Area

Nagas are basically tribal people and every tribe had its own effective system of self-governance from time immemorial. The present Nagaland was only a district called "Naga Hills" within the State of Assam till 1957. A tribe is distinguished by its language, mores and customs. Each tribe tends to treat itself as a race apart. The patrilineal descent is the vehicle of continuity which provides stability to the Naga social structure. The social structure has its special ethical and moral values which enjoying a member to clearly recognize what is its own, what belongs to the neighbour and what belongs to the village as a whole. In the Naga society, elaboration of the descent groups provides a scaffold for organizing social relationships amongst the territorially divided social groupings, particularly the clans and lineages. In Naga society, there is no class or caste. Socially, a tribe consists of subdivisions called clans. These are strictly exogamous.

A Naga village may more appropriately be defined as a cluster of independent clans occupying distinct clan-territories. These clan localities had come to be described as *khels* during the British period. Each clan traditionally enjoys its autonomy in terms of its exclusive political, social and economic rights over well-defined land and forest areas including water resources and fishing areas.

In the classless, caste-less Naga society, women have traditionally enjoyed a high social position, with a pivotal role in both family and community affairs. However, being a patriarchal society with strong warrior tradition, it is considered an honour to be born as a man. The traditional culture and customs expect a Naga woman to be obedient and humble; also expect her to perform the roles of wife, mother, child bearer, food producer and household manager. She also supplements the household income by weaving colourful shawls, an activity which is done exclusively by women. Women are highly respected and given a great deal of freedom, however, they are traditionally not included in the decision-making process of the clan or the village.

Nagaland has an agrarian economy with over 70 per cent of the population dependent on agriculture, and maintains a rich genetic diversity in crops such as rice, millet, maize, pulses, sugarcane, potato, coffee, cardamom, tea, etc. Rice is the important food grain (Singh, 2010).

Agro-Climate of Study Area

High rainfall Agro-climatic condition of a place plays a vital role in crop planning, irrigation scheduling, water harvesting as well as in design of infrastructures for green houses for horticultural, floricultural, etc. The classification of agro-climatic zones of North-Eastern Region of India (excluding Assam) have been based on altitude, rainfall pattern, temperature variations, topography, soil, etc. Nagaland is classified into six agro-climatic zones namely: Alpine zone, Temperate and sub-alpine zone, Sub-tropical hill zone, Sub-tropical plain zone, Mild Tropical Plain zone and Mild tropical hill zone (Borthakur, 1992). The annual mean maximum temperature varies from 21.0°C to 30.0°C whereas annual mean rainfall varies from 920.0 mm to 2500 mm (Fig. 6.2).

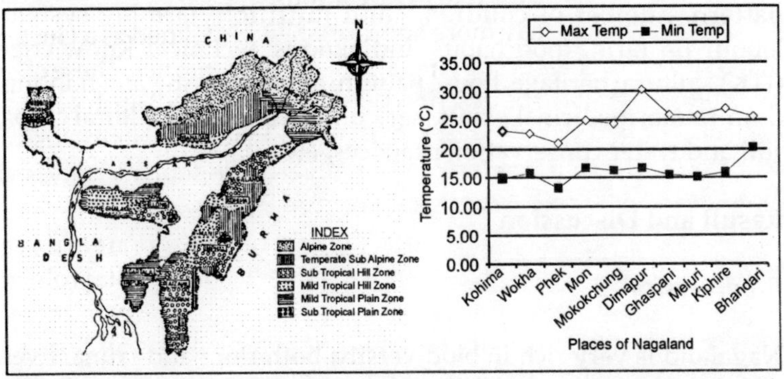

Fig. 6.2: Agro-Climatic Zones and Temperaure Variation of Nagaland

Methodology

A wide range data has been collected on socio-cultural, demographic, reproductive history and other health aspects has collected which are basic to all living beings, are manifested through an intricate series of changes that give a definite shape to human being under the influence of both heredity and environment. The methodology for the study of the target area, flora, fauna, biodiversity, conservation and preservation, etc., has been given in detail in this chapter. A format was designed and for the benchmark survey all the households were selected from Nagaland (Angami dominated). The indicators included bio-physical, socio-economic as well as infrastructure related and including practicing of indigenous/traditional farming system. The survey was conducted during 2005-2006 by Senior Research Fellow/ contractual workers under the supervision of scientists and anthropologists. The study envisages covering nine villages namely *Viswema, Jakhama, Kigwema, Mima, Phusama, Jytosoma, Mesoma, Khonama and Kohima* about 100-800 farm families in each village. The considerable indicators are food sufficiency, land quality, forest area, preservation of biodiversity and ecological conservation.

The questionnaire was designed with a schedule for evaluating biodiversity conservation as well as socio-economic characteristics of the participants in the survey. The schedule was containing question on age, gender, household size, total annual income, total land owned, total land cultivated, land tenure system, land-use pattern, number of children, child nutrition, farming system, labour on farm, food habits, Indigenous Technical Knowledge (ITK), cultural heritage, house pattern, animal rearing and hunting, flora-fauna, medicinal plants, agricultural and horticultural crops, soil and water conservation practices, etc.

Result and Discussion

Biodiversity

Nagaland is very rich in biodiversity, both flora and fauna. Even today some pockets of forests are covered with gigantic trees, where sunrays cannot penetrate. Due to reckless and uncontrolled cutting of trees for timber, firewood, continued *jhum* cultivation and annual fire in vast tracts of land, forests got degraded and barren, which accelerated diminishing of the most of the original characteristics of the forests. Though geographically being a small State, Nagaland has several types of forests, mainly because the State is mostly tropical, and the altitudes range from a few hundred metres to about four thousand metres. The major types of forests found in the State, as per the classification of Champion and Seth, are as follows:

1. Northern tropical wet evergreen forests.
2. Northern tropical semi- evergreen forests.
3. Northern sub-tropical broad leave wet hill forests.
4. Northern sub-tropical pine forests.
5. Northern montana wet temperate forests.
6. Temperate forests.

The local population are intricately involved with the forests for their sustenance, be it agriculture, timber, items of woods for day-to-day or the uses of medicinal plants, etc. These forest products are also their main source of economy. Therefore, when the main stay of the people is dependent on forest, destruction of forests is imminent and thereby endangering many valuable species. Due to the primitive method/practice of cultivation (*i.e.,* slash and burn) the rich biodiversity of the State is dwindling year by year. Most of the species, both flora and fauna, appears to be endangered due to heavy biotic pressure/ interference and reckless deforestation.

Flora

Out of two biodiversity hotspots of North-East India, Nagaland belongs to Indo-Burma hotspot (Mittermeier *et al.,* 2004). The State is having 2,250 floral species out of 8550 floral species of the region. Among these species world's tallest Rhododendron tree were also found. Rhododendron has been found in Japfu Mountain of Kohima district is recorded in the *Guinness Book of World Record.* Commonly found floras in the survey are as follows:

Dipterocarpous macrocarpous (Hollong), *Shorea assamica* (Makai), *Rododendron* Spp., *Mesua ferra* (Nahar), are rare and endangered spp. *Panax gensing* (Gensing) is found only in Tuensang district at higher altitude which is endangered. *Aquilaria agallocha* (Agar) is also an endangered species.

Bamboo

There are 22 species of bamboos available in the State. The important species of bamboos are as given in Table 6.1.

Canes

Around 5 numbers. of species namely, *Calamus rotang, Calamus flagellum, Calamus erectus, Calamus gracilis and Calamus floribundu* found in the survey.

Coniferous

About 4 number of coniferous species namely, *Pinus khasyia (Indigenous), Pinus caribiae* (exotic), *Pinus petula* and *Cryptomeria japonica* (exotic) were found.

Table 6.1 : List of Bamboo Species found in Nagaland

No.	Species	No.	Species
1.	*Sinarundinaria griffithiana* (Munro) Chao & Renv. (*Arundinaria griffithiana* Munro) *Saramati.*	10.	*Dendrocalamus hookeri* Munro Kohima, Wokha.
2.	*Sinarundinaria elegans* (Kurz) Chao & Renv. (*Arundinaria elegans* Kurz) *Puliebadze*, near Kohima.	11.	*Dendrocalamus hamiltonii Nees et Am* ex Munro, Dimapur - Kohima Road and Wokha.
3.	*Sinarundinaria rolloana* (Gamble) Chao & Renv. (*Arundinaria rolloana* Gamble) Japfü Range, Kohima.	12.	*Dendrocalamus giganteus* Munro Kohima, Mao.
4.	*Sinarundinaria nagalandiana* Naithani Niriyo Peak, Wokha.	13.	*Dendrocalamus calostachys* (Kurz) Kurz Phikrokezema, Dimapur and Kohima.
5.	*Chimonobambusa callosa* (Munro) Nakai (*Arundinaria callosa* Munro) *Puliebadze* above Kohima and Mao.	14.	*Schizostachyum polymorphum* (Munro) Majumdar (*Pseudostachyum polymorphum* Munro) Longsachu near Wokha
6.	*Neomicrocalamus prainii* (Gamble) Keng f. (*Arundinaria prainii* Gamble) *Puliebadze*, Japfü Range.	15.	*Schizostachyum dullooa* (Gamble) Majumdar (*Teinostachyum dullooa* Gamble) Yikum near Wokha
7.	*Bambusa balcooa Roxb.* Wokha.	16.	*Schizostachyum fuchsianum* (Gamble) Majumdar (*Cephalostachyum fuchsianum* Gamble) Kohima, Zulhama-Kilomi.
8.	*Bambusa tulda* Roxb. Kohima, Jaluki.	17.	*Melocanna baccifera* (Roxb.) Kurz. (*M. bambusoides Trin.*) Jaluki
9.	*Bambusa palliada* Munro Wokha, Kohima and Zeliang village.		

Broad Leaved

Survey revealed around 50 numbers. of following broad leaved species in Nagaland.

Lagerstromia speciosa (Ajhar), *Tectona grandis* (Teak), *Mangifera indica* (Am), *Alnus nepalensis* (Alder), *Morus laevigata* (Bola), *Tetrameles nudiflora* (Bhelu), *Trewia nudiflora* (Bhelkar), *Betula alnoides* (Betula), *Canarium resiniferum* (Dhuna), *Gmelina arborea* (Gomari), *Cinnamomum cecicodaphne* (Gonsoroi), *Nyssa javanica* (Gahorisopa), *Terminalia myriocarpa* (Hollock), *Adina eligocephala*

(Haldisopa), *Cedrela toona* (Jatipoma), *Podocarpus nerifolia* (Jinari), *Altingia exelsa* (Jutuli), *Duabanga grandiflora* (Khokon), *Albizzia procera* (Koroi), *Anthocephalus kadamba* (Kadam), *Shorea assamica* (Mekai), *Endospermum chinensis* (Phulgomari), *Melia azadirach* (Ghoora-Neem), *Stereospermum chelonoides* (Paroli), *Magnolia* spp. (Sopas), *Cassia fistula* (Sonaru), *Bombax ceiba* (Semal), *Ficus nervosa* (Robar), Spondias axillaris (Hog plum), *Michelia champaca* (Titasopa), *Bischofia javanica* (Uriam), *Juglans regia* (Walnut), *Mansonia dipikai* (Badam), *Phoebe goalparensis* (Bonsom), *Dipterocarpus macrocarpus* (Hollang), *Terminalia chebula* (Hilika), *Schima wallichii* (Gogra), *Mesua ferrea* (Nahar), *Albizzia lebbeck* (Siris), *Quercus* Spp. (Oaks), *Artocarpus chaplasha* Sam), *Chukrasia tabularis* (Bogipoma), *Terminilia bellerica* (Bahera). *Hovenia dulcis (Coral tree), Acrocarpus fraxinifolius (Mandani), Bucklandia populnea (Pipli), Pseudostreblus indicus (Tsüngkoh).*

Medicinal Plants

The prominent species which are found in Nagaland are: *Panax pseudo-gensing* (Gensing), *Taxus baccata* (Yew), *Aquilaria agallocha* (Agar), *Solanum khasianum, Ocimum sanctum* (Tulsi), *Aegle marmelos* (Bel), *Rauvolfia serpentina* (Sarpgandha), *Elaeocarpus ganitrus* (Rudraksha), *Dioscorea deltoides* (Kath Aloo), *Emblica officinalis* (Amla), *Swertia chirata* (Chirata), *Rubia cordifolia, Oroxylum indicum, Clerodendrum colebrookianum, Passiflora edulis.* Some of the medicinal plants are listed in below which are using by Angami Naga in Nagaland:

Orchids

Nagaland has about 344 spp. out of 1250 spp. of orchids found in India. Most of the Orchids here are epiphytes or lithophytes. A few terrestrial orchids are also found in the state. Rarely found and endangered species of Orchids available in the state are: *Thunia*- 1no.species, *Arundinaria graminifolia* (Bamboo orchid), *Renenthera* (Red vanda), Rhynchostylis (Fox-tail), *Pleoni, Phauis* (Ground orchid)-2nos of species, *Paphiopedilum*-1no. species, *Cymbidium tigrinum*-1no. species.

Table 6.2 : List of Plants that are used for Curing Different Ailments of Angami Naga

Local name (Tenydie)	English name	Scientific name	Parts used	Uses
Wapa		*Heliotropium indicum*	Leaf	It is used for eye problem and also as feed for pig.
Satu	Wild Tulsi	*Oeimum sanctum*	'Leaf & juice	Headache, fever. Also used in pickle preparation
Wara	Pennywort	*Centella asiatica*	Leaf & juice	Leaf is used for stomach problem & as vegetable. Juice is for conjunctivitis
Mepyo		*Leonurus sibinicus*	Juice of leaf	Headache & fever
Allovera (Prickly pear)	Alloe vera	*Cactaceae sps.*	Leaf	Leaf juice used for stomach & skin problem
Ova	Seasam (wild)	*Sesamum indicum*	Seed	Used as vegetable & as ointment
Rupro	Alder	*Alnus nepalensis*	Leaf	Leaf paste used for cuts
Muduram	Guava	*Psidium guyava*	Leaf boiled	Used in dysentery & Diarrhoea
Rummu		*Rubus ellipticus*	Root	High fever
Kekhronhasi		*Tamarindus indica*	Seed	Snake bites
	Touch me not	*Mimosa pudica*	Root	Roasted rice paste & juice of root together used in taking out pus from boils
Tomato	Wild tomato	*Solanaceae sps*	Leaf	Juice is used in kidney pain
	Goose berry	*Phyllanthus embica*	Fruit	Juice is used in dysentery
Kikoise	Wild brinjal	*Solanum torum*	Fruit	Juice used for stomach problem
Kipfu		*Solanum kurzi*	Fruit boiled	Used for stomach pain
Zepne		*Solanum sps.*	Leaves boiled	Used for stomach ache
Parazhi		*Meriea esculata*	Bark boiled	Used for stomach ache
Mekrinipu		*Jropotum sps.*	Leaf juice	Applied on boil to take out pus
Kuchurabi		*Side acuta*	Stem piece	Tie around the neck with thread with clothes
Thayie	Banana	*Musa sps.*	Stem boiled	Boiled juice drink for diarrhoea
Peza		*Menea explanata*	Bark	As powder mixed with water and drink for dysentery
Lemon + Keshu	Lemon + Snail shells	*Citrus sps.* + snail shells	Snail shells dissolved in lemon juice	The juice drink for malaria
Zerpru		*Solanum sps.*	Leaf boiled	Juice drink for malaria
Tsomhu		*Rhus javanica*	Fruit	As powder mixed with water and drink for cholera
Metsuniu		*Phlogacanthus pubinaris*	Leaf boiled	Drink for gastric problem

Table 6.3 : List of orchids found in Nagaland

Sl. No.	Name	Sl. No.	Name
1.	Acampa papillosa	48.	Bulbophyllum polyrhizum
2.	Acampa rigida	49.	Bulbophyllum reptans
3.	Acampa wightiana	50.	Bulbophyllum rigidum
4.	Acanthephippium striatum	51.	Bulbophyllum rothschildianum
5.	Acanthephippium sylhetense	52.	Bulbophyllum roxburghii
6.	Aerides crassifolium	53.	Bulbophyllum secundum
7.	Aerides fieldingii	54.	Bulbophyllum striatum
8.	Aerides multiflorum	55.	Bulbophyllum umbellatum
9.	Aerides odoratum	56.	Bulbophyllum uniflorum
10.	Anoectochilus crispus	57.	Bulbophyllum viridiforum
11.	Anoectochilus elwesil	58.	Bulbophyllum wallichi
12.	Anoectochilus grandiflorus	59.	Calanthe alismifolia
13.	Anoectochilus griffithi	60.	Calanthe alpina
14.	Anoectochilus roxburghii	61.	Calanthe angusta
15.	Anthogonium gracile	62.	Calanthe biloba
16.	Aphyllorchis montana	63.	Calanthe brevicornu
17.	Aphyllorchis prainii	64.	Calanthe chloroleuca
18.	Appendicula cornuata	65.	Calanthe clavate
19.	Arachis bilinguis	66.	Calanthe densiflora
20.	Arachis cathcartii	67.	Calanthe foestermannii
21.	Arundina graminifolia	68.	Calanthe gracilis
22.	Ascocentrum ampullaceum	69.	Calanthe herbacea
23.	Ascocentrum curvifolium	70.	Calanthe manni
24.	Ascocentrum micranthum	71.	Calanthe musuca
25.	Ascocentrum miniatum	72.	Calanthe plantaginea
26.	Brachycorythis obcordata	73.	Calanthe puberula
27.	Bulbophyllum aculiflorum	74.	Calanthe tricarinata
28.	Bulbophyllum affine	75.	Calanthe triplicata
29.	Bulbophyllum andersonii	76.	Calanthe vaginata
30.	Bulbophyllum careyanum	77.	Calanthe vestita
31.	Bulbophyllum caudatum	78.	Calanthe whiteana
32.	Bulbophyllum cylindraceum	79.	Cephalanthera ongifolia
33.	Bulbophyllum dyeranum	80.	Ceratostylis himalaica
34.	Bulbophyllum elatum	81.	Ceratostylis teres
35.	Bulbophyllum eulepharum	82.	Cheirostylis griffithii
36.	Bulbophyllum gambeiel	83.	Cheirostylis pusilla
37.	Bulbophyllum guttulatum	84.	Cleisocentron trichromum
38.	Bulbophyllum gymnopus	85.	Cleisostoma aspersum
39.	Bulbophyllum helenae	86.	Cleisostoma filliforme
40.	Bulbophyllum hirtum	87.	Cleisostoma simondii
41.	Bulbophyllum hymenanthum	88.	Cleisostoma striatum
42.	Bulbophyllum leopardinum	89.	Cleisostoma subulatum
43.	Bulbophyllum leptanthum	90.	Cleisostoma racemiferum
44.	Bulbophyllum odoratissimum	91.	Coelogyne barbata
45.	Bulbophyllum ornatissimum	92.	Coelogyne corymbosa
46.	Bulbophyllum pencillium	93.	Coelogyne cristata
47.	Bulbophyllum piluliferum		

Table 6.3 : (*Contd.*)

Sl. No.	*Name*	*Sl. No.*	*Name*
94.	Coclogyne flaccida	140.	Dendrobium devonianum
95.	Coelogyne fuscescens	141.	Dendrobium eriaeflorum
96.	Coelogyne griffithi	142.	Dendrobium falconeri
97.	Coelogyne hitendrae	143.	Dendrobium farmeri
98.	Coelogyne longipes	144.	Dendrobiumfimbriatum
99.	Coelogyne micrantha	145.	Dendrobium formosum
100.	Coelogyne nitida	146.	Dendrobium gibsonil
101.	Coelogyne occuitata	147.	Dendrobium heterocarpum
102.	Coelogyne ovalis	148.	Dendrobium hookerianum
103.	Coelogyne prolifera	149.	Dendrobium infundibulam
104.	Coelogyne punctulata	150.	Dendrobium jenkinsii
105.	Coelogyne raizada	151.	Dendrobium lindleyi
106.	Coelogyne rigida	152.	Dendrobium longicornu
107.	Coelogyne schultesii	153.	Dendrobium moschatum
108.	Coelogyne stricta	154.	Dendrobium nobile
109.	Coelogyne viscosa	155.	Dendrobium ochreatum
110.	Corymborkis veratrifolia	156.	Dendrobium porphyrochilum
111.	Cremastra wallichiana	157.	Dendrobium primulinum
112.	Cryptochilus lutea	158.	Dendrobium pulchellum
113.	Cryptochilus sanguineus	159.	Dendrobium stuposum
114.	Cymbidium aloifolium	160.	Dendrobium terminate
115.	Cymbidium cochleare	161.	Dendrobium thysiflorum
116.	Cymbidium devonianum	162.	Dendrobium transparens
117.	Cymbidium elegans	163.	Dendrobium wardianum
118.	Cymbidium ensifolium	164.	Dendrobium williamsonii
119.	Cymbidium eburneum	165.	Diplomeria hirsuta
120.	Cymbidium iridioidea	166.	Diplomeria pulchelia
121.	Cymbidium lancifolium	167.	Diplomeria championi
122.	Cymbidium longifolium	168.	Epigeneium amplum
123.	Cymbidium lowianum	169.	Epigeneium fuscescens
124.	Cymbidium macrorhizon	170.	Epigeneium rotundatum
125.	Cymbidium mastersii	171.	Eria acevata
126.	Cymbidium pendulum	172.	Eria alba
127.	Cymbidium tigrinum	173.	Eria amica
128.	Cymbidium tracyanum	174.	Eria bambusifolia
129.	Dendrobium acinaciforme	175.	Eria biflora
130.	Dendrobium anceps	176.	Eria bractesces
131.	Dendrobium aphyllum	177.	Eria coronaria
132.	Dendrobium bensoniae	178.	Eria dasyphylla
133.	Dendrobium bicameratum	179.	Eria excavata
134.	Dendrobium candidum	180.	Eria graminifolia
135.	Dendrobium chrysanthum	181.	Eria muscicola
136.	Dendrobium chrystoxum	182.	Eria paniculata
137.	Dendrobium crepidatum	183.	Eria pannea
138.	Dendrobium densiflorum	184.	Eria spicata
139.	Dendrobium denudans	185.	Eria stricta

Table 6.3 : *(Contd.)*

Sl. No.	*Name*	*Sl. No.*	*Name*
186.	Eria vittata	222.	Liparis nervosa
187.	Eulophia bicallosa	223.	Liparis odorata
188.	Eulophia graminea	224.	Liparis pardoxa
189.	Eulophia nuda	225.	Liparis petiolata
190.	Flickingeria fimbriata	226.	Liparis plantaginea
191.	Flickingeria fugax	227.	Liparis platyrachis
192.	Galeola falconeri	228.	Liparis pulchella
193.	Galeola lindleyana	229.	Liparis resupina
194.	Gastrochilus acutifolium	230.	Liparis viridiflora
195.	Gastrochilus calceolaris	231.	Luisia inconspicua
196.	Gastrochilus distichus	232.	Luisia prachystachys
197.	Gastrochilus inconspicuum	233.	Luisia prachystachys
198.	Gastrochilus pseudodisticus	234.	Luisia teritifolia
199.	Geodorum densiflorum	235.	Luisia trichorhiza
200.	Goodyera foliosa	236.	Luisia zeylanica
201.	Goodyera fusca	237.	Malaxis acuminata
202.	Goodyera hispida	238.	Malaxis biaurita
203.	Goodyera procera	239.	Malaxis cylindroatachya
204.	Goodyera repens	240.	Malaxis josephiana
205.	Goodyera schiechtendaliana	241.	Malaxis khasiana
206.	Goodyera secundiflora	242.	Malaxis latifolia
207.	Goodyera viridiflora	243.	Micropera mannii
208.	Habennaria acuifera	244.	Micropera rostrata
209.	Habennaria dentate	245.	Monomera barbata
210.	Habennaria ensifolia	246.	Neogyne gardneriana
211.	Habennaria furcifera	247.	Neotianthe secundiflora
212.	Habennaria intermedia	248.	Neottia listeroides
213.	Habennaria malleifera	249.	Nephelaphyllum cordifolium
214.	Habennaria pactinata	250.	Nervilia aragoana
215.	Habennaria stenopetala	251.	Nervilia prainiana
216.	Herminium lanceum	252.	Oberonia acaulis
217.	Herminium macrophyllum	253.	Oberonia clarkel
218.	Herminium monorchis	254.	Oberonia ensiformis
219.	Hetaeria rubens	255.	Oberonia griffithiana
220.	Hygrochilus parishii	256.	Oberonia iridifolia
221.	Kingidium deliciosum	257.	Oberonia longilabris
212.	Kingidium taenialis	258.	Oberonia mannii
213.	Liparis assamica	259.	Oberonia micrantha
214.	Liparis bistriate	260.	Oberonia obcordata
215.	Liparis biturberculata	261.	Oberonia orbicularis
216.	Liparis bootanensis	262.	Oberonia pachyrachis
217.	Liparis caespitosa	263.	Oberonia pyrulifera
218.	Liparis cordifolia	264.	Oberonia recurva
219.	Liparis delicatula	265.	Oreochis foliosa
220.	Liparis distans	266.	Ornithochilus difformis
221.	Liparis longipes	267.	Otochilus alba

Table 6.3 : (*Contd.*)

Sl. No.	*Name*	*Sl. No.*	*Name*
268.	Otochilus fusca	306.	Pteroceras suaveolens
269.	Otochilus lancilabius	307.	Renanthera imschootiana
270.	Pachystoma senile	308.	Rhynchostylis retuasa
271.	Panasia unifllora	309.	Robiquetia succisa
272.	Paphiopedilum hirsutissimum	310.	Satyrium napalense
273.	Papiopedilum insigne	311.	Schoenorchis gemmata
274.	Paplionanthe longicornu	312.	Smitinandia micrantha
275.	Paplionanthe teres	313.	Spathoglottis ixioides
276.	Pecteilis gigantea	314.	Spathoglottis plicata
277.	Pecteilis susannae	315.	Spathoglottis pubescens
278.	Pelanthanthera insectifera	316.	Spiranthes sinense
279.	Perisrtylus affinis	317.	Sunipia bicolor
280.	Perisrtylus chloranthus	318.	Sunipia candida
281.	Perisrtylus constictus	319.	Thelasis longlifolia
282.	Perisrtylus densus	320.	Taeniophyllum khasianum
283.	Perisrtylus falla	321.	Thunia alba
284.	Perisrtylus goodyeroides	322.	Thunia marshlliana
285.	Perisrtylus mannii	323.	Tropidia curculigoides
286.	Perisrtylus prainii	324.	Tylostyles discolor
287.	Phalus flabus	325.	Uncifera acuminata
288.	Phalus longipes	326.	Uncifera obtusifolia
289.	Phalus mishmensis	327.	Vanda alpina
290.	Phalus tankervilliae	328.	Vanda bicolor
291.	Pholidota articulate	329.	Vanda coerulea
292.	Pholidota calceolate	330.	Vanda cristata
293.	Pholidota convallariae	331.	Vanda pumila
294.	Pholidota grifithii	332.	Vanda tesselata
295.	Pholidota imbricate	333.	Vanda testacea
296.	Pholidota protacta	334.	Vanda undulata
297.	Pholidota rubra	335.	Vandopsis vandarum
298.	Phreatia elegans	336.	Yoania prainii
299.	Platanthera arcuata	337.	Zeuxine abbreviata
300.	Platanthera stenantha	338.	Zeuxine flava
301.	Pleione hookeriana	339.	Zeuxine goodyeroides
302.	Pleione humilis	340.	Zeuxine gracilis
303.	Pleione maculata	341.	Zeuxine nervosa
304.	Pleione praecox	342.	Zeuxine strateumatica
305.	Poneoorchis chusua		

Table 6.4 : Commonly found Mammals in Nagaland are as follows :

Common Name	Scientific Name
Mammals	
1. Asian Elephant	*Elephas maximus.*
2. Gaur (Indian Bison)	*Bos gaurus.*
3. Jackal	*Canis aurius*
4. Tiger	*Panthera tigris.*
5. Sambar	*Cervus unicolor*
6. Leopard	*Panthera pardus.*
7. Barking Deer	*Muntaiqus muntijak*
8. Wild boar	*Sus scrofa*
9. Sloth Bear	*Eelursus arsinus*
10. Serow	*Capricornis sumatraensis*
11. Hoolock	*Hylobatus hoolock*
12. Common Langur	*Presbytis antillus*
13. Macaque	*Macaca* spp.
14. Leopard Cat	*Filis bengalensis*
15. Himalayan Squirrel	*Callosciuras pygerythru*
16. Pangolin.	*Manis crasicaudata*
17. Civet.	*Vivirra* spp.
18. Wolf	*Canis auririus*
19. Fruit bat	*Cynoptirus sphinx*
20. Porcupine	*Hystrix indica*
21. Hispis hare	*Caprogus hispisdus*
22. Slow Loris	*Nycticebus causeang*
23. Otter	*Lutra lutra*
24. Wild Dog	*Cuon alpinus*
25. Orange billed Himalayan Squirrel	*Cirrus unicolor*
26. Mangoose	*Herpester spp.*
27. Musk Deer.	*Moschus moschiferous.*
28. Binturong	*Arctictis binturong*
29. Jungle cat	*Filis chaus.*
30. Mole rat	*Bandicota bengalensis*
31. Indian hare	*Lypus nigricolis.*
32. Martin	*Martis* spp.
33. House Mouse	*Mus musculus*
34. Field Mouse	*Mus booduga*
35. Goral	*Nemarahidus goral*
36. Clouded Leopard	*Niofolis nibulosa*
37. Palm Civet	*Paguna larvata*
38. Wood cat	*Rattus blaufardi*
39. House cat	*Rattus rattus*
40. Fulvous fruit bat	*Tousettus leschinuitas*
41. Indian fox	*Vulpis bengalensin*
Reptiles.	
Monitor lizard	*Varanus albigularis*
Tortoise (desert)	*Gopherus agassizii*
Python (reticulate)	*Python reticulatus*
King cobra	*Ophiophagus hannah*
Common cobra	*Naja naja*

(Contd)

Table 6.4 : *(Contd)*

Common Name	Scientific Name
Common krait	*Bungarus caeruleus*
Banded krait	*Laticauda colubrina*
Viper	*Bitis nasicornis*
Bluethreated barbet	*Mengalaima lineata*
Birds.	
Greyheaded fishing eagle	*Ichuophaga nana*
Crested serpent eagle	*Pilernia cleala*
Bearded vulture	*Gypactus barbatus*
Forest eagle owl	*Bubo nipalensis*
Collared pigmy owlet	*Tus bakkameena*
Collared scope owl	*Laucidium brodei*
Tragopan	*Tragopan blythii*
Kaleej Pheasants	*Lophura leucemelona*
Common hill patridge	*Arboraphila forqueola*
Common pheasants	*Entropus simensia*
Red Jungle fowl	*Gallus gallus*
Peacock pheasants	*Polyplectron bicalcaratum*
Pintailed green pigeons	*Treron apicauda*
Rutous turtle dove	*Streptopolia orientalia*
Marrnbacked imperial pigeon	*Ducula badia*
Emarald dove	*Chalcophapa indica*
Himalayan Jungle nightjar	*Caprimulgus indicus*
Indian roller	*Coracias bengalensis*
Chestnut threaded bee-eater	*Morapa leschanaulti*
Bluethreaed barbet	*Mengalaima lineata*
Great barbet	*Megalaima virens*
Great pied hornbill	*Buceros bicornis*
Rufousnecked hornbill	*Aceros nipalensis*
Goldenbacked throated woodpecker	*Dimopium shorii*
Darjeeling pied woodpecker	*Picoides darjellensis*
Red eared pied woodpecker	*Lythipicus pyrrhotis*
Bluenapped pitta	*Pitta nepanlensis*
Mrs. Gould's sunbird	*Aethopyga gapldinale*
Nepal Yellow backed sunbird	*Aethopyga nipalensis*
Black breasted sunbird	*Aethopyga saturata*
Firetailed yellow backed sunbird	*Aethopyga ignicauda*
Longtailed broadbill	*Serilophus lunatus*
Red drumped swallow	*Hirundedaurice*
Tyflers swallow	*Hirunderustice tyleri*
Balcknapped ariole	*Oriolus chinesis*
Himalayan tree pie	*Dendrocitta formosee*
Bronzed drongo	*Dicrurus aeneus*
Large brown thrush	*Zoothera menticola*
Lesser racket-tailed drongo	*Dicrurus renifer*
Large racket tailed drongo	*Dicrurus paradiseau*
Black drongo	*Dicrurus adaimilis*
Grey drongo	*Dicrurus leucephaecus*
Clouded Leopard	*Niofolis nibulosa*

Conservation Measures and Practices

About 85-90 per cent of land in Nagaland was under community ownership. Originally, the Nagas were head hunters and food gatherers. They have land for shifting cultivation, settled cultivation and forests reserves to meet food, vegetables, medicine, fruit, fuel, timber and other requirements. Wild meat was an integral part of tribal culture in Nagaland. Indigenous gun for hunting were present in almost every house. Degrading of forests and high rate of hunting has led to a quick decline in the population of wild animals, density of orchids, wild medicine, fruits (wild products). In spite of some student organizations and village councils, adoption of rules to prevent the collection of any wild products, people do not follow the rules. But it has been observed that the people of Khonoma village have accepted the wild life protection act. They have formulated rules and regulations for the management of the Khonoma sanctuary and ecosystems. The villagers do not destroy the forests and its products for which Khonoma has been declared as *Green village*.

They have taboos as well as rituals related to conservation of forest, wild products, the ultimate objective of which is the conservation of ecosystem. For example, Angami people as a team of young girls and boys go and collect bamboo (small and thin) and broom grass from the forest for chasing chicken fishing and sweeping purposes before Sekhreni festival, which indicate they do not disturb the forest in all the times.

Fauna

The largest Asian mammal, Elephant is endangered spp. The other endangered spps are *Melurses ursinus* (Sloth Bear), *Prionodon pardicolor* (Spotted linsang, Tiger-civet), *Panthera tigris* (Tiger), Macaca assamensis (Tailed Pig). The Gaur, or Indian Bison in habitats in Intangki National Park and Fakim Wildlife Sanctuary and other hilly areas is facing extinction from Nagaland The different Horn bills and Tortoise are also endangered. There are

41 nos. mammals, 8nos. Reptiles, 43 nos. of birds have been found in Nagaland.

Conservation of Soil and Water

The soil conservation practices in agriculture aimed to maintain productivity for sustained production of crops. The term soil conservation includes the preservation and restoration of lands (Singh, 2002). In most of the agricultural fields, soil erosion is minimized through traditional methods such as by bamboo clums, stones and gunny bags filled with soil (NIC, 2001). A form of bamboo fence (called *Tempale*) is erected (especially in the slope) to prevent the top soil and fertile soil from being washed away by rain. A sort of small stones and logs (small) are placed hither and thither or wherever necessary to check soil being carried away by rain. Trees are planted, especially in the sloppy areas to hold soil and thus prevent soil erosion. Adopted terrace cultivation to prevent soil erosion. Some non-cereal crops such as grass clover (*Trifolium repens* Linn) and alfalfa (*Medicago sativa)* conserve the organic matter in the soil. Thus growing these crops tend to conserve soil even if some minerals are carried aways in the removal of crops (*Singh, 2002* and *Chinnamani, 1977*). Applying green leaf and farmyard manure is the traditional method of improving the condition of the soil, in which green leaves and farmyard manure are ploughed into the soil. It helps in improving soil fertility through fixation of nitrogen using microorganisms (Sarma, 2002, Satapathy, 2002 and Laxminarayan, 2002).

Conservation of Agricultural Diversity (Crops and Vegetables)

Paddy

Rice is the principal food crop of the region and was extensively cultivated (72 per cent of the total cultivated area) in upland, lowland and deep-water conditions (Hore, 2005). Paddy, after harvest were collected and kept in a very big container made of bamboo called *Mosem/Okhi* which has a capacity of 200–250 bags (Molule). A kind of funnel shaped structure called *Tsukbong* were kept in the middle of the container so that air was allowed to circulate inside the container and thus prevent the paddy from getting spoilt/rot, in Angami areas they use net type structure as innerwall of the okhi made of bamboo for the same purpose as like Ao tribe and they cover with orha and the join between grannery and orha (lid) they plaster with mud to prevent from insects. In this way paddy were kept throughout the year without being spoilt. Thus about 5–7 bamboo containers (*Mosem/ Okhi)* were kept in a special hut meant for paddy called granary which were constructed at a distance away from residential house in Ao houses but in Angami houses they keep granary in front of the drawing room or both side of the main door to show their socio-economic status. Moreover in Angami areas outsiders were not allowed to touch their granary. Rice (*Oryza sativa* L.) spp. was found in the survey.

Maize

Maize after harvest are tied in a bunch and hung in the open air usually away from fire, i.e., dry and airy place. But in Angami areas they hung in the kitchen for eating and sowing (seed) purposes. In this way, they can be kept for long till the next season. Maize (*Zea mays* L.) spp. was found in the survey.

Naga *Dal* and Other Cereals

After harvesting, these were stored in a light container usually made out of bamboo. These are stored in the container and are made use throughout the year. Wheat (*Triticum aestivam* L.) and Sorghum (*sorghum bicolor* L.) were found in the survey.

Bamboo Shoot

Bamboo shoots after collection from the forest could be preserved in different ways.

Liquid Form

Bamboo shoots were crushed and made into paste. After that they were wrapped lightly in a banana leaf and a stone was placed over it so that by its pressure and weight, the juice present in the bamboo were drained well and collected in a container placed below it. The juices were stored in a bottle or big bamboo in an air tight condition. It was used in making different dishes.

Solid Form

The remaining solid form, i.e., after the juice has been drained properly it was stored again in different container and was kept throughout the year. It was considered as one of the special food item among Ao Naga in particular and also Naga in general.

Dried Form

The solid form is again dried in the sun properly and stored in container. It is used throughout the year without being spoiled.

Yam

Yam bulb: After harvested, it is kept in the open cool, dry place so that moisture is removed from the bulb so as that it does not get spoiled.

Yam stem: Stem is cut into pieces and dried properly and kept in a bamboo container.

Yam leaf: Leaves are collected and cut into small pieces, dried and stored in an indigenously made pouch made out of palm leaves.

Sweet Potatoes

After harvesting they are kept in cool, dry place and are utilized throughout the year.

Gooseberry

After collection, they were boiled with little salt and dried after which they were stored in a container.

Chilly

After harvesting they dry and wrapped with banana leaf and hung inside the *Chullah* and use throughout the year.

Knoll-khol (Squash)

Tanghkul, Angami and other community of Naga tribes in order to conserve knoll-khol, dig pit whose length and width depends on the quantity of knoll-khol to be conserved. The depth is usually three-fourth of a meter. The knoll-khol is kept covered with earth. By this indigenous method, knoll-khol remains fresh for 6 months to 1 year.

Conservation of Land by Customary Law

Individual ownership of land was absent in Naga society. The land was classified as either clan land or village land. Even today their traditional land holding systems are prevailing in the society. All clan land will be village land but all village land will not be clan land. Only those who are very rich purchase land. And that is how private or individual ownership come into existence. But that land should be permitted from the seller party's clan members. Till today they do not have any specific measuring unit for land or any given area. To measure the land they have some kind of boundaries (demarcated area) through laws which is called customary law. Customary law is very strong among all the Naga tribes, be it in Nagaland or Manipur (Tangul/Zeliangrong) or Arunachal Pradesh. Transfer of land is going on from generation to generation. The land is divided among the sons and not the daughters. The ownership differs from community to community among the Naga tribes. For example among the Ao, Sema, Lotha, etc., the first son of the family owns the main share of the land but in Angami tribe, the youngest son gets major part of the property. Though the land can be used for cultivation, they lack the authority to sell, lease or deal with any monetary work of the land. They have specific land for cultivation either for *jhum* or terraced cultivation.

Major Customary Rules and Regulations in Naga Society

(1) For purchase of land by any person, he needs to consult with other members of the clan. It is only after the consent granted by the other members of the clan that the land can be purchased.

(2) For share cropping and shifting cultivation they do not have specific tenure. They shift from one place to another depending on the variety of crops, types of cultivation.

(3) An individual cannot take his sole decision regarding share cropping. It depends on other members of the clan.
(4) All the members of the clan participate for lease to land or any monetary decisions by all the members of the clan.
(5) The benefits whether to be shared by individual or all the members depends on the decision taken by the clan members.
(6) Clan fund is used for purchasing of land. All the members of clan contribute equal amount of money and that money is used for purchase of land which will be called as clan land.
(7) Restricted forests are not allowed for cultivation and any other purposes. They have specific forests for fuel or furnitures/constructive purposes.
(8) An important rule is that forest products can be sold but not forests. They are of the belief that forests are their traditional property/right and should be preserved. And for this reason, the percentage of forest land is more than in any other areas. They feel that the sale of forest is giving away their tradition/identity.
(9) If any one migrates from one place to another he need to donate his share of forest land to other members of the clan but the sale of forest land cannot be done.
(10) If any one in the clan wants to sell land for need of money in time of emergency, he should make known his problem to the other members of the clan. The members of the clan will try to solve the problem by themselves without the involvement of any outsider. The land is either purchased by an individual or a group of members in the clan.
(11) Plantation in forest with clan to clan or any other, there should be agreement for tenure and monitory benefit or products. Everything will be decided by the members of the clan and not individually.
(12) For any land dispute or other problems that arise in clan will be solved by clan members; for inter-clan, the Village Council Chairman. But inter-clan affairs from Village Council will again come to clan members to make situation normal. The punishment will be shared by the other members of the clan for inter-clan affairs.

Conservation of Forest /Ecology/Ecosystem

Nagaland has been endowed with a wide variety of forest types on account of its unique geographic locations and wide range of physiographic terrain obtained in the State. Forest occupy an area of approximately 8,62,930 ha, of which government forest account for 11.7 per cent. The private forests vested with the villagers are being haphazardly, unscientifically exploited without taking into consideration the future supply.

Though in olden times, the people were not aware about the conservation of ecology or ecosystems, they were having a sense of conserving the forest and ecosystem in traditional way. The villagers were not allowed to cut trees without taking permission from the other members of their respective clan. Permission has to be sought for fishing and other aquatic products from the local authority. Generally permission is granted to the groups rather than a single person alone so as to share it among a larger number of people. In order to maintain and regulate water supply to the fields, the surrounding hills were covered with forests.

Restricted forests are not allowed for cultivation and any other purposes. They have specific forests for fuel or furniture or for constructive purposes. An important rule is that forest products can be sold but not the forest. They are in the belief that forests are their traditional property/right and it should be preserved. Due to which, the percentage of forest land is more than in any landholdings. They are in the feeling of sale of forest is the giving away of their traditional/identity. Moreover, no member of the clan can sale of his forest while migrating from one place to another except donation of his share to any of his clan. Plantation in forest could be done among the clan members.

Department of Forest has initiated Joint Forest Management (JFM) during the year 1997 with an objective to conserve Forest ecology/ecosystem. They have involved a total of 55 forest communities managing an area of 650 ha. More than 85 per cent forests are privately owned in Nagaland with a provision to provide the share to the private owner at the time of harvesting. But the private owner should not utilize the land for own forestry purposes.

Conservation through Some Indigenous Farming System

Several farm-level water management innovations and traditional practices have been tried in the past namely, integrated watershed management with a water harvesting structure as an integral part, sustainable multi-commodity farming systems, *Zabo* system of cultivation, *Bamboo drips, Pani-kheti, Apatani system* and more recently storing rainwater in plastic-lined ponds *(jalkund)* or ferro-cement tanks.

Survey also revealed that indigenous farming systems are playing a vital role for natural resource conservation and on farm resource recycling in North-Eastern hilly region as well as in Nagaland. The indigenous farming system that are predominant in Nagaland are Zabo system, Alder based system, shifting cultivation and *Pani-kheti* system. These indigenous agricultural practices are mainly based on scientific knowledge of plants, conservation practices and land-use systems.

Zabo Farming System:

The word *'Zabo'* means impounding of water which is a superb system of rain water harvesting (Fig 5.7). Zabo system is locally known as *Zura* system is practiced by Chakesang tribes. This system is a combination of forestry, soil and water conservation. *Zabo* is practiced in Phek district of Nagaland State. This farming system has a combination of forestry, agriculture and animal care with a well-founded conservation base, soil erosion control, water resources development and protection of environment. This farming system is followed on the hill slopes up to 100 per cent or even more. (Mishra and Sharma, 2001).

It has a combination of forest towards the top of hill, water harvesting tanks in the middle for agriculture and paddy field followed by cattleyard at the lower side with well-founded soil and water conservation base. The tank is used for storage of water for the crops as well as for irrigation during the crop period. Special techniques for seepage control in the paddy plots are followed. Paddy husk is used on shoulder bunds and puddling is done thoroughly so that seepage of water through the bund is checked. Special techniques for seepage control in the paddy plots are followed. Paddy husk is used on shoulder bunds and puddling is done thoroughly. The catchment area is generally kept under forest cover without disturbing by activities such as cutting and burning of trees. The water carries with it the dung and urine of the animals to the fields. This serves as good source of nutrition for the crops.

The Zabo farming system is a traditional agriculture and forestry land-use system which has an inbuilt water harvesting and recycling systems with well founded conservation base to control soil erosion, proper management of soil fertility and available water. It is a viable practice of resource management and maintenance of ecological balance.

Alder Based Farming Systems

In this system soil fertility is maintained by planting Alder (*Alnus nepalensis*) in the system which can fix atmospheric nitrogen (Fig. 5.9). This involves planting of the alder trees to enhance the soil fertility with crops such as maize, Job's tears, millet, potato, chilli, pumpkin, barley, etc. The alder grows well on lands varying in altitude from 800 to 3,000 m. It is a non-leguminous tree that fixes atmospheric nitrogen through nodules on the roots. Besides fixing atmospheric nitrogen, the litter of the trees adds to the soil phosphorus, potassium, calcium, and other nutrients through the addition of biomass. The Nepalese Alder *(Alnus nepalesis)* tree based TEK which is incorporated both during the cropping and the fallow phases of *jhum,* widespread throughout the Angami tribe of Khonoma village near Kohima. This fixes up to 120 kg N per ha. per year, and is the starting point and the basis for identifying a number of other tree species, for a redeveloped *jhum* (Ramakrishnan, 2008).

Pruning of alder tree is done regularly to maintain required height and green biomass is recycled in the system. Whereas, branches are used as fire wood and Alder leaves are also a medicine used for blood coagulation. The *jhumia* of Khonoma village under Kohima district of Nagaland plant alder trees in the *jhum* cycle area and traditional agricultural crops basically with the idea that their root nodules improve soil fertility by fixing atmospheric nitrogen. It also increases crop yield and reduces soil erosion, besides providing shades to plantation crops like coffee at lower altitude and cardamom at higher altitude. Normally, a *jhumia* cultivates the field for 2 years within a nine-year span, but the alder-based system allows two harvests in every 4 to 5 years. The system involves pollarding of alder trees in two phase, i.e., (i) Initial pollarding, and (ii) cyclical/subsequent pollarding. This practice has been in use since about 100 years by the whole community. The ability of the alder trees to develop and retain fertility of the soil has been fully utilized by farmers in Angami, Chakhesang, Chang, Yimchunger and Konyak area in Nagaland at varying altitudes (Gokhle *et al.*, 1985).

Large Cardamom Alder Based Farming System

The large cardamom (*Amomum subulatum* Roxb.) based farming system is one of the most important among them. Large cardamom as an under growth occupies the middle tier in the three-tier forest constitution with alder (*Alnus nepalensis*) as the dominant companion (Fig 5.11). Large cardamom is one of the most stable cash earners for the people of Khonama. Normally large cardamom has been observed to thrive well in association with the Himalayan Alder (*Alnus nepalensis* D. Don) and hence, this companion is also called as the large cardamom–*Alnus* farming system.

Shifting Cultivation

The Shifting cultivation developed in Mizoram and Nagaland for survival of people living on the slopes was the best way to sustain soil fertility and productivity, and to conserve and use the bio-resources in a sustainable manner. This highly organized agro-ecosystem called *jhum* is based on empirical knowledge accumulated over centuries. It involves slashing of vegetation, burning it before the onset of monsoon, raising a mixture of crops on temporarily enriched soil for a year or two, leaving it fallow for a few years and returning for another cropping cycle after a gap of 5-15 years (Singh, 2008). This type of cultivation system is also called as *Slash and Burn* agriculture and still prevalent in Nagaland (Fig. 5.12). The area under shifting cultivation (*Jhum or Swidden cultivation*) is about 74,040 hectares and under terraced cultivation is 61,060 hectares during 1994-1995. Shifting cultivation covers over 73 per cent of the total arable area of the State. It is mostly concentrated in the districts of Mokokchung, Tuensang, Wokha, Zunheboto and Mon (Sharma, 2010). The farmers have started maintaining agro-biodiversity in *jhum* fields by sowing agricultural crops amidst naturally regenerated plants preserved in *jhum* cycle. Boundaries are demarcated through the cultivation of creeper crops like cucumber, pumpkin, etc. Almost all the crops grown in the field are also found near the household. Due to such agricultural bio-diversity practiced by the farming community in Nagaland, the villagers are almost self-dependent. Due to such agricultural bio-diversity practiced by the farming community in Nagaland, the villagers are almost self-dependent. The practice of shifting cultivation is an important factor for village life through a wide range of food, medicine, fibre and fuel crops. The main advantage of the practice is that the ecosystem is maintained and preserved, besides ensuring availability of food, fuel, etc., including medicinal plants for immediate local use. Local varieties of paddy, maize, soybean, millets, root crops, mustard and wide range of vegetables besides timber like teak, hollock, titachap and alder in specific areas. Almost all the farmers in higher altitude have been practicing this since 50-60 years. Proper support of the laid log/bamboo is ensured to last for at least three years, as the farmers go up to third year. Thus, the soil erosion and speed of the run-off water are checked and moisture is conserved in the soil and on the bund to strengthen the bund and serve as additional barrier as also to get additional harvest. This practice results in increased crop yield (Fig 5.12).

During the month of February/March natural vegetation is slashed for clearing the jungle and the dried biomass is burnt. rice, maize, minor millets, tapioca, cucumber, pumpkin, chillies, etc., are the major crops grown under shifting cultivation which also serves as vegetative barrier for soil conservation. Almost all the crops grown in the field are also found near the household. After cultivating for 1-3 years, the land is abandoned for regeneration of fertility and a new area is searched for *jhuming*. The productivity of crops are very low, e.g., rice productivity is 0.5-1 t/ha in *jhum*. Under a mixed cropping system in *jhum* land, the farmer harvests crops sequentially as and when the crop matures over a period of a few months; after harvesting the economically useful component, they recycle the biomass into their agricultural plot, which decomposes rapidly. Weed biomass pulled out of their plots were put back into the system for similar reasons; about 20 percent biomass of weeds, which they leave *in situ* without being pulled out serves as important nutrient conservation role on the hill slope, which otherwise could be lost through erosive/ leaching process. Socially selected and/or valued species of indigenous agricultural systems and those from natural systems often have ecologically significant keystone value; these keystone species often play a key role in nutrient enrichment of the soil; such species helps in redeveloped land-use systems with community participation.

Pani-Kheti System (Rice Cultivation in Terrace)

In this system runoff from forest area on hill top is diverted into rice fields by contour terracing on the hill slopes to ensure water pounding (Fig 5.14). This ensures availability of water to rice and check weed growth in paddy field. All the left over crop and weed biomass are recycled into the system. Terrace cultivation is widely practiced by the tribal communities. The major crops include rice, maize, millets, pea, oilseeds (rapeseed/mustard and niger), fibres, sugarcane, tobacco, potato, etc. The farmers also cultivate a variety of temperate, subtropical, and tropical vegetables, which includes pea, carrot, chili, onion, melon, spinach, cucumber, brinjal (eggplant), tomato, brassicas, yam, and arums in home garden as well as in terraced field. They may be a monocrop or in mixed cropping system with diverse ingredients. The important cropping systems are rice-mustard, rice-pea, maize-mustard, ginger-mustard (Singh, 2010). All the indigenous farming systems are that local crop varieties and animal breeds are used which varieties are also needed to preserve in quality in terms of nutrient content. All the works are done manually or with animal power and in organic farming methods. Therefore, all the indigenous farming systems are very important for keeping natural resources intake position.

Bench Terracing

Department of Soil and Water Conservation, Nagaland has initiated land development programme with terracing through farmers' participation during the year 2003-04. The terraced construction has been taken up in the land up to 30 per cent slope with 50 per cent subsidy by the Government and remaining 50 per cent has been contributed by the beneficiaries. The scheme will stabilize 5574.00 ha. of hill slopes and foot hill areas during the whole project period which otherwise will be subjected to heavy soil erosion and environment degradation.

Conclusion

The survey in nine villages of Nagaland revealed that bio-diversity of the State is rich and varied in nature. Biodiversity also changes with the variation of physiographic and geo-climatic condition of the State. Variation of topography also gave the State as a unique biodiversity in the region. Under this survey, 2250 number. of floral species out of 8,550 floral species of the region, 17 species of bamboo, 5 species of canes, 15 species of medicinal plants, 344 species of orchids, 41 species of mammals, 8 species of reptiles, 43 species of birds have been found. Among all the flora species, worlds tallest Rhododendron tree were also found in Japfu Mountain of Kohima district which has already been recorded in the Guinness Book of World. Study revealed that most of species, both flora and fauna, appears to be endangered due to heavy biotic pressure/interference and reckless deforestation. Some of exotic flora and fauna species has already become extinct. Some flora and fauna are also preserved by the Naga society. They have taken lots of conservation practices like *Pani-kheti*, bamboo drip irrigation, *Terrace cultivation*, community land ownership; *Zabo* farming system, *Alder based* farming system, and *green manuring*. This type off conservation practices and farming systems has increased at least three times higher socio-economic return of Nagaland than any other conservation practices. Hence, bio-diversity of Nagaland varied with fertile soil, agro-ecological situations of plains as well as valleys, hills, tilla land, immense water resources, human resources of ethnic diversity and cultural groups, could be potential sources for economic development of Nagaland and the North-East region as a whole. To preserve the biodiversity of the State, ecology and gene pool, judicious management and care of natural resources are necessary. Local systems of conservation and traditional knowledge may also to be given importance.

REFERENCES

Borthakur, D.N.,1992. *Agriculture of the North Eastern Region with Special*

Reference to Hill Agriculture. Beecee Prakashan, Guwahati, Assam, India. 9-10.

Chinnamani S., 1977. Soil and water conservation in the hills of Western Ghats. *Soil Conservation* Dig. 5:33

Gokhle, A.M.; Zeliang, D.K.; Kevichusa, R.; Angami, T. and Bendangnugsang, S., 1985. *The Use of Alder Tree*. State Council of Education Research & Training. Govt. of Nagaland, Kohima, India: 20.

Hore, D.K., 2005. Rice diversity collection, conservation and management in noth eastern India. *Genetic Resources and Crop Evaluation*. 52:1129-1140.

Laxminarayan, K., 2002. Agroforestry for fertility improvement and management of soils, in: *Natural Resources Conservation and Management of Mountain Development*. International Book Distributor, Dehra Dun, India, 331

Lalsiemlien P., 2009. *Linkage between Indigenous Agriculture and Sustainable Development – Evidences from Two Hill Communities in North-East India.*

Mittermeier, R.A.; Gil, P.R.; Hoffmann, M.; Pilgrim, J.; Brooks, T.; Mittermeier, CG.; Lamoreux, J.; and Da Fonseca, GAB., 2004. *Hotspots Revisited: Earth's Biologically Richest and Most Endangered Terrestrial Ecoregions*. Cemex Books on Nature, USA.

Munda, G.C.; Das, A.; Ngachan, S.V.; Satapathy, K.K.; Biswas, S. and Malanging, S., 2010. *Livelihood improvement through Farming System and Sustainable Activities in Disadvantageous Districts of North-East India*. ICAR Research Complex for NEH Region, Umiam, Meghalaya.

Mishra, A.K. and Sharma U.C., 2001. Traditional wisdom in range management for resource and environment conservation in North Eastern region of India. *ENVIS Bulletin: Himalayan Ecology and Development*, 9(1): 48.

NIC, 2001. *Soil and Water Conservation, Meghalaya*. (National Informatics Centre, Meghalaya State Centre, Shillong), (http://megsoil.nic.in/shifting_cul.htm).

Ramakrishnan, P.S., Knowledge Systems, Socio-ecological System Resilience and Coping with Environmental Uncertainties in the Context of Global Change. *Glimpses of Geoscience Research in India*. 64-70.

Singh, R.K., 2002. Soil conservation measures in agricultural land, in: *Integrated Watershed Management for Sustainable Development*. 104.

Sarma, B.K., 2002. Watershed management and biodiversity conservation in: *Integrated Watershed Management for Sustainable Development*. ICAR Research Complex for NEH Region, Umiam, Meghalaya 202.

Satapathy K.K., 2002. Natural resources conservation and management for mountain development in North-Eastern region, in: *Natural*

Resources Conservation and Management of Mountain Development. International Book Distributor, Dehra Dun, India, 322.

Singh, A. K and Varaprasad, K.S., 2008. Criteria for identification and assessment of agrobiodiversity heritage sites: evolving sustainable agriculture. *Current Science,* 94(9):1131–1138.

Singh, A.K., 2010. Probable Agricultural Biodiversity Heritage Sites in India: VI. *The Northeastern Hills of Nagaland,* Manipur, Mizoram, and Tripura. Asian Agri-History. 14(3): (217–243).

Sharma, B. Riaz; M.V.; Pant, D.; Adhikary, D.; Bhatt, B.P. and Rahaman, H., 2010. *Water Poverty in the North-East Hill Region (India): Potential Alleviation Through Multiple-Use Water Systems.* IWMI-NAIP Report No. 1:3.

7

Antibacterial Activity of Some Plants belonging to the Family Rubiaceae : A Review

Katyayani Dutta Choudhury and *M. Dutta Choudhury*

Introduction

Infectious diseases remain a serious threat to public health. Infectious diseases are world's leading cause of premature death, killing almost 50,000 people everyday all over the world (Anonymous, Centres for Disease Control and Prevention, 2000). Rapid resistance development among major pathogens makes antibiotics more and more ineffective, raising the need to find novel structural classes of antimicrobials (Breithaupt H., 1999). The use of and search for drugs and dietary supplements derived from plants have accelerated in recent years. Ethno pharmacologists, microbiologists, and natural-products chemists are combing the Earth for Phytochemicals which could be developed for treatment of infectious diseases. Plants are rich in a wide variety of secondary metabolites, such as tannins, terpenoids, alkaloids, flavonoids etc., the efficacy of which in treating diseases has been away from belief. Research work is carrying out extensively in this line for isolating pure compounds with antimicrobial properties and widely using these for clinical trials.

Many higher plants accumulate extractable organic approaches, substances in quantities sufficient to be economically management of disease. Plants have been a rich source of medicines because they produce wide array of bioactive molecules, most of which probably evolved as chemical defence against predation or infection. It is estimated that only one per cent of 2,65,000 flowering plants on earth have been studied exhaustively for their chemical composition and potential against important medicinal value (Cox *et al.*, 1994).

The Rubiaceae is one of the five largest plant families. According to the World Rubiaceae checklist, 611 genera and 13,143 species were recognised (Davis, 2009). A large number of members belonging to the family are ethnomedicinally important and also reported to have a wide variety of biological activities such as antimicrobial, antimalarial, hepatoprotective, antioxidant, and so many other interesting biological activities. Investigations have been carried out on various members of this family regarding their antimicrobial activities and found to be active against large number of pathogenic bacterial strains. Some of the important genera of this family are *Borreria, Gardenia, Morinda, Mitragyna, Uncaria, Mussaenda, Nauclea, Psychotria, Rubia,* etc. which have been reported to possess antibacterial properties. *Borreria hispida* is widely distributed in throughout India, up to 900m in hills and on all dry lands as a weed. The seed of *Borreria hispida* is used as PPAR-alpha gene expression, antioxidant redox status, protein metabolism in STZ diabetic rats, in ameliorating cardiovascular risk factor (Vasanthi *et al.*, 2009). *Gardenia jasminoides* has been included in traditional medicinal formulations for the treatment of inflammation, jaundice, headache, fever, hepatitic disorders and hypertension (Aburada *et al.*, 1976; Miyasita, 1976; Tseng *et al.*, 1995). *Gardenia jasminoides* has demonstrated effective pharmacological actions, such as protective activity against oxidative damage, as well as cytotoxic, anti-inflammatory and fybrolytic effects (Tseng *et al.*, 1995; Jagedeeswaran *et al.*, 2000; Koo *et al,*, 2006). *Morinda citrifolia* is commonly known in various cultures as Indian Mulberry, Nono, Noni, Cheese fruit and Nhau (Wang *et al.*, 2002). The leaves are used to treat cough, nausea and colic and to treat gout, tuberculosis and ringworm. In the Philippines, the seeds are eaten in order to expel intestinal worms. This plant has also been popular as a source of red, yellow and purple dyes (Gurib and Brendler, 2004). The leaves of *Mitragyna speciosa* has been reported for its antitussive, anaesthetic, antinociceptive, stimulant, analgesic and narcotic-like actions properties (Idid S.J., 1998; Perry, L.M., 1980). Parthasarathy S. *et al.*, carried out investigation on antimicrobial and antioxidant activity of the leaf extracts of this plant and also estimated total phenolic and flavonoid contents of the extracts (Parthasarathy, S. *et al., 2009).* Fruit of Randia dumatoram, which is commonly known as emetic nut have been screened for their anti-inflammatory, antibacterial, antipyretic, emetic, anthelmintic and antitumour activity (Nadkarni, A.K. *et al.*, 1976; Agrawal, S.S. *et al.*, 1999; Kirtikar, K.R. *et al.*, 1991). *Nauclea* species are used traditionally for difficult urination, menstruation problems and ear infections (Perry L.M., 1980). The underground parts of *R. peregrina* have been used as a natural dye in Turkey (Baytop, T., 1984). The review attempts to summarize the current status of antimicrobial screening efforts conducted on the members of the family Rubiaceae.

Antimicrobial Activity of the Members belonging to the Family Rubiaceae

Bacterial pathogens have been causing serious diseases all over the world and even leading to death in severe cases. *Staphylococcus aureus* can cause a range of illnesses from minor skin infections, such as pimples, impetigo, boils, cellulitis folliculitis, carbuncles, scalded skin syndrome and abscesses, to life-threatening diseases such as pneumonia, meningitis, osteomyelitis, endocarditis, toxic shock syndrome, bacteremia and sepsis (Whitt, *et al.*, 2002). *Bacillus subtilis* is not considered as a human pathogen, it may contaminate food but rarely causes food poisoning (Ryan, K.J. *et al.*, 2008). *Klebsiella pneumoniae* is among the most common gram-negative bacteria encountered by physicians worldwide. It is a common hospital-acquired pathogen, causing urinary tract infections, nosocomial pneumonia, and intraabdominal infections (Podschun, R. *et al.*, 1998). *Pseudomonas aeruginosa* typically infects the pulmonary tract, urinary tract, burns, wounds, and also causes other blood infections (Balcht *et al.*, 1994). *Micrococcus luteus* is non-pathogenic and usually regarded as a contaminant, it should be considered as an emerging nosocomial pathogen in immunocompromised patients (Greenblat, C.L. *et al.*, 2004). Pathogenic strains of *E. coli* are responsible for three types of infections in humans: urinary tract infections, neonatal meningitis and intestinal diseases (Evans *et al.*, 2007). *Streptococcus mutans*, a dental pathogen, is the leading cause of tooth decays worldwide (Proceedings of National Academy of Science, 2002). *Porphyromonas ingivalis* is found in the oral cavity, where it is implicated in certain forms of periodontal disease, as well as the upper gastrointestinal tract, respiratory tract, and in the colon (Naito *et al.*, 1995).

The number of multi-drug resistant microbial strains and the appearance of strains with reduced susceptibility to antibiotics are continuously increasing. This increase has been attributed to indiscriminate use of broad-spectrum antibiotics, immunosuppressive agent, intravenous catheters, organ transplantation and ongoing epidemics of HIV infection (Graybill, J.R., 1988; Ng, P.C., 1994; Dean, D.A., 1996). In addition, in developing countries, synthetic drugs are not only expensive and inadequate for the treatment of diseases but also often with adulterations and side effects. Therefore, there is need to search new infection-fighting strategies to control microbial infections. The search for compounds with antimicrobial activity has gained increasing importance in recent times, due to growing worldwide concern about the alarming increase in the rate of infection by antibiotic-resistance microorganisms (Davis, P.H., 1982).

Various secondary metabolites isolated from plants like alkaloids, flavonoids, tannins, terpenoids, etc. have shown various biological activities which indeed has formed the basis for their applications in some pharmaceuticals, alternative medicines and natural therapies. *Uncaria tomentosa* presents components like oxindole alkaloids, triterpenes, vegetal steroids, phenolic compound, glicosides, tannin and flavonoids. These compounds may be related to its microbial activity (Otake, S. *et al.*, 1991). Mukherjee *et al* reported a triterpene with antimicrobial property from *Borreria articularis* from chloroform extract. Cardiac glycosides isolated from *Borreria ocymoides* significantly inhibited *S. aureus* (Ebana *et al.*, 1991). Enolethers isolated from some medicinal plants are found to be responsible for significant antibacterial activities (Milata V., 2008). A new anthraquinone, Rubiacordone was isolated from the dried roots of *Rubia cordifolia* and showed considerable antimicrobial activity against Gram-positive bacteria (Lix, *et al.*, 2009).

Some recent publications have shed substantial light on the

antimicrobial activities of some useful medicinal plants of this family Rubiaceae. Plant parts like root, stem, bark, leaf (Jayasinghe, U.L.B., 2001) or whole plant in case of small herbs (Muthu, K. *et al*, 2010) are powdered and extracted with various solvents like petroleum ether, ethyl acetate, methanol, ethanol, etc and their antimicrobial activities were found out against various pathogenic strains of bacteria (Jayasinghe, U.L.B., 2001). The method employed by most of the workers for antibacterial investigations is Filter Paper Disc Diffusion Method (Vincent and Vincent, 1944). Values of Minimum Inhibitory Concentration also have been reported by some workers by using several methods like Serial Dilution Technique (Petersdorf and Plorde, 1963).

Table 7.1 represents all the genera belonging to the family Rubiaceae on which antibacterial screening have been performed till date and Table 7.2 represents some of the important medicinal plants of the family Rubiaceae and their reported antibacterial activities against some specific bacterial inoculums applying Disc Diffusion Method along with their zone of inhibitions.

Table 7.1: List of Genera belonging to Rubiaceae Family showing Antibacterial Activity

Benkara	Damnacanthus	Ixora	Pentanisia	Tarenna
Borreria	Diodia	Massularia	Phyllanthus	Uncaria
Calycophyllum	Fadogia	Mitracarpus	Plectronia	Vangueria
Canthium	Gaertnera	Mitragyna	Plocama	Viola
Carphalea	Gardenia	Morinda	Prismatomeris	Wendlandia
Cephalanthus	Genipa	Mussaenda	Psychotria	
Chassalia	Haldina	Nauclea	Putoria	
Chiococca	Hamelia	Neonauclea	Randia	
Coffea	Hedyotis	Oldenlandia	Rubia	
Corynanthe	Heterophyllaea	Paederia	Saprosma	
Coutarea	Hydnophytum	Palicaurea	Sarcocephalus	
Craterispermum	Hymenodictyon	Pavetta	Spermacoce	

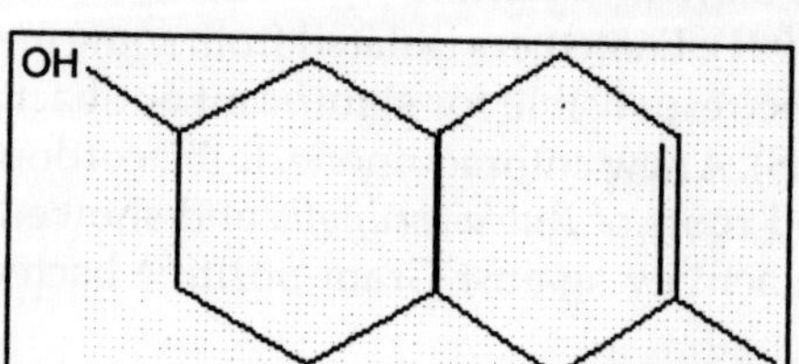

Fig. 7.1 : Structure of 6-methyl-5-cyclodecen-1-01 isolated from *Borreria articularis*

Table 7.2 : Antibacterial Activities of Some Plants belonging to the Family of Rubiaceae

Plants	*Plant Part(s) Used*	*Plant Extract(s)*	*Bacterial Pathogens*	*Zone Diameter (mm)*	*References*
Benkara malabarica (Lam.) D.D.Tirvengadum	Bark	Hexane	*Bacillus cereus*	8	Jayasinghe, U. L. B., 2001
			Escherichia coli	10	
Borreria articularis (L.f.) Will.	Whole plant	Chloroform	*Bacillus subtilis*	10	Sultana, *et al.*, 2008
			Vibrio cholerae	12	
			Shigella dysenteriae	11	
			Shigella sonnei	9	
		Ethyl acetate	*Bacillus subtilis*	11	
			Escherichia coli	10	
			Shigella dysenteriae	10	
			Shigella sonnei	11	
			Salmonella typhi	10	
		Ethanol	*Staphylococcus aureus*	14	
			Bacillus cereus	14	
			Bacillus megaterium	11	
			Bacillus subtilis	10	
			Escherichia coli	20	
			Vibrio cholerae	10	
			Shigella dysenteriae	10	
			Shigella dysenteriae	11	
			Salmonella typhi	11	
Borreria hispida L.	Whole plant	Methanol	*Bacillus subtilis*	15	Muthu *et al*, 2010
			Bacillus pumilus	16	
			Staphylococcus aureus	15	

(Cont.)

Table 7.2 (*Contd.*)

Plants	*Plant Part(s) Used*	*Plant Extract(s)*	*Bacterial Pathogens*	*Zone Diameter (mm)*	*References*
			Escherichia coli	18	
			Klebsiella pneumoniae	17	
		Ethanol	*Bacillus subtilis*	19	
			Bacillus pumilus	21	
			Staphylococcus aureus	19	
			Pseudomonas aeruginosa	19	
			Escherichia coli	20	
			Klebsiella pneumoniae	19	
Borreria latifolia (Miq.) Steyerm.	Leaf	Methanol	*Bacillus cereus*	14	Ali, A.M.*et al* ,1995
			Pseudomonas aeruginosa	20	
			B. megaterium	16	
Canthium coromandelicum Roxb.	Leaf	Dichloromethane	*Bacillus subtilis*	9	Jayasinghe U. L. B., 2001
		Methanol	*Bacillus subtilis*	13	
Chassalia kolly (Schumach.)Hepper.	Whole plant	Methanol (100mg/ml)	*Bacillus subtilis*	22	Onocha, P.A. *et al*, 2010
			Salmonella typhii	20	
			Staphylococcus aureus	14	
			Escherichia coli	15	
			Pseudomonas aeruginosa	16	
Gardenia jasminoides Ellis.	Flower	Essential oil	*Staphylococcus aureus*	17.3	Chaichana. J *et al*, 2009
			Staphylococcus epidermidis	20.7	

(*Contd.*)

Table 7.2 *(Contd.)*

Plants	Plant Part(s) Used	Plant Extract(s)	Bacterial Pathogens	Zone Diameter (mm)	References
		5% chloramphenicol (100 mg/ml)	*Staphylococcus aureus*	30.3	
			Staphylococcus epidermidis	38	
			Escherichia coli	27.7	
			Pseudomonas aeruginosa	14	
Hedyotis nudicaulis (Roth.) Wight & Arn.	Whole plant	Methanol	*Bacillus cereus*	18	Ali, A.M.*et al* ,1995
			Pseudomonas aeruginosa	21	
Hedyotis diffusa Willd.	Whole plant	Methanol	*Bacillus cereus*	13	Ali, A.M.*et al*, 1995
			Pseudomonas aeruginosa	22	
Hymenodictyon parvifolium Oliv.	Stem bark	Methanol (800mg/disc)	*Bacillus cereus*	18	Kariba R. M., 2002
			Pseudomonas aeruginosa	14	
			Staphylococcus aureus	16	
			Escherichia coli	10	
Ixora calycina Thw.	Bark	Dichloromethane	*Bacillus cereus*	14	Jayasinghe U. L. B., 2001
			Escherichia coli	11	
Ixora coccinia L.	Leaf	Ether	*Bacillus cereus*	18	Annapurna J. *et al*,2003
			Bacillus licheniformis	18	
			Staphylococcus aureus	22	
			Escherichia coli	20	
Morinda eclipta L.	Root	Methanol	*Bacillus cereus*	13	Ali, A.M. *et al* ,1995
			Pseudomonas aeruginosa		
Morinda citrifolia L.	Leaves	Water	*Staphylococcus aureus*	20	Usha, R *et al*, 2010

(Cont.)

Table 7.2 (*Contd.*)

Plants	*Plant Part(s) Used*	*Plant Extract(s)*	*Bacterial Pathogens*	*Zone Diameter (mm)*	*References*
Morinda tinctora Roxb.	Leaves	Hexane	*Bacillus subtilis*	10	Jayasinghe U. L. B., 2001
			Escherichia coli	12	
Mitragyna speciosa Roxb.	Leaf	Methanol(100mg/ml)	*Salmonella typhi*	29	Parthasarathy, S. *et al*, 2009
			Bacillus subtilis	30	
		Chloramphenicol (100mg/ml)	*Salmonella typhi*	23	
			Bacillus subtilis	24	
			Escherichia coli	22	
			Pseudomonas aeruginosaa	23	
Mussaenda frondosa L.	Leaves	Dichloromethane	*Bacillus subtilis*	11	Jayasinghe U. L. B., 2001
	Bark	Methanol	*Bacillus subtilis*	12	
Nauclea observifolia L.	Stem bark	Ethanol	*Bacillus cereus*	14	Khan *et al*,2001
			Bacillus coagulans	14	
			Micrococcus luteus	13	
			Lactobacillus casei	12	
			Staphylococcus pneumonia	14	
			Salmonella typhii	14	
			Proteus mirabilis	12	
Oldenlandia umbellata L.	Whole plant	Methanol	*Staphyllococcus aureus*	18	Arun, P. *et al*,2010
			Proteus sp	18	
			Klebsiella sp	20	
			Escherichia coli	21	
Psychotria gardneri (Thw.) Hook.	Bark	Methanol	*Bacillus cereus*	15	Jayasinghe U. L. B., 2001

(*Contd.*)

Table 7.2 (*Contd.*)

Plants	*Plant Part(s) Used*	*Plant Extract(s)*	*Bacterial Pathogens*	*Zone Diameter (mm)*	*References*
			Escherichia coli	11	
Psychotria reevesii Wall.	Aerial parts	Petrol ether	*Staphylococcus aureus*	12.3	Glang P.M. *et al*,2006
			Shigella flexneri	9.7	
Psychotria stenophylla (Thw.) Hook.	Bark	Dichloromethane	*Bacillus subtilis*	11	Jayasinghe U. L. B., 2001
	Bark	Methanol	*Micrococcus luteus*	21	
Randia dumetorum Lamk.	Fruit	Methanol (100mg/ml)	*Staphylococcus aureus*	16	Movalia D., 2009
			Staphyllococcus epidermidis	15	
			Bacillus subtilis	10	
			Escherichia coli	21	
			Salmonella typhi	17	
Rubia peregrine L.	Roots &rhizomes	Methanol	*Bacillus subtilis*	18	Ozgen G. *et al*,2003
		Ethanol	*Bacillus subtilis*	21	
			Staphylococcus aureus	28	
Saprosma foetans (Wight.)K.Schum.	Leaves	Hexane	*Escherichia coli*	11	Jayasinghe U. L. B., 2001
Tarenna asiatica (L.) Als.	Leaves	Hexane	*Escherichia coli*	10	Jayasinghe U. L. B., 2001

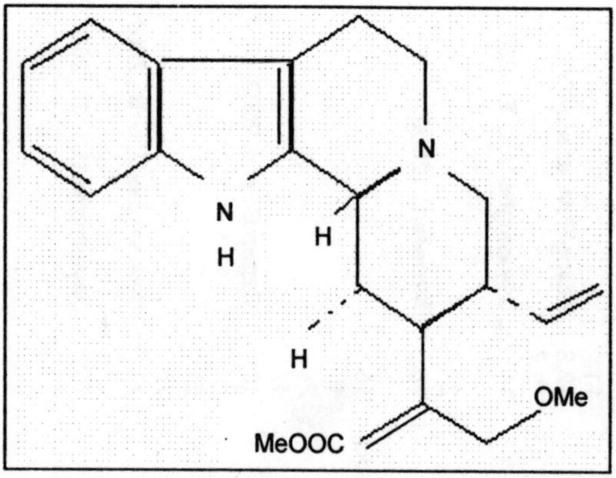

Fig. 7.2 : Structure of Hirsuteine isolated from *Mitragyna parvifolia, Uncaria* sp.

Discussion

Antimicrobial properties of several plants have been investigated as alternatives with low toxicity for the prevention and treatment of infectious diseases. Almost all the plants mentioned above are multi-resistant against a number of bacterial pathogens and may have the potentiality for broad range of clinical practices.

Rubiaceae is a family of flowering plants which possess a large collection of medicinal plants. Literature survey reveals that research works on antibacterial activity have been conducted on only 48 genera of Rubiaceae out of 611 genera. Most of the plants under investigation have shown significant activity against multiple bacterial pathogens. Available data regarding the zone of inhibitions indicate that the bacterial pathogens whose activities have been inhibited most by the plant secondary metabolites are *Bacillus* sp., *Staphylococcus* sp., and *Pseudomonas aeruginosa.* Maximum inhibition have been observed in case of 5 per cent chloramphenicol flower extract of *Gardenia jasmonoides* executing 38 mm zone diameter against *Staphylococcus epidermidis* and 30.3 mm against *Staphylococcus aureus.* In all the research papers studied, zone of inhibition of the plant extracts against bacterial inoculums have been compared with the zone of inhibition exhibited by the standard antibiotics to find out their level of significance. Methanol, ethanol, chloroform and chloramphenicol plant extracts have been found to be more active against bacterial pathogens, this clearly indicates the presence of potent bioactive principles in these crude extracts which might be very useful as antibacterial. During these recent years research works also have been carrying out with water extracts and in some plants it has shown significant antimicrobial activity (Usha, R *et al.*, 2010).

Now-a-days there is a worldwide movement towards finding out chemical constituents from various plant sources and the bioactivity studies of the novel drugs isolated. As significant antibacterial activities have been displayed by some of the members of the family Rubiaceae, they need special attention by researchers for isolating their chemical backgrounds and their related biological applications.

As antibacterial activity screenings have been performed on only 48 genera of Rubiaceae out of 611 genera, data from a large number of genera are lacking in this field. Attention should be paid by the workers to carry out extensive researches on those genera which may enrich the area of medicinal chemistry by providing valuable drugs with better efficacy. Attention should also be paid for implementation of proper protection strategies to conserve all these valuable medicinal plants in nature and their proper utilisation in the field of medical sciences.

Conclusion

48 genera belonging to the family Rubiaceae out of 611 genera have been recorded to show antibacterial properties. Extensive studies should be carried out on isolation and characterization of pure chemical constituents from these plants and their successful clinical application in curing various infectious diseases.

REFERENCES

Aburada, M.; Sasaki H.; Harada M. (1976). Pharmacological studies of gardenia fruits. II. Contribution of the constituent crude drugs to choleretic activity of Inchinko-to in rats. *Yakugaku Zasshi,* 96, 147-153.

Agrawal, S.S. and Singh, V.K. (1999). Immunomodulators—A review of studies on Indian medicinal plants and synthetic peptides, Part-1, Medicinal plants, *Proc. Indian Natl. Sci. Acad.,* B (65), 179-204.

Ali A.M. *et al.* (1995). Antimicrobial Activity of Selected Malaysian Plants. *Pertanikaj. Trop. Agric. Sci.* 18(1), 57-61.

Anonymous (2000). Centres for Disease control and prevention. *Preventing emerging infectious diseases : A Stratagy for 21st Century.* 1-3.

Balcht, Aldona; Smith, Raymond (1994). *Pseudomonas Aeruginosa:* Infections and Treatment. *Informal Health Care.* 83–84.

Baytop, T. (1984). Therapy with medicinal plants in Turkey, *Istanbul University Publications,* 32 (55), 43-54.

Breithaupt, H. (1999). The new antibiotics. *Nat. Biotechnol.* 17, 1165-1169.

Cox, P.A., Balick, M.J. (1994). The ethnobotanical approach to drug discovery, *Scientific American* 270, 60-65.

Davis, P.H. (1982). *Flora of Turkey and East Eagean Island,* Edinburg. Edinburg University Press, 7, 947.

Davis, Aaron P.; Rafaël Govaerts; Diane M. Bridson; Markus Ruhsam; Justin Moat; Neil A. Brummitt (2009). A global assessment of distribution, diversity, endemism, and taxonomic effort in the Rubiaceae. *Annals of the Missouri Botanical Garden* 96 (1), 68–78.

Dean, D.A. and Burchard, K.W. (1996). Fungal infection in surgical patients. *Am. J. Surg.,* 171, 374-382.

Dharmishtha, M. and Falguni, G. (2009). Antibacterial activity of methanolic fruit extract of *Randia dumatorum* Lamk. *Int.J. Pharm. Tech. Res.,* 1(3).

Ebana *et al.,* (1991). Microbiological exploitation of cardiac glycosides and alkaloids from *Garcinia kola, Borreria ocymoides, Kola nitida* and *Citrus aurantifolia. Journal of Applied Bacteriology, 71,* 398-401.

Evans, D.J. and Evans, P.G. (Ed.) 2007. *Escherichia coli. Medical Microbiology.* The University of Texas Medical Branch at Galveston.

Gurib, Fakeem A., and Brendler (2004). T-Medicinal and Aromatic plants of the Indian Ocean Islands. *Boca Raton, FL: CRC Press,* 331-332.

Graybill, J.R. (1988). Systemic fungal infections: diagnosis and treatment. I. Therapeutic agents. *Infectious Disease Clinics of North America.* 805-825.

Greenblat, C.L.; Baum, J.; Klein, B.Y.; Nachshon, S.; Koltunov, V.; Cano, R.J., (2004). Micrococcus luteus – Survival in Amber. *Microbial Ecology* 48, 120–127.

Idid, S.Z. and Saad, L.B. (1988). Evaluation of Analgesia Induced by Mitragynine, Morphine and Paracetamolon Mice. *ASEAN Review of Biodiversity and Environmental Conservation.* Bangi, Malaysia. 2:1–7.

Jaime Nifio, Diana M. Narvaez, Oscar M. Mosquera, Yaned M. Correa (2006). Antibacterial, Antifungal and Cytotoxic Activities of Eight Asteraceae and two Rubiaceae plants from Colombian Biodiversity. *Brazilian Journal of Microbiology.* 36, 566-570.

Jayasinghe, U.L.B. *et al.* (2002). Antimicrobial Activity of some Sri Lankan Rubiaceae and Meliaceae. *Fitoterapia,* 72, 424-427.

Lelono, R.A.A.; Tachibana S. and Itoh K. (2009). Isolation of antifungal compounds from *Gardenia jasminoides*. *Pak. J. Biol. Sci.*, 12: 949-956.

Kariba, R.M. (2002). Antimicrobial activity of *Hymenodictyon parvifolium*. *Fitoterapia*. 73(6): 523-525.

Kirtikar, K.R. and Basu, B.D. (1991). *Indian Medicinal Plants*. Panni Office, Bhuwaneswari Ashrama, Bahadurganj, Allahabad. 648-652.

Koo, H.J., Lim K.H., Jung K.J., Park E.H. (2006). Antiinflammatory evaluation of *Gardenia* extract, Geinpin and Geniposide. *J. Ethnopharmacol.*, 103: 496-500.

Milata, V. (2008). Naturally occurring enolethers. *Acta Chimica Slovaca*, 1(1): 221-237.

Muthu, K.A. *et al.* (2010). *International Journal of Pharma Sciences and Research*. 1(2): 127-130.

Li, X.; Liu, Z.; Chen, Y.; Wang, L.J.; Zheng, Y.N.; Sun, G.Z.; Ruan, C.C. (2009). Rubiacordone A: A new anthraquinone glycoside from the roots of *Rubia cordifolia*. *Molecules*. 14(1): 566-72.

Nadkarni, A.K. and Nadkarni, K.M. (1976). *The Indian Materia Medica*, Popular Prakashan. 1047-1048.

Naito, M.; Hirakawa, H.; Yamashita, A. *et al.* (2008). Determination of the genome sequence of Porphyromonas gingivalis strain ATCC 33277 and genomic comparison with strain W83 revealed extensive genome rearrangements in *P. gingivalis*. *DNA Res.* 15(4): 215–25.

Ng, P.C. (1994). Systemic fungal infections in neonates. *Arch Dis of Childhood*. 71:130-135.

Onocha, P.A., Ali, S.M. (2010). Insecticidal, antimicrobial, phyto- and cyto-toxicity of *Chassalia kolly* plant extract. *Archives of Applied Science Research*. 2 (4): 151-156.

Otake, S.; Makimur, M.; Kuroki, T.; Nishihara, Y. and Hirasawa, M. (1991). Anticaries effects of polyphenolic compounds from Japanese green tea. *Caries Res.* 25(6):438-43.

Ozgen, G. *et al.* (2003). Antioxidant and antimicrobial activities of *Onosma argentatum* and *Rubia peregrina* . *Fitoterapia*. 74(7-8): 682-685.

Parthasarathy, S. *et al.* (2009). Evaluation of Antioxidant and Antibacterial Activities of Aqueous, Methanolic and Alkaloid Extracts from *Mitragyna Speciosa* (Rubiaceae Family) Leaves. *Molecules* 14:3964-3974.

Perry, L.M. (1980). *Medicinal Plants of East and Southeast Asia*; MIT Press: Cambridge, MA, USA.

Podschun, R. and Ullman, U. (1998). *Klebsiella* spp. as Nosocomial Pathogens: Epidemiology, Taxonomy, Typing Methods, and Pathogenicity Factors. *Clinical Microbiology Reviews*. 11 (4):589-603.

Perry, L.M. (1980). *Medicinal Plants of East and Southeast Asia: attributed Properties and Uses*. The MIT Press, Cambridge, Massachusetts and London. 334-360.

Petersdorf and Plorde. (1963). *Ann. Rev. of Med.* 14, 41.

Renzo, Alberto *et al.* (2007). Antimicrobial activity of *Uncaria tomentosa* against oral human pathogens. *Braz Oral Res* 21(1):46 50.

Ryan, K.J. and Ray, C.G. (ed.) 2004. *Sherris Medical Microbiology*. McGraw Hill.

Tseng, T.H.; Chu C.Y.; Huang J.M.; Shiow S.J. and Wang C.J. (1995). Crocetin protects against damage in rat primary hepatocytes. *Cancer Lett.*, 97: 61-67.

Vasanthi, Hannah R.; Mukherjee, S.; Lekli, Istvan M. Farm, Ray.; Veeraraghavan, G. and Das, D.K. (2009). Potential Role of *Borreria hispida* in Ameliorating Cardiovascular Risk Factors. *Journal of Cardiovascular Pharmacology*. 53(6): 499-506.

Vincent, J.G. and Vincent, H.W. (1944). Filter Paper Disc Modification of Oxford cup Penicillin determination. *Proc. Soc. Exp. Med.* 55:162-164.

Wang, M.Y., West, B.J.; Jensen C.J.; Nowicki, C.S.; Palu, A. and Anderson G. (2002). *Morinda citrifolia* (Noni). a literature research. *Acta Pharmacologica Sinica.* 23(12):1127-1141.

Whitt, D.D. and Salyers, A.A. (ed.) 2002. *Bacterial Pathogenesis: A Molecular Approach*. USA, ASM Press.

8
Resource Conservation in Agriculture and its Practices in NEH Region

Mandira Chakraborti[1], A.K. Singh[1] and M. Datta[2]

Intensive agriculture and excessive use of external inputs lead to degradation of soil, water and genetic resources and adversely effect crop productivity. Widespread soil erosion, nutrient mining, depleting water table and eroding biodiversity are the global concern which are threatening the food security and livelihood opportunities of farmers, especially the poor and underprivileged. Soil degradation due to erosion and compaction process is the most serious environmental problem caused by conventional agriculture. Many global treaties have raised the concern to conserve natural resources for improving livelihood opportunities and enhancing the quality of the million of small and marginal farmers living in abject poverty. Conservation agriculture has been identified as one of the technological options, to meet the global challenges of increasing food production and conserving environment, thereby to improve food and nutritional security and alleviate poverty.

Conservation agriculture is a range of soil management practices that minimize effects on composition, structure and natural biodiversity and reduce erosion and degradation. Largely, the conservation agriculture practices includes: (i) direct sowing/ no tillage, reduced tillage/minimum tillage, (ii) surface incorporation of crop residue, and (iii) establishment of cover crops in both annual and perennial crops. Recently, Food and Agriculture Organisation of the United Nations (FAO) focused conservation agriculture as resource saving agricultural crop production. As per FAO definition, the conservation agriculture is to (i) achieve acceptable profits, (ii) high and sustained production levels, and (iii) conserve the environment. It further argues that conservation agriculture is based on enhancing natural biological processes above and below the soil surface. These go beyond zero tillage and provide a range of technology and management options. Conservation agriculture practices are applicable to virtually all the crops including cereals, horticultural and plantation crops. However, these are more popular in maize, soybean, rice and wheat. The conservation agriculture practices promises tremendous potential for different soils and agro-ecological systems. The adoption of conservation agriculture is most urgently required by small farmers to reduce their cost of production, increase profit and save resources.

Conservation tillage is a more appropriate strategy for rainfed production systems. Practices like contour cultivation and cultivation on graded bunds, sod seeding, stale bed, ridge till etc. help in effective conservation of moisture. These practices reduce runoff up to 40 per cent and contribute to yield up to 25 to 30 per cent depending on the rainfall situation. The most acceptable conservation practices to farmers are the ridge and furrow system of planting. Ridge and furrow reduce runoff and help *in situ* moisture conservation. Straw and soil mulching are other simple practices that conserve moisture. The effect of mulching is seen more in rabi crops than kharif crops. Suitability of different conservation tillage in the soils of humid tropics is given in Table 8.1.

Table 8.1: Suitability of different conservation tillage in the soils of humid tropics

Soil type	*Rainfall (mm/year)*	*Slope (%)*	*Cropping System*	*Conservation tillage system*
Alfisols, Oxisols. Inceptisols. Ultisois, Entisols	1500-4000	< 5	Cereal and pulses crops	No-till, sod seeding, slot tillage strip-tillage
Alfisols, Oxisois, Ultisols	1500 4000	< 5	Root crops	Ridge tillage, tied ridges, rough seedbed
Alfisols, Inceptisols, Ultisols	1000-1500	5-10	Grain ridges	Ridge tillage, tied-ridges, chisel-tillage, pare-plow
Histosols, Mollisols	150C-4000	5	Root crops	No-till, chisel-till, para-plow, ridge tillage

Source: http://unu.edu, 14th December 2010

A permanent soil cover is important to protect the soil against the deleterious effects of exposure to rain and sun and to provide the micro and macro organisms in the soil with a constant supply of food, congenial microclimate in the soil for optimal growth and development of soil organism including plant roots. Cover crops improve the stability of the conservation agriculture system, not only on the improvement of soil properties but also for their capacity to promote an increased biodiversity in the agro ecosystem.

Table 8.2: Effects of Mucuna fallowing on runoff and erosion as compared with alley cropping and maize-cowpea rotation

Treatment	First season		Second season		Annual Total	
	Runoff (mm)	Erosion (kg/ha)	Runoff (mm)	Erosion (kg/ha)	Runoff (mm)	Erosion (kg/ha)
Maize-cowpea	12.9	0.0	5.2	0.0	18.1	0.0
Mucuna	8.1	0.0	3.4	0.0	11.5	0.0
Alley cropping	4.6	0.0	1.9	0.0	6.5	0.0
Forest fallow	0.0	0.0	0.3	0.0	0.3	0.0
Rainfall (mm)	615.2		223.6		838.8	

Source: Lal 1992.

In region where smaller amounts of biomass are produced, as in semi arid regions or areas of eroded and degraded soils, cover crops are beneficial as they protect the soil during fallow periods, mobilize and recycle nutrients, improve the soil structure and break compacted layers and hard pans, permit a rotation in a monoculture and to control weeds and pests. The principal benefit of a cover crop lies in erosion control. The data in Table 8.2 show that runoff and soil erosion under a Mucuna cover crop were low and the cover was extremely effective in decreasing erosion losses, even on eroded and compacted soils.

In general, management of leguminous cover crops gives good result. There is considerable scope for selecting appropriate species and cultivars for suitable cover crops. The choice of an appropriate cover crop for different soils and ecological regions depends on many considerations, including the ease and economics of establishment, including the availability of seed; quick ground cover and growth rate during the off-season; N-fixing rather than N-consuming; deep-root system and low consumptive water use- feed value for livestock, low possibility as alternative hosts for pests and cover for wildlife, low canopy height; ability to suppress weeds, growth duration (i.e., permanent versus annual); shade tolerance; and ease of management for growing a food crop with conservation tillage. Some cover crops used for soil and water conservation in the humid tropics are given in Table 8.3.

Table 8.3: Cover crops used for soil and water conservation in the humid tropics

	Cover Crops
Grasses	*Axonopus micay*
	Brachiaria brizantha
	Brachiaria decumbens
	Brachiaria mutica
	Cenchrus ciliasris
	Chlorea gayanu
	Eragrostis curvula
	Glycine wightii
	Panicum antidotala
	Panicum coloratum
	Panicum maximum
	Paspalum conjugatum
	Pasoalum notatum
	Pennisetum purpurcum
	Setaria sphacelata
Legumes	*Centrosema pubescens*
	Desmodium buegeri
	Mucuna pruriens
	Phaseolus aconitifolius
	Psophocarpus palustris
	Pueraria phaseoloides
	Stizolobium deeringianum
	Stylosanthes guinetances
	Vigna catijang

Source: Modified from Lal, 1984

In NEH Region, farmers practices some unique efficient resource conservation systems based on topographical situation, sources, amount of water available and crop to be irrigated. The major indigenous methods of irrigation which have been in vogue since centuries and have remained sustainable are discussed below:

Zabo System of resource conservation: 'Zabo' means impounding of water. The place or origin of this system is the Kikruma village in Phek district of Nagaland, located at an attitude of 1270 m above mean sea level. The Zabo system has forest land on the top of the hill, water harvesting and desiltation tanks in the middle and fields at the foot hills. The rain water from the catchment area or top hill slopes is diverted to dug-out tanks. Usually there are one or two desiltation tanks where the runoff water is stored for desiltation for days before taking it to the main tank below. The size of these tanks depends on the catchment area and expected water harvest. Sometimes, excess water from desiltation tank is taken directly to the rice fields. These tanks are desilted and the material is put in the fields for improving soil fertility as it contains lot of organic matter due to forest litter accumulated. This also helps in maintenance of the desiltation tanks. These tanks are rammed and compacted from inner surfaces to avoid water loss through seepage. Water from the desiltation tanks is taken to the main tank for storage. This is plastered from inside using rice husk and mud to avoid water loss. The bottom of the tank is rammed and compacted by trampling by the animals which are allowed freely in the tank before storage of water. The water from the main tank is passed through animal yard before taking it to the fields for irrigation. The water carried with it the dung and urine of the animals to the fields and the soil fertility is maintained properly. The water by this method is not only used efficiently, but soil loss due to erosion is reduced to the minimum.

Resource management in Apatani Plateau: The Apatanis have developed an efficient system of water management for rice and fish culture. All streams averaging out from the surrounding hills are tapped, channelised at the beginning of the valley and diverted by a network of primary, secondary and tertiary channels. At the short distance above the terraces, occurs the first diversion from the stream. Some water is allowed to flow in the first feeder channel, which the stream continues its course. The feeder channel branches off at angles which leads water to *terraced rice fields* in a way that blocking or opening the connecting ducts (Huburs) any field can be flooded or drained as need be. This system involves peoples participation for common works and the available water from natural streams is used most judiciously in a planned way for crop production. The system has remained sustainable since centuries

Bamboo drip irrigation: Bamboo drip irrigation system is mainly followed in *Jaintia* and *Khasi* hills of Meghalaya. This is a very good system for the area where the water is scarce, soils have poor water holding capacity, the topography is undulating and rocky and the irrigation is required for such crops whose water needs are low. Natural perennial as well as seasonal streams are the main source of water, because the topography of the region is undulating, the cost involving for the construction of irrigation channels for carrying water to desired sites would be very high and the proportional land area available for irrigation is expected to be low. The most convenient technique would be to transfer water from upper reaches of hill to lower level through gravitational flow. This concept has been fully utilized by the tribal farmers. The water is carried from the source to the place of use with the help of bamboo pipes cut in to different shapes and forms. The flow of water can be controlled as per requirement with the help of blocking and opening slits at diversion points. The rate of water flow varies from 800 to 1200 litres per hour. The water is allowed to trickle down drop at the plant site by having small holes at appropriate points. Irrigation by this system is provided to plantation and horticultural crops

Conservation of water in Panikheti: One can see beautiful rice terraces in many states of NEH region which is locally known as Panikheti. *Angami* and *Chakhesang* tribes of Nagaland have developed a system of irrigating rice fields. Due to high rainfall in the region the growth of weeds in upland rice is a serious constraint for higher productivity. Since only hills were available for rice cultivation terracing became necessary for keeping the rainwater standing in the fields. The farmers acquired the skill and ingenuity for construction of terraces for keeping the water standing in the field.

Traditional vegetative barriers to erosion control measures

in *Jhum*: Converting slopes into flat lands require heavy labour, technical know-how and many other inputs. Hill slopes, when cultivated, are prone to soil erosion through rain and wind. The farmers of Nagaland, in spite of the difficult terrain, have adapted well to the conditions and practice *Jhum* cultivation. These farmers have developed a number of mechanical and vegetative barriers to sustain cultivation in these conditions.

Jhum farmers in Nagaland grow about 15 to 60 different crops. They normally plant crops and vegetables in rows across the slopes of the *Jhum* fields to check sheet erosion.

- *Maize, Millet, Job's Tear barriers:* Farmers grow these crops in rows across the slopes to check soil erosion. These are the stable food crops for farmers in higher altitudes having an evaluation of at least 1500 m. farmers also plant these crops along the boundaries of their *Jhum* fields.
- *Soybeans and Velvet Beans*: Soybeans are generally grown in rows along the contours to check soil erosion. On the other hand, velvet beans, which spread over vast areas, are gown as cover crops to prevent the loss of top soil from rain action.

In addition, a unique and highly productive form of *Jhum* has been developed in Khonoma village (Kohima) based on the alder tree. The village is interspersed with alder trees, some of these are more than 200 years old and are still healthy. It helps in controlling the soil erosion.

Bun method of resource conservation: Bun is an indigenous method of cultivation in Meghalaya. It involves putting of dried vegetation in the form of raised beds along the slopes and covering the same with soil collected from the surroundings, burning of the covered vegetation and planting on the soil afterwards.

All the traditional system of land and water management of NEH region discussed above is partly community managed and partly self-managed. The approximate average cost involved in making various systems operational in terms of man days, longevity of the system, cost benefit ratio of the systems are given in Table 8.4.

Table 8.4. Approximate average cost in making various systems operational

System	Longevity of the system	Man days required	Benefit Cost ratio
Zabo	30 to 40 years	192 days	1.0:1.9
Apatani plateau	30 to 40 years	128 days	1.0:1.7
Bamboo Drip Irrigation	3 to 4 years	36 days	1.0:1.4
Terraced Rice Cultivation system	30 to 40 years	108 days	1.0:1.6

The methods adopted traditionally by the tribal farmers of the region due to their skill and experience are simple, make use of locally available resources, and are most suitable for hilly terrains. These methods have combination of soil and water conservation techniques and do not involve deforestation and, therefore, are eco-friendly and help in resource conservation.

Benefits of Conservation Agriculture

- Improve the sustainability of different production system
- Provides soil as sink for carbon dioxide, thereby improves soil organic carbon content and contribute in reducing global warming.
- Improves water infiltration and thereby reduces run-off of surface and ground water and enhance ground water recharge.
- Improves habitation of organism, from larger insects down to soil borne fungi and bacteria, which improve soil biological, physical and chemical properties, and contribute in increasing crop productivity.
- Reduce cost of production (15 to 16%) by saving energy, labour and water, and thereby increase farm income.
- Restore biodiversity and reduces environmental pollution.
- Enhance food and nutritional security due to higher, more stable yields and lower food prices.

Conclusions

Farming community of our country already have the mindset that intensive agriculture and use of external input will increase the agricultural production as farmers have realized huge economic benefit in the past by practicing intensive agriculture. Thus the shift from intensive agriculture to conservation agriculture will need massive awareness programme regarding conservation agriculture. Institutional arrangements are needed to be evolved so that small and marginal farmers can afford the equipments for practicing conservation agriculture. Training programme on capacity building of farmers on conservation agriculture by KVK and Extension wing of line department should be emphasized.

REFERENCES

Masod Ali and Venkatatesh, M.S.((2009). Pulses in improving Soil Health. *Indian Farming,* 58(11): 18-22

Reddy, S.R. (2000). *Principals of Agronomy,* Kalyani Publishers, New Delhi, India.

Sharmah, R.K., Chhokar, R.S., Gill, S.C. and Jagshoran.(2009). Efficient Crop Residue Management: A Key to Conservation Agriculture, *Indian Farming,* 58(11):27-31.

Singh, H.P.(2009). Impact of Horticulture in Conservation Agriculture. *Indian Farming,* 58(11):9-13.

Part 2
Threat to Biodiversity

9 Varietal Screening against Bacterial Wilt Disease of Under Subtropical Humid Climate of Tripura

Pranab Dutta, Britan Rahman and *A.K. Singha*

Introduction

Bacterial wilt of tomato (*Lycopersicon esculentum* Mill.), incited by *Ralstonia solanacearum* (Smith) Yabuuchi *et al.*,(Syn. *Pseudomonas solanacearum* E.F. Smith) is one of the devastating bacterial disease affecting vascular bundles of plants (Sood and Singh, 1993). The pathogen has a very wide host range and almost all the solanaceous vegetables are susceptible. In India, plant species belonging to 37 families are attacked by bacterial wilt pathogen (Shekhawat *et al.*, 1992). Resistance to this disease is rarely available. Therefore, to identify resistant sources against bacterial wilt for Tripura, some popularly grown tomato varieties and hybrids were screened in naturally infested farmer's field.

Materials and Methods

Seedlings of 11 different varieties of tomato were raised in formaline sterilized nursery beds and transplanted in natural bacterial wilt infested sick soil at Khowai subdivision of West Tripura district at five different locations, viz., Sonatola, Kamalnagar, Mahabir Chowmohini, Bhabatoshpara and Uttar Chebri in November 2008 in a plot size of 3 × 3 m^2 having three replications with spacing of 60 × 45 cm^2 between row to row and plant to plant. Thirty plants were maintained in each plot and regularly observed for the appearance of disease symptoms. Wilted plants were observed critically to confirm the association of bacterium and to record the extent of vascular bundle discolouration. Observation on per cent plant mortality was also recorded starting from 15 days of transplanting till final harvest at an interval of 10 days by following the method of Biswas and Singh, 2008. The plant showing symptoms were examined by ooze test to confirm the disease. The varieties were categorized into different classes: 0 – no vascular discolouration, 1 – up to 1/3rd root zone showing vascular discolouration, 2 – up to 2/3rd root zone showing vascular discolouration, 3 – complete root portion showing vascular discolouration, 4 – vascular discolouration extended up to 5 cm of the stem and 5 – vascular discolouration extended to more than 5 cm. Vascular bundle discolouration index (VBDI) was calculated for each varieties by the formula VBDI = Sum of all class ratings/numbers of roots examined. Plant varieties were categorized on the basis of wilt incidence by modified scale of Sinha *et al.* (1990) as Resistant - R (<10%), Moderately resistant – MR (>10 – 20%), Moderately susceptible – MS (>20 – 30 %), Susceptible – S (>30 – 70%) and Highly susceptible – HS (>70 – 100%).

Results and Discussion

Eleven tomato cultivars popularly grown by the farmers of Tripura were evaluated in bacterial wilt sick soil at five different locations and data on per cent disease incidence was collected. Except "All Rounder" none of the cultivars was as resistant having plant mortality of 8.98 per cent. Four cultivars, viz., Swarakhsha, Rakshak, Trishul and Arka Alok were found moderately resistant (>10 – 20 %). Of the remaining six varieties, four (Yash – F1 Hybrid, TO – 1458, Hybrid – 7610 and F1 – Amulya – 1744) were moderately susceptible (>30 – 70%) and two (Loknath and Arka Vikash) were highly susceptible (>70 – 100%). In all the varieties tested, typical symptoms were developed in the infected plants, which are confirmed by ooze test. The extent of damage to the vascular tissue was reflected in the severity of bacterial wilt, which was assessed in all the cultivars and expressed as VBDI. Highest (4%) VBDI was recorded in Arka Vikash followed by Loknath (4.5%). Both these cultivars were recorded as highly susceptible to wilt (Fig. 9.1). These were further followed by moderately susceptible cultivators viz.,

TO-1458, T1-Amulya-17444, Hybrid-76110 and Yash FF1 Hybrid having VBDI of 22.9, 2.8, 2.7 and 2.6 respectively. Rakshak, Trishul and Arka Alok recorded as moderately resistant cultivars with VBDI of 1.6, 1.3 and 1.9 respectively. Lowest VBDI (1.0) was recorded in All Rounder showing resistant (<< 10% plant mortality) action toward bacterial wilt disease (Table 9.1). In the present study on performance of tomato genotype against bacterial wilt by VBD was earlier done by Kumar and Sharma (2004). They reported that higher VBDI in Highly susceptible genotypes followed by susceptible, moderately susceptible and moderately resistant with absence of VBDI in genotypes recorded as resistant towards bacterial wilt disease.

Table 9.1: Reaction of Tomato Cultivars against Bacterial Wilt Disease

Cultivars	Marketed by	Reaction*
Yash–F1 Hybrid	Century Seed Pvt Ltd., New Delhi	MS
Swarakhsha	Namdhari Seed Pvt. Ltd., Bangalore	MR
TO – 1458	Syngenta India Ltd., Pune	MS
Rakshak	Pehuja Seeds Pvt. Ltd., New Delhi	MR
Loknath	Indus Seeds, Bangalore	HS
Hybrid – 7610	Nunhems Seeds Pvt. Ltd., Hyderabad	MS
F1–Amulya–1744	Gaden Seed, Delhi	MS
All Rounder	Syngenta India Ltd., Pune	R
Arka Vikash	IIHR, Bangalore	HS
Trishul	Syngenta India Ltd., Pune	MR
Arka Alok	IIHR, Bangalore	MR

Note: Data are meant of three replications of different locations.

R = Resistant; MR = Moderately resistant; MS = Moderately susceptible; S = Susceptible; and HS = Highly susceptible; under sick soils in natural condition. The differences in reaction towards wilt carrying pathogen reported as resistant, moderately resistant and moderately susceptible. Moderately resistant may be due to the presence of modifying genes and/or influence of the environment.

REFERENCES

Biswas, S. and Singh, N.P. (2008). *Journal of Mycology and Plant Pathology*. 38(1): 18-20.

Kumar, R. and Sharma, S.K. (2004). *Journal of Mycology and Plant Pathology*. 34(2): 480-481.

Shekhawat, G.S.; Gadewar, A.V. and Chakraborti, S.K. (1992). *Bacterial Wilt Newsletter ACIAR*, 8: 5-6.

Sinha, S.K.; Mishra, B.; Singh, D.R. and Jain, B.P. (1990). *Bacterial Wilt Newsletter ACIAR*, 6: 6.

Sood, A.K. and Singh, B.M. (1993). ACIAR Proceeding. 45: 358-361.

10
e-Waste : Downside of e-Revolution

Sajal Debnath

Introduction

Waste Electrical and Electronic Equipment (WEEE) or in short e-Waste is the term used to describe old, end-of-life or discarded appliances using electricity. It includes computers, consumer electronics, fridges, etc., that have been disposed of by their original users.

We can refer "e-waste" as a generic term embracing all types of waste containing electrically powered components. e-Waste can be categorized into three categories, i.e., household (like refrigerator and washing machine, micro oven), IT and Telecom (PC, mobile etc.) and consumer equipment (TV, DVD etc.).

Within every electronic device lie toxic materials that make up the bits and bytes, a complex trash of lead, mercury, cadmium, plastics, and a host of other often-harmful ingredients. Hi-Tech trash is a wake-up call to the importance of the e-waste issue and the health hazards involved.

e-Waste contains both valuable materials as well as hazardous materials which require special handling and recycling methods. We should regard electronic waste as a rapidly expanding issue. Technical solutions are available, but in most cases a legal framework, a collection system, logistics, and other services need to be implemented before a technical solution can be applied.

The Wall Street Journal has defined e-waste as "the world's fastest growing and potentially most dangerous waste problem".

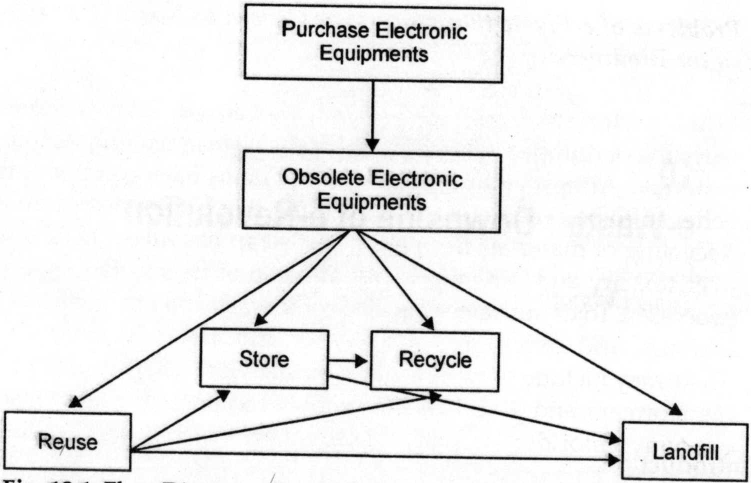

Fig. 10.1: Flow Diagram of e-product

Facts Behind e-Waste

Rapid changes in technology, low initial cost, and planned obsolescence have resulted in a fast-growing surplus of electronic waste around the globe. Surplus electronics have extremely high cost differentials. A single repairable laptop can be worth hundreds of dollars, while an imploded CRT is extremely difficult and expensive to recycle. An estimated 50 million tonnes of e-waste is produced each year. The USA discard 30 million computers each year and 100 million phones are disposed of in Europe each year. The Environmental Protection Agency estimates that only 15-20 per cent of e-waste is recycled, the rest of these electronics go directly into landfills and incinerators.

In the United States, an estimated 70 per cent of heavy metals in landfills come from discarded electronics, while electronic waste represents only 2 per cent of America's trash in landfills. 75 per cent of all personal computers ever sold are now gathering dust as surplus electronics. While some recycle, 7 per cent of cellphone owners still throw away their old cellphones. We are slowly, subtly, sometimes unknowingly polluting our environment with electronic goods.

Problems of e-Waste that needs to be Curved to Avoid Damages to the Biodiversity

When materials cannot or will not be reused, conventional recycling or dumped in landfill, where it is dismantled for precious materials. Almost all obsolete electronic items have components believed to be carcinogenic is something that cannot be ignored. Recycling of materials from electronic scrap has raised concerns over toxicity and carcinogenicity of some of its substances and processes. Toxic substances in electronic waste may include lead, mercury, and cadmium. Carcinogenic substances in electronic waste may include polychlorinated biphenyls (PCBs). Capacitors, transformers, and wires insulated with or components coated with polyvinyl chloride (PVC), manufactured before 1977, often contain dangerous amount of PCBs.

- Large quantities of used electronics are typically sold to countries with very high repair capability and high raw material demand, which can result in high accumulations of residue in poor areas without strong environmental laws.
- The complexity of the various items to be disposed of, the cost of environmentally approved recycling systems, and the need for concerned and concerted action to collect and systematically process equipments are challenges. One study indicates that two-thirds of executives are unaware of fines related to environmental regulations.
- Environmental groups claim that the informal processing of electronic waste in developing countries causes serious health and pollution problems. Some electronic scrap components, such as CRTs, contain contaminants such as lead, cadmium, beryllium, mercury, and brominated flame retardants. Activists claim that even in developed countries recycling and disposal of e-waste may involve significant risk to workers and communities and great care must be taken to avoid unsafe exposure in recycling operations and leaching of material such as heavy metals from landfills and incinerator ashes.

Protective Measures : *Bassel Convention*

The Bassel Convention on the Control of Transboundary Movements of Hazardous Wastes and their disposal, usually known simply as the Bassel Convention, is an international treaty that was designed to reduce the movements of hazardous waste between nations, and specifically to prevent transfer of hazardous wastes from developed to less developed countries.

The Bassel Convention controls trade in electronic waste. The Bassel Convention Parties have considered the question of whether exports of hazardous used electronic equipments for repair or refurbishment are not considered as Bassel Convention hazardous wastes unless they are discarded. The burden of proof that the items will be repaired and not discarded rest on the exporter, and any ultimate disposal of non-working components is subject to control under that Convention. In the Guidance document produced on that subject, that question was left up to the Parties.

Toxic substances in electronic wastes may include lead, mercury, and cadmium. Carcinogenic substances in electronic waste may include polychlorinated biphenyls (PCBs). Capacitors, transformers, and wires insulated with or components coated with polyvinyl chloride (PVC), manufactured before 1977, often contain dangerous amount of PCBs.

Up to 38 separate chemical elements are incorporated into electronic waste items. Many of the plastics used in electronic equipment contain flame retardants. These are generally halogens added to the plastic resin, making the plastics difficult to recycle. Due to the flame retardants being additives, they easily leach off the material in hot weather, which is a problem because when disposed of, electronic waste is generally left outside.

General Obligations of Bassel Conventions

- It is prohibited to export or import hazardous wastes or other wastes to or from a non-party State;
- No waste may be exported if the State of import has not given its consent in writing to the specific import;
- Information about proposed transboundary movements must be communicated to the States concerned, by means of a notification form, so that they may evaluate the effects

of the proposed movements on human health and the environment;

- Transboundary movements of wastes must only be authorised where there is no danger attached to their movement and disposal;
- Wastes which are to be the subject of a transboundary movement must be packaged, labelled and transported in conformity with international rules, and must be accompanied by a movement document from the point at which a movement commences to the point of disposal;
- Any party may impose additional requirements that are consistent with the provisions of the Convention.

The Convention establishes notification procedures regarding:

- Transboundary movements between parties;
- Transboundary movements from a party through the territory of States which are not parties.

e-Waste and Global Concerns

The importance and seriousness of the issue is well felt by the developed and developing nations.

The United Nations Conference on Trade and Development (UNCTAD) tends to support the repair and recycling trade. Mining to produce the same metals, to meet demand for finished products in the west, also occurs in the same countries, and UNCTAD has recommended that restrictions against recycling exports be balanced against the environmental costs of recovering those materials from mining. Hard rock mining produces 45 per cent of all toxins produced by all industries in the United States.

Legislations to Address this Problem in Asia

Many Asian countries have legislated for electronic waste recycling. South Korea, Japan and Taiwan ensure manufacturer responsibility by demanding that they recycle 75 per cent of their annual production.

China: Chinese laws are primarily concerned with eliminating the import of e-waste. China has ratified the Bassel Convention as well as the Bassel Ban Amendment, officially banning the import of e-waste. In October 2008, The Chinese State Council also approved a "draft regulation on the management of electronic waste". This regulation is intended to promote the continued use of resources through recycling and to monitor the end-of-life treatment of electronics. Under the new regulations, recycling of electronics by the consumer is mandated. It also requires the recycling of unnecessary materials discarded in the manufacturing process.

Australia: The Australian and New Zealand Environment and Conservation Council (now replaced by the Environment Protection and Heritage Council (EPHC) was the first body to identify electrical and electronic waste as a concern. The EPHC again declared that e-waste needed action. The Electrical Equipment Product Stewardship Sub-Group examined the issue and decided that computer and television wastes were "wastes of concern". Since that time the television and computer industry has been working with the EPHC to identify a suitable way to manage end-of-life televisions and computers.

Canada: Canada has imposed a fee which was added to the cost of purchasing new televisions, computers, and computer components and also implemented an electronics recycling fee in February 2007.

Europe: Some European countries implemented laws prohibiting the disposal of electronic waste in landfills. This created an e-waste processing industry in Europe.

In Switzerland, the first electronic waste recycling system was implemented in 1991, beginning with collection of old refrigerators. Over the years, all other electric and electronic devices were gradually been included in the system. Legislation followed in 1998, and since January 2005 it has been possible to return all electronic waste to the sales points and other collection points free of charge.

The Waste Electrical and Electronic Equipment (WEEE) Directive has now been transposed in national laws in all member countries of the European Union. It was designed to make equipment manufacturers financially or physically responsible for their equipment at the end of its life, under a policy known as EPR. Users of electrical and electronic equipment from private households should have the possibility of returning WEEE at least free of charge, and manufacturers must dispose of it in an environmentally friendly manner, by ecological disposal, reuse, or refurbishment. EPR is seen as a useful policy as it internalizes the end-of-life costs and provided a competitive incentive for companies to design equipment with fewer costs and liabilities when it reached its end of life. Since August 13, 2005, electronics manufacturers have become financially responsible for compliance to the WEEE Directive.

The Directive on the Restriction of the Use of Certain Hazardous Substances in Electrical and Electronic Equipment commonly referred to as the Restriction of Hazardous Substances Directive (RoHS Directive), was also adopted in February 2003 by the European Union. The RoHS Directive took effect on July 1, 2006, and is required to be enforced and become law in each Member-State. This directive restricts the use of six hazardous materials in the manufacture of various types of electronic and electrical equipment.

e-Waste in India

e-waste is growing rapidly in India because of the faster rate of obsolescence of electronic equipment. Previous studies on e-waste management in India have pointed out the problems and hazards of widespread informal e-waste recycling as it takes place in many bigger cities such as Delhi, Mumbai and Bangalore.

In these cities a complex e-waste handling infrastructure has developed mainly based on a long tradition of waste recycling. This is mainly operated by a very entrepreneurial informal sector. Rag pickers and waste dealers found it easy to adapt to the new waste stream, resulting in a large number of new businesses focusing on the re-use of components or extraction of secondary raw materials. So far, the e-waste recycling system is purely market driven and viewed as profit making entrepreneurship.

According to a national survey conducted by an international NGO, India generates a whopping four lakh tonnes of hazardous e-waste from electronic products such as computers, television sets, etc. every year.

Centre's draft policy on the disposal of hazardous e-waste could well become a landmark law. In its draft rules, the Ministry of Environment and Forests (MoEF) has proposed that manufacturers and dealers of electrical and electronic products be made accountable for the "end of-life" disposal of the goods, once they become obsolete or are ready to be recycled.

Manufacturers will not only be made responsible for setting up collection centres to oversee the process, but have to also ensure that the hazardous products are handled by registered dismantlers or recyclers in order to control the possible damage to the environment and human health.

While the draft policy does not deal with individual consumers, bulk clients like banks, MNCs and other big companies will now have to deposit their e-waste at authorized collection centres instead of selling them to local wholesale scrap shops.

Bulk consumer will also have to file annual returns on the quantity of the e-waste disposed. After Europe and the US, India is the first nation among developing countries to draft such a proposal. Records of e-waste that have been handled will have to be maintained by all concerned parties.

While environmental agencies like Greenpeace and Toxics Link have hailed the move as a step in the right direction, activists have expressed concern over whether the draft policy will be notified in its entirety. This draft rule can bring in some positive changes and will make the manufacturer, dealer and the consumer more accountable while disposing e-waste.

Even if the MoEF's proposals become the law—something that activists are actively campaigning for—many say that the government's task would not be easy in the face of stiff resistance from manufacturers and dealers. Officials in the Ministry admitted that the efficacy of what has been proposed will also depend on a proactive approach from the industry.

So far only 20 odd companies are actively involved in collecting e-waste from their consumers and routing it to recycling plants. We should hope more companies come forward and form a consortium in setting up additional centres and recycling units. The draft rules say the dealers will also have to collect e-waste by providing consumers a box or bin or a demarcated area to deposit the used goods. The Extended Producer Responsibility (EPR) is yet to become a reality in India. The draft rule also mandates that the manufacturer provide each item with a unique serial number to help track the product.

Tamil Nadu has become the first State in the country to come up with a separate e-waste policy in the country. While welcoming the move and the policy on collection by community-based organisations (CBO), activists and organisations are awaiting specific details.

Electronics Corporation of Tamil Nadu Limited (ELCOT) was one of the key organisations that worked on preparing the policy for the State. The 11-12 members who were on the Board were drawn from several allied sectors were given the mandate to keep in tune with the national guidelines.

While at this point of time, the e-waste policy remains a mere document, it will be followed in the next six months with a series of government orders and a set of rules that will ensure the implementation of all the features mentioned in the policy.

The government would also take up a massive awareness programme to tell consumers of the huge quantities of e-waste they are accumulating, and suggesting responsible means of getting rid of them.

The research by the Department of Scientific and Industrial Research estimates that 25,000 people in India's slums are employed in an unregulated e-waste recycling industry, with just five per cent of waste going through official channels.

Some of the recycling processes are extremely harmful and have negative impacts on the workers' health and the environment. A study on the burning of printed wiring boards that was conducted 2004 showed an alarming concentration of dioxins in the surrounding areas in which open burning was practiced. These toxins cause an increased risk of cancer if inhaled by workers and local residents or by entering the food chain *via* crops from the surrounding fields.

Proposals to Control e-Waste in India

Guideline must be designed to serve as a current and definitive information resource on the issues, problems and opportunities created by e-waste, focusing on the present scenario in India.

Rules or laws has to be imposed for e-waste management, recycling methodologies and to protect workers and the environment. Scrap industry officials agree that electronic waste should be managed with great caution.

We should regard electronic waste as a "rapidly expanding"

issue. Technical solutions are available, but in most cases a legal framework, a collection system, logistics, and other services need to be implemented before a technical solution can be applied.

The state of Maharashtra of India planned to crack down on e-waste by penning new regulations to address the problem in cities such as Mumbai and Pune which produce some 28,000 metric tonnes of electronic waste annually.

Government and Industries need advanced e-waste recycling facilities which do not pose a threat to both workers and to the environment. This can be made possible with enactment of existing e-waste guidelines into legislation.

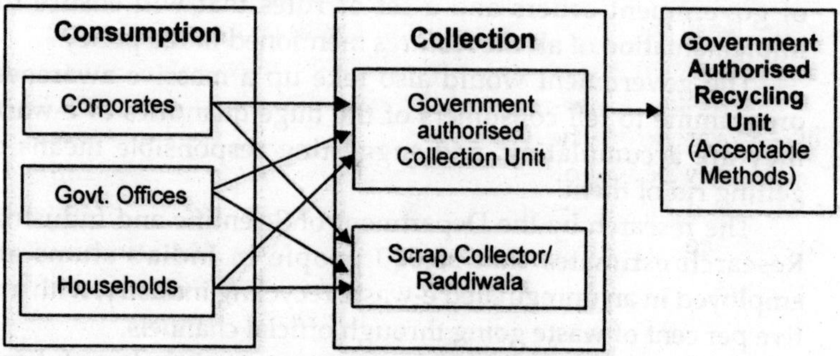

Fig. 10.2: Proposed e-waste recycling mechanisms.

As depicted in Fig. 10.2, Government or Government authorized collection centre can be build-up across the country where all e-waste can be gathered from corporate offices, Governmental offices and from households by own initiatives or by raddiwalas network. Those collected e-waste can be treated in safe and hazard free scientifically acceptable procedure in Government authorized recycling units.

Even the manufacturer must find out more technical methods to help after production managing of e-products. Such as using :

- Environmental sustainable production process.
- More renewable material and energy.
- Creating e-products with biodegradable material.
- Looking at green packaging solution.
- Utilize minimum packaging for the materials.
- Recovery and reuse.

Partnership among all stakeholders is necessary to make the process successful.

Conclusion

The tangible impact of e-waste on environment and human health may be out of sight for many people but this is by no means a story of abstraction or its impacts are far remote. The need of the hour is an urgent approach to curb the growth of e-waste by technical and policy interventions.

Once the rules were in place, key stakeholders including manufacturers, pollution control boards, local bodies and last but not the least, the consumer consider it with prime importance.

Also, the population must be educated about the seriousness of the issue and made aware of the need of e-waste management. Citizen awareness is the first step in trying to address this problem.

The way people of India are aware of dangers in application of DDT and other pesticides and made it an issue of National importance; hence an initiative should be taken from the government and public, regarding bringing the world's attention about the impact of e-waste and India's sincerity to deal with the issue.

REFERENCES

All India e-waste Recyclers Association

Boralkar D.B., *Perspective of electronic waste management,* from www.mpcb.mah.nic.in

Computer and the Environment, Kluwer Academic Publishers, pp. 5-12, 25-29.

e-waste, Indian Perspective, available from www.nswai.com

Harder, B, Toxic "e-waste"gets cashed in poor nation. www.news.nationalgeographic.com/news/

Hi-tech Trash, Elizabeth Grossman, Island Press, pp. 2, 3, 13.

http://india.ewasteguide.info/Initial

MoEF reports

Pandve, HT, *e-waste management in India: an emerging environmental and Health Issue.*

RushPRnews \ technorati.com/tag/articles

Ramesh Babu, Parande AK Ahmed Basha C. *Electrical unul Electronic Waste: A Global Environmental Problem*, p. 25, 307-18.

Sinha, S. *Downside of Digital Revolution*. Available at http://www.toxicslinlk.org

www.ewasteproject.org

Part 3
Role of Media in Conservation of Biodiversity

Part 3

Role of Media in Conservation of Biodiversity

11
Biodiversity and Media Advocacy

K.V. Nagraj

In recent times, there is a welcome media focus on biodiversity and climate change. The media attention to biodiversity is invariably linked to the future of humankind on this planet. In fact, environmental communication, after a long period of gestation is slowly emerging as a distinct discipline under a broad umbrella called science communication. Science has always advocated social welfare, equity and distributive justice besides access to economic and knowledge resources. The very existence of a knowledge society has its own significance for media and biodiversity.

The process of development chosen by societies all over the world is perhaps responsible for the need to revisit our priorities. This planet, a unique home for varieties of species of living beings, is under a continuous assault, by the new priests of development and modernization. Development has become an ism across the globe overshadowing all other politico-cultural ideologies. Now we are living in an era of developmental ideology, irrespective of capitalism, socialism, Gandhism, or any other ism, for that matter. And this unflinching enthusiasm for hyper modernization has affected environmental causes in a way.

Biodiversity as seen by experts does really matter for ecological balance. It also includes environmental concerns raised by well-meaning individuals and institutions. Environment, as we perceive, includes the physical environment of biodiversity. This in turn can be either natural or human environment that encompasses varieties of animals, plants, their habitats, climate, land, water and air. Biodiversity is a natural order for all other creatures should be free from unnatural human intervention. We, the human beings, should understand that we live in a world of limited resources. In the name of development, unfortunately, we have created a world of unlimited wants. In the process, we have inflicted a heavy blow to the ecological balance, endangering both biodiversity and physical environment.

There is no need to repeat that the world is interdependent of all natural systems. As has already been repeatedly pointed out, the first and foremost concern for biodiversity because of the extensive use of DDT appeared in Silent Spring (1962), authored by Rachel Carson. The unbridled use of chemicals in the form of fertilizer, pesticide or insecticide, as all of us know, has the impact of transmutation. This book, *Silent Spring*, heralded an era of environmentalism, besides injecting a new news value for media attention.

In India, the first policy document to make a reference to the environmental aspect of developmental strategy was made in the Fourth Five Year Plan proposal, in which the Planning Commission clearly stated:

> It is an obligation for each generation to maintain the productive capacity of land, air, water and wildlife in a manner which leaves its successors some choice for the creation of a healthy environment. The physical environment is a dynamic, complex and inter-connected system in which any action in one part affects others. There is also the inter-dependence of living things and their relationships with land, air and water. Planning for harmonious development recognizes this unity of nature and man .... It is necessary, therefore, to introduce the environmental aspect into our planning and development. Along with effective conservation and rational use of natural resources, protection and improvement of human environment is vital for national well-being (Planning Commission, 1975, p. 275).

Let us now discuss the role of mass media in advocating the preservation of biodiversity. The Chipko, the Appiko and other related movements hogged media limelight in 1970s, 1980s and even in 1990s as they were reflective of mass protests. Since these were the formative years of television and the electronic media were under the control of the Union Government, the print media played a dominant role in exposing the conflict between decision-makers in the government and masses of farmers. For some activists, industrialization, in the present day context, means destruction of biodiversity. The Bedthi power project in Karnataka is another instance of the press diligently publicizing the mass movement against the proposal, as the project would submerge both fertile agricultural and forest land. Noted Kannada author and popular science writer Shivaram Karanth lent his support to the movement.

A major event of the mass movement to project biodiversity pertained to the Silent Valley. When the Kerala State Government proposed a power project in the Silent Valley, a strong public opposition under the leadership of Kerala Sastra Sahitya Parishad (KSSP) surfaced. As all of us know, Silent Valley is one of the very few existing hotspots of biodiversity in the world. Incidentally, the KSSP is an organization spearheading the popularization of science education. The local people who had initially welcomed the project were later educated by the activists, of its harmful effects on the biodiversity of the region. The mainstream press, especially the language press, lent its unwavering support to the movement against the project, which was ultimately shelved.

It is also a fact that the third sector initiatives and its environmental has received coverage in the media, but not adequate. Similar is the case with the judgements of green judges. The media advocacy of protection to biodiversity has been in patches, neither regular nor consistent. The controversies surrounding the Narmada Bachav Andolan can be a good topic for an in-depth case study of media approach to environmental and biodiversity, and also to the issue of development. Such multi-dimensional issues should be debated widely by the media for collective education and good.

No doubt, the ideology of environmentalism exists in India today, but it is not coherent. Though claim to be a pluralistic democracy, there exists a kind of feudal attitude in all sectors of our polity including scientific and media establishments. The greatest danger to the inculcation of scientific temperament and ethos is the absence of democratic debates and tolerance of dissent. Unless diverse scientific views are democratically inspected, the very edifices of science will crumble. Here comes the need for media activism and advocacy. The recent media persons has somewhat proved the dictum that communication is power.

In recent times, the mass media have received a great amount of flak from media scholars themselves for ignoring their obligations and responsibilities. It is alleged that mass media have become business enterprises and the news supply, a commercial trade. The non-stop supply of information in the garb of infotainment has only one objective of earning super profits. The mass media no longer sport the missionary zeal for public service, but have become private enterprises. Market forces rule the roost and dictate terms for the supply of news and views, from gathering of news for dissemination, the media have moved towards manufacturing of news and views. Media advocacy of sensitive issue like protection to biodiversity is influenced by contradictions of definitions between market forces and public service.

With the world moving from the concept of modernization to hyper-modernization, newer and newer questions as to the issue of media advocacy are raised especially with regard to environmentalism. The concept of objectivity, the hallmark of traditional journalism is given a decent burial in favour of advocacy or campaign journalism. Partisan stances are permeated with impunity. The distinction between different economic ideologies is getting blurred leading to confounded ideological anarchy. The serious nature of issues of biodiversity and climate change, which are, of course, inter-related, have been relegated to the background.

Media corporatization has become so much pervasive, everything including biodiversity is seen through the prism of market value. In India, it has been noted that environmental issues are of three perspectives. M. Gadgil and R. Guha (1995) have described them as Gandhian, Marxist and technological. The Gandhian view is the rejection of western ways of life. Environmental problem is discussed from the moralist viewpoint. Materialistic and consumerist lifestyle is dubbed wasteful. It is basically a moral problem and the solution lies in village republics that foster socio-ecological harmony (Nandy, 1989).

Of late, we have come across new concepts like corporate ethics, corporate morality and corporate social responsibility. Marketization of morality has its own connotation in which means are not important, only the goals are. The Gandhian precept emphasizes the morality of means to achieve societal objectives.

The Marxist view considers ecological issues in terms of political and economic equations, the unequal distribution of resources as the core of the entire debate.

Environmental Marxists are closely identified with the people's Science movements, Kerala Sastra Sahitya Parishad being a fine example. The appropriate technology philosophy seeks a functional relationship between agriculture and industry. It is the middle road between Gandhian and Marxist prescriptions. Media persons who subscribe to these precepts can be found in India also. However, a major allegation is that most of them subscribe to western corporate imperatives, tilting towards capitalist-economic ethos, i.e., nature takes care of itself, and we should continue to follow the existing path of development.

The concept of green politics is still alien to middle and upper class urbanites and urban-centric mass media in India. Forget elections being fought on the basis of green issues. The India mass media have never attempted to educate the political class on any issue of environment or biodiversity. Media persons and politicians alike appear to support big projects without proper evaluation and irrespective of their ideological nomenclatures. Clearly, mass media should be the natural forum for a discourse of ecological construct and realities. However, the moot question is whether a performance audit should be held in the case of mass media *vis-a-vis* ecological issues like biodiversity. The media obsession with salacious contents such as sex, crime and celebrities has unmasked the real issues of poverty, environment, health and others. Through the concept of advocacy journalism become perceptible in 1970s, it underwent ups and downs along environmental disasters and issues. According to a study of the media in the United States, their environmental coverage was less than two per cent of the media contents in 1990s (Beder, 1998). Ecological tragedies become news, making negativity a high news value. Basically, this is the Western news value which declares that no news is good news.

While deciding the issue of biodiversity and environment and content selection, regular media persons do not have the expertise to interpret the significance of the issue involved. Nor the science advocates have the skill to communicate their expertise to the masses. This problem was evident initially in the coverage of the Silent Valley imbroglio by mainstream media. The recent cry for the resurrection of the project is a testimony for media failure. Perhaps, the media persons have not yet grasped the gravity of serious ecological issues. However, some media experts find a fine functional relationship between media and environmental activities. The emergence of magazines devoted to environment in 1990s is an indicator of its importance attached to the issue in recent times. Added to this is the media recognition of environmental groups as a credible news source.

A study of environmental news coverage in Indian newspapers (2000) revealed that the environmental coverage between 1980 and 1998 in select English daily newspapers of the country was as low as 1.25 per cent of the editorial whole. The study also found out that governmental policies and actions had an impact on the media coverage. Besides, the media attention was event-centric and lacked consistency and constancy. *The Hindu* gave more coverage to the environmental issue and *The Times of India*, the least. *The Hindu* was the only newspaper to employ green specialists. The positioning of news on environment mostly in the inside pages, unless the story was related to a major disaster. Stories of deforestation, water pollution and air pollution were the focus areas in order. The study pointed out that problems like soil erosion, resource depletion, sea pollution, global warming and damage too much ozone layer did not receive much coverage. According to the study, the India Press did not play any advocacy role when it came to green issues, including biodiversity. The study also revealed that in most cases, editorial remained neutral.

Another important finding of this study is the complacency among journalists who averred that the coverage given to green subjects and issues was adequate. While most men journalists belonged to this category, woman journalists held a contrary view of inadequacy of media coverage. Media advocacy of green issues did not appeal to most men journalists while women journalists favoured it.

Media advocacy itself has generated a lot of heat and dust. Now media advocacy is accepted as a routine signpost. However, a cause of worry is that issues like biodiversity and climate change are turning out to be a big business. The billion dollar question is how to make media advocate green causes and perform their social obligations. Is it really possible in a market driven environment of development? The issue is complex, so also the solution. Here comes the importance of language media in India which can reach out to the huge masses of audience without much ado, unlike their English language counterparts that cater to a microscopic minority of pseudo elites. What we need now is an omnibus media advocacy movement for green issues. Let us pledge ourselves for this onerous task.

REFERENCES

Beder, S. (1998), *Global Spin: The Corporate Assault on Environmentalism*: Chelsea Green Publishing Company.

Carson, Rechel (1962), *Silent Spring*, Boston: Houghton Miffin.

Chapman, G. Kumar; K.J., Fraser; C. Gaber I. (1997): *Environmentalism and the Mass Media: The North-South Divide*, London: Routledge.

Gadgil, M. and Guha, R. (1995): *Ecology and Equity*, New Delhi: Penguin.

Hannigan, J.A. (1995), *Environmental Sociology: A Social Constructionist Perspective*, London: Routledge.

Hachten, W.P. (1992), *The World News Prism*, Ames: Iowa State University.

Khanna, G.N. (1993), *Global Environmental Crisis and Management*, New Delhi: Ashis Publishing House.

Lewis, M.W. (1992), *Green Delusions: An Environmental Critique of Radical Environmentalism*, Durhan, NC: Duke University Press.

Rubin, C.T. (1994), *The Green Crusade: Rethinking the Roots of Environmentalism*; New York: The Free Press.

Poorhananda, D.S. (2000), *Press and the Environment: A Study of Environmental News in Indian Newspapers*, Mangalore University: Unpublished doctoral thesis.

12

Media Advocacy for Biodiversity Conservation Study on North-East

Biswendu Bhattacharjee and *Deepak Upadhyaya*

Introduction

The so-called failed Copenhagen UN Summit on Climate Change was not a "failure" altogether. It did give birth to the consciousness for concerted media advocacy across the globe for which similar sentiment was echoed from a world leader none other than the stature of Jacques Chirac, former President of France. There is no reservation on the statement from global media community at large though differences of approach in reporting were observed around the Summit. It is a fact that the issue of climate change hit the media because of their affinity with higher echelons of "power" and not because of any earnest concern for biodiversity. World media became bi-polar during Copenhagen Summit – pro-US and pro-BRIC, which finally became a part of global politics.

Design

With this view in mind, a qualitative content analysis of two English newspapers in the region was undertaken for a period of six months to gauge the media mind before and after the Copenhagen summit was held. The study took a sample population of articles that were exclusively reported in the *Assam Tribune* and The *Times of India*. The *Assam Tribune* is the highest circulated regional English daily, whereas The *Times of India* is the highest circulated mainstream English daily of the country. Purposive random monitoring was done to locate the environment related articles /news/features running all through the pages of the said two papers for a period of six months (November 2009 to March 2010).

Findings

The study reveals a gloomy scene of media portrayal on biodiversity conservation and other environmental issues of North-Eastern India. Although North-East (NE) India is regarded as one of the two biodiversity hotspots even in international forums, the media coverage of biodiversity issues of NE was not found satisfactory to most of them who would love to see ample media coverage in both the reputed dailies. The record says, The *Times of India*, which has circulation of two exclusive editions for North-East – early Kolkata edition and Guwahati edition covered only eleven news items on environment and biodiversity issues over a period of six months. Unfortunately, the portrayal was lopsided because it was beating round the bush by concentrating on *catastrophe frame* without due coverage on *advocacy and conservation frames*. The few news items those touched the biodiversity and environment issues when they went on to speak of Commonwealth Games, Livelihood issues, Politics and Insurgency, Smuggling of animal body parts, Abduction of forester's family, etc. Barring others, these two stories were observed in positive frame and promoting the biodiversity resources of North-East.

However, The *Times of India* (1st December, 2009) portrayed the region, *"The North-East, which contains one-fourth of India's forest cover, is peculiar due to traditional practices of shifting cultivation which make a steady assessment difficult. While Mizoram saw a gain of 640 sq km and Manipur of 328 sq km, Nagaland suffered a loss of 201 sq km and Tripura 100 sq km to shifting agriculture"*. It also highlighted that *Forest Cover in 2007—21.02 per cent of geographical area, Tree Cover in 2007—2.82 per cent, Forest cover growth in a decade—3.13 million ha. Out of the 728 sq km increase in 2005-07, 690 sq km gained in the 188 tribal districts of the country and the forest cover in the hill States is 53.72 per cent of the possible forest area.* Another news story (*ToI*, March 12, 2010) termed North-East as India's Battery referring the statement of P.D. Rai, a Sikkim Democratic Front MP and General

Secretary of North-East MPs' Forum. It said, "*This region...., is the battery of India. It has a power potential of about 80,000 MW. It is sitting on a colossal amount of hydrocarbons. The region has nearly 33 per cent of India's biodiversity reserves. How much better can it get? So its important for the country that there is development in the region*".

It is to be mentioned that The *Times of India* has got a substantial reader base in the North-East but it is expected that the newspaper should feed the people with stories emanating from the region for the region along with other parts of the country. It has been observed that the Guwahati edition of The *Times of India* has concentrated mainly on issues primarily like violence, terrorism, politics and other related topics of Assam and the same edition is being fed to people of Assam and a few adjoining States (except Tripura and Mizoram)—here it loses its national character. Moreover, it has been noticed that The *Times of India* has its news network in almost all the districts of North-East whereas the reporting of news from all the corners does not get reflected. There is a serious imbalance observed between circulation and the presence of news items across the region. The edition available in Mizoram and Tripura is not covering the news of North-East rather it contains stale items from Eastern India. At the same time, issues and events on biodiversity of the region do not get reflected in the metro editions. A point to be observed here is that the Guwahati edition has only been started in early part of the new millennium but decadence has crept in the reportage pattern of such an iconic newspaper of India.

On the other, content analysis study of the 75 years old English daily of the North-East—the *Assam Tribune* brings in a mixed scenario so far as coverage of environmental and biodiversity issues are concerned. The content analysis reveals that the *Assam Tribune* covers about 20 stories related to biodiversity and environment but most of the news items covered in wire of local character pertaining to Assam. It has been observed that although the *Assam Tribune* has covered a few news stories on environment issues in the last six months, the coverage is little in comparison to other issues. Most of the news items had highlighted the events and not the outcome or advocated for any action. It seems, the newspaper is concerned with announcement and pagination with no regard to follow up.

Curiously, the mast head of the *Assam Tribune* equivocally

pronounces that it is a paper echoing the voice of the whole of the North-East region; however, it hardly devotes space to environment related coverage from other States except Assam and Arunachal Pradesh. The regional claim of the newspaper is thus, confined to its State of nativity. Both qualitative and quantitative analysis of the news coverage of the contents appears that they are just declarative in nature and the analysis as well as inducement to action is absent. The news items were also basically repetitive in nature with the only difference in headlines.

Discussions

In general it has been found that the press in the region has not been shouldering the responsibility of educating and informing the masses on various facets of biodiversity loss and conservation. Both the objectivity and subjectivity of the news items published in different newspapers including the editions of so-called national newspapers, regional newspapers and State/local dailies are subject to the mismatch. The agenda setting role of the press of North-East region is found to be slowly on the wane. Print media, which is at the vanguard of setting political and policy agenda of the region, is failed miserably in regard to environment protection and biodiversity conservation. So far it has been observed that the political issues are main beat that is being covered by most of the newspapers of the region. Burning issue like biodiversity conservation and environment protection, if not portrayed with all fairness by the press could have disastrous consequences in near future.

The gate keeping role of the media is yet to be sensitized by itself to include environment journalism in practice. The newspaper journalists are not trained or motivated to cover environment in a critical manner. As a result, the few news items those are published only when there are "sensational" or a "celebrity association". Half of the blame has to be shared by academicians and bureaucrats who consider that biodiversity, environment and technological interface are a hardcore science subject, so, beyond the domain of understanding and action by general masses. Even though, so-called guardians of environment protection are voicing their concern and welcome the participation of the common people, which remains to mere observance of events like Earth Day, Environment Day, Water Day, etc., with no concerted action to implement the resolution on the next day.

Right from Obama to Manmohan Singh who made tall talks in Copenhagen Summit hardly directed their administration to stick to *carbon credit reduction mechanism*. Developing countries like India rely heavily on fossil fuels as much as the developed countries like the United States for its means of transport and communication. Reduction in Carbon Emission level would come down drastically, if environment norms are observed in switching over to *cleaner fuels* by breaking the monopoly of big automobile manufacturers who cash in on with their hands in glove with the petroleum companies.

Observations

The banks operating in the region provides easy loans for owning individual cars to customers these days through their thousands of branches while the government does not have any concrete policy to dissuade individuals from owning car. The spirit of nationalism seems to be neglected by the ethos of the banking scenario of the region that prefer to provide loans for luxury but hesitate to provide the same to needy unemployed youths for self-enterprising pursuits. The argument of the bankers in regard to recovery from unemployed is nothing but a callous attitude.

Similarly, the government's apathy in promoting better means of public transport in smaller cities of the North-East goes a long way in destroying the eco-balance. Poor means of public transport, congested roads in cities like Agartala, Guwahati, Kohima, Aizawl and Imphal have given impetus to alternative means of communication like small auto-rickshaw and taxis, which has become detrimental to eco-sustainability as well as social values. Had the government been conscious enough to contribute its mite in earning *"carbon credit"* by introducing mass-means of public transport system?

Biodiversity conservation does not only mean conservation of flora and fauna. Fresh water is also a non-renewable natural resource, which has been mindlessly explored by a few companies who harp on the lucrative business of package drinking water. Unlike other natural resources, water is also recognized as a *"community asset"*—no individual/company has the exclusive right to extract ground water for commercial purposes. The failure of government to contain such unethical business which is mushrooming in the country due to apathy and short sightedness of the policy makers and bureaucrats, would spell a dooms day by next few decades. Depleting ground water level is to be blamed for rampant explosion by the industrial and commercial groups, and calls for a serious intervention in both legal and policy frame. The commercial concerns can do well by exploring alternative avenues by harvesting rain water, storm water, liquid sewerage, river water and sea water, which would not be readily fit for human consumption but could well be used for industrial purposes.

In recent years, many developed countries have introduced *"Green Tax"* as a measure to discourage pollution. Green taxes are those taxes that put an additional cost on the polluters. In case of a polluting company, the social cost of production exceeds the private cost as their activities cause loss of welfare of society, which is uncompensated. With "green taxes", the cost of activities that damage the environment is increased and the cost of activities that people want to encourage for environmental reasons is decreased. Green taxes operate under the premise that economic activity impacting the environment on a large scale is not accountable for the cost of such impacts. It provides incentives to companies for utilizing renewable resources to reduce pollution. Suppose a company cuts production cost by discharging its effluents in a nearby river. A tax is, therefore, imposed on the company. The company may prefer to pay the tax when the tax burden is more than the private benefit obtained from polluting the river. So the challenge lies in the fiscal policy to fix the rate in such a way that it becomes cheaper not to pollute. Green tax will not work as a license to destroy natural resources. Rather, "pay as you burn, not pay as you earn" approach would benefit both the environment and the economy. Green taxes can complement the need for regulatory or command and control measures. Command and control measures refer to environmental policy that relies on regulation, permission, prohibition, standard setting and enforcement as opposed to economic instruments of cost internalization.

Again, taxation shift from capital and labour to discharges and resource use will have positive impact on the economy. Taxes like payroll, income or sales tax, corporate tax, property tax, etc., can be lowered by a green tax shift. Of course, it requires ecological fiscal reforms. Sweden implemented the world's first environmental tax shift. It enacted a carbon tax on the use of oil, coal, natural gas, and LPG, petrol and aviation fuel used in domestic travel. Since 1991, a number of European governments have cut conventional taxes on income and raised certain taxes that discourage harm to the environment.

The UK's Green Fiscal Commission in its October 2009 report makes a strong pitch for green tax. Green taxes that penalize carbon emission make high carbon substitutes less attractive and encourage investment in low carbon alternatives. It discourages what is bad and encourages what is good for the economy. UK has already imposed fuel tax known as fuel duty escalator as a result of which fuel consumption in the road transport sector has dropped and the average fuel efficiency of trucks has increased by 13 per cent. India can follow the example of the UK. Our economy demands such measures to discourage and reduce the use of environmentally destructive products.

After the Copenhagen Summit, Tata Steel expressed its commitment to curb emission. It is aiming to reduce its carbon emission by 10 per cent by 2012 and 25 per cent by 2020. From the example of Tata, it cannot, of course, be expected that other companies will do the same. So a three-in-one approach like green tax is needed. By penalizing the polluters, reducing harmful emissions and raising revenue, will save both the environment and economy. So carbon tax, pesticides and fertilizer tax, virgin fibre tax, ozone depletion tax, company car parking, etc., can be tried. Similarly, green tax can be imposed on low energy efficiency electronic products.

Case Study

1. In a first of its kind initiative in India, Himachal Pradesh decided to impose a green tax on vehicle users to generate a fund for combating climate change. The Government fund will be utilized for protecting nature from certain death and making the State a carbon-neutral zone. Green tax has also been levied by Karnataka on vehicles older than 15 years.
2. In Tripura, ARPAN Society had filed a Public Interest

Litigation (PIL) in 2008 in Guwahati High Court against poor transport system and mobility in Agartala. Pronouncing the judgement, in March 2010, the High Court's division bench, comprising Justices H.N. Sharma and H. Barua, issued direction to the State Government to take immediate action and ensure vibrant transport system in the State. The judgement criticized the police for forcing drivers and riders of two-wheelers to wear non-standard headgear and its inaction against overloading and over-speeding by public vehicles, besides indiscriminate stoppages on the roads. ARPAN prayed to the High Court for strict enforcement against the use of vehicles causing pollution, air-horns and improper use of high-beam lights in the vehicles, reckless driving, and legal action against both drivers and passengers for overloading in public vehicles.

REFERENCES

Papers published in Periodical, Journals and Dailies

Green taxes can safeguard the environment by Dr. Susmita Priyadarshani Lecturer in Economics at DCB College, Jorhat, published in March 1, 2010 in *Assam Tribune*.

Boykoff, M., and Boykoff, J. (2007). Climate change and journalistic norms: A case study of US mass-media coverage. *Geoforum* 38, 1190-1204.

Edited Books

Boykoff, M., and Boykoff, J. (2004). Balance as bias: Global warming and the U.S. prestige press. *Global Environmental Change* 14, 125-136.

Carvalho, A. (2005). Representing the politics of the greenhouse effect: Discursive strategies in the British media. *Critical Discourse Studies*, 2 (1), 1-29.

Carvalho, A. (2007). Ideological cultures and media discourses on scientific knowledge: Re-reading news on climate change. *Public Understanding of Science*, 16, 223-243.

Chapman, G.; Kumar, K.: Fraser, C. and Gaber, I. (1997). Environmentalism and the Mass Media: *The North-South Divide*. London: Routledge.

Chouliaraki, L. (2006). *The Spectatorship of Suffering*. London: Sage.

Cottle, S. (2000). TV news, lay voices and the visualisation of environmental risks. In S. Allan, B. Adam, C. Carter (Eds), *Environmental Risks and the Media* (pp. 29-44). London: Routledge.

Cottle, S. (2003). News, public relations and power: Mapping the field. In S. Cottle (Ed.) *News, Public Relations and Power* (pp. 3-24). London: Sage.

13
The Role of SHGs in Propagation of Information to Rural India with Special Reference to Tripura

Bijit Debbarma

Introduction

The dictionary meaning of information is "facts or knowledge that are provided or learnt". This is an established fact that information is one of the most important ingredient towards development of a country. It is noticed that people blame it to the information needs for underdevelopment or low level development of a region or sector. The term information age is used today which has helped organizations numerously towards accurate levels of productions and communications at more target level.

India is a vast country where majority of its population lives in rural (around 73%). It has been noticed that the concentration of different organisations, be it government or business, is more of urban centric. So the rural is left with lots of problems specially infrastructure development, and the current need is *Bijli, Sadak and Paani* (Electricity, Road and Water) which is a big shift from the earlier one "*Roti, Kapda and Makan*" (i.e., Food, Clothing and Shelter). But above all is the need for communication and information.

Tripura a small State in North-Eastern region of India, has got the similar kind of requirement and as it is situated in the extreme corner, with Bangladesh bordering its three sides. So the gateway of information to rural Tripura is similar in nature and the problems are equal to, as faced by the other States of North-East region. As looking deeper one can find out that the current information providers are different government agencies, NGOs, Panchayats and others are not too effective. What is noticed is though the agriculturists and the other consumers seek information, but there is a lack of mechanism for effective information dissemination.

Role of Information : Different Initiatives

Information is one of the most important factor responsible for development or underdevelopment and it is applicable to any country or region. Numerous reports have been published where a region has witnessed slow development because of lack of a proper information system or negligence of the authority towards dissemination of information.

If we look into the process of communication we can notice the role Sender plays, where a media is used to send a message in an encoded form to the Receiver. The receiver decodes the message and sends feedback. The whole process could be disrupted by Noise.

Organisations trying to communicate to the audiences in Rural India face numerous problems, because of its inadequate infrastructure and other non-development related issues.

Though government has developed different windows to disseminate information, but they are not as effective as they are supposed to be.

Mentioned below are the ways or sources through which different government departments of Tripura seek information as well as passes information.

Handloom, Handicraft and Sericulture Department

Sericulture department in the process of selecting and training farmers to start mulberry plantation, approaches Panchayat Samiti for collecting information regarding the farmers or families below poverty limits who would become the beneficiaries to start mulberry plantation. The Panchayat Samiti after checking sends list of people who are willing to do mulberry plantation. Meanwhile the department sends its employees for baseline survey to match the details of people given by Panchayat Samiti. After the department is convinced, next process is to prepare land. Next step is to create awareness among BPL family and women's. Then training is undertaken followed by Plantation.

What can be noticed here is the department is further doing a baseline survey to confirm the truthfulness of the Panchayat's list of beneficiaries.

Department of Agriculture

Department of Agriculture has got its research centre which conducts adaptability study of the research finding of agricultural products developed by ICAR. And once it is found the products suitability, the department decides for its distribution or training to the farmers.

The department follows a pyramid system where information are passed from the head office to the offices located in different districts and Sub-Divisions. The different Agricultural Officers and Block superintendents contact the 3-tier Panchayat to pass information regarding the product and also to collect information regarding the beneficiaries. The Panchayat through village level workers or Gram Sewaks gets information about the target groups.

Other Problems

A visit to any government department and it is noticed that a person have to knock different doors to ultimately get the right and actual information. Most important, the process is lengthy and cumbersome and needs lots of patience from the information seekers end.

It has also been noticed that information regarding different schemes of the government, fails to reach to the target groups most of the time. And that proves the role that different information providing government machineries inability and ineffectiveness in passing the information to the right groups.

Insight to the Problems

Reach

Reaching the most dispersed farmers geographically is one of the challenges faced by organizations—government and non-government/ business.

Education

Most of the farmers or beneficiaries who are the target audience to communicate are illiterates or semi-literates, so talking in their own languages is another challenge.

Big Farmers get more Attention

It is often seen that the beneficiaries are the big farmers who are better resourced with larger scale of farming operations. And in the process the small farmers are the less fortunate regarding the benefits provided.

Public Duty and Information Providing

Opportunity for corruption and less productive government employees has given rise to the importance of information providers close to the farmers or beneficiaries.

Accountability Worries

Another important issue is regarding accountability of farmers or the beneficiaries.

Bureaucratic Procedures

Bureaucracy is one of the big problems faced by different government organizations, as it is more time consuming.

Self Help Groups: A Solution to the Problems

Looking at the problems, a scope for Self Help Groups to come into picture and play an active role in providing information to the real peoples.

What rural India lacks is absence of an effective media, followed by illiteracy and semi-literacy, which also acts as barriers to communications.

Rural India also witnessed the changing role of opinion leaders. In such a situation it is proposed to utilize the Self Help Groups and act as medium to two-way information provider—first the any organization seeking information about a particular Block or village; and second to the target groups whom these organizations are trying to reach.

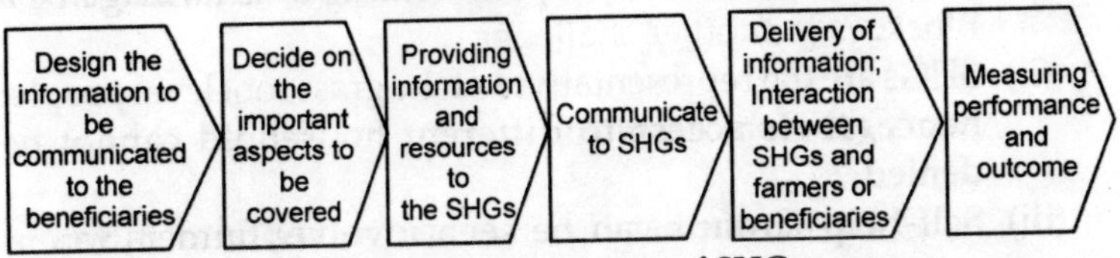

Fig. 13.1: Proposed Model of Participation of SHGs

What is a Self Help Group?

SHG is group of rural poor who have volunteered to organise themselves into a group for eradication of poverty of the members. They agree to save regularly and convert their savings into a Common Fund known as the Group Corpus.

Generally a self-help group may consist of 10 to 20 persons. However, in difficult areas like deserts, hills and areas with scattered and sparse population and in case of minor irrigation and disabled persons, this number may be from 5-20.

Generally all members of the group should belong to families below the poverty line. However, if necessary, a maximum of 20 per cent and in exceptional cases, where essentially required, up to a maximum of 30 per cent of the members in a group may be taken from families marginally above the poverty line living contiguously with BPL families and if they are acceptable to the BPL members of the group. This will help the families of occupational groups like agricultural labourers, marginal farmers and artisans marginally above the poverty line, or who may have been excluded from the BPL list to become members of the Self Help Group.

The group shall not consist of more than one member from the same family. A person should not be a member of more than one group. The BPL families must actively participate in the management and decision making, which should not ordinarily be entirely in the hands of APL families.

Why SHGs?

Mentioned below are the reasons behind proposing Self Help Groups as information gateway:

(i) SHGs belong to a particular village or a Block and they are aware about the peoples residing in the village or a Block.

(ii) SHGs are the representatives of the grass root level people; hence, their access to different household cannot be denied.

(iii) Self-help Groups can be seen involved into different activities like cattle and poultry farming, fisheries and village artisans, etc. So based on their area of interest they can be approached, as they would be the best and suitable source of information.

(iv) SHGs can act as a goldmine of information as they can give the true picture about beneficiaries for any scheme.

Examples of Organisations

Mentioned below are the organizations that considered SHGs to play a vital role in reaching target groups.

Tripura AIDS Control Society

Tripura AIDS control society undertakes preventive training and workshops regarding making people aware of HIV/AIDS. The target groups who attend workshop/training are :

Representatives of :

(i) The Panchayat Raj Institutions;
(ii) Nehru Yuva Kendra;
(iii) NSS;
(iv) Anganwadi workers;
(v) ASHA;
(vi) Drivers-government and private operators;
(vii) Tea garden workers; and
(viii) Government officers.

Tripura AIDS Control Society has also included Self-Help Group in the list. According to data of financial year 2008-09, 600 SHGs have participated in different workshops/ training. And the targets of 2010-11 are 800 SHGs. According to the Society, the reasons behind selecting SHGs are their origin from grass root level.

Hindustan Unilever Limited

HUL the number one MNC in India has used Self Help Groups to market its products to rural markets. HUL initiated "Project Shakti" which aims at involving the self help groups to sell FMCG products. Objectives of the SHGs are to encourage members to save from the daily wages or crop sales of the members and to find ways to make their collective savings grow. Adopting the direct model from AMWAY and AVON, HUL's Shakti aims at involving SHGs to buy the company's products at a cost, which they can sell to their friends and to other community groups to sell at a margin and earn a profit.

This effort is HUL's huge departure from stratified distribution channels and highly trained sales representatives and adopting a direct sales model, because of SHGs access to different rural homes.

Conclusion

Self Help Group can be very effective in dissemination of information to rural. Though we do not deny the important role three-tier Panchayat is performing, but another model could be developed where Self Help Groups could actively participate in propagation of information. And that could act as a probable solution to the problems of passing information into rural India.

REFERENCES

Feder G. Anderson J. R., Birner R., Deininger K. (2010), *Promises and Realities of Community based Agricultural Extension*, IFRI.

http://www.tn.gov.in/dtp/shg.htm

Interaction with Officials of different departments.

Literatures of Department of Agriculture, Govt. of Tripura.

14
Biodiversity and Media Advocacy Concerns: A Few Reflections

Deepak Upadhyaya

Introduction

How many people from the North-East have seen a polar bear or would miss it if it went extinct? The fragile balance of plants and animals that share the Earth took millions of years to develop. Some life-forms have persisted in nearly their original state, thus, surviving episodes of mass extinction. Some, like us, are relatively newcomers. The ones that have perished will not return. The web of life connects the smallest bacterium to the giant redwood and the whale. When we put that web in peril, we become agents of calamity.

In February 2007, the IPCC (Inter-governmental Panel on Climate Change), report gave its strongest statement on climate change and loss of biodiversity. It is said that human activities were more than 90 per cent likely to be the cause and the impacts could be abrupt and irreversible. It, further added that if steps are not taken immediately it could be disastrous. World leaders have failed to deliver commitments made in 2002 to reduce the global rate of biodiversity loss by 2010, and have instead overseen alarming biodiversity declines. More than 100 countries have signed on to the Copenhagen Accord—the non-binding agreement to combat climate change—hastily agreed to this in December (year) at a summit of world leaders. As signatories, the countries agree to cut greenhouse gas emissions to keep global average temperatures from warming more than 2 degrees Celsius. The countries that have signed up, to date are responsible for more than 80 per cent of the global emissions of such heat-trapping gases.

The Media is Still Catching Up

In journalism conflict sells more than consensus. For more than two decades, the so-called mainstream media have preached the dangers of man-made global warming, insisting that the American businesses and consumers must make massive economic sacrifices to ward off a global climate catastrophe. The journalists have been balancing science with skepticism, offsetting evidence with emotion. Since 1995, there has been a strong scientific consensus that humans influence climate change. On the other hand, companies and politicians with vested interests in maintaining their *status quo* have tried to undermine science and subvert journalism. In this process media coverage of biodiversity issues has only served to confuse and misinform public and has helped to delay actions to address climate change.

Going back to the late 1980s shows just how reporters from the developed countries have started pushing the liberal line on global warming and started setting media agenda on biodiversity concerns. Here are just some of the many examples: [please quote the references]

> *"Global warming could mean economic upheaval. It could bring suffering. It could bring starvation....The causes of global warming are no mystery. The biggest culprit is carbon dioxide, or* CO_2*, a bi-product when man burns fossil fuels to run cars or generate electricity....If we fail to act, there may be hell to pay in a hotter world....Global warming is not a fact, just a widely-held theory. The problem is, if man waits for proof, it may be too late."* (1)
>
> *"If the world is to head off the risk of global warming, with its danger of massive crop failure, or rising sea levels, or spreading starvation in the poorest countries, then America — the largest producer of the gases that cause global warming — is in the spotlight."* (2).
>
> *"After decades of rancorous debate, only a handful of the most*

> ***doctrinaire die-hards still dispute the idea that human activity is heating up the planet."*** (3)

Communication research on media advocacy for biodiversity conservation suggests that messages like those on climate change will resonate more with people if they are "framed" to suit diverse audiences, which is, told with a strong focus on a certain aspect of the story. For instance, the "scientific uncertainty frame" might struck a chord with people who do not want to change or the "catastrophe frame" might inspire inaction while the "national security frame" might inspire action from the same people.

This underscores the need for journalists to think imaginatively when proposing stories to their editors. The polar bear's prospects might be less bleak if the discourse focused more on what climate change means for price of wheat, maize or rice. Here then is the challenge for media.

While the future looks bleak, but change is not impossible. One has to focus more on the solutions to climate change and ways to adapt to its effects, and less on the frightening statistics to move from denial and despair to action. Media can help share the voices and concerns of the poorest, who are most valuable people contributed least to the problem but will suffer most from its impacts. They must adapt and they need financial support to do this. But this aspect of climate change is underreported. The voices of the valuables are rarely heard by those in power.

Communicating Biodiversity Loss

The failed UN Climate talks in Copenhagen became a prelude to the observance of the International Year of Biodiversity in 2010. The need for global political action to stop the threat of large scale biodiversity loss is growing everyday. At a meeting on biodiversity organized in January 2010 in London, the former head of the IPCC Dr. Robert Watson had warned that the damage to the natural environment was approaching a point of no-return and urged world community and politicians for an urgent need to take action.

Watson further echoed a concern that at the root is the conflict between the need to change our use of natural resources and the desire to maintain current forms of economic growth in both developed and developing countries. He, further, feels that part of the answer in each case lies in enhancing the media's ability to communicate messages emerging from underlying science, so that these reports accurately reflect both the urgency of the situation, and how ordinary people's lives may be affected.

Getting these messages across is no easy task. And so far, in the case of biodiversity, efforts have largely failed. It is already clear that governments signed up to the Convention on Biological Diversity (CBD) have missed their 2010 targets, set in 2002 achieving a significant reduction in the rate of biodiversity loss. "Climate change is one of the most important challenges humanity faces today", said Felipe Calderon Hinojosa, President of Mexico.

As part of signing on, countries also listed their national goals for emission reductions. Mexico, for its part, pledged to cut 50 million metric tonnes of greenhouse gas emissions annually by 2012. The U.S. pledged to reduce emissions by 4 per cent below 1990 levels, pending legislation, whereas China promised cuts of 40 to 45 per cent of the total CO_2 per unit of economic production, so-called carbon intensity. And it will fall to Calderon and his colleagues in the Mexican Government as hosts of the next climate change negotiation meetings in Cancun in November 2010 to continue progress towards an international binding agreement. After all, without a legally binding treaty there will be no accountability on greenhouse gas emissions, warned United Nations Secretary General Ban Ki-Moon at the conference. Citing the various national action plans announced since Copenhagen, and in some cases listed therein, Desai, a former U.N. Under Secretary General argued that "what really matters is the degree of legal force behind national action", such as India's commitment to at least a 25 per cent reduction in its carbon intensity. That means U.S. governmental action will be vitally important; details of legislation to reduce Greenhouse Gas (GHG) emissions are currently being worked on in the Senate while the House of Representatives has passed a bill that would match the Barak Obama administration's pledge under the Copenhagen Accord. "It is up to the U.S. now to cut our carbon emissions, if the rest of the world can reasonably be expected to do anything", said climate expert, Mark Cane of Columbia University's Earth Institute.

At the same time, the U.S. is pushing for international monitoring and verification of emission reductions in emerging countries, such as India, China, and Brazil. But political scientist Zha Daojiong of Peking University noted from Beijing that "in the West, if something is not put into law then that won't work." In China, when the government comes out and says, 'We have a target', we are going to do this, because the culture and political institutions are different. They are going to do it look at the past 30 years".

The key to doing it, according to Calderon, is "to find out a new model of development that will allow us to grow in harmony with the environment, which will imply a new Industrial Revolution based on *low carbon growth*."

In essence, the challenge is "how to link Fighting poverty, which is a main concern of developing countries, with Fighting climate change", he added. Mexico has begun to address it by providing direct cash payments to impoverished residents to purchase energy-efficient goods or *preserve local forests*.

A bigger part of any linkage between Fighting climate change and poverty alleviation will be building a more comprehensive energy infrastructure. "When hundreds of millions of Indians *don't have access to electricity*, it's unrealistic to expect India to cut growth", noted Jyoti Parikh, Executive Director of Integrated Research and Action for Development, New Delhi. But economic growth can be paired with climate change solutions. For example, the Government of India has instituted a goal of 20,000 mega watts of new *solar power* installations by 2022. "With the solar energy programme, the strongest pressure is not from green groups," Desai noted. "The corporate sector in India is showing huge interest in getting into this area." At the same time, locally appropriate technologies must play a role, such as using cattle to drive a generator or using livestock *waste to produce biogas*, Devin Narang, Chairman of the Freeplay Group, a maker of consumer electronics, New Delhi.

Using *clean technologies to promote economic growth* is already a reality. India has a long way to go. While China has surpassed the U.S. and other nations in total clean energy investment—securing $ 34.6 billion in investments and finance for wind, solar and hydropower, among other renewable energy technologies in 2009 alone. The key will be further speed and scale in efforts to reduce Greenhouse Gas (GHG) emissions from energy, agriculture, buildings and other sectors. "All the science shows that technology is not a silver bullet. We'll have to see lifestyle changes, as well", said Johan Rockstrom, Executive Director of the Stockholm Environment Institute. "This is the most decisive decade, when we have to start bending the curve on Greenhouse Gas emissions and biodiversity. What if we push this too far"?

The scientific community has not been able to effectively communicate its concerns to decision makers—at least not in a way that sufficiently prioritizes biodiversity conservation within a political agenda predominantly concerned with employment and economic growth. Discussions on a new set of targets for protecting biodiversity over the next decade are already underway, are due to be agreed. The new targets must not only be more realistic but must also be accompanied by a more sophisticated communications strategy.

The new strategy to disseminate communication messages for bringing seedy transformation to halt further biodiversity degradation must address the weakness found in current approaches. For example, the issues which scientists think most important often seem abstract and far removed from the day-to-day concerns of the ordinary people. The rate at which the world is losing species is a typical example. Forging an effective communication strategy that avoids these pitfalls is clearly one of the biggest challenges facing the biodiversity community as it plans for the next decade. And, if researchers are to rise to the challenge, they must first firm up the scientific case for action. The damage that recently aired scientific flaws are causing climate change campaigns is a reminder that, with the stakes as high as they are, sloppy scientific reasoning can have a broad and lasting impact. Equally important is the need to embed this scientific evidence into viable but sustainable economic growth and development strategies. And that means generating a public discourse that directly relates the needs of the environment to social priorities such as jobs, food and health. The components for such a dialogue—such as how natural products are potential sources of new medicines– already exist. But much more needs to be done to forge these into a viable and effective political strategy to reverse current trends.

Media Coverage

Journalists worldwide stand accused of creating hype by focusing too much on attention-seeking issues, and in the process marginalizing "less glamorous" topics such as biodiversity, that are critical to secure livelihoods—a vital foundation in which humanity is built. And the North-Eastern region is no exception. It seems, apart from a handful of journalists working in the North-East region, the media rarely tells the story of biodiversity loss in depth. Journalists could do much to improve their coverage, to hold politicians to account on the promises they have made, and to empower people to make better informed choices about their lives. Where a fair amount of reporting has been done, the account has been mostly flat and one-sided. The untold side of the story needs to be told if only the media is all aware of its social responsibility role in such a perilous time, when the world is in between the sea and the devil.

Stories often describe a promise such as researchers "bioprospecting" for potential drugs from rainforest plants in Assam, Tripura, Arunachal Pradesh, Manipur and Mizoram which has world famous biodiversity hotspots, or a threat such as "biopiracy", sale in animal body parts, rampant poaching of rare and endangered animals like tiger, gangetic dolphins and rhinoceros, etc., when researchers misappropriate biological resources and, or traditional knowledge for commercial gain. But only rarely do the press in the region present a balanced appraisal of two competing claims. The press can have a big role in investigating a case of a sudden death of a rhino in Kaziranga National Park, the administration say it as natural death, whereas locals believe it to be a case of poaching In both of the dominant narratives, the negative and the positive, there is often another, untold side to the story. The North-East is one of the most biodiversity-rich regions in the country, according to Endangered Wildlife Trust (EWT), which laments that biodiversity, is under great pressure. Intellectuals say loss of natural habitat is one of the major causes of the country's biodiversity loss. Yet, some observers believe that very little reporting has been done in this regard to highlight the problem. Biodiversity reporting in North-East is concise and outward and often lacks human nature—a trend blamed on lack of interest and inadequate skills and resources to undertake a deep investigative report. The few reports get published in newspapers of the region are basically elite/politician or announcement framed. Reports of biodiversity loss rarely ask hard questions about how much we can afford to lose. They tend not to mention that some biodiversity loss may be essential to sustain and improve human livelihoods. The case of shrinking Deepar *Beel* near Guwahati is a case in point. Journalists from NE rarely cover these issues in depth, but this is perhaps unsurprising. And the few positive stories that get published, have to compete with other news items for space, rarely spare time to analyse whether environmental conservation initiatives or apparently biodiversity-friendly products are fair or truly sustainable, and who stands to gain from them. It seems Radio and TV, especially cable TV channels operating in the region has no regard for social responsibility ethics. In a cut throat competition to attract more and more eye balls and garner higher TRPS, they have forgotten that environment issues are not worthy to be covered unless there is sensation angle in it.

A story of how humanity depends on nature but is driving its destruction needs to be told in a more sophisticated way. While warnings about the current extinction crisis do hit the headlines, they tend to melt away from the media agenda as soon as the day, say Environment day, Water Day, Earth Day is over. What is often missing is the human angle, and this serves to distance the problem from people's minds.

There are plenty of opportunities to tell stories with strong human angles that demonstrate directly the benefits the natural world brings to local people's lives. These stories also need to be told to the people what is at stake if the destruction of nature goes unchecked.

Biodiversity is Much More than just Wildlife and Wild Places

However, reporting mostly on climate change and the plight of rare charismatic species such as tigers, or on threats to tropical forests and coral reefs is not enough. Looking at the media now; it would be easy to assume that climate change is the sole global environmental challenge. Biodiversity means more than just wildlife or wild places. It encompasses the full variety of genes, species and ecosystems on the planet. It includes the crops we eat and the insects that pollinate them, the plants we use for both traditional medicines and improve human livelihoods. It would do well, if journalists report extensively on many issues revolving landscapes, forests, fringe village dwellers, river siltation, floods etc. Once, the NE region of the country was very rich in biodiversity species or habitats because humans have not modified the environment. The media also tends not to air voices and views of those most dependent on nature, such as indigenous people and rural communities in developing countries.

Experts Need to Communicate Better

Scientists and environmentalists are people, who are often custodians of biodiversity and have a wealth of relevant traditional knowledge, but they have little say in deciding what is important to save, and how to conserve and make best use of it. They have the knowledge but their scientific knowledge is not intelligible to the reporters who might not be educated in environment sciences and as a consequent they might not be able to perceive, retain and reproduce the same in their news stories what they have understood. As a result, what the common people will understand will be obviously less than what the scribes have themselves understood. This is how, the scientific issues like environmental degradation, biodiversity loss and its ecological impact with all its subtlety is seldom properly grasped by the people at large. If this be the reality, how would these issues go on to climb the hierarchy ladder of social agenda, media agenda, national agenda and international agenda. The media agenda of today will become national agenda tomorrow, which will command political attention and resources would be pooled to Fight biodiversity conservation programmes tooth and nail. The general people fail to appreciate the gravity of the issues partly because of lack of information. Teach them why and how they should conserve biodiversity and they will work towards it earnestly. After all who would not love flora and fauna that grows in the small portion of earth which belongs to them!

Putting the blame solely on journalists seems unfair, partially, because experts are also to be blamed, for not properly communicating complex biodiversity issues to the reporters in a lucid manner intelligible to them. Experts, whom journalists rely on for information, have often failed to communicate these issues in a meaningful way and the element of *noise (communication barrier)* cannot be ignored here, altogether. The experts would have done more by describing the importance of nature to human well-being and explained the real costs of its loss. It would be advisable to the journalists and media professionals to avoid jargon—including the word "biodiversity", which is often and poorly understood by layman. Journalists need to gear up to tell this story better by learning more about the issues and framing them in ways that make sense to their audiences. Researchers and policymakers must also do more to explain the importance of nature to people, using jargon-free language and examples that help make the issues real.... Key to successful communication will be an ability to show that people are part of biodiversity, reliant on its richness and deeply affected by its loss. This will grow in importance in the coming years, as major international storylines unfold and climate change takes hold.

The introduction of biodiversity beat in the press of the region would have been interesting but it also remains that climate change reporting is also complex business. However, with proper training and instruction, the media coverage, would have improved. There has to be a *balanced reporting*, that is, it should not only speak of the *"catastrophic narrative"* (reporting that depends on scenarios of potential imminent disaster for audience interest) but also in the lines of *"emphatic narratives"* (reporting that encourages action and empowerment). Balanced reporting ensure relevance to audiences, including ways to address climate change that might bring benefits, is a challenge, along with raising the profile of adaptation and the perspectives of the economically poor.

A content analysis survey of studies on climate change reporting shows that, though the media of climate change profile has never been higher, the news may not be reaching all people equally and is particularly missing in economically poorer communities of country. Senior editors and reporters often do not have science backgrounds to report on highly politicized climate issues. It also reveals that the media's need to appear unbiased has led to imbalances and public confusion, ignoring presentation of the scientific consensus, sometimes due to corporate vested interests. Training and access to experts will be key especially for under-resourced reporters in the poorest countries. With a little time and training, non-scientific journalists can cover climate change well.

The use of "the catastrophe frame" results in narratives those are "confusing, contradictory and chaotic, with the likely result that the public feels disempowered and uncompelled to act". Suggested alternatives to the discourse on catastrophe are: (1) focus more on the solutions to climate change and ways to adapt to its effects, and less on the frightening statistics—to move from denial and despair to action; and (2) connect in minds of audience the emissions in one place and impacts in another, and to share the voices and concerns of the economically poorest, most vulnerable people who have contributed least to the problem but will suffer most from its impacts.

The ICT and internet-based new media could also be of immense help to tide the wave of biodiversity degradation. Citizen journalism and the power of bloggers, who create rumour and dispel rumour by revealing its origins, could be harnessed for the cause. The media messages can have the effect of behaviour change, for some people some of the time, but the media gives the public mixed messages on climate change and includes advertising that might contravene climate change messages. However, growing demand for "green" (environmentally safer) products and environmental news may result in changes in media content.

Media reports should provide a positive parallel to the disaster narrative, one that highlights the economic and social benefits of preserving the natural world, including analyzing whether conservation initiatives or apparently biodiversity-friendly products are fair or truly sustainable, who stands to gain from them, who are the custodians of biodiversity that have a wealth of relevant traditional knowledge, and whether they have a say in deciding what is important to save, and how to conserve and make best use of it.

Media should tell stories that relate the wealth of nature to people's everyday lives, using the lenses of money, human rights, international politics, climate change, health, and religion. Befitting example to illustrate the point is the story of the economic value of the natural goods and services the mangroves forests in India provide. Local communities have for generations obtained food, medicines and building materials from the mangroves. Many species of commercially important fish breed among the mangrove trees' submerged roots and the forests help to remove toxins from rivers before they enter the sea. The trees also protect coastal areas from the force of cyclones and tidal surges. Research has shown that the economic value of the natural goods and services mangroves provide is many times greater than what their conversion to agriculture or shrimp farming would bring. Sadly, it took the devastation wrought by the 2004 tsunami in the Indian Ocean for many policy-makers to realize the risks of mangrove deforestation.

Thus, we have seen that the structure of the media itself is a big hindrance to serious and systematic coverage of biodiversity. Noted journalist P. Sainath who had done excellent field level coverage of poverty and deprivations referring to the absence of reporting on the poor in India says: "You see it in the simplest and most direct way: the organization of beats. Many beats have become extinct. Take the agriculture beat—in most newspapers the idea does not exist anymore. If you lack correspondents on these beats, you are saying 70 per cent of the people in this country do not matter".

Conclusion

Environment concerns and biodiversity conservation is quite a tricky question as the issue covers almost each and every walk of our lives. As communication is highly interdisciplinary medium, there is the need for utilizing the vast potential of mass media for expanding the cause of biodiversity concerns. There is an urgent need for incorporating the subject in the curriculums in the courses of study in Journalism and Mass Communication in universities and colleges. India urgently requires a media literacy movement.

The media suffers from yet another serious structural deficiency. The media does an excellent job of covering events. But media fails in covering the process that leads to an event. In fact the procedural coverage shall prevent a crisis like biodiversity degradation. Media also suffers from a deep elitist bias. This bias is blatantly clear when the human rights of the rich and the poor are under question.. Nothing wrong in upholding the rights of the privileged, but the rights of the underprivileged should receive same attention if not greater. Media advocacy should, therefore, become the voice of the voiceless. Media also suffers from a content disease called celebrity gauging and crime chasing syndrome. In such a media milieu, biodiversity coverage is an obvious casualty. The civil society should act as watchdog.

At the same time it should also be kept in mind that there can be no alternative than using mass media vehicles for spreading awareness about biodiversity concerns. This would mean proper training and allotment of beats to journalists to cover the issue on a war front until a public agenda is not set in motion in the society. Only an all out effort like this can save us from the disastrous future as echoed by Watson and IPCC. If the failure in Copenhagen can act as a wake-up call to the biodiversity conservation across the globe, that itself would have been a positive achievement.

REFERENCES

Don, Harrison, narrating CNN's Primetime Climate in *Crisis Special*, August 1, 1989.

Ned, Potter, ABC reporter on *World News Tonight*, April 7, 1992.

Michael, Lemonick, *Time Magazine* in a special edition for Earth Day, 2000.

Boykoff, M.T. and Roberts J.T., Media coverage of climate change: current trends, strengths and weakness background paper published by United Nations Development Programme—Human Development Report, 2007.

Lester, Libby and Cottle, Simon, Visualizing Climate Change: TV news and ecological citizenship, published in the *International Journal of Communication* Vol. 3 (2009), pp. 920-936.

Antilla, L. (2004). Climate of scepticism: U.S. newspaper coverage of the science of climate change. *Global Environmental Change* 15, pp. 338-352.

Barthes, R. (1977). Rhetoric of the image. In R. Barthes, *Image, Music, Text* (pp. 32- 51). London: Fontana.

Beck, U. (1992). *Risk Society: Towards a New Modernity*. London: Sage.

Beck, U. (1999). World Risk Society. Cambridge, UK: *Polity*.

Boykoff, M., & Boykoff, J. (2004). *Balance as Bias: Global Warming and the US.*, Presitige Press, Global Environment Change 14, pp. 125-136.

Boykoff, M., & Boykoff, J. (2007). Climate Change and Journalistic Norms: A Case Study of the US Mass Media Coverage. Goeforum 38, pp. 1190-1204.

Chapman, G.; Kumar, K.; Fraser, C; and Gaber, I. (1997). *Environmentalism and the Mass Media: The North South Divide*, London, Routlage.

Part 4
Biodiversity and Human Interface

15
An Account of Local Rice Germplasm for Abiotic Stress Tolerance in Tripura

M. Datta, S.P. Das and *S.V. Ngachan*

Introduction

Major advances have been made in increasing rice production worldwide as a result of large-scale adoption of modern high-yielding varieties and improved cultural practices. World rice production increased from 257 million tonnes in 1966 to 560 million tonnes in 1997. The present world population of 6 billion is likely to reach 8 billion by 2025. More than 70 per cent of this increase will occur in Asia where rice is the staple food. It is estimated that we will have to produce 50 per cent more rice to satisfy the growing demand for food. This increased demand will have to be met from less land, with less water, less labour and less chemicals. Thus, the challenges for the rice improvement are to develop varieties with higher yield potential, more durable resistance to diseases and insects, and higher levels of tolerance to abiotic stresses.

The collection of rice at International Rice Research Institute, Manila, Philippines is of genetically diverse in nature because the acquisition and field collection efforts were implemented in the appropriate places and at opportune time before advanced genetic erosion occurred (Chang *et al.*, 1989). However, it has been estimated that a total of 100,000 rice cultivars exist in Asia alone (Chang, 1985). Therefore, the collection and acquisition of rice germplasm must be a continuous effort. Moreover, the important point is that only a small proportion of the total genetic diversity of rice has been conserved (Chang *et al.*, 1989).

The exact number of Oryza species is controversial. However, the genus Oryza is generally thought to include between 20 to 24 species. Approximately 15 species have the same diploid number (2n=24) as *O. sativa;* whereas, nine species are tetraploid (2n=48). Rice germplasm collection in India was initiated in 1911 and the list of rice collection is presented in Table 15.1.

Table 15.1 : Rice Germplasm Collection in India

S. No.	Agency/ Area	Year	No. of collections
1.	Base collection from Coimbatore (AC)	1911-47	2,000
2.	Jeypore Botanical Survey (JBS)	1955-59	1,745
3.	Manipur Collection (MNP)	1965-70	904
4.	West Bengal Collection Chinsurah, Bankura and Kalimpong	1960-71	5,550
5.	Assam Rice Collection (ARC)	1968-71	6,630
6.	Dr. RIchharia's Collection from M.P.	1971-81	19,000
7.	Collection from various States (Upland)	1976-77	1,431
8.	National Collaborative Programme (NCS)	1978-80	6,439
9.	U. P. Hill collection by Pantnagar Univ. VPKAS, Almora	1978-90	2,580
10.	Lowland and saline types from Orissa	1980-82	300
11.	Collection by NBPGR from different parts of India	1976-84	8,353
12.	Collection by P.A.U., Kapurthala	1982-84	1,178
13.	Collection by H.A.U., Kaul	1982-86	960
14.	Collection by NBPGR/CRRI from Goa, Gujarat, Karnataka, Sikkim, Mizoram, Arunachal Pradesh and Orissa	1984-88	3,092
15.	Collection from Rajasthan and Maharashtra	1980-90	3,489
16.	Collection by NBPGR from Orissa, W.B.	1986-95	3,122
17.	Collection by CRRI from Orissa	1990-95	717
18.	Wild Rice Collection by NBPGR/IRRI/IGKWI CRRI	1984-97	840
		Total	68,330

The number of germplasm deposited in the National Gene Bank is estimated to be around 42,000 and out of which collection from Tripura Centre is 60 (Table 15.2).

The variable traits of both biotic and abiotic stresses present in rice germplasms collected in different places in India are presented in Table 15.3.

Table 15.2 : Number of Germplasm Accessions Deposited in National Gene Bank

Centre	*No. of Accessions*
NBPGR, Trichur	1,086
NBPGR, Cuttack	1,299
NBPGR, Shillong	1,270
NBPGR, Bhowali	270
NBPGR, New Delhi	15
IARI New Delhi	20
ICAR Res. Comp.,Tripura	60
DRR, Hyderabad	3,900
CRRI Cuttack	21,874
IGKW, Raipur	8,712
MSSRF, Chennai	43
IRRI Philippines	3.455
Total	**42,004**

It may be pertinent to mention that the desirable traits for rice collection in North-East India are as follows:

- Tolerance to low temperature at vegetative stage.
- Tolerance to low temperature at reproductive stage.
- High spike fertility at low temperature.
- Tolerance to lodging.
- Glutinous.
- Higher yield in low land.
- Dwarf.
- Drought tolerance.
- Tolerance to iron toxicity.
- Aroma.

Materials and Methods

Local rice varieties collected in Tripura (Sardana, 1997) are 142 in numbers and the varieties are as follows:

Aduma-1, Aduma-2, Abar-b1, Abar-b2, Arsinsail-1, Arsinsail-2, Billrong, Beti, Bethi, Badia-1, Badia-2, Boral Binni-1, 2, 3, Badia Bichi, Binni Rangi, Berain, Binni Goria, Binni Marang, Binni Karma, Bangbuh-1, 2, 3, 4, Bhusaki-1, 2, Charui-1, 2, 3, 4, Chalti Rangi 1, 2, Chanmuri, Chingrijail, Dhup Amli, Dhup Gellong, Dula Kamrang, Dullo-A, Dyngri, Dhamodhar, Ermala, Fareta-1, 2, Full Badam,

Gellong-1, 2, 3, 4, 5, 6, 7, Gellong Kupri, Gori Gellong, Garo Malati, Goduma, Guisail, Harpi, Jhum Malati, Jumira Red-1, 2, Jagli Boro, Jali, Kamrang-1, 2, 3, Kalobrak, Kaltongman, Kalamunia, Kalia Surit-1, 2, 3 Kalahatya, Kong Koi, Kang Poi, Kali Kasha, Kubra,

Table 15.3 : Variable Traits of Rice Germplasm in India

Collection	*Traits*	
CRRI (old collection)	Abiotic stresses	Upland with adequate moisture, Upland with moisture stress, Saline and alkaline soils, low-lying areas with waterlogging flood and deep water conditions
	Biotic stresses	Blast, Helminthosporiosis, Bacterial leaf blight, Stem rot, Stem borer, Gall midge
CRRI (JBS collection)	Agronomic/ yield	High number of grains per panicle, high 1000-grain weight, Early and good tillering, Scented kernel
ARC	Biotic stresses	Blast, Bacterial blight, Gall midge, RTV
	Agronomic/ yield	Dwarf with Indica type grain, Dwarf with Japonica type grain, Javanica plant habit, Glaberrima type plant habit
	Abiotic stresses Biotic stresses	Tolerant to flood Biotic stresses Blast, Bacterial blight, Stem rot, Stem borer, Gall midge, RTV, WBPH, brown plant hopper, Multiple resistance to GM, SB, BLB, BLS, BL, RTV
DRR / ARC	Biotic stresses	Blast, Bacterial leaf blight, Stem borer, Gall midge, RTV, Green leaf hopper
DRR	Biotic stresses	Blast, Bacterial leaf blight, Sheath blight, RTV, Green leaf hopper, Stem borer, WBPH, Brown plant hopper, Gall midge, Leaf folder, Yellow stem borer
ICAR Research Complex for NEH Region	Agronomic/ yield	Rainfed upland, lowland, earliness, Non-lodging tall habit, finegrain, glutinous rice, scented rice, Suitable for high altitudes (1300 m), Suitable for medium altitudes (800-1300 m), Suitable for low altitudes (<800 m)
	Abiotic stresses	Drought tolerance, tolerance to cold at flowering, tolerance to iron toxicity,
Raipur	Biotic stresses Abiotic stresses Biotic stresses	Blast Drought Bacterial blight, Panicle midge, Stem borer, Gall midge, WBPH, Brown plant hopper, Brown spot
Assam	Agronomic/ yield Abiotic stresses Biotic stresses	High protein content, High aromatic oil content Drought tolerance, flood, submergence, low light Biotic stresses Blast, Bacterial leaf blight, Sheath blight, Root knot nematode, Brown plant hopper,

Kanchali Bitchi-1, 2, Khurpi, Katak Tara, Kartik Sail, Lati Sail, Lai Gelong, Maidani-1, 2, 3, 4, Maro, Maima, Maibra-1, 2, 3, Mamyyathiok, Makumymokul, Mamysuprang, Mai Misaria, Maichikan, Mirikarak, Munri-1, 2, Metisera, Maiwasa-1, 2, 3, Mulasail-1, 2, Maimikarma, Mipia, Maimi, Mamimasag, Maimisahay, Monobakra, Moriphi, Matri Mangal, Mali, Nowrah, Nowgri, Pan Bawh, Pan Foophag, Plapin, Pitaram, Rangkai-1, 2, Reliong, Reliong Khasa, Ranga Gellong, Sarendyma, Sonamukhi, Symrit-B, Subhashi, Tipra Binni, Topra Binni-2, Thoripi, Țangar, Trical-1, 2, 3, Thakurbhog, Tarakok.

The variability in grain size/shape is quite large and such variability is depicted below :

Fig. 15.1 : A view of local rice grain in Tripura

The field experiment was conducted at ICAR Research Complex, Lembucherra, Tripura, Fifty-eight local rice genotypes were evaluated under treatments of no P and 30 kg P_2O_5/ha. A uniform dose of 60 kg N and 30 kg P_2O_5 /ha was applied. The experiment was laid out in a randomized block design with 3 replications. Grain yield was recorded at 14 per cent moisture. Rice grain dried at 60°C was digested and analysed for P (Jackson,

1967). Response of some local rice germplasm was also studied with no zinc and $ZnSO_4$ (20 mg/kg). Datta and Dhiman (2001) reported the significant response of 15 kg $ZnSO_4$/ha to rice grown in acid soils of Tripura. Similarly, pot experiment with the soils (Typic Paleochralf) having 14.6 mg./kg DTPA-Fe was conducted in local rice in simulated iron (60 mg Fe/kg) toxic condition and per cent change in grain yield of rice was recorded at maturity. Ravichandran *et al.* (2000) reported that the effective anaerobiosis resulted in the reduction of Fe^{3+} to Fe^{2+} leading to high concentration of ferrous form of iron in waterlogged soil.

Results and Discussion

In acid soils of Tripura, P is one of the limiting factors for crop productivity and more than 60 per cent soils are highly deficient in available P (< 10 kg/ha) (Laskar *et al.*,1983). Further, a high P-fixation upon application of soluble phosphatic fertilizers causes its severity (Datta *et al.*, 1992). On P-deficiency in acid soils, red/ purple colour may develop in rice.

Fig. 15.2 : P-deficiency symptom in rice

It is evident from the perusal of the data presented in Table 15.4 that some local rice genotypes like 'Aduma', 'Badia', 'Batteswar', 'Bhushakhi', 'Guasail', 'Garo Malati', 'Kangpui', 'Kanchali Bitchi', 'Kartik Sail', 'Latika', 'Subashi', 'Thakurbhog' underwent a decline in grain production ranging from 4 to 74 per cent upon P-application thus indicating tolerance to P deficiency. Rasi, an improved rice variety was kept as control produced 29 per cent decline in grain yield upon application of phosphate. All other varieties showed an increase in grain yield, indicating their persistent response to P-application. P content as estimated in grain, showed a wide variation among the genotypes and was

Table 15.4: Effect of P-application on Performance of Local Rice Germplasm

Genotype	Grain yield (g/plant)		P-content in grain (mg/kg)		Change over control (%)	
	Control	Treated	Control	Treated	Grain yield	P-content
'Aduma'	2.80	2.95	69	82	(–)5	19
'Arsin Sail-I'	1.97	261.00	88	89	33	1
'Arsin Sail-2'	1.72	2.43	49	70	41	43
'Badia'	2.78	2.67	69	148	(–)4	115
'Bethi-5'	1.32	4.04	298	447	206	46
'Batteswar'	4.38	2.48	43	48	(–)43	12
'Bhushakhi'	1.58	0.53	36	37	(–)66	3
'Binni Guria'	3.79	2.37	27	30	11	25
'Binni Karma'	1.11	3.36	720	1326	203	216
'Binni Merang'	5.01	5.72	2361	2401	14	2
'Binni Rangai'	4.51	5.00	39	52	11	33
'Biral Binni-1'	2.37	2.70	333	436	14	31
'Dauri'	2.14	3.46	41	54	62	32
'Dhup Gellong'	1.75	3.75	317	317	114	0
'Dulla Kamang'	1.62	3.29	165	186	103	13
'Farete'	1.01	1.85	37	41	83	11
'Full Badam'	1.16	2.41	32	36	108	13
'Garo Mality'	3.87	1.48	34	49	(–)62	44
'Gellong'	0.95	1.39	212	376	46	77
'Gellong Kupu'	0.99	1.54	27	37	56	37
'Gori Gellong'	2.95	2.07	33	48	70	45
'Guasail'	2.08	1.12	32	75	(–)46	134
'Guria Karma'	1.73	2.99	24	31	73	29
'Irrimala'	1.18	21.93	102	244	148	139
'Irrimala-I'	2.97	0.93	227	329	(–)69	45
'Kalahatia'	2.39	3.77	31	125	58	303
'Kalia Surit'	0.96	2.74	199	272	185	37
'Kalikhasa'	0.59	2.09	28	42	254	50
'Kanchali Bitchi'	1.69	1.17	27	41	(–)31	52
'Kangpui'	3.06	2.61	120	341	(–)15	184
'Kaminisail'	0.71	1.78	309	475	150	54

(Contd.)

Table 15.4: (*Contd.*)

Genotype	*Grain yield (g/plant)*		*P-content in grain (mg/kg)*		*Change over control (%)*	
	Control	*Treated*	*Control*	*Treated*	*Grain yield*	*P-content*
'Kamrang'	0.95	3.02	24	36	218	50
'Kartiksail'	3.27	2.92	140	265	(–)11	89
'Khasa'	1.55	2.59	267	299	67	12
'Khurpi'	1.42	1.61	320	419	14	31
'Laitika'	3.12	2.33	53	115	(–)25	117
'Latisail'	2.36	0.61	208	222	(–)74	7
'Maichika'	1.79	1.87	24	26	4	8
'Mality'	3.42	2.06	1020	1151	(–)40	13
'Matrimangal'	1.63	1.71	45	53	66	18
'Mibra'	0.59	2.46	24	35	317	46
'Mibra-2'	1.03	1.15	388	413	12	6
'Mipla-1'	0.69	1.23	70	105	78	50
'Monobakra'	3.24	5.41	40	44	67	10
Mulaisailo'	3.26	3.07	26	29	4	12
'Mulasail'	1.09	2.77	55	87	154	58
'Nizersail'	1.25	2.54	55	75	103	36
'Plapia-1'	1.85	1.98	209	647	7	209
'Ranga Gellong'	1.95	2.29	30	32	17	7
'Sonamukhi'	1.46	0.91	25	30	(–)38	20
'Subhashi'	1.99	1.74	313	516	(–)13	65
'Tarical'	1.24	3.38	21	33	172	57
Thakurbhog'	1.45	0.81	491	539	(–)44	10
'Composalek'	2.19	3.85	100	113	76	13
'Goduma'	1.05	1.85	236	342	76	45
'Ngoba'	2.14	2.41	42	70	13	67
'BG 34-8'	1.09	1.25	76	174	15	129
'Rangia'	2.09	2.10	2095	2265	0.5	8
'AR-11' (HYV)	0.94	2.78	39	52	195	33
'TRC-246'	–	–	–	–	–	–
'C-10' (HYV)	1.18	1.39	2558	2612	18	2
'Rasi' (Control)	2.57	1.83	103	141	(–) 29	37
	SE (+)	CD(5%)	–	–	–	–
'Variety'	0.35	0.69	–	–	–	–
'Treatment'	0.06	0.12	–	–	–	–
'Variety x Treatment'	0.49	0.97	–	–	–	–

raised upon P application. Rice genotypes that showed a decline in grain yield also produced 3 to 115 per cent increase in P content upon P application. So this tolerant rice genotypes could be a good source of donor genes for development of rice varieties tolerant to P deficient condition.

Zinc deficiency is the most widespread nutritional disorder in Indian soils for rice cultivation as about 43 per cent soil samples in India have available Zn content in the deficient range (Takkar, 1996). Data on the response of Zn to local rice cultivars were presented in Table 15.5. It was found that some local varieties producing 5.7 to 56.7 per cent and 5.5 to 50.0 per cent decline in grain and straw yield upon application of $ZnSO_4$, were tolerant to Zn stress. The varieties which did not require the supply of additional Zn, showing their tolerant behaviour in Zn stress condition, were 'Dhupani', 'Thakurbhog', 'Binni Merang', 'Kalikhasa', 'Nigersail', 'Laitika', 'Guria Karama', 'Binni Guria', 'Biral Binni'. Such Zn stress condition was more pronounced in lowlands having abundance in Fe and Mn as reported by Datta and Dhiman (2001).

Fig. 15.3 : Zinc application to rice in Tripura

Fe toxicity is a phenomenon generally occurring in lowlands having impeded drainage. Reduction of Fe oxyhydroxides and its enhanced solubility in wetland rice cultivation under anaerobic condition (Schwab and Lindsay, 1983) often caused Fe toxicity (Ponnamperuma *et al.*, 1955; Moor and Patrick, 1989). Available Fe varied from 7.6 to 21.9 mg/kg in acid soils of Tripura (Datta and Munna Ram, 1993), indicating the presence of adequate amounts as its critical limit was 4.5 mg/kg. Occurrence of Fe toxicity is widely spread in lowlands comprising 40.05 per cent of total

Table 15.5 : Response of Zn to local rice cultivars

Cultivar	Treatment			
	Grain (g/pot)	Straw (g/pot)	Grain (g/pot)	Straw (g/pot)
'Sonamukhi'	15.0	57.0	26.75	96.25
'Arsin Sail'	12.8	89.0	19.0	98.75
'Billrong'	11.0	39.25	14.25	53.75
'Kanchati Bithchi'	14.3	10.80	20.0	130.0
'Gori Gellong'	11.75	86.25	13.5	90.0
'Kartik Sail'	16.25	56.25	18.0	68.75
'Kalia Surit'	23.50	88.50	29.75	92.5
'Jatihet'	24.50	56.75	29.75	97.5
'Lati Sail'	17.25	79.25	24.75	91.25
'Dhupami'	14.0	45.5	6.25	32.0
'Kamini Sail'	19.75	73.75	27.0	87.5
'Binni'	16.0	67.5	30.0	98.75
'Thakurbhog'	21.75	71.25	17.5	60.0
'Binni Merang'	30.0	102.5	13.0	51.25
'Monobakra'	6.75	31.25	21.0	62.50
'Kali Khasa'	17.5	72.5	15.5	66.75
'Niger Sail'	21.75	91.25	20.5	86.25
'Laitika'	23.75	78.75	17.5	60.0
'Guria Karma'	14.75	50.0	11.0	52.5
'Binni Guria'	25.5	77.5	18.0	76.25
'Biral Binni'	25.5	77.5	16.75	55.0
'Binni Karma'	20.5	93.75	23.0	80.0
'Matri Mangal'	13.0	52.50	16.0	70.0
Variety Treatment	6.09	30.17	–	–
CD (P=0.05)	8.61	42.67	–	–

cultivable area, thereby inducing toxicity symptoms in most of the improved rice cultures grown in areas having impeded drainage (Datta and Laskar, 1992). On the other hand, available Zn was found negatively correlated (Datta and Munna Ram, 1993) with available Fe and Mn, indicating antagonistic relationship. The mechanism by which iron toxicity symptoms become prominent in lowland soils in Tripura is illustrated in Fig. 15.4.

Iron toxicity symptoms in rice are as follows :

- Tiny brown spots develop on the leaf tip and spread towards the leaf.
- Leaves turn orange brown and die.
- Stunted growth and greatly reduced tillering.
- Coarse, sparse and damaged root growth.

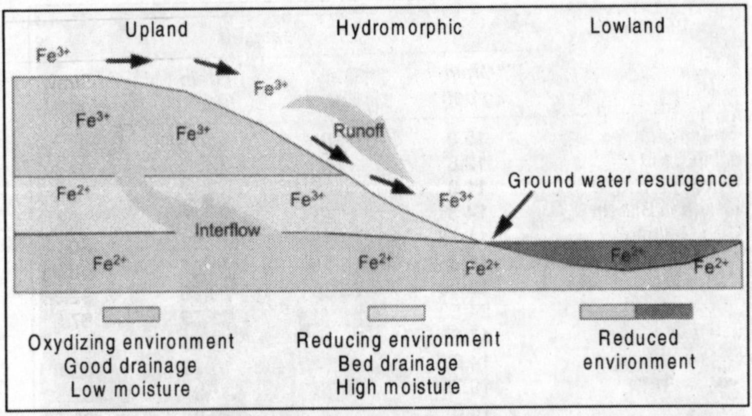

Fig. 15.4 : A view of toposequence showing movement of iron and reduction process

Fig 15.5 : A view of flooded rice field with high iron concentration

Under toxic condition simulated in pot experiment (Table 15.6), it was found that some local varieties like 'Arsinsail', 'Billrong', 'Binni Merang', 'Chingrijoli', 'Gelong Kufru', 'Kaliahatie', 'Kanchani Bitchi', 'Lathisail', 'Maliti, Nigersail' producing an increase in grain yield from 8.24 to 65.04 per cent upon application of Fe, were tolerant in nature.

Fig. 15.6 : Rice plant with bronzed flag leaf and small panicles in the area with iron toxicity

Similarly Patra and Mohanty (1988) reported a striking variability in critical Fe level for inducing toxicity in rice cultures (Table 15.3). As indicated from the data (Table 15.3), rice varieties markedly differ in their ability to survive Fe toxicity stress. Similarly it was also reported that variety IR 8 had the maximum DTPA- Fe (75.2 mg/kg) in its rhizosphere, while IR 22 had the minimum (68.2 mg/kg). Studies have also shown that Fe content of rice grain may vary widely among the rice genotypes (Senadhira *et al.*, 1998; Promuthai and Rekasem, 2001).

Conclusion

So, local rice varieties which were found to be tolerant to abiotic stress, could be used as donor genes for rice improvement programme. Following are the observations as summarized herein.

Table 15.6 : Response of rice to Fe toxic condition

Local varieties	*Change in grain yield over control (%)*	*Local varieties*	*Change in grain yield over control (%)*
'Aduma'	–4.18	'Kalahaitia'	30.0
'Arsin Sail-I'	26.67	'Kaliasurit'	8.24
'Badia'	13.64	'Kalikhasa'	12.50
'Batteswar'	–43.22	'Kanchali bitchi'	25.48
'Bhushakhi'	–5.78	'Kaminisail'	–26.79
'Billorng'	27.26	'Kamrang'	–16.37
'Binni'	–29.09	'Kartiksail'	–28.91
'Binni Guria'	–12.91	'Khasa'	–35.43
'Binni karma'	–43.30	'Khurpi'	–42.67
'Binni Merang'	32.52	'Laitika'	–5.12
'Biral Binni-1'	0	'Latisail'	41.29
'Biral binni-2'	–58.12	'Maichikan'	–7.12
'Chanmuri'	–19.59	'Malati'	33.31
'Chingri Joly'	65.04	'Matrimangal'	38.58
'Dauri'	–26.14	'Mipla-I'	–16.49
'Dhupamei'	0	'Monobakra'	–18.18
'Dulla Kamang'	–14.99	'Mulasail'	–28.90
'Farete'	22.17	'Mizersail'	27.53
'Full badam'	23.70	'Plapin'	–12.33
'Garomalati'	8.96	'Ranga gellong'	–14.12
'Gellong'	–27.06	'Rellong'	27.63
'Gori Gellong'	–6.54	'Sonamukhi'	–5.96
'Guasail'	–36.07	'Tarical'	18.99
'Guria Karma'	–19.93	'Thakurbhog'	–38.70
'Irrimala'	10.97	'RP-44-119-1 (Control)	68.07
'Jatihet'	–8.33	SE (±)	0.67
'Joly'	–10.17	Mean	0.70

- Some local rice genotypes like 'Aduma', 'Badia', 'Batteswar', 'Bhushakhi', 'Guasail', 'Garo Malati', 'Kangpui', 'Kanchali Bitchi', 'Kartik Sail', 'Latika', 'Subashi', 'Thakurbhog' underwent a decline in grain production ranging from 4 to 74 per cent upon P-application thus indicating tolerance to P deficiency.
- The varieties which did not require the supply of additional Zn, showing their tolerant behaviour in Zn stress condition, were 'Dhupani', 'Thakurbhog', 'Binni

Merang', 'Kalikhasa', 'Nigersail', 'Laitika', 'Guria Karama', 'Binni Guria', 'Biral Binni'.

- Some local varieties like'Arsinsail', 'Billrong', 'Binni Merang', 'Chingrijoli', 'Gelong Kufru', 'Kaliahatie', 'Kanchani Bitchi', 'Lathisail', 'Maliti, Nigersail' producing an increase in grain yield from 8.24 to 65.04 per cent upon application of Fe, were tolerant in nature.

REFERENCES

Chang, T.T. (1985). *Preservation of Crop Germplasm*. Iowa State J. Res. 59(4):365-378.

Chang, T.T., S.M. Dietz, and M.N. Westwood. (1989). Management and use of plant germplasm collections. *Biotic Diversity and Germplasm Preservation, Global Imperatives*. Beltsville Symposia in Agriculture Research (13).

Datta, M. and Laskar, S. (1992) Differential reaction of local rice races to iron in Tripura. *Oryza* 29: 388-391.

Datta, M., Banik, S. and Laskar, S. (1992). Effect of inoculation of phosphate-dissolving bacteria on rice *(Oryza sativa)* in acid soil. *Indian Journal of Agricultural Sciences* 62 (7): 482-485.

Datta, M. and Munna Ram (1993). Status of Micronutrients in some soil series of Tripura. *Journal Indian Society Soil Science*. 41 (4): 776-777.

Datta, M. and Dhiman, K.R. (2001). Yield and response of rice (*Oryza sativa*) as influenced by methods and sources of micronutrient application. *Indian Journal of Agricultural Sciences*, 71(3): 190-192.

Jackson, M. L., (1967). *Soil Chemical Analysis,* Prentice Hall of India Pvt. Ltd., New Delhi.

Laskar, S., Dadhwal, K. S. and Prasad, R. N. (1983). *Soils of Tripura and Their Fertility Management*. Bulletin ICAR Research Complex 23: 25-35.

Moore, P. A. Jr. and Patrick, W. H. Jr. (1989). Iron availability and uptake by rice in acid sulfate soils. *Soil Science Society America Journal*. 53: 471-76

Patra, B. N. and Mohanty, S. K. (1988). Effect of iron on dry matter production, nutrient contents and uptake by rice. *Oryza*, 25: 149-56.

Ponnamperuma, F. N., Bradfield, R. and Peech, M., (1955). Physiological disease or rice attributable to Iron toxicity. *Nature*, 175: 265.

Promuthai, C., Rekasem, B. (2001). Grain iron concentration in Thai rice germplasm. *Development Plant Soil Science*, 92:350-351.

Sardana, S. (1997). Rice genetic resources in Tripura—Neglected Treasure, Debacle, July-September and October-December 22-24.

Senadhira, D., Gregorio G, Graham RD (1998) Breeding iron and Zinc tolerant rice. Paper presented at the International Workshop on Micronutrient Enhancement of Rice for Developing Countries, 3 September, 1998, Rice Research and Extension Centre, Stuttgart, Arkansas, USA.

Schwab, A.P. and Lindsay W. L., (1983). Effect of redox on the solubility and availability of iron. *Soil Science Society American Journal*. 47: 201-5.

Takkar, P. N. (1996). Micronutrient research and sustainable agricultural productivity in India. *Journal of Indian Society of Soil Science*. 44(4): 562-587.

Weeraratna, C.S., (1976). Phosphorus, iron and manganese uptake of some low and high yielding rice varieties. *International Rice Commission Newsletter*. 25:45-55.

16

Genetic Variability and Contribution of Seed Protein Content in Diversity of Some Indigenous Rice Germplasm from North-Eastern Region of India

Krishnendu Chattopadhyay, Avijit Das and *S.P. Das*

Introduction

North-Eastern region of India is considered as one of the secondary centre of origin of rice. Fortunately, due to inaccessible geographic situations and traditional cultivation practices, some of the indigenous rice cultivars still exist. These germplasm are having intermediate to poor vigour, shy in tillering habit, open to semi-compact culm angle, fairly well panicle exertion and poor thresh ability (Sardana, 1997). Most of the lines are low yielder. But, evaluation based on agronomic and morphological characters and resistance to biotic and abiotic stresses are required to be done extensively to find out valuable and unique genotypes. They may not be competent enough to meet the demand of ever increasing population. But some of their unique features, related to stress tolerance or nutritional quality can be utilized in the breeding programme for developing rice varieties with the aim of food and nutritional security. Seed Protein content in rice is one of the important nutritional parameter. Strong efforts have been invested over the past five decades to improve the protein content of rice, mainly *via* conventional breeding techniques and induced mutations (Khush and Juliano, 1984). Screening germplasm collections of cultivated rice for protein content has shown that protein content in cultivated rice ranges from about 5 to 18 per cent with an average of 9.5 per cent, indicating the presence of genetic variability for high protein content and suggesting the feasibility of breeding high-protein rice cultivars. However, these efforts have been largely unsuccessful, as indicated by the lack of modern high-protein rice cultivars. The lack of success may have been caused by the universal complexity of the inheritance of endosperm traits. In addition, seed protein content tends to have low heritability due to the significant environmental effects and to show negative correlation with yield and some eating/cooking quality criteria (Vasal, 2002). A very little understanding on the genetical basis of inheritance was pursued for this quantitative character (Shi *et al.*, 2006). In the present study, agro-morphological parameters and protein contents were measured and used in genetical analysis as well as selection of suitable crossing combination for breeding high protein rice genotypes using rice germplasm from North-Eastern India.

Materials and Methods

15 cultivars from North-Eastern region of India along with two check variety (high protein containing ARC-10075 and low protein containing Basmati 370) were planted for evaluation in kharif season 2009 at CRRI farm, Cuttack (Table 16.1). They were planted in two replications in randomized block design (RBD) with 20 cm row to row and 15 cm plant to plant distances. N:P:K ratio was 80 : 40 : 40. Urea and MOP were applied in two split doses. Data were recorded on 10 plants from each replication. Seed protein content was measured by standard Micro-Kjeldahl method. Analysis of variance (ANOVA) for all parameters and correlation among them were calculated using standard procedure. The analysis of genetic divergence was carried out by using Mahalanobis D^2 statistics. The genotypes were grouped into clusters as per Tochar's method (Rao, 1952).

Results and Discussion

All the yield attributing traits were found significantly differ except number of panicles/plant. Days to maturity, panicle length, panicle

Table 16.1: Varieties with their Yield, Yield Contributing Traits and Protein Content

No.	Variety	Days to maturity	Plant height (cm)	Panicle length (cm)	Panicle number/ plant	Seed/ panicle	100 seed wt (g)	Crude protein (%)	Seed wt/ plant (g)	Protein yield/plant (g)
1.	Aduma	124.00	139.20	26.73	7.00	134.00	1.72	8.88	17.02	151.18
2.	Garomalati	125.50	136.20	26.48	7.10	133.63	1.87	8.83	18.76	165.52
3.	Makumi mokul	137.50	147.00	27.75	5.50	118.25	2.45	8.56	12.08	103.09
4.	Mamy yathlok	123.50	127.70	23.35	10.00	128.25	1.84	10.80	18.14	196.31
5.	Beti	128.50	144.17	22.38	10.67	104.13	1.82	9.44	18.70	176.34
6.	Full Badam	122.50	112.50	19.90	9.80	94.50	1.91	11.06	15.45	170.96
7.	Mykachak	115.50	118.70	23.85	8.70	124.75	1.91	11.09	14.30	158.76
8.	White gelong	124.00	113.30	21.95	10.60	138.25	1.86	8.89	16.17	143.97
9.	Ngoba	137.50	121.50	26.43	9.57	128.58	2.25	9.95	24.52	243.81
10.	Kataktara	124.50	122.20	23.73	7.50	140.50	1.90	8.54	13.61	116.10
11.	Khasha	152.00	151.50	27.08	16.17	216.75	1.41	7.70	34.62	266.65
12.	Kali khasha	146.50	162.17	25.00	12.00	158.50	1.47	8.47	23.86	201.96
13.	Binni	144.00	167.58	26.79	10.25	130.75	2.09	8.53	25.28	214.91
14.	Pyzum white	153.00	112.25	26.83	12.25	235.20	2.00	8.13	37.96	308.72
15.	RCPL-1-87-4-1	144.50	124.67	26.00	10.67	172.17	1.61	7.67	27.64	212.47
16.	Basmati-370	129.50	133.17	27.50	10.17	122.38	2.18	6.87	17.67	121.54
17.	ARC-10075	144.00	166.20	27.48	7.70	122.75	2.77	10.43	21.20	220.24
	Mean	133.91	135.29	25.25	9.74	141.37	1.94	9.05	21.0	186.62
	SEm +/-	*1.27*	*3.31*	*0.78*	*1.44*	*15.14*	*0.05*	*0.18*	*1.53*	*14.34*
	CD 5%	*3.93*	*10.22*	*2.41*	*4.46*	*46.77*	*0.16*	*0.56*	*4.71*	*44.31*

number /plant, seeds/panicle were significantly and positively associated with seed yield/plant. But CP content was found negatively associated with seed yield (r = –0.41) as well as most of the important yield attributing traits like, number of seeds/panicle (r = –0.61) (Table 16.2).

Table 16.2 : Correlation coefficients among different parameters

Parameters	*Maturity*	*Plant Height*	*Panicle length*	*Panicle number/ plant*	*Seeds/ panicle*	*100 seeds wt*	*Crude protein*
Maturity	1.00						
Plant Height	0.46**	1.00					
Panicle length	0.64**	0.51**	1.00				
Panicle number/ plant	0.66**	0.00	–0.12	1.00			
Seeds/panicle	0.76**	–0.11	0.43*	0.72**	1.00		
100 seeds wt	0.01	0.16	0.33	–0.73**	–0.44**	1.00	
Crude protein	–0.51**	–0.2	–0.57**	–0.44**	–0.61**	0.27	1.00
Seed yield/ plant	0.86**	0.12	0.43*	0.82**	0.93**	–0.3	–0.41*

Diversity of genotypes was found significant using D^2 statistics. CP contributed highest (51%) followed by seed weight (14.7%) and maturity (14%) to the D^2 values. Genotypes were grouped under 4 clusters. Cluster-II contained three genotypes, viz., Khasha, RCPL-1-87-4 and Pyzum white. Cluster-III and Cluster-IV contained one genotype each. Ngoba and ARC-10075 belonged to Cluster-III and Cluster-IV, respectively. Rest of the varieties belonged to Cluster-I. Inter-cluster distance was highest (52.7) between cluster-II and Cluster–IV. Khasha, RCPL-1-87-4 and Pyzum white (in Cluster-II), having highest Cluster mean for number of panicle per plant (13.03), seed per panicle (208.04), seed yield per plant (33.41 g) and protein yield per plant (262.61 g) could produce valuable diverse segregants while hybridizing with ARC-10075 (only genotype in Cluster-IV) with highest mean CP content (10.43%).

Seed protein content was found negative related with grain yield in most of the varieties under this study (Fig. 16.1). Therefore, more selection pressure for achieving more seed yield may negatively contribute to total seed protein. We know that rice is a main source of calories as well as protein intake for billions of people. Therefore, enrichment of protein through hybridization

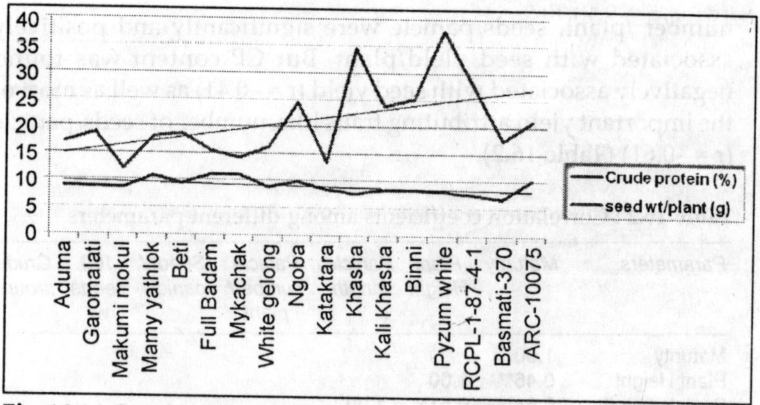

Fig 16.1 : Graphical Presentation of Seed Yield Per Plant and Crude Protein Content of 17 Varieties

and selection could be a positive impact on millions of poor and malnourished people in developing countries (Mahmoud *et al.*, 2008). In the present study we found some genotypes with high crude protein content, like, Mykachak (11.09%) and Full Badam (11.06%). We also found some potential cross combination for developing high yielding and high protein rice genotypes by using germplasm from North-Eastern region of India.

Acknowledgements

We are indebted to Joint Director at ICAR Research Complex for NEH Region, Tripura centre for providing the seed materials of rice germplasm for this study.

REFERENCES

Khush, G.S. & Juliano, B.O. (1984). Status of rice varietal improvement for protein content at IRRI. In *Nuclear Techniques for Cereal Grain Protein Improvement*; Proceedings of research coordination meeting; IAEA: Vienna, Austria, pp. 199–202.

Mahmoud, A.A.; Sukumar, S. and Krishnan, H.B. (2008). Interspecific rice hybrid of *Oryza sativa* × *Oryza nivara* reveals a significant increase in seed protein content. *J. Agric. Food Chem.* 56 (2) 476–482.

Rao, C.R. 1952. *Advanced Statistical Method in Biometrical Research*. John Wiley & Sons, New York.

Sardana, S. (1997). Rice genetic resources in Tripura—Neglected treasure. *Debacle.* July-September and October-December. 22-24.

Shi, C.H.; Ge, G.K.; Wu, J.G.; Ye, J. and Wu, P. (2006). The dynamic gene expression from different genetic systems for protein and lysine contents of *Indica* rice. *Genetica 128*- 297–306.

Vasal, S.K. (2002). The role of high lysine cereals in animal and human nutrition in Asia. In *Protein Sources for the Animal Feed Industry*; Food and Agriculture Organization of the United Nations: Rome, Italy, pp. 97–108.

17

Edible Fruit Plants of Cachar District, Assam and their Ethno-Medicinal Uses

M.K. Baruah, G. Chakraborty, P.D. Choudhury, K.D. Choudhury, and *M. Dutta Choudhury*

Introduction

Fruits provide food diversity and beneficial nutrients and phytochemicals in diets. Most of the fruits available from Cachar district show high nutraceutical value and have been reported to possess both therapeutic and dietary functions. In India, the nutraceutical market pegged at rupees sixteen billion is still evolving. The value of the neutraceuticals among the people is increasing day by day with the increasing awareness towards health and lifestyle disorders. (*Ref.* Nutraceutical product market in India, 2005).

Nutraceutical, a term combining the words "nutrition" and "pharmaceutical", is a food or food product that provides health and medical benefits, including the prevention and treatment of disease. Such products may range from isolated nutrients, dietary supplements and specific diets to genetically engineered foods, herbal products, and processed foods such as cereals, soups, and beverages. With recent breakthroughs in cellular-level nutraceuticals agents, researchers, and medical practitioners are developing templates for integrating and assessing information from clinical studies on complementary and alternative therapies into responsible medical practice (Kalra, E.K., 2003).

Cachar district of South Assam is surrounded by North Cachar hills district and Khasi and Jaintia hills on the North, Manipur on East, Mizoram on South and Tripura State on West (Fig. 17.1). The district Cachar covers an area of 3,786 sq. km. The area has been at an altitude of 26-27 m above sea level and lies between longitude 92°-24′ E and 93°-15′ E and latitude 24°– 22′ N and 25°- 8′ N. Barak, Jiri and Siri are the main rivers in the district. The soil type is

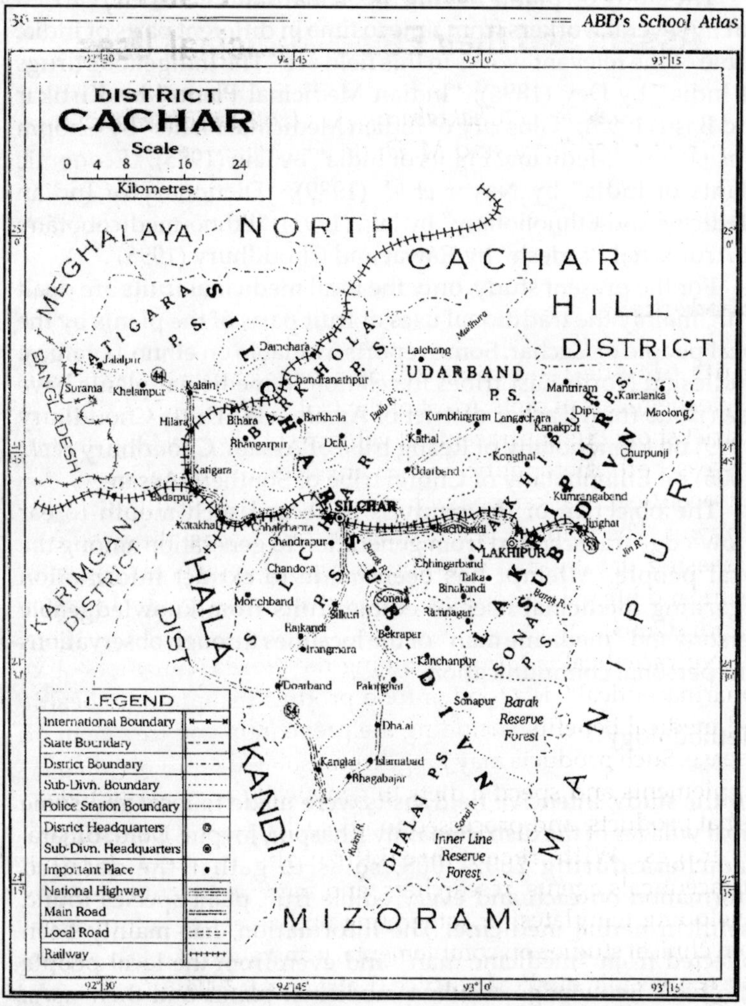

Fig. 17.1 : Map showing the Study Area (Cachar District of Assam)

alluvial and texture is sandy, loamy and silt type depending on their silt and sand content. The pH of the soil varies between 5.0-6.5 or around neutral. The climate of the district is very hot with dry cold season. The average temperature of the district lies in between 15-35°C. The average annual rainfall of the district is around 300 mm and average atmospheric humidity is 75-85 per cent.

The study on plants having medicinal values has been carried out by several workers from time to time in different parts of India. Some of the relevant works in this field are "The Indigenous drugs of India" by Dey (1896); "Indian Medicinal Plants" by Kirtikar and Basu (1993); "Glossary of Indian Medicinal Plants" by Chopra *et al.* (1956); "Medicinal Plants of India" by Jain (1985); "Economic Plants of India" by Nayar *et al.* (1989); "Dictionary of Indian Medicine and Ethnobotany" by Jain (1991); "Ethno-medicobotany of Arunachal Pradesh" by Rawat and Choudhury (1998) .

For the present study, only the local medicinal fruits are dealt with, mainly the traditional uses of fruit parts of the plants by the local people of Cachar. Some reports available on ethno-botanical studies on North-East tribes in relation to medicinal plants have been done from Cachar district of Assam, viz., Dutta Choudhury (1999) on Ethnobotany of Reang tribe of Assam; Choudhury *et al.*, (2005) on Ethnobotany of Chorei tribe of Southern Assam.

The objective of the study is to record such mouth to ear knowledge transcended from generation to generation among the local people. Attempt has been made to extract information regarding medicinal uses of edible fruits from knowledgeable persons and "medicine man" of the localities through observations and personal communication.

Methodology

For the study, intensive field visits were made to local and some tribal villages of the district mainly Khaspur, Joypur, Dolu, Bihara, Damchera during 2007-2008, so as to gather the detailed information on each and every edible fruit plant species found useful in herbal medicine. The information, has mainly been collected from "medicine man" and even from the local people who have knowledge of ethno-medicinal plants and their uses. Surveys were also conducted in the nearby forests with the help of local people. Routine methods of botanical collection and herbarium techniques were followed as suggested by Jain and Rao (1977).

Thorough observations were made on the spot collection of individual species and for identification of plants a number of flora had been consulted specially *Flora of British India*, Vol. 1-7 (Hooker, 1872-1897), *Flora of Assam*, Vol. 1-4 (Kanjilal *et al.*,1934-40). Finally, confirmation on identification was done by consulting Herbaria of Botanical Survey of India EC, Shillong. As far as possible, sufficient information were collected for plants with regard to vernacular names, fruits used for the preparation of medicines and application in the diseases.

Results

Collected ethno-medicinal plants are enumerated in a tabular form (Table 17.1) classifying them disease-wise one or more plant species, correct scientific name with author citation, vernacular name, name of family, parts used and applications are provided.

Discussion

During the survey it was observed that most of the people are aware about the medicinal value of fruit plants of *Aegle marmelos, Emblica officinalis, Avorrhoea carambola, Terminalia belerica, T. chebula, Psidium guayava*, etc., against different kinds of ailments. Some of the fruits plants are not only used in medicinal purposes, but also in religious functions. So the protection of plants which are commonly used in our day-to-day traditional remedies for common ailments has a significant role in bio-diversity conservations. The potential of Cachar district in this respect is no less than any other region of the country. These indicate that its soil and climate can be utilized in due course to develop fruit plants having medicinal values.

During the course of recent investigation, it has been observed that a particular plant is sometimes prescribed for different ailments in different localities and different plants are used to prepare medicine of a particular disease (Table 17.2)

Altogether 28 species of fruit plants having medicinal value of fruit were ascertained in this study. Among them, some species

Table 17.1: Ethno-Medicinal Plants

Diseases	*Name of species*	*Vernacular name*	*Family*	*Parts used and Application*
Antidandruff	*Dillenia indica* L.	Chalta	Dilleniaceae	Decoction of the fruit is applied to scalp for curing dandruff and falling hairs.
Antiseptic	*Elaeocarpus floribundus* Bl.	Jolphai,	Elaeocarpaceae	Fruit are used as antiseptic.
Headache	*Terminalia belerica* Roxb.	Boyar,	Combretaceae	Dry fruits is used in diarrhoea, headache.
Eye diseases	*Emblica officinalis* Gaertn.	Amloki	Euphorbiaceae	Fruit juice is given in eye diseases.
Fever and Cough	*Punica granatum* L.	Dalim	Lythraceae	Fruit juice is given in cough and throat troubles.
	Tamarindus indica L.	Tatul	Caesulpiniaceae	Fruit pulp mixed with water is used in cough.
	Avorrhoea carambola Linn.	Kamranga	Malphigiaceae,	Unripe fruits are given in fever.
Indigestion	*Aegle marmelos* Correa.	Bel	Rutaceae	Pulp of roasted green fruit is given in chronic stomach disorder, and also ripe fruit juice is given for digestion.
	Citrus aurantium L.	Kagji lebu,	Rutaceae	Fruit juice is used for digestion.
	Mangifera indica L.	Aam	Anacardiaceae	Fruit is given in digestive purpose.
	Psidium guyava Linn.	Sopri	Myrtaceae,	Fruit is used as digestive and nutritive purpose
Dysentery and Diarrhoea	*Emblica officinalis* Gaertn.	Amloki,	Euphorbiaceae	Fruits are given in diarrhoea and dysentery.
	Grewia asiatica L.	Solpha,	Tiliaceae,	Fruits are given in diarrhoea and dysentery.
	Mangifera indica L.	Aam	Anacardiaceae	Unripe fruit is given in constipation and also in dysentery and diarrhoea.
	Musa superba Roxb.	Athiya Kola	Musaceae	Unripe boiled fruit is given in dysentery and diarrhoea; ripe fruit is used as astringent in dysentery and also used as vegetable.
	Cocos nucifera L.	Narikel	Aracaceae	Coconut water is given after Dysentery to reduce dehydration.
	Citrus decumara Linn.	Jambura,	Rutaceae,	Fruit juice is used in dysentery.

(Contd.)

Table 17.1: (*Contd.*)

Diseases	*Name of species*	*Vernacular name*	*Family*	*Parts used and Application*
	Terminalia belerica Roxb.	Boyar	Combretaceae	Dry fruits are used in diarrhoea.
Diabetes and to purify Blood	*Annona squamosa* L.	Ataphal,	Annonaceae	Ripe fruit is used in diabetes.
	Citrus decumara Linn.	Jambura,	Rutaceae,	Fruit juice is used in purifying the blood.
	Eugenia jambolana Linn.	Kalajam	Myrtaceae	Fruit juice is given in diabetes and to purify blood.
	E. cymosa Linn.	Panijam	Myrtaceae	Fruit juice are given to purify blood and in dehydration.
	E. bracteata Roxb.	Luk-luki	Myrtaceae	Fruit juice is used to purify blood.
	Punica granatum L.	Dalim	Lythraceae	Seeds with honey are given for diabetes.
Jaundice	*Avorrhoea carambola* L.	Kamranga	Malphigiaceae	Fruit extract is given in jaundice.
	Emblica officinalis Gaertn.	Amloki	Euphorbiaceae	Fruits are given in jaundice
	Punica granatum L. .	Dalim	Lythraceae	Decoction of seeds with honey is given for jaundice.
Skin Diseases	*Carica papaya* L.	.Pepe	convolvulaceae	Latex of fruit used skin diseases.
	Terminalia chebula Gaertn.	Haritaki	Combretaceae	Burnt fruit is applied to old skin diseases.
Toothache	*Solanum ferox* L.	Gummite	Solanaceae	Smoke of burning fruit is used as a remedy for toothache.
Piles	*Avorrhoea carambola* Linn.	Kamranga	Malphigiaceae	Unripe fruits are given in piles.
Stomachache	*Carica papaya* L.	Pepe	Convolvulaceae	Fruits are used in stomachache.
	Dillenia indica L.	Chalta	Dilleniaceae	Fruits are also used in abdominal pains.
Tuberculosis	*Spondias mangifera* Willd.	Amra	Anacardiaceae	Fruit juice is given to TB patient.
Nerve problem	*Litchi chinensis* Sonn.	Lichu	Sapindaceae	Seeds are used as nerve problem.
	Solanum ferox L.	Gummite	Solanaceae	Fruit after boiling with water are used in muscle and nerve problem.
Abdominalpain and worms	*Ananas cosmosus* L.	Anaras	Bromeliaceae.	Fruit juice are used for killing worms, unripe fruit juice is used in abdominal pain

Table 17.2 : List of Plant Species with Multiple Medicinal Values

Plants	Application in Diseases
Mangifera indica L.	Indigestion, Dysentery and Diarrhoea
Punica granatum L.	Fever and cough, Jaundice, Diabetes and to purify blood.
Citrus decumara Linn.	Dysentery and Diarrhoea, Diabetes and to purify blood.
Emblica officinalis Gaertn.	Jaundice, Dysentery and Diarrhoea
Avorrhoea carambola L.	Piles, Jaundice
Dillenia indica L.	Tuberculosis, Antidandruff
Carica papaya L.	Stomachache, Skin Diseases
Ananas cosmosus L.	Abdominal pain and worms

like *Psidium guyava, Musa superba, Mangifera indica, Citrus medica,* etc., are recorded to be used as nutraceuticals. Most of the fruit plants are cultivated for their fruits. The plants noted here are in vogue as remedy of different types of diseases; such as fever, indigestion, cough and cold, dysentery, jaundice, acidity, stomachache, abdominal pain and worms, piles, ulcers, diarrhoea, etc. It is apparent from the foregoing account that local people and rural inhabitants of the district have knowledge of medicinal uses of plants available in the area. They exploit them for the treatment of a wide variety of ailments. Further, it has been observed that in this district most of the diseases are related to stomach troubles and skin diseases and in the present observation many fruits of the plants mentioned are used for these purposes.

Acknowledgement

The authors are grateful to Deputy Director, B.S.I., Eastern Circle, Shillong, Ministry of Environment and Forest, Government of India, for providing Herbarium and Library facilities for identification of plants. Authors are also thankful to all the persons for their cooperation who are related to this survey works.

REFERENCES

Bennet, S.S.R. (1987). *"Name Changes in Flowering Plants of India and Adjacent Regions"* Triseas Publishers, Dehradun, India.

Borthakur, S.K., (1981). Certain plants in the folklore and folk life of the

Karbis (Mikirs) of Assam In: *Glimpses of Indian Ethno-Botany*. Ed. S.K. Jain, New Delhi. pp. 170-181.

Borthakur, S.K., (1976a). Less known medicinal plants of tribes of Karbi Anglong (Mikir Hills). Bulletin of Botanical Survey of India 18(1-4): 166-177.

Borthakur, S.K., (1992). Native phytotherapy of child and women diseases in Assam, North Eastern India. *Pitoterpia* 63(6):486-488.

Gogoi, P. and Boissya, C.L. (1984). Information about a few herbal medicines used by the people of Assam (India) against jaundice. *Himal. Res . Dev.* 2: pp. 141-144.

Hajra, P.K. and Baishya, A. K (1981). Ethno-botanical notes on the Mikir (Mishings) of Assam. In S.K. Jain (ed) *Glimpses of India,* New Delhi: pp. 161-169.

Hooker, J.D. (1872-1897). *The Flora of British India,* Vol. 1-7, London.

Jain, S.K. and Rao, R.R. (1977). *A Hand Book of Field and Herbarium Methods*. Today and Tomorrow Printers and Publishers, New Delhi.

Jain, S.K. and Dham, N. (1979): Some ethno-botanical note from North Eastern India. *Eco Bot*. 33(1): pp. 52-56.

Kalra EK (2003). *Nutraceutical—Definition and Introduction* AAPS Pharm Sci 5 (3): E25. doi:10.1208/ps050325. PMID 14621960.

Kanjilal, U.N. and Bor, N.L. (1934-1940). *The Flora of Assam,* Vol. 1-5, Government of Assam, Shillong.

Nayar, M.P.; Ramamurthy, K.; and Agarwal, V.S. (1989). *Economic Plants of India,* Vol. 1, B.S.I., Calcutta.

Sharma, G.D.; Bhattacharjee, S.; Sinha, M. and Das, A.K. (2002): Status of Plant Bio-diversity of Cachar district and its Conservations. *J. Econ. Taxon. Bot.*, Vol. 25, No. (1), pp. 94-101.

18
Biodiversity of Mushroom in Eastern Region of India

Jai Prakash Sharma

Introduction

The fungi are one of the most diverse groups of organisms. Mushroom is a general term used mainly for the fruiting body of the macro fungi (*Ascomycota* and *Basidiomycota*) and represents only a short reproductive stage in their life cycle. Wild mushrooms have a profound biological and economical impact. They have had a long association with human kind. Wild mushrooms have been consumed by man from ancient times with delicacy probably, for their texture and pleasing flavour. Edible fungi are not only beautiful but play a significant role in the daily life of human beings besides their utilization in industry, agriculture, medicine, food industry, textiles, bioremediation, natural cycling, as biofertilizers and many other ways. Fungal biotechnology has become an integral part of the human welfare (Manoharachary *et al.*, 2005). The variety and galaxy of fungi and their natural beauty occupy prime place in the biological world and India has been the cradle for such fungi. Only a fraction of total fungal wealth has been subjected to scientific scrutiny and mycologists have to unravel the unexplored and hidden wealth. One-third of fungal diversity of the globe exists in India. Hawksworth (1997) reported about fungal 70,000 species of fungi have been described since then 270,000 plant species are known which suggests that the total number of fungal species may approach 1.5 million. On an average

700 species were described as new to science each year from 1920 to 1950. However, the annual total catalogued fungi reached around 1,400 in 1961, 1,500 in 1968 and averaged 1,700 each year for 1986 to 1990. Fungi are regarded as being the second largest group of organisms in the biosphere after the insects. Out of about 70,000 described species of fungi, it has been suggested that around 14,000-15,000 species produce fruiting bodies of sufficient size and suitable structure to be considered as macro fungi. Of these, about 5,000 of the species are considered to possess varying degrees of edibility, and more than 2,000 species from 31 genera are regarded as prime edible mushrooms. But only 100 of them are experimentally grown, 50 economically cultivated, around 30 commercially cultivated, and only about 6 to have reached an industrial scale of production in many countries. Furthermore, about 1,800 are medicinal ones. The poisonous mushrooms is relatively small (approximately 10%), of these some 30 species are considered to be lethal (Miles and Chang, 1997). Out of 1.5 million of fungi, only 50 per cent are characterized until now and only around 5–10 per cent of fungi can be cultured artificially. Over 2,000 species of edible fungi known to man out of a total of 10,000 species of macro fungi reported to be growing in the world (Dhar and Singh, 1999).The people have been eating mushrooms for a long time. They used to go to the forests and other wild places and based on their personal knowledge of edible and poisonous mushrooms they used to collect the edible ones. Even now some people collect wild mushrooms from the forest and eat them. Sometimes they turn out to be poisonous and have harmful effects. In India the "Guchhi" mushroom was a delicacy known to the people prior to the 1950s. Jain (2005) stated that mushroom cultivation in India was started by Dr. S.S. Jain (First Mycologist) in the early 1950 who has grown *Agaricus* and other species successfully on rotting apple tree twigs and branches, cow dung and wheat straw, etc., popularised among the farmers of Himachal Pradesh. Previously, the edible mushrooms were grown in France and Japan. Several reports on wild edible mushrooms have been collected and consumed by people since thousands of years. Archaeological evidences reveal edible species associated with people living 13,000 years ago in Chile (Rojas and Mansur, 1995) but in China where the eating of wild fungi was first reliably noted several hundred years before the birth of Christ (FAO, 2004). Hobbs

(1995) stated that many cultures have been identified that certain mushrooms could have profound health-promoting benefit. China is the world's largest edible mushroom producer (*Anonymous*, 2003) produces about half of all cultivated mushrooms, and around 2.7 kilograms (6.0 lb) of mushrooms are consumed per person per year by over a billion people and 95 per cent of mushroom production in China is consumed locally, the consumption per capita is likely to be over 10 kg/person/year (Chang, 1999, 2006). This is drastically higher than in US and many European countries where it is around 3 kg/person/year. India produced over 1.13 lakh tonnes during 2010 and exported about 60-70 per cent of it, our per capita consumption is low around 30-40 g/person/year (Wakchaure, 2010).

Mushrooms have been exploited commercially world over and may be cultivated or gathered from the wild. Of the 14,000 mushroom species, nearly 7,000 species are well studied to possess varying degree of edibility, and more than 3,000 species spread over in 31 genera are regarded as prime edible. Thus far, only 200 of them are experimentally cultured, 100 economically cultivated, approximately 60 commercially grown and about 10 have reached an industrial scale (Chang and Miles, 2004).

Table 18.1: Total World Mushroom Production and China's Contribution since 1978

Year	*Total Production (in 1000 tonnes)*	*China Production (in 1000 tonnes)*	*China contribution (%)*
1978	1060.0	60.0	5.7
1983	1453.0	174.5	12.0
1990	3763.0	1083.0	28.8
1994	4909.0	2640.0	53.8
1997	6158.4	3918.0	63.6
2002	12250.0	8650.0	70.6
2006	—	14000.0	—
2008	26000.0	18200.0	70.0

Nutrition Value of Wild Edible Fungi

They have rich nutritional value with high content of proteins, vitamins, minerals, fibres, trace elements and low/no calories and cholesterol. Many of them have been used in folk medicine for thousands of years. Some of them are neutralceuticals while some can produce potent nutriceuticals.They are the sources of various bioactive substances like, antibacterial, antifungal, antiviral, antiparasitic, antioxidant, anti-inflammatory, antiproliferative, anticancer, antitumour, cytotoxic, DNA damaging, anti-HIV, hypocholesterolemic, antidiabetic, anticoagulant, hepatoprotective, etc. A number of mushrooms form mutual associations (mycorrhizal) with the roots of several forest trees. This beneficial association enhances absorption of water and nutrients amongst trees and is indispensable for the growth and development of these trees and mushrooms. Mushrooms are not of course always beneficial to mankind. Detrimentally, a large number of mushrooms are the wood-rotters causing serious damage to the forest trees hence causing considerable economic loss to timber industry every year. The wild mushrooms are edible; it can be difficult to identify them correctly in the field. Besides, some are toxic, even deadly when eaten (Das, 2009). Fatality due to unwise consumption of wild mushrooms is a common affair amongst regional poor. In India wild mushroom have been reported since its inception from India (Ahlawat *et al.*, 2008). Das (2010) reported that wild mushrooms have manifold impacts in biology; ecology and economy. They have been a part of our daily life since time immemorial. Some nutritional work of wild edible fungi from North-East India has been done earlier by Longvah and Deosthale (1998). The Food and Agricultural Organization has recommended the use of edible mushrooms as food supplement for protein deficient populations of developing and underdeveloped countries due to the following benefits because it is available in open and unrestricted access to the forests and grasslands, No expenditure is involved for mushroom gathering. Economic benefits in which income generated from the sale of collected mushroom resources goes directly to these inhabitants. As a result, majority of the rural people besides practicing traditional subsistence hunting and agriculture also participate in wild mushroom collection. As a nutritional supplement, mushrooms could help diversify an otherwise monotonous diet during the rainy season when there was a paucity of other food resources. There could be several other social and cultural benefits including the healthy bonding between the families and the market place.

Wild Edible Fungi

The North-Eastern Hills bordering China, Burma and Bangladesh and marked by high rainfall have also yielded rich mushroom floras as a result of extensive surveys were done by (Verma *et al.*, 1985, 1987, 1989, 1995). Apart from their importance as a source of food for the regional poor and as mycorrhizal partners of host trees, some are huge sources of bioactive compounds showing medicinal importance and reported 126 wild mushrooms collected from Sikkim. Bhaben *et al.* (2011) reported that more than 13 species of fleshy fungi under 9 genera and six families were identified from Nagaland. No reports are available for artificial cultivation of wild edible fungal flora from India if a technology can be developed which will be beneficial to uplift the economy of people of (Lakhanpal, 1994). Little work on biodiversity on mushroom has been done from Jharkhand by Sinha (2003). Several workers have reported from Himalayan range mainly by Lakhanpal and his associates (Lakhanpal, 1994, 1997; Sohi and Upadhyay 1986). Kaul and associates have reported fleshy fungi from Jammu and Kashmir (Kaul and Kachroo, 1974; Abraham and Kachru, 1989; Kaul, 1997; Sagar *et al.*, 2005). A few isolated forays into the UP Hills (Harsh and Bist 1985; Singh 1988) have and J&K State need to be augmented to a great extent. Recently a systematic work on wild mushroom diversity from Jammu and Kashmir have been undertaken by Kumar and Sharma (2011). Similarly, the large tract of Indo-Gangetic plains of U.P. and Bihar have remained almost unattended to, although plains of Punjab (Saini and Atri, 1995; Atri *et al.*, 1997, 2005) and those of Bengal, (Purkayastha and Chandra 1985) have yielded rich dividends and Assam (Boruah *et al.*, 1997). Madhya Pradesh (a rich tribal belt) has also received very limited attention (Kumar and Shukla, 1995 a ıd Harsh *et al.*, 1993, 1996) and different agro-ecological zones from desert ecosystem of Rajasthan (Doshi and Sharma 1997), Vishwakarma *et al.* (2012) reported from Uttaranchal 40 taxa belonging to 11 families were identified. Two families and 2 taxa belonged to class-A scomycetes, viz., Family-Helvellaceae and Morchellaceae, and nine families and 38 taxa to class-Basidiomycetes, viz., Family-Agaricaceae, Amanitaceae, Boletaceae, Cantharellaceae, Coprinaceae, Ganodermataceae, Hydnagiaceae, Lycoperdaceae and Russulaceae. Some macro fungi are also being used as medicine, viz., *Morchella esculenta, Hydnum repandum, Agaricus campestris, Cantharellus cibarius, Coprinus comatus and Ganoderma lucidumfrom* from Uttranchal . Similarly, the North-Eastern region particularly in Jharkhand no work has been done about the diversity of mushroom and reported herewith.

Jharkhand meaning the "forest area" is geographically known as the Chotanagpur plateau, forming the North-Eastern portion of peninsular plateau of India which lies between 21° 58′10″ to 25° 16″ latitude and 83° 22″ to 87° 57″ longitude. The climate in general is sub-tropical and sub-humid. The agro climatic zones are described Bhatt (2004) below: Climatically, it lies within the tropical zone but the high elevation has an ameliorating effect. The climate of plateau on the whole is salubrious and is one of the rainiest tracts but rainfall is unevenly distributed over the Plateau. About 80 per cent of the annual rain is received in rainy season. The winter season is the period from November to February. December is the coldest month though January is also almost equally cold. There is six agro climatic zones and altitude, latitude annual rainfall and details of Jharkhand are shown in Figure 18.1.

Agro Climatic Zones of Jharkhand

1. *The North and North-Western Zone:* Palamau and part of Hazaribagh district, temperature over 44.4°C, and min. 3.9°C with rainfall ranging from 1160 mm to 1280 mm. It is driest part of Jharkhand. Summer *loo* and dust storm and winter frost are common. This part is the least cloudy and rainy.
2. *The Central Zone*: Chatra-Kadarma Plateau. Summer is hot but winter is keen and bracing. Rainfall varies from 1280 mm to 1660 mm.
3. *The Marine-Influence Zone*: The east and west Singhbhum. Summar is hot but winter is milder. *Loo* is uncommon in the ara except in Jamshedpur. Rainfall varies between 1280 mm to 1310 mm.
4. *The South-Western Rainy Zone*: Western half of Singhbhum and Southern part of Ranchi district. Summer is hot and dry with temperature varying from 15.5°C to 32.2°C/ Winter is severe and rainfall 1530 mm.

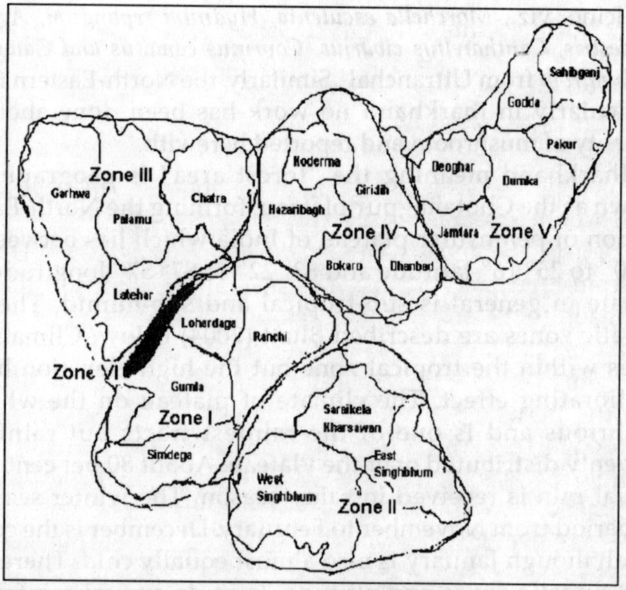

Fig. 18.1: Details of six agro climate zones of Jharkhand

Capital: Ranchi.	Latutude: 22.5° to 23.6°N and 84.9° to 85.9°E
Area: 7,698 sq. km.	Annual Rainfall: 1462.7 mm
Altitude: 652 Meter MSL.	Temperature: 41.8°C (max) and 5.3°C (min)

People living below poverty line	69.83%	Blocks	212
Tribal	30	Town	152
Districts	24	Panchayats	3765
Sub-division	33	Villages	31615

5. *The Keen-Bracing Zone*: Plateau of Ranchi, Hazaribagh, and high lands of Santhal Paraganas. Excellent climate, elevation over 600 m. temperature rise above 32° C only in the hottest month of May. Winter is extremely bracing Rainfall is heavy about 1300 mm in Hazaribagh andover 1530 mm in Ranchi plateau.
6. *The Pat Region*: It includes South-Western corner of Palamau and North-Western part of Ranghi deistrict. The climate is similar to Ranchi plateau. The area is rainier and cloudier in rainy season, cooler in summer and colder in winter than Ranchi plateau. Nights are chilly, especially

during winter. Temperature down to freezing point in winter. Rainfall is over 2050 mm.

Wild Edible Mushrooms

Collection forays were conducted in collaboration of Directorate of Mushroom Research, Solan (HP) more frequent in May to July and August to September months during rainy season of 2002 to 2011 from local market as well as several forest area of Ranchi, Bandhgaon forest of West Singhbhum and Khunti of Jharkhand by Sharma *et al.* (2012). However, the best period for wild mushroom collection in the study area starts with the onset of rains, the period when the conditions are conducive for the mushroom growth and they are available in plenty. The study also indicated that several reasons probably enabled rural folks to participate successfully in the harvest of wild edible mushrooms.

Thirty eight local germplasms of wild and edible mushrooms were collected and preserved. Eighty eight wild mushrooms were identified. The majority of genera belongs to order Agaricales, viz., *Agaricus, Termitomycetes, Macrolepiota, Cococybe cyanopus, Calocybe* and *Volvariella* sp. of four families, Table 18.2. Among the order agaricales majority of wild six species were of *Termitomycetes (Bada Khukhri)* belongs to family Agaricaceae which are sold at high prices in Ranchi market. Similarly *Cococybe cyanopus (Tecnas)* of order Agaricaceae belongs to family Bolbitaceae were the most popular in Ranchi market (Fig 18.2).

However, two species of order Agaricales viz; *Amanita* and *Chlorophylum* were poisonous of family Agaricaceae and Amanitaceae, respectively. Eight species of *Ganoderma* spp. (medicinal) belongs to order polyporales were preserved. Seven species of *Russula* belongs to order Russulales, Four species of *Boletus* belongs to Bolataceae of order Bolatales were sold at cheap rate. Two species of *Lycoperdon* belongs to order Lycoperales in which *Scleroderma* sp. was the most popular and sold at high prices, *Pleurotus, Calocybe, Auricularia, Polypore,* were seen in the forest and preserved. The photographs of the above wild mushroom have been shown in Fig 18:1. Considerable biodiversity of mushrooms and potentials of their utilization have been reported earlier by Verma and Upadhyay (1999) from South Bihar and various species of mushrooms are growing in wild as saprophytes, ligninolytic,

Table 18.2 : Diversity of Wild Mushroom in Jharkhand

S. No.	*Order*	*Family*	*Scientific name / (Number of Species)*	*Common Name*	*Price (Per kg) (Rs.)*	*Availability*
1.	Agaricales	Agaricaceae	*Agaricus* sp. (1)	*Khumbhi*	100	July-Aug.
2.	Agaricales	Agaricaceae	*Chlorophylum* sp. (1)	*Poisonous Khumbi*	—	July-Aug.
3.	Agaricales	Agaricaceae	*Termitomycetes* spp. (5)	*Bada Khukhuri/ Namak Khukhuri*	200 to 600	July–October
4.	Agaricales	Amanitaceae	*Amanita vegenatae* (1)	*Poisonous Khumbi*	—	July-Sept.
5.	Agaricales	Bolbitiaceae	*Cococybe cyanopus* (1)	*Tecnus*	200	July-Sept.
6.	Agaricales	Lyophyllaceae	*Calocybe* sp. (1)	*Dudhiya Khukhuri*		July-Sept.
7.	Agaricales	Lepiotaceae	*Macrolepiota* sp. (1)	*Bada Khukhuri*	200	July-Sept.
8.	Agaricales	Pleuotaceae	*Pleurotus* sp. (1)	Oyster / *Kher Khukhuri*	150	July-Aug..
9.	Agaricales	Pluteaceae	*Volvariella sp.* (1)	*Tormai khukhri* or *Pagla khukhri*	150	June-Aug.
10.	Auriculariales	Auriculariaceae	*Auricularia* sp. (1)	*Kanchapra*	—	July-Sept
11.	Aphyllophorales	Polyporaceae	*Lentinus* sp (1)	*Bans Khukhuri (Dingli)*	200	Sept -Oct
12.	Boletales	Boletaceae	*Boletus* spp. (4)	*Jamun Khukhuri*	150	July-Sept
13.	Boletales	Sclerodermataceae	*Scleroderma* sp. (1)	*Rugra*	200	May-July
14.	Lycoperales	Lycoperdonaceae	*Lycoperdon* sp. (2)	*Gene khukhuri /Rugra*	60 to 200	July-Aug..
15.	Polyporales	Polyporaceae	*Ganoderma* spp. (8)	*Ganoderma*	—	July-Sept.
16.	Polyporales	Polyporaceae	*Polypores* sp. (1)	—	—	July-Sept
17.	Russulales	Russulaceae	*Russula* spp. (7)	*Patra*	60	July-Sept
18.	Russulales	Russulaceae	*Lactarius* sp. (1)	*Patra*	—	July-Sept
	Total		**39**			

or mycorrhizic types in the forests of Bihar and they could be utilized for domestic consumption and commercial exploitation. Those genera were to be looked into *Agaricus, Agrocybe, Calocybe, Kuehhneromyces, Lentinus, Macrolepiota, Pholiota, Stropharia, Tricholoma, Termitomyces and Volvariella* spp. Various spp. widespread in their distribution in temperate to tropical conditions could be collected from the forest during rainy season and marketed. The people of South Bihar have to be made aware of these macro fungi. Various members of Gasteromycetes like *Melanogaster* spp. (Phootka) are collected and sold in the market. *Lycoperdon* spp. (Rugra), *Malanogaster* spp, *Calvatia* spp. and *Rhizopogon* spp. are worth collecting for consumption. *Terminella* is also grown naturally (Ram and Singh, 1997). It has been reported that the tribal are habitual of mushroom eating in their culture since time immemorial. They collect wild mushroom from the forest and sale them in the market at high prices to cater the need for their survival. As per record 200 kg per week of Rugra (*Lycoperdon* sp) is marketed in Ranchi urban (Sinha, 2003). According to survey done by Sharma *et al.* (2002) 10 quintal per season of Rugra (*Lycoperdon* sp) is marketed and Bada Khukhri (*Macrolapiota* sp) 8 quintal per season and Tecnus (*Termitomycetes* sp.) 2 quintal per day by the tribal and oyster mushroom (*Pleurotus* spp. red strain locally known as *Kher khukhri* or *Patra*) are sold in Ranchi alone.

In addition to above the other mushroom are *Bansh khukhri* (*Dingli*) (*Auricularia* spp.), *Jamun khukhri* (*Boletus* spp.), Paddy straw mushroom (*Volvariella* spp. locally known as *Tormaikhukhri* or *Pagla khukhri*), *Balu khukhri, Ganoderma* spp. and *Namak khukhri*. Some of the salient features of the wild species are described below. The mushroom is in food habit and their culture for long time, hence, it can be popularized easily by training them properly and ensuring the availability of quality spawn. Atri *et al.* (1997) reported *Russula* Pers. is the most common mushroom of coniferous and broad leaves of the Himalayas and as many as 74 taxa spread over 287 collections have been listed. A lot of work has been conducted (Verma, 1997; Verma and Singh, 1981, Verma, *et al.*, 1985, 1987, 1989; 1995) in North-Eastern region and reported that the natural wealth of edible fungi of India if exploited for cultivation, may further augment the species diversification of cultivated mushroom scenario of the country.

Some of the important wild mushroom characteristics are described below:

Rugra (Lycoperdon/ Scleroderma sp.)

Two species of *Lycoperdon/ Scleroderma* were commonly available.They appear first immediately after onset of monsoon (May-June) locally known as *Manie* in Oraon and the second one appears in July-August and known as *Chiraya* in Oraon. It is found in the sandy upland where stale and burnt leaves are scattered. They are found near the Sal (*Shorea robusta*) trees/ bushes and sold at higher price in urban area. The sporophores of first one are elliptical in shape 0.5 cm to 2.5 cm dia. and brown in colour whereas inner portions are white at young stage and cracks at matured stage while the other one are spherical in shape, 1 to 2 cm dia. and white in colour at matured stage and burst.The tribals like to eat this mushroom very much.

Bada khukhri (Termitomycetes spp. *and Macrolepiota* spp.)

It is found in rainy season (July–October) near termite nests in the forest and garden soil. The stripes are long about 30 cm and pileus diameter is about 6.5 cm. They are excellent in taste like meat and sold at higher prices in the market. People like it too much. It is not given to pregnant ladies as well as small kids as it may prove harmful to them. Tamarind is used in the preparation of dishes mushroom. Powder of *bada khukhri* is used in fish as well as vegetable preparations.

Jamun khukhri (Boletus spp.)

It is found near the base of the Jamun (*Syzygium cuminii*) tree during July-October. The fruiting bodies are fleshy; the pileus is greater than 15 cm in diameter, about 600 g in weight, and brown in colour. It is eaten after removing the external layer and its taste is just like liver. Over matured fruiting bodies spoil rapidly and insects' larvae appear.

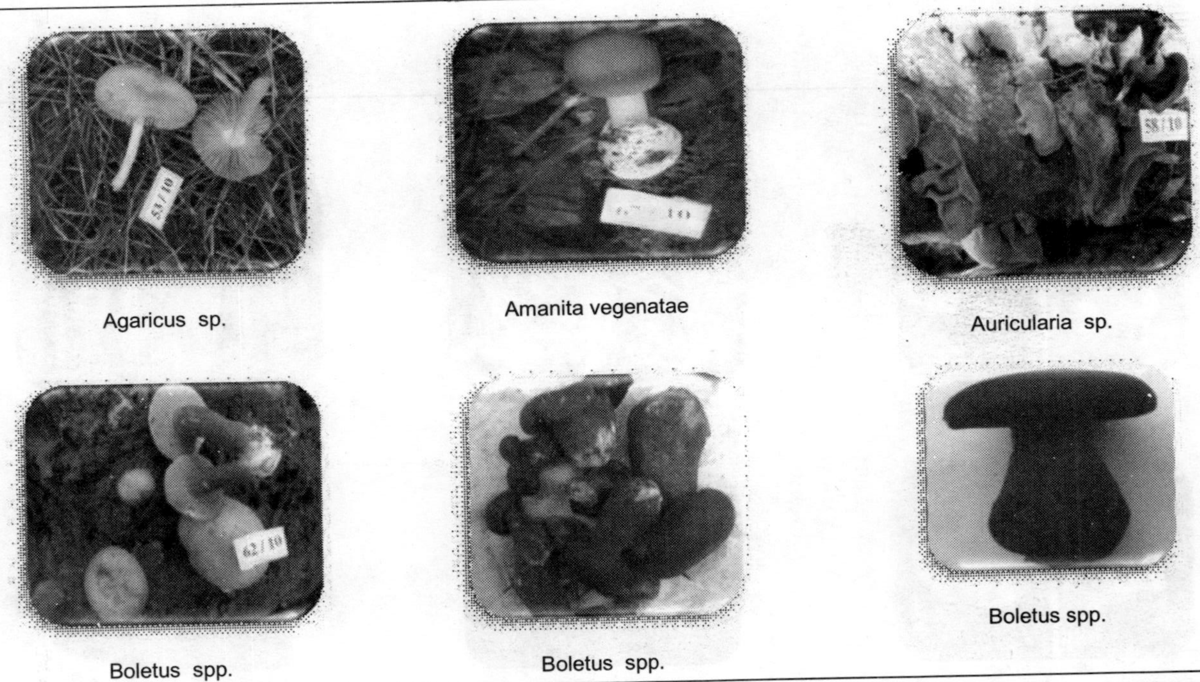

Fig. 18.2: Biodiversity of Wild Mushroom in Jharkhand

(Contd.)

Fig. 18.2 : *(Contd.)*

Boletus spp.

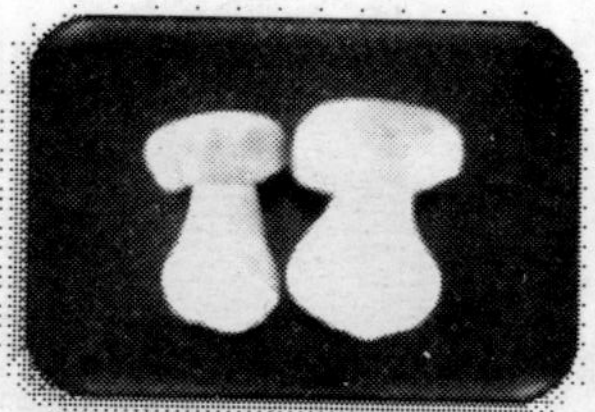

Calocybe sp.

Chlorophylum sp.

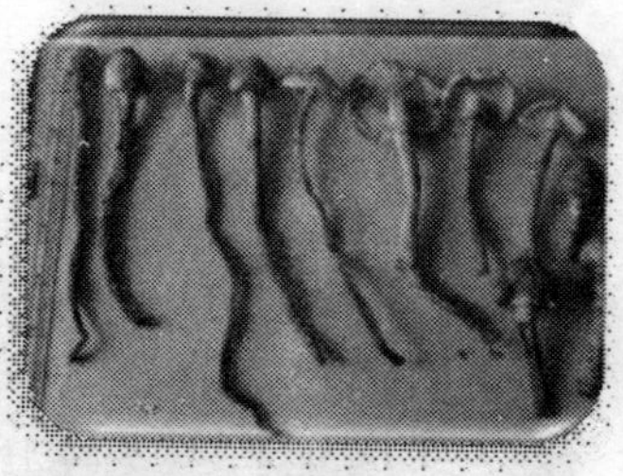

Cococybe cyanopus

Ganoderma sp.

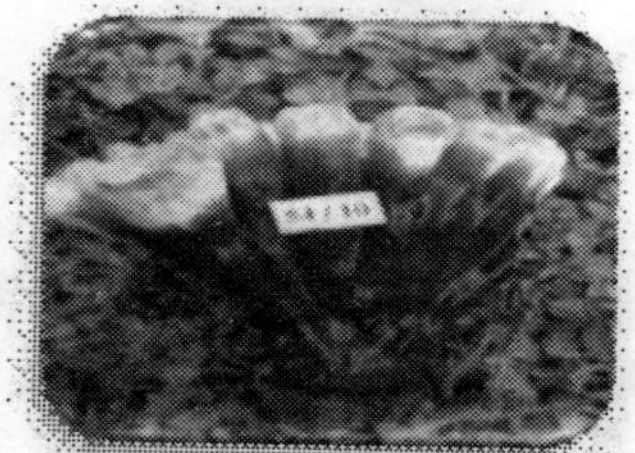

Ganoderma sp

(Contd.)

Fig. 18.2 : (*Contd.*)

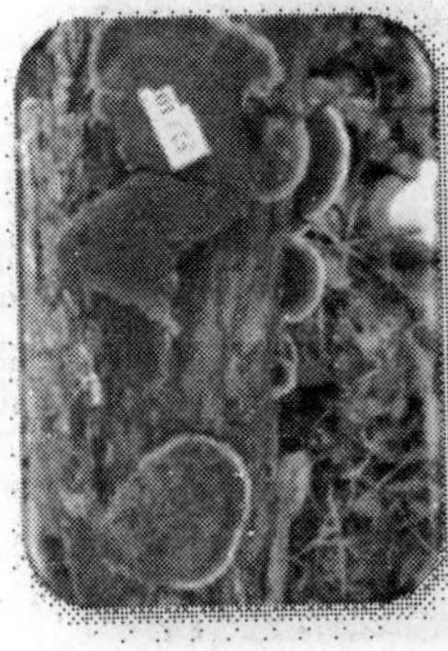

Ganoderma sp.

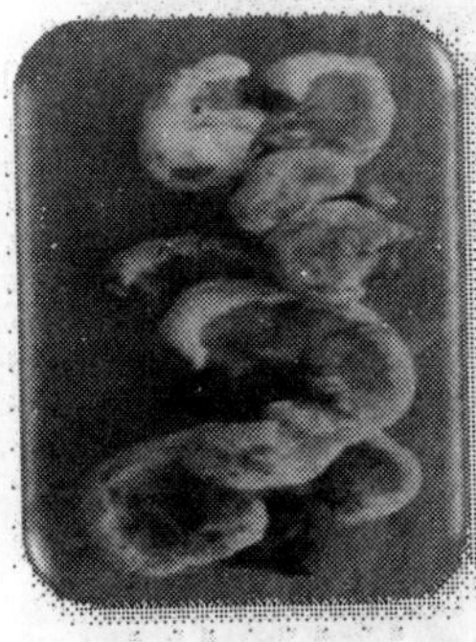

Ganoderma sp.

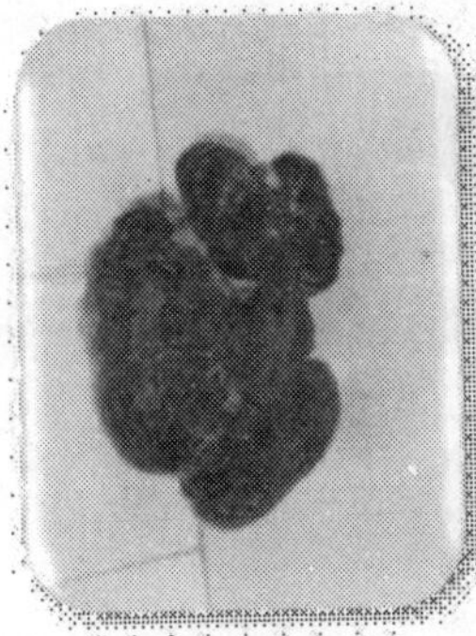

Ganoderma sp.

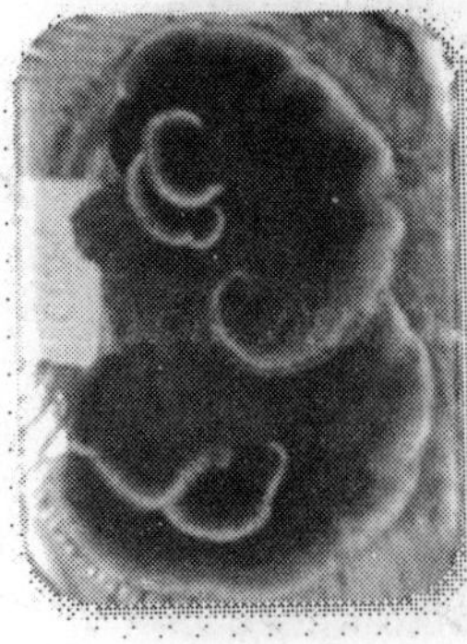

Ganoderma sp.

Ganoderma sp.

Ganoderma sp.

(*Contd.*)

Fig. 18.2 : (*Contd.*)

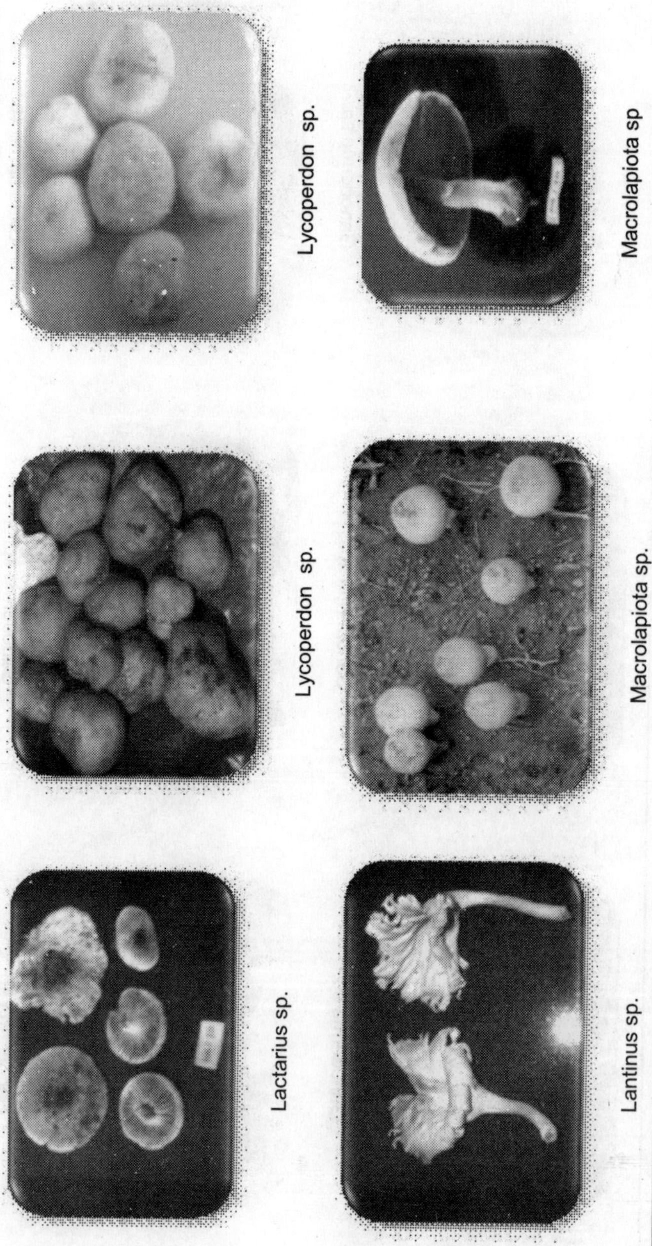

(*Contd.*)

Fig. 18.2 : (Contd.)

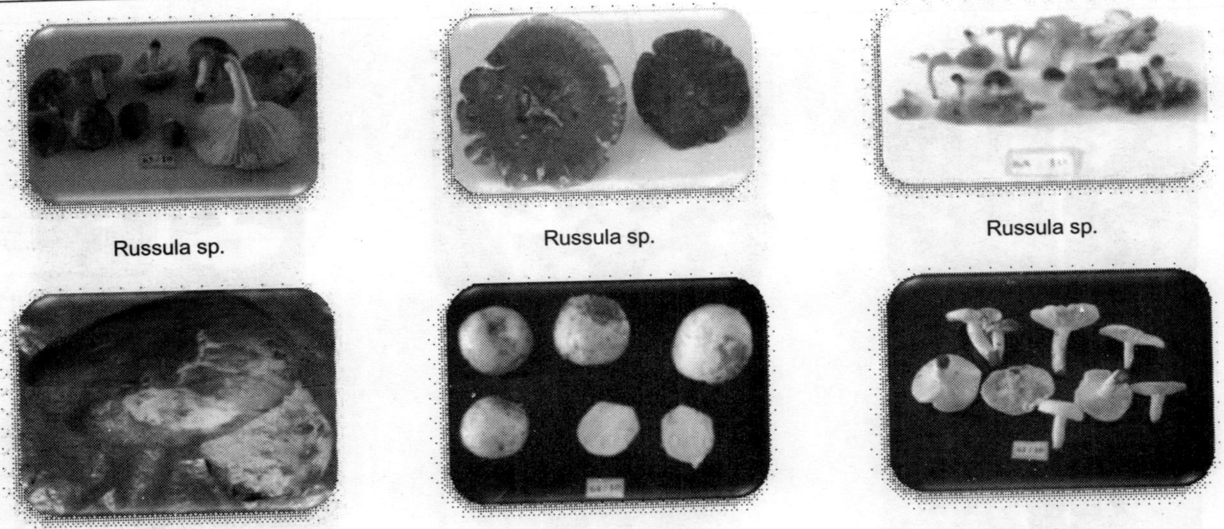

Russula sp. | Russula sp. | Russula sp.

Russula sp. | Russula sp. | Russula sp.

(Contd.)

Fig. 18.2 : *(Contd.)*

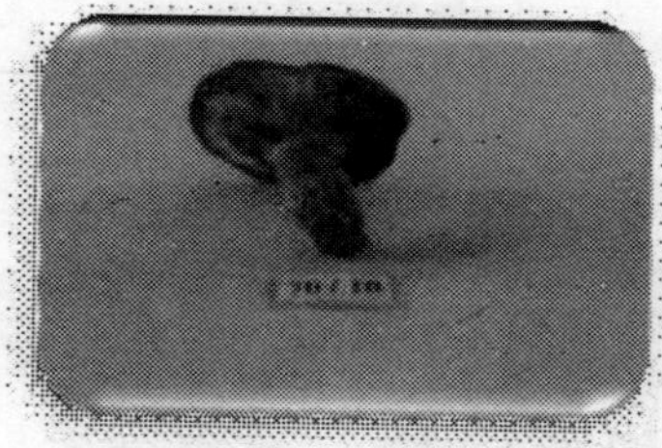

Russula sp.

Scleroderma sp..

Termitomycetes sp

Termitomycetes sp.

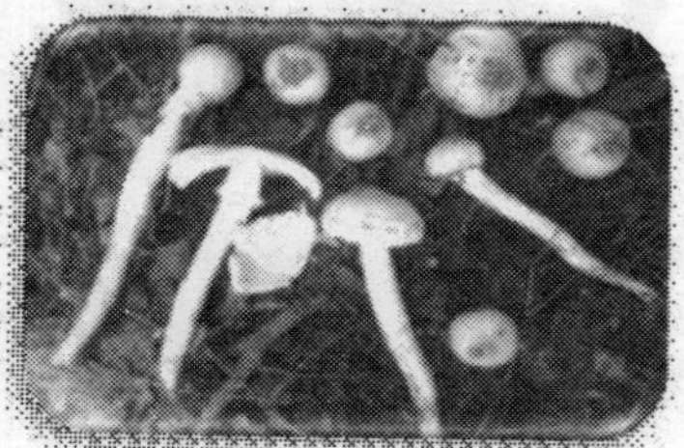

Termitomycetes sp

Termitomycetes sp.

(Contd.)

Fig. 18.2 : *(Contd.)*

Termitomycetes sp

Termitomycetes sp

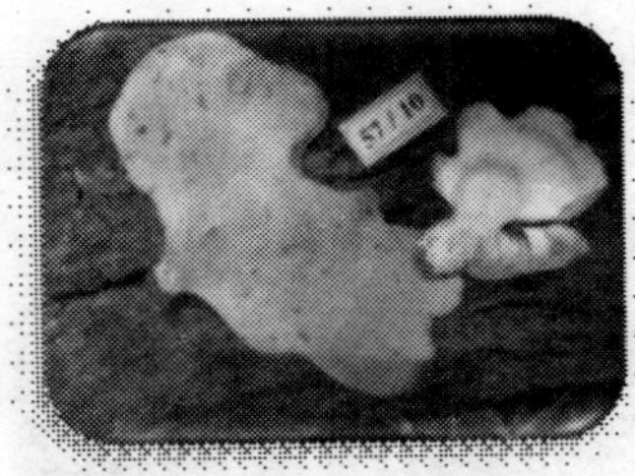

Polypores sp.

Volvariella volvacea

(Contd.)

Local Wild Mushroom Sale in Market

Scleroderma sp.

Scleroderma sp & Tecnas

Tecnas

Tecnas

Tecnas

Tecnas

Fig. 18. 3 : Scene of Sale of Wild Mushroom in Local Market

(Contd.)

Russula sp. Lantinus sp. Termitomycetes sp.

Fig. 18.3 : (Contd.)

Nutritive Value of Common Wild Edible Mushrooms

The earlier on nutritive value of wild mushroom by Gbolagade *et al.* (2006) from Southern Nigeria and assessed the nutritive value from young and matured carpophores of twelve common wild edible mushrooms collected from different locations. Of the entire wild mushroom tested, *T. globulus* was the richest containing highest amount of protein, ash, calcium, phosphorus and iron. This was followed in order by *T. microcarpus, V. esculenta, L. giganteum* and *L. pusilum* ($p < 0.05$). The highest amount of moisture (98.5%) was found in the matured fruit bodies of *L. pusilum* followed by *A. polytricha* (97.1%) and *L. giganteum* (96.9%). *Lycoperdon giganteum* contained greatest amount of soluble sugars and glycogen while *V. esculenta* was the richest in total lipid containing 17.7 per cent of the mushroom dry weight. Generally, the young fruit bodies of all the tested fungal samples were found to be richer than the matured fruit bodies. *T. microcarpus, P. atroumbonata, L. pusilum* and *V. esculenta* contained abundant amount of K, Na, Mn and Cu respectively. No works on this aspect on wild mushroom have been done so far from Jharkhand.

Nutrient composition in wild and cultivated edible mushroom, *Lentinus tuberregium* (Fr.) isolated from the wild and cultivated was analyzed on dry weight basis for their proximate nutrient compositions have been done from Tamil Nadu by Manjunathan and Kaviyarasan, (2011). The cultivated mushroom accumulated higher concentrations of carbohydrates (58.05%), protein (25%), moisture (12.51%), total ash (5.14%), crude fibre (14.69%), fat (1.54%), potassium (90.8 mg/gm), calcium (87 mg/gm), magnesium (30.4 mg/gm), sodium (37.3 mg/gm), iron (6.5 mg/gm), copper (1.0 mg/gm), zinc (4.9 mg/gm), manganese (1.7 mg/gm), energy (338 kcal). Of the nutritive value analyzed, potassium was the most dominant with concentration as high, followed by calcium, magnesium, sodium respectively. Whereas the wild mushroom proximate value such as carbohydrates (55.8%), protein (25%), moisture (9.4%), total ash (4.7%), crude fibre (3.6%), fat (1.6%), potassium (7.53 mg/gm), calcium (2.66 mg/gm), magnesium (2.45 mg/gm), sodium (1.2mg/gm), iron (0.53 mg/gm), copper (0.11 mg/gm), zinc (0.41 mg/gm), manganese (0.08 mg/gm), energy (331 kcal).

Cultivated Mushroom Diversity

Mushroom has a great potential in India and its production is exponentially increasing in areas of favourable climate and where the technological back up is available. Today, over 100 countries are practising mushroom farming and world production of this commodity is increasing at an annual rate of 7 per cent (Tiwary, 2004). The commercial mushroom farming exhibited good growth during the last decade of the twentieth century and reached the projected target of 1 lakh ton in India. Himachal Pradesh, Punjab and Haryana are major white button mushroom (*Agaricus bisporus*) growing States in North India with average yield of 20-22 kg per quintal of compost. It is now becoming popular in other States. Several species of edible fungi have been reported from North-Eastern hills of India (Verma and Singh, 1981).

In Bihar, Oyster mushroom was grown in Bhagalpur, Purnia, Hazaribagh and Ranchi districts and production was very scanty before 1992-93 (Ram and Singh, 1997). The production of mushroom have been reported 5 tonnes during 1992-93 and 10 tonnes in 1994-95 in Bihar by Sharma and Rai (1994). Now its the total production in undivided Bihar was 31.83 tonnes (Fig. 18.4) from 1986-2001 (Fig. 18.3). However, in Jharkhand was estimated to be 67.6 tonnes from 2001 to 2011-12 (Fig. 18. 5).

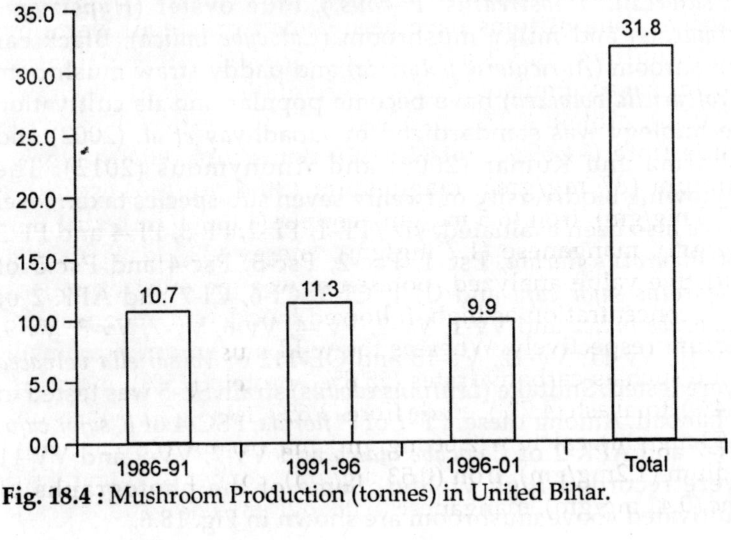

Fig. 18.4 : Mushroom Production (tonnes) in United Bihar.

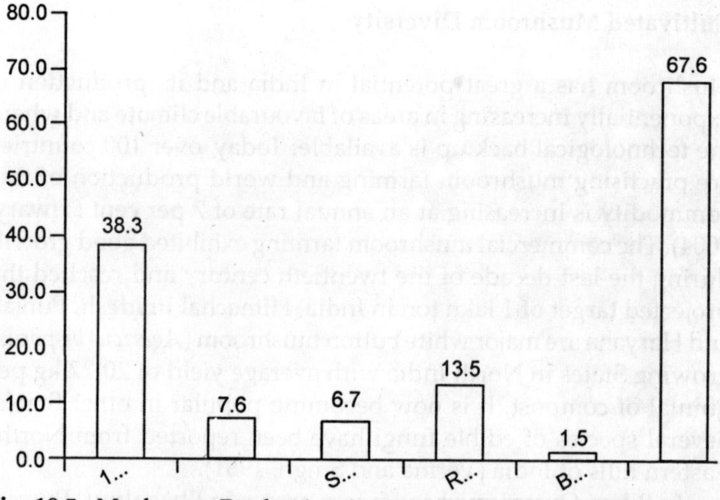

Fig. 18.5 : Mushroom Production (tonnes) in Jharkhand (April 2002 to March 2012)

In addition to wild mushroom, cultivated mushroom are also getting popularity in tribal and urban areas of Jharkhand and adjoining States of eastern region. Of late, eight cultivated mushrooms *viz.*, white button mushroom (*Agaricas bisporus*), summer button (*A. bitorqis*), oyster mushrooms (*Pleurotus florida, P. sajorcaju, P. ostreatus, P. eous,*), blue oyster (*Hypsizygus ulmarius*) and milky mushroom (*Calocybe indica*), Black ear mushroom (*Auricularia polytrica*) and paddy straw mushroom (*Volvariella volvacea*) have become popular and its cultivation technology was standardized by Upadhyay *et al.* (2002) and Sharma and Kumar (2006) and Anonymous (2012). The following biodiversity of twenty seven sub-species taxon level have also been evaluated, viz., PF-1, PF-2, PF-3, PF-4 and PF-5 of *Pleurotus florida*, Psc-1, Psc-2, Psc-3, Psc-4 and Psc-5 of *Pleurotus sajor caju* and CI-1, CI-3, CI-6, CI-7 and APK-2 of *Calocybe indica* and Vv-1, Vv-2, Vv -4, Vv-6, Vv-7, Vv-8, Vv-9, Vv-10, Vv-11, Vv-12, Vv-13 and OE-112 of *Volvariella volvacea* were tested. Shiitake (*Lentinus edodus*) strain SL-5 was tested in Dhanbad. Among these, PF-1 of *P. florida*, PSC-4 of *P. sajor caju*, CI-7 and APK-2 of *Calocybe indica* and VV-7, VV-9 and VV-11 were recorded high yielder. Some of the photographs of cultivated above mushroom are shown in Fig. 18.6.

Biodiversity of Cultivated Mushroom

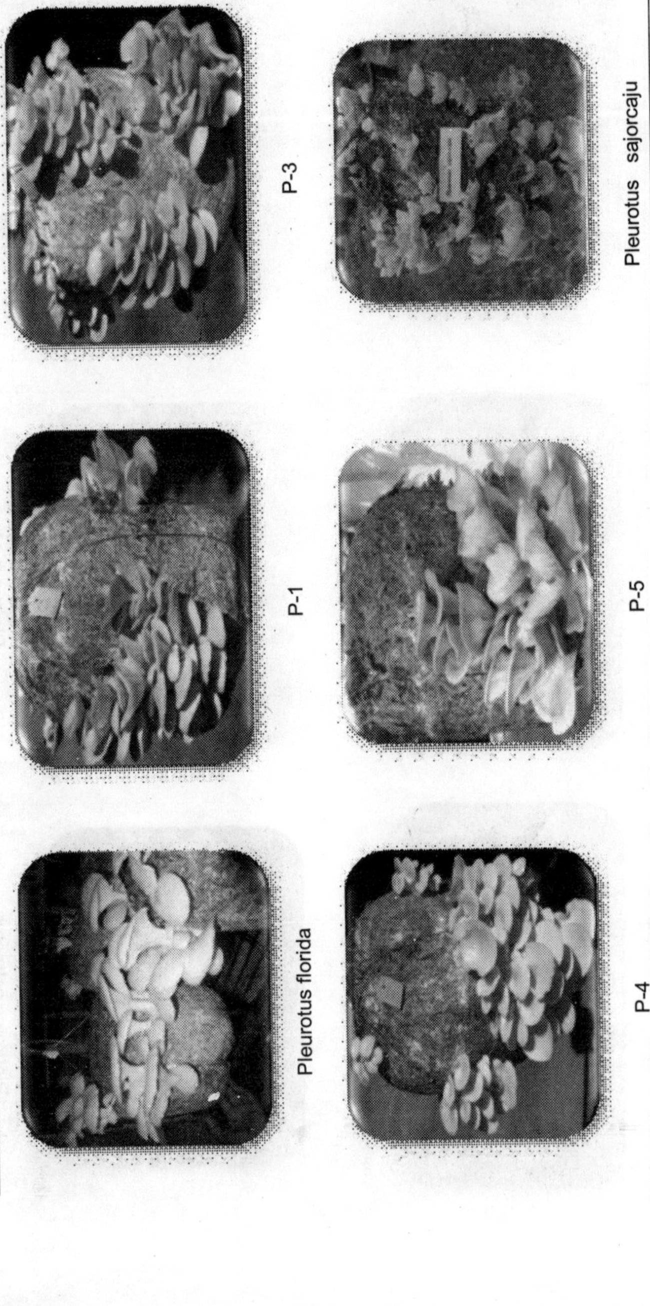

Fig. 18.6 : Cultivated Mushroom Varieties

(Contd.)

Fig. 18.6 : *(Contd.)*

(Contd.)

Fig. 18.6 : *(Contd.)*

(Contd.)

Fig. 18.6 : *(Contd.)*

CI-1

CI-7

APK-2 (On Wheat straw)

APK-2 (on paddy straw)

Agaricus bisporus

Agaricus bitorquis

(Contd.)

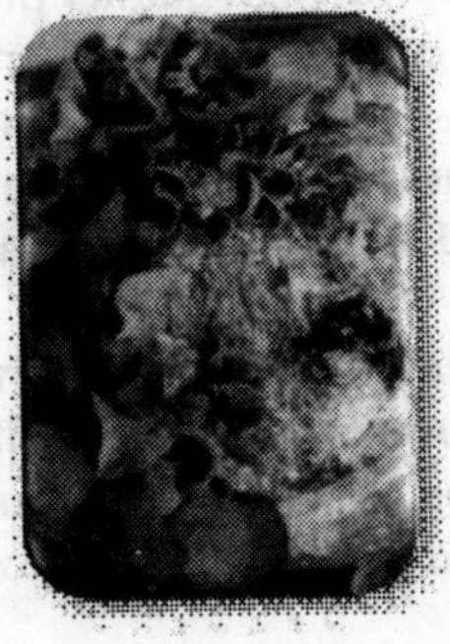

Auricularia polytricha

Fig. 18.6 : (*Contd.*)

Advantages of Mushroom Cultivation

1. Wastes such as cereal straws are largely burnt by the farmers, which causes air pollution. However, these raw materials can actually be used for the cultivation of mushrooms. This kind of bioconversion exercise can greatly reduce environmental pollution.
2. Mushroom cultivation can be a labour intensive activity. Therefore, it will serve as means of generating employment, particularly for rural women and youths in order to raise their social status. It will also provide additional work for the farmers during winter months when the farming schedule is light.
3. It will provide the people with an additional vegetable of high quality, and enrich the diet with high quality proteins, minerals and vitamins which can be of direct benefit to the human health and fitness. The extractable bioactive compounds from medicinal mushrooms would enhance human's immune systems and improve their quality of life.
4. Mushroom cultivation is a cash crop. The harvested fruiting bodies can be sold in local markets for additional family income or exported for an important source of foreign exchange that will definitely improve the economic standards of the people.
5. Some warm mushrooms, e.g., *Volvariella volvacea* (Straw mushrooms) and *Pleurotus sajor-caju* (Oyster mushrooms) are relatively fast growing organisms and can be harvested in 3 to 4 weeks after spawning. It is a short return agricultural business and can be of immediate benefit to the community.

Mushroom farming is both a science and an art. The science is developed through research and the art is perfected through curiosity and practical experience. However, mushroom farming is a business which requires precision. Indeed, it is not as simple as what some people often loosely stipulate.

Conclusion

Thirty nine wild edible fungi were identified in mushroom diversity of Jharkhand. Among them, nine species belongs to the order of Agaricales in which six species were *Termitomycetes* (*Bada Khukhri)* which belongs to family Agaricaceae and two species were found as poisonous, viz., *Chlorophylum* sp.and *Amanita vegenatae*. Similarly, *Cococybe cyanopus* (*Tecnas*) of order Agaricales belongs to family Bolbitaceae were popular in Jharkhand. Nine species belong to Polypoales viz., *Ganoderma* and *Polypore*. Eight species belong to Russulales. The important species of edible fungi belong to *Scleroderma, Boletus* and *Lycoderma*. Eight cultivated species were standardized and evaluated. Among them, P-1 of *P. florida*, Psc-4 of *P. sajor-caju*, CI-7, APK-2 of *C. indica* and Vv-7, Vv-9 and Vv-11 of *V. volvacea* were recorded high yielders.

REFERENCES

Abraham, S.P. and J.L. Kachroo (1989). Larger fungi from Kashmir, India, VI. The genus Amanita. *Micol. Neotrop. Apl.* 2: 41-51. Agricultural Engineering and Machinery (APCAEM). Convention Centre No. 12, Yumin.

Ahlawat, O.P.; Kumar, S.; Arumuganathan, T. and Tewari, R.P. (25 Years) of AICRP (Mushroom) All India Coordinated Research Project on Mushroom National Research Centre for Mushroom (Indian Council of Agricultural Research) Chambaghat, Solan-173 213 (HP).

Anonymous (2003). "China Becomes World's Biggest Edible Mushroom Producer". Allbusiness.com. August 21, 2003. Retrieved 2010-08-04. Road, Chaoyang District, Beijing 100029, P.R. China. www.unapcaem.org.

Anonymous (2012). *Training Manual on Mushroom Cultivation Technology. Asian and Pacific* Copyright© 2012 UNAPCAEM.

Atri, N.S., Saini, S.S. and Saini, M.K. (1997). Studies on Genus *Russula* Pers. from North Western Himalaya .In *Souvenir and Abstracts. Indian Mushroom Conference* 1997 (Abs) p. 11.

Atri, N.S.; Kaur, A. and Kaur, H. (2005).Wild Mushrooms-Collection and Identification. In Frontiers in Mushroom Biotechnology (Eds. R.D. Rai, R.C. Upadhyay and S.R. Sharma. NRC Solan p. 9-26.

Bhaben, T.; Lisha, G. and Chandra, S.G. (2011). Wild edible fungal resources used by ethnic tribes of Nagaland, India. *Indian Journal of Traditional Knowledge* 10(3):512-515.

Bhatt, R.P. and Lakhanpal, T.N. (1990). Fleshy fungi of North-Western Himalayas V. *Indian Phytopathol.* 43 (2), 156-164.

Bhatt, S.C. (2004). *The District Gazetteers of Jharkhand*. Gyan Publication House, New Delhi, p. 354.

Boruah, P.; Kailta, P.; Bordoloi, D.; Gogi, P. and Adhikary, R.K. (1997). Some fleshy fungi of ethnobotanic use from North-East India. *Advances in Forestry Research in India,* 16:165-171.

Chang, S.T. (1999), Global impact of edible and medicinal mushrooms on human welfare in the 21st century: *International Journal of Medicinal Mushrooms,* 1:31-62.

Chang, S.T. (2006). The World Mushroom Industry: Trends and Technological Development, *International Journal of Medicinal Mushrooms,* 8 (4): 297-314.

Chang, S.T. and Miles, P.G. (2004). *Mushrooms- Cultivation, Nutritional Value, Medicinal Effect and Environmental Impact.* CRC Press, Washington, D.C. pp. 451.

Das, K. (2009). Mushrooms of Sikkim I: Barsey Rhododendron Sanctuary. Sikkim State Biodiversity Board, Gangtok and Botanical Survey of India, Kolkata. 1-160.

Das, K. (2010). Diversity and conservation of wild mushrooms in Sikkim with special reference to Barsey Rhododendron Sanctuary *NeBIO,* 1(2):1-13.

Dhar, B.L. and Singh, S.K. (1999). Current status of mushroom genetic resources in India. In Proceedings *of the 3rd International Conference on Mushroom Biology and Mushroom Products* & AMGA's 26th National Industry Conference Sydney. pp. 40-46.

Doshi, A. and Sharma, S.S. (1997).Wild mushrooms of Rajasthan. In: Rai D, Verma (eds) *Advances of Mushroom Biology and Production.* Mushroom Society of India. Solan, India.

FAO. (2004). *Non Wood Forest Products, Wild Edible Fungi: A Global Overview of their Use and Importance.* (ed. Boa, E). FAO Publication, Rome, pp. 17-147.

Gbolagade, J.; Ajayi, A.; Oku, I. and Wankasi, D. (2006). Nutritive Value of Common Wild Edible Mushrooms from Southern Nigeria, *Global Journal of Biotechnology & Biochemistry,* 1 (1): 16-21.

Harsh, N.S.K.; Rai, B.K.; Ayachi, S.S. (1993). Forest fungi and tribal economy—a case study in Baiga tribe of Madhya Pradesh. *J. Trop. Forest,* 9: 270-279.

Harsh, N.S.K.; Tiwari, C.K.; Rai, B.K. (1996). Forest fungi in the aid of tribal women of Madhya Pradesh. *Sustainable Forestry* 1: 10-15.

Hawksworth, D.L. (1997). The fascination of fungi: Exploring fungal diversity.*Mycologist,* 11: 18-22.

Hobbs, C. (1995). *Medicinal Mushrooms: An Exploration of Tradition, Healing, and Culture.* 2nd edition. Santa Cruz CA, USA. *Botanica* Press. pp. 252.

Jain, R.K. (2005). *The History of Mushroom Cultivation in India.* Environment.Bhologi.com

Kaul, T.N. (1997). *Introduction to Mushroom Science (Systematics).* Oxford and IBH Publ. Co. Pvt. Ltd, New Delhi. p. 198.

Kaul, T.N. and Kachroo, J.L. (1974). Common edible mushrooms of Jammu and Kashmir. *Ind. Mush. Sci.* 71:26-31.

Kumar, S. and Sharma Y.P. (2011). Diversity of wild mushrooms from Jammu and Kashmir (India), *Proceedings of the 7th International Conference on Mushroom Biology and Mushroom Products* (ICMBMP7) 568-577.

Kumar, S.M. and Shukla, C.S. (1995). *In Advances in Horticulture,* Vol. 13 Mushrooms. Malhotra Publish. House, New Delhi, pp. 277-316.

Lakhanpal, T.N. (1994). Prospect of mushroom from the wild. In *Advances in Mushroom Biotechnology,* edited by Nair, M.C., Gopalan, C. and Das, L. Scientific *Publisher,* Jodhpur, India p. 15-22.

Lakhanpal, T.N. (1997). Diversity of mushroom mycoflora in the North-West Himalaya. In *Recent Researches in Ecology, Environment and Pollution* (Eds. Sati, S.C.; Saxena, J. and Dubey, R.C.), Today and Tomorrow's Printers and Publishers, New Delhi. 1997, pp. 35–68.

Longvah, T. and Deosthale, Y.G. (1998). Compositional and nutritional studies on edible wild mushroom from North-East India, *Food Chem.* 63:331-334.

Manjunathan, J. and Kaviyarasan, (2011). Nutrient composition in wild and cultivated edible mushroom, *Lentinus tuberregium* (Fr.) Tamil Nadu., India *International Food Research Journal,* 18: 809-811.

Manoharachary, C.; Sridhar; Singh, R.; Adholeya, A.; Suryanarayanan, T.S. Rawat; S. and Johri; B.N. (2005). Fungal biodiversity: Distribution, conservation and prospecting of fungi from India. Special Section: Microbial Diversity. *Current Science,* 89(1):58-71.

Miles, P.G. and Chang, S.T. (1997). *Mushroom Biology, Concise Basics and Current Developments. World Scientific Publ.,* London.

Purkayastha, R.P. and Chandra, A. (1985). *Manual of Indian Edible Mushroom.* Today and Tomorrow's Printers and Publishers, New Delhi.

Ram, D. and Singh, A.R. (1997). Mushroom cultivation in Bihar-Present Status and Future Prospects. *Souvenir and Abstracts,* Indian Mushroom Conference (September 10-12, 1997). Poster 4. 34 p. 82.

Rojas, C. and Mansur, E. (1995). Ecuador: Informaciones generales sobre productos non madereros en Ecuador. In *Memoria, consulta de expertos sobre productos forestales no madereros para America Latina Y el Caribe,* pp. 208-223.

Sagar, A.; Chauhan, A.; Sehgal, A.K. (2005). Ethnobotanical study of some wild edible mushrooms of tribal district Kinnaur of Himachal Pradesh. *Indian J. Mush.* XXIII: 1-8.

Saini, S.S. and Atri, N.S. (1995). In *Advances in Horticulture,* Vol. 13,

Mushroom, Malhotra Publishing House, NewDelhi, pp. 375-386.

Sharma, J.P.; Ajit, Jha; S. Kumar and M. Rai (2002). *Jharkhand Mei Khumbh Utpadan (Khukhri) Chotanagpur Horticulture Special Issue* -2002: 30-1.

Sharma, J.P. and Kumar, S. (2006). Effect of supplementation with bran and oil cake on yield of (*Pleurotus* spp.) in Jharkhand. Souvenir and Abstract, National symposium on Emerging plant disease, diagnosis and management (Jan. 31- Feb. 2) p. 126.

Sharma, J.P., Kumar, S. and Upadhyay, R.C. (2012).Biodiversity of wild and cultivated mushroom in Jharkhand State. In Book of Abstract. National Seminar on plant genetic research for eastern and North-Eastern India held at ICAR Research Complex for NEH Region (May 11-12). IC: 5 P7.

Sharma, S.R. and Rai, R.D. (1994). Aiming for the world market .*The Hindu Survey of India.* pp. 191-7.

Sinha, B.K. (2003) Biodiversity and its economics: A case study of Ranchi urban agglomeration. *Jharkhand Journal of Development and Management Studies* XISS, Ranchi. Vol. 1 No 3. pp. 349-360.

Sohi, H.S. and Upadhyay, R.C. (1986). Occurrence of *Cladobotryum variospermum* (Link) huges on polyporous fungi under natural condition. *Current Science* 55:1037-1038.

Sohi, H.S. and Upadhyay, R.C. (1989). Effect of temperature on mycelial growth of *Pleurotus* species and their yield parameters or selected substrates. *Mushroom Science 12* (2) 49-56.

Tiwari, R.P. (2004). Now in Limelight. *The Hindu Survey of Indian Agriculture,* pp. 132-33.

Upadhyay, R.C.; Verma, R.N.; Singh S.K. and Yadav M.C. (2002). Effect of organic nitrogen supplementation in *Pleurotus* species. *Mushroom Biology and Mushroom Products. Sánchez et al. (eds). 2002UAEM. ISBN 968-878-105-3.*

Verma, R.N. and Singh, G.B. (1981). Investigation on edible fungi in the North Eastern Hills of India. *Mushroom Sci.* 11: 89-99.

Verma, R.N.; Singh, G.B. and Singh, S.M. (1985). *Meghalaya Sci. Soc. J.* 7 and 8: 6-9.

Verma, R.N.; Singh, G.B. and Bilgrami K.S. (1987). In *Proceedings of the International Conference on Science and Cultivation Technology of Edible fungi,* RRL (J&K) 414-421.

Verma, R.N., Singh, S.M., Singh, G.B. and Bilgrami, K.S. (1989). *Gomphus flocculus*—A new record for India. *Curr. Sci.* 58: 1370-1371.

Verma, R.N.; Singh, G.B. and Singh, S.M. (1995). Mushroom flora of North Eastern Hills. In *Advances in Horticulture Mushroom,* edited by Chadha, K.L. & Sharma, S.R. Molhotra Publishers House, New Delhi, 329-349.

Verma, R.N. (1997). The mushroom Scenario of India—a need for species diversification. In *Souvenir and Abstracts. Indian Mushroom Conference* 1997 (Abs) p. 12.

Verma, R.N. and Upadhyay, R.C. (1999). Biodiversity of mushroom and potential of their utilization in tribal belts of Bihar. In *National Seminar on Sustainable Horticulture Production in Tribal Region* (July 25-26) HARP pp. 140.

Vishwakarma, M.P.; Bhatt, R.P. and Joshi, S. (2012). Macro fungal diversity in moist temperate forests of Garhwal Himalaya. *Indian Journal of Science and Technology* 5 (1): 1928-1932.

Wakchaure, G.C. (2010). Production and Marketing of Mushroom: Global and National Scenario. In *Mushrooms cultivation, Marketing and Consumption*. (Eds. Singh, M.; Vijay, B.; Shwet Kamal and Wakchaure, G.C.). Directorate of Mushroom Research (ICAR) Chambaghat, Solan pp. 15-22.

19
Bioactivity of Colocasia species

Saswati Roy, Rumki Nath and M. Dutta Choudhury

Introduction

Higher plants, as sources of medicinal compounds, have continued to play a dominant role (Farombi, 2003) in the maintenance of human health since ancient times. Over 50 per cent of all modern clinical drugs are of natural product origin (Stuffness *et al.*, 1982) and natural products play an important role in drug development programmes in the pharmaceutical industry (Baker *et al.*, 1995) There has been a revival of interest in herbal medicines and this is due to increased awareness of the limited ability of synthetic pharmaceutical products to control major diseases and the need to discover new molecular structures as lead compounds from the plant kingdom. Plants are the basic source of knowledge of modern medicine. The basic molecular and active structures for synthetic fields are provided by rich natural sources. This burgeoning worldwide interest in medicinal plants reflects recognition of the validity of many traditional claims regarding the value of natural products in health care. The relatively lower incidence of adverse reactions to plant preparations compared to modern conventional pharmaceuticals, coupled with their reduced cost is encouraging both in consuming public and national health care institutions to consider plant medicines as alternatives to synthetic drugs. The medicinal value of drug plants is mainly due to the presence of some chemical substance in the tissues known as secondary metabolites. These chemical substances are mainly C, H, O and N containing alkaloids, terpenoids, flavonoids, etc., which if introduced into the human body produce a definite physiological effects causing even death. Gums, resins, essential oils, glucosides, tannins, etc. are also used in drugs. Several plants have medicinal values and bioactivity and some plants of *Colocasia* species of family Araceae are also well known. The Araceae is a large family comprising some hundred genera and more than fifteen hundred species. Most of the aroids prefer to grow in moist or shady habitats. Some are terrestrial while others are vines, creepers or climbers. Many species of the aroids are also epiphytes. The major edible aroids are classified into two tribes and five genera; Lasioideae (*Cyrtosperma* and *Amorphophallus*) and Colocasiodeae (*Alocasia, Colocasia and Xanthosoma*). Plants of the genus *Colocasia* are herbaceous, often with large leaves and bearing one or more underground stems or corms. The root system of taro is adventitious and fibrous. The flower of taro is composed of a spathe 20 to 40 cm in length surrounding a spadix measuring 6 to 14 cm that contains unisexual flowers. All parts of the taro plant contain acrid principles which are irritating to the mouth and oesophagus (Lee, http://www.siu.edu/-ebl/leaflets/taro.htm. Acridity is due to the presence of the calcium oxalate crystals in the taro plant. Calcium oxalate crystals in taro exist in two forms: raphides and druses. The number and density of the crystals is higher in early development, then level off, and eventually decrease in older larger corms (Leslie *et al.*, 1979). The corms are considered as a good source of carbohydrates and potassium. They also contain greater amounts of vitamin B complex than whole milk. The taro leaf, like most higher plant leaves, is rich in protein and ash. It is also a rich source of calcium, phosphorus, iron, vitamin C, thiamine, riboflavin and niacin, which are important constituents of the human diet (Inno, 1999).

The liver plays a central role in transforming and clearing chemicals and is susceptible to the toxicity from these agents. Smooth endoplasmic reticulum in liver is the principal metabolic clearing house for both endogenous chemicals (e.g., cholesterol, steroids hormones, fatty acids and proteins) and exogenous substances (e.g., drugs) (Donald *et al.*, 2006). More than 900 drugs have been implicated in causing liver injury (Friedman and Schott *et al.*, 2003) and it is the most common reason for a drug to be withdrawn from the market. Drug induced liver injury is responsible for 5 per cent of all hospital admissions and 50 per cent of all acute liver failures (McNally and Peter., 2006), (Ostapowiez *et al.*, 2002). Cytochrome P-450, is the most important family of metabolizing enzymes in the liver. Cytochrome P-450 is not a single enzyme, but rather consists of a family of closely related 50 isomers; six of them metabolize 90 per cent of drugs (Skett, *et al.*, 2001), (Lynch and Price, 2007). Many substances can influence P-450 enzyme mechanism. Drugs interact with the enzyme family in several ways (Michalets, 1998). Drugs that modify cytochrome P-450 enzyme are referred to as either inhibitors or inducers. There are various factors influencing drug induced hepatotoxicity (Keefe, Emmet B. *et al.*, 2004). Adverse drug interactions are classified as type A (pharmacological) or type B (idiosyncratic) (Davies, 1985). Type A drug reaction accounts for 80 per cent of all toxicities (Pirmohammed *et al.*, 1998). Idiosyncratic (type B) injury occurs without warning; when agents cause non-predictable hepatotoxicity in susceptible individuals which is not related to dose and has variable latency period (Zimmerman, H.J., 1978). Biochemical markers (i.e., alanine transferase, alkaline phosphatase, bilirubin) are often used to indicate liver damage. Liver injury means either rise in ALT level, rise in ALP level or rise in bilirubin level when associated with increased ALT or ALP (Mumoli *et al.*, 2006), (Benchou, 1990). An elevation in serum bilirubin level of more than 2 times upper limit of normal (ULN) with associated transaminase rise is an ominous sign which indicates severe hepatotoxicity, is likely to lead to mortality in 10 per cent to 15 per cent (Arora and Goldhaber, 2006). Some important specific drug or toxin of liver injury mainly includes acetaminophen (paracetamol), non-steroidal anti inflammatory drugs, glucocorticoids (Manov *et al.*, 2006), isoniazed (Ianchu *et al.*, 1986), (commonly used drug for tuberculosis), industrial toxin (arsenic, ccl_4 and vinyl chloride), natural products (amanita mushrooms), etc. Liver diseases are therefore, a major problem of worldwide population, however, the number of drugs actually used successfully in human is very small (Muriel and Rivera-Espinoza, 2008).

Colocasia antiquorum (L) Schott, (Araceae), is an ancient crop grown throughout the humid tropics. Hepatoprotective effect of the ethanolic extract of corms of Colocasia antiquorum was evaluated in paracetamol and ccl_4 intoxicated rats. The ethanolic extract of C. antiquorum at a dose of 500 mg/kg was administered orally for 7 days. The protective effect was evident from serum biochemicals parameters and histopathological analysis. Rats treated with extract of C. antiquorum significantly ($P<0.001$) inhibited the elevation of serum Glutamic Oxaloacetic acid Transaminase (SGOT) and serum Glutamic Pyruvic Transaminase (SGPT) in paracetamol and ccl_4 treated rats. Histopathological changes induced by paracetmol and ccl_4 were also significantly reduced by the extract in similar dosage. Extract of. C antiquorum was found nearly similar to that of silymarin. Active constituents identified in ethanolic extract were anthocyanins such as cyanidin 3-glucoside, pelargonidin 3-glucoside and cyanidin 3-rhamnoside in corms of C. antiquorum which may be responsible for the hepatoprotection (Patil M. *et al.*, 2008).

Antioxidant and Anticancer Activity of *Colocasia*

Poi is a pasty starch made from the cooked, mashed corm of the taro plant (*Colocasia esculenta* L.). Poi has been used as a probiotic – defined by FAO/WHO as live microorganisms which when administered in adequate amount confer a health benefit to the host. No scientific studies have explored the possibility of poi being used as a probiotic but an investigator determined that predominant bacteria of poi are *Lactobacillus lactis* and *Lactibacilii* (Amy C. Brown, *et al.*, 2004). Soluble extract of poi were incubated at 100 mg/ml *in vitro* for antiproliferative activity against the rat YYT colon cancer line. 3H thymidine incorporation studies were conducted to demonstrate that poi inhibited the proliferation of these cancer cells in a dose dependent manner. The greatest suppression of YYT colon cancer growth occurred when 25 per cent concentration was used. When poi was incubated with YYT cells, after 2 days the YYT cells underwent apoptotic changes as evidenced by a positive terminal deoxynucleotide transferase mediated by dUTP nick end labelling (TUNEL) stain. Poi consumption lower the colon cancer by two mechanisms—by inducing apoptosis within colon cancer cells and by non-specifically activating lymphocytes, which in turn can lyse cancerous cells (Army C. Brown, *et al.*, 2005). The corms of taro plant contain cyanidin 3-glucoside, cyanidin 3-rhamnoside and pelargonidin 3-glucoside. These substances have antioxidant and anti inflammatory properties which could protect the intestine from carcinogens (Cambie, R.C., *et al.*, 2003).

A 22,4-kDa dimeric hemaglutinin was isolated from tubers of Colocasia esculenta acv. Small taros by employing a purification protocol that involved ion exchange chromatography on Q-sepharose, fast protein liquid chromatography (FPLC)—ion exchange chromatography on Mono Q and FPLC gel filtration on Superdex 75. The bhemaglutinin was isolated from the fraction of the taro extract adsorbed on Q-sepharose and subsequently adsorbed on Mono Q. The hemaglutinin exhibited slight antitumour activity toward hepatoma Hep G2 and weak mitogenic activity toward murine splenocytes. It induced expression of the cytokinines interleukin-1beta, interleukin-2, interferon-gamma and tumour necrosis factor alpha. But hemaglutinin was devoid of any antifungal activity (Yau Sang Chan *et al.*, 2009).

Six C-glycosylflavonoids and O-glycosylflavonoid have been identified from the shoot system of Taumu (*Colocasia esculenta*). They were identified as schaftoside, isoschaftoside, orientin, isovitexin, isoorientin, vitexin and luteolin 7-O-sophoroside. The presence of catechol moiety in the B-ring of isoorientin, orientin, luteolin 7-O-sophoroside showed strong antioxidant activity with different mechanisms of action in DPPH radical, B-carotene bleaching and superoxide radical inhibition assays. Isovitexin was the main compound of water extract of the stem. The results suggest the potential of the leaf of Taumu as a source of dietary antioxidant (Abraham Cheng, 2009).

Antimicrobial Activity of *Colocasia*

Plants with possible antimicrobial activity should be tested against an appropriate microbial model to confirm the activity and to ascertain the parameters associated with it. The effects of plants extract on bacteria have been studied by a very large number of researchers in different parts of the world (Reddy *et al.*, 2001), (Erdo Urul, 2002), (Ateb and Erdo Urul, 2003). Much work have been done on ethnomedicinal plants in India (Maheshwari *et al.*, 1986), (Rai, 1989), (Negi *et al.*, 1993). Interest in a large number of traditional natural product has been increased (Taylor *et al.*, 1996). It has been suggested the aqueous ethanolic extracts from plants used in allopathic medicine are potential sources of antiviral, antitumours and antimicrobial agents (Chung *et al.*, 1995), (Vlietinok *et al.*, 1995).

Colocasia esculenta Schott. (PSN-748) is thought to be a native of India. The young leaves are rich in vitamin C and roots rich in starch. It contains thiamine, riboflavin, niacin, oxalic acid, calcium oxalate and sapotoxin. The tubers contain amino acid and proteins. The corms contain cyaniding 3-glucoside, cyanidin 3-rhamnoside and pelargonidin 3-glucoside. The methanolic extract of this plant showed antibacterial activity against *Klebsiella pneumoniae* (Nair R., *et al*, 2005).

The methanolic leaf extract of *Colocasia esculenta* showed no active antimicrobial activity but its aqueous extract showed effect against *Vibrio alginolyticus, Vibrio parahaemolyticus, Vibrio harveyi, Vibrio vulnificus, Vibrio cholerae, Citrobacter freundi* (Lee Seong Wei, *et al.*, 2008).

9,12,13-trihydroxy-10(E)-octadecenoic acid isolated from *Colocasia antiquorum* inoculated with *Ceratocystis fimbriata* possess antifungal activity. The 80 per cent ethanolic extract of leaves of *Colocasia gigantea* Hook showed weak effect against *Alternaria alternata* (Suhaila Mohammed, *et al.*, 1996).

Anti Inflammatory Activity of *Colocasia*

The majority of naturally occurring phenolics retain antioxidative and anti-inflammatory properties which appear to contribute to their chemopreventive or chemoprotective activity. Cyclooxygenase-2 (COX-2) inducible and nitricoxide synthase (iNOS) are important enzymes thatb mediate inflammatory processes. Improper upregulation of COX-2 and or iNOS has been associated with pathophysiology of certain types of human cancers as well as inflammatory disorders. Since inflammation is closely linked to tumour promotion, substances with potent anti-inflammatory activities are anticipated to exert chemopreventive effects on carcinogensis, particularly in the promotion stage. Recent studies have demonstrated that eukaryotic transcription factor nuclear factor kappa B (NF-kappa B) is involved in regulation of COX-2 and iNOs expression. Multiple lines of compelling evidence indicate that extracellular-regulated protein kinase and p38 mitogen activated protein kinase are key elements of the intracellular signalling cascades responsible for NF-kappa B activation in response to wide array of external stimuli. One of the possible mechanisms underlying inhibition of NF-kappa B activation by aforementioned phytochemicals involves repression of degradation of the inhibitory unit I kappa B alpha which hampers subsequent nuclear translocation of the functionally active sub-unit of NF-kappa B (Surh Y.J., *et al.*, 2001).

Taro roots are rich in starch (amylase 28 per cent and amylopectin 72%) and the corms of taro contain the anthocyanins cyaniding 3-glucoside, cyaniding 3-rhamnoside and pelargonodin 3-glucoside, reported to have antioxidant anti-inflammatory properties (Hegnaeur, 1963).

An ethanolic extract study of the leaves of *Colocasia esculenta* in wister rats showed significant anti-inflammatory activity (N. Shah Biren *et al.*, 2007).

Inhibition of human lanosterol synthase *Colocasia esculenta*

Ethanolic extract of *Colocasia esculenta* showed the inhibition of human lanosterol synthase at 300 micro g/m*l*. Examination of activity variation among eight taro cultivars indicated that "Aichi-wase" and "Yatsugashira" had the most potent activity for human lanosterol synthase (hOSC) inhibition. In order to identify the active constituent of taro, ethanol extract of "Aichi-wase" were partitioned with hexane and aqueous methanol, and fractionated by silica gel column chromatography. Inhibitory activity was concentrated in two major active fractions. Further purification of these fractions by preparative HPLC gave three monogalacto-syldiacylglycerols and five digalactosyldiacylglycerols as active cmpounds that showed 28 to 67 per cent inhibitory activities at the concentration 300 micro g/m*l* (Sakano Yuichi, *et al.*, 2005).

Chemical Constituents from *Colocasia* Species

Active constituents identified in ethanolic extract of corms of *Colocasia antiquorum* were anthocyanins such as cyanidin 3-glucoside, pelargonidin 3-glucoside and cyanidin 3-rhamnoside, which may be responsible for the hepatoprotective activity (Patil *et al.*, 2008).

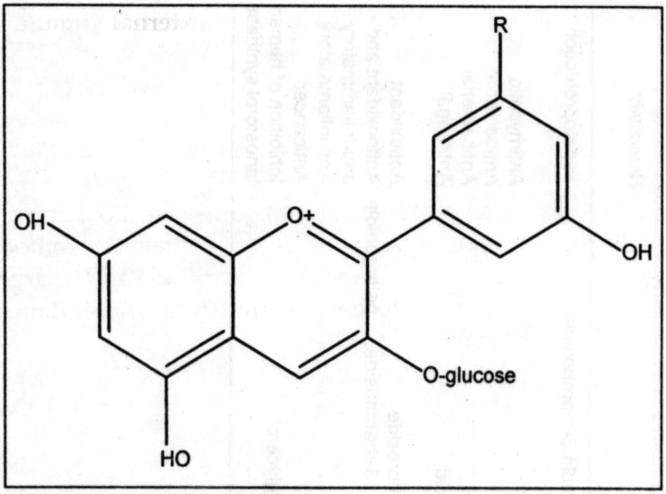

Fig. 19.1:

Cyanidin 3-glucoside (R=OH)
Pelargonidin 3-glucoside (R=H)

(Cambie and Lynette, 2003)

Six C-glycosylflavonoids and One O-glycosylflavonoid have been isolated from the shoot system of Taumu (*Colocasia esculenta*). They were identified as schaftoside, isoschaftoside, orientin, isovitexin, isoorientin, vitexin and luteolin 7-O-sophoroside. The presence of catechol moiety in the B ring of isoorientin, orientin and luteolin 7-O-sophoroside showed strong antioxidant activity (Abraham, 2009). 9,12,13-trihydroxy-10(E)-octadecenoic acid isolated from *Colocasia antiquorum* inoculated with *Ceratocystis fimbriata* are known to possess antifungal activity (Masui *et al.*, 1989). Aqueous acetone extract of corms of *Colocasia* sp. When examined by TLC and HPLC showed the existence if a range of phenolic compound which includes gallic acid, chlorogenic acid, (+)-catechin, (–)-epigallocatechin and the possible presence of proanthocyanidin and flavonoids (Tom and June, 2006). The ethanolic extract of *Colocasia esculenta* ("Aichi-wase", a taro cultivars) gave three monogalactosylacylglycerols and digolactosylacylglycerol by preparative HPLC which showed 28 to 67 per cent inhibition of human lanosterol synthase at the concentration 300 micro g/ml (Sakano *et al.*, 2005).

Table 19.1 : Bioactivity and Chemical Constituents of Colocasia

Name of the plant	*Parts used*	*Extract/ compound*	*Bioactivity*
Colocasia antiquorum (L) Schott	Corms	Ethanolic, cyanidin 3-glucoside, cyanidin 3-rhamnoside, pelargonidin 3-glucoside	Hepatoprotection
Colocasia gigantea Hook	Leaves	80% ethanolic extract	Antimycotic
Colocasia esculenta	Leaves	Aqueous extract	Antibacterial
Colocasia esculenta	Corms	Methanolic extract	Antibacterial
Colocasia antiquorum inoculated with *Ceratocystis fimbriata*		9,12,13-trihydroxy-10(E)-decenoic acid	Antifungal
Colocasia esculenta	Leaves	Isoorientin, orientin, luteolin 7-O-sophoroside	Antioxidant
Colocasia esculenta	Corms	Cyanidin 3-glucoside, cyanidin 3-rhamnoside, pelargonidin 3-glucoside	Antiooxidant and anti-inflammatory
Colocasia esculenta	Leaves	Ethanolic extract	Anti inflammatory
Colocasia esclenta	Corm	Poi	Anticancer
Colocasia esculenta	—	Ethanol extract (monogalactosylacylglycerol, digalactpsylacylglycerol)	Inhibition of human lanosterol synthase

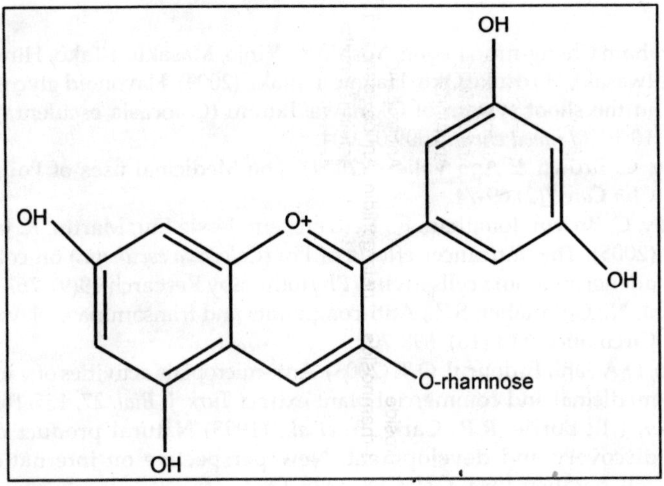

Fig. 19.2

Cyanidin 3-rhamnoside

Conclusion

The efficiency of medicinal plants in the treatment and prevention of diseases is a promising and controversial matter in the field of research. From our current discussion it can be concluded that *Colocasia* species showed diverse types of bioactivities and the active cmpounds isolated from the corms of *Colocasia* species are anthocyanins such as cyanidin 3-glucoside, cyanidin 3-rhamnoside, pelargonidin 3-glucoside. These compounds may be responsible for hepatoprotection, antimicrobial activity, anticancer activity, antioxidant activity and anti-inflammatory activity. Some other compounds have also been isolated from *Colocasia* and some of them are also bioactive. Therefore, genus *Colocasia* of family Araceae can be considered as one of the important bioactive plant. So further research can be done with other species of *Colocasia* as well as with other varieties of *Colocasia esculenta* for screening of pure compounds and to analyse the bioactivity of those compounds.

REFERENCES

Abraham Cheng-ning Leong, Yoshinori Kinjo, Masakuni Tako, Hironori Iwasaki, Hirosuke Oku, Hajime Tamaki, (2009). Flavonoid glycosides in the shoot system of Okinawa Taumu (Colocasia esculenta) doi 10:1016/ *j.food chem*. 2009.07.004.

Amy, C. Brown & Ana Valiers (2004). The Medicinal uses of Poi *Nutr Clin Care* 7(2) 69-74.

Army, C. Brown; Jonathan, E.; Reitzenstein, Jessie Liu; Martin, R. Jadus (2005). The anticancer effects of Poi (*Colocasia esculenta*) on colonic adenocarcinoma cells invitro Phytotherapy Research 19(9), 767-771.

Arora, N.; Goldhaber, S.Z.; Anti-coagulants and transaminase elevation Circulation 113 (15), 698-702.

Ateb, D.A., and Erdourul, O.T. (2003). Anti-microbials activities of various medicinal and commercial plant extract *Turk. J. Biol.* 27, 157-162.

Baker, J.T.; Borris, R.P.; Carte, B. *et al.*, (1995) Natural product drug discovery and development: New perspective on international collaboration *Prod. J. Nat.* 58, 1325-1357.

Benichou, C. Criteria of drug induced liver disorders. Report of an international consensus meeting *J. Hepatol.* 11 (2), 272-6.

Cambie, R.C.; Lynnete, R. Ferguson (2003). Potential functional foods in the traditional Maori diet,. Mutation Research/Fundamental and Molecular Mechanisms of Mutagenesis, 523-524,109-117.

Chung, T.H.; Kim, J.C.; Kim, M.K. *et al.*, (1995). Investigation of Korean plant extracts for potential phytotherapeutic agents against B-virus hepatitis, *Phytotherapy Res*, 9, 429-434.

Davies, D. (1985). Textbook of adverse drug reactions. Oxford [Oxfordshire]: Oxford University Press. 18-45. ISBN 0-19-261479-7.OCLC 12558288.

Donald, Blumenthal; Laurence, Brunton; Keith, Parker; Lazo; John, S.; Iain, Buxton (2006). Goodman and Gilman's Pharmacological Basis of Therapeutics Digital Edition. McGraw-Hill Professional. ISBN 0-07-146804-8.

Erdourul, O.T. (2002). Antibacterial activities of some plant extracts used in folk medicine *Pharmaceutical Biol*, 40, 269-273.

Farombi, E.O. (2003). African indigenous plants with chemotherapeutic potentials and biotechnological approach to the production of bioactive prophylactic agents *African J. Biotech.* 2 662-671.

Friedman, Scott E.; Grendell, James H.; Mcquaid, Kenneth R., (2003). *Current Diagnosis and Treatment in Gastroenterology*. New York; Lang Medical Books/McGraw-Hill. 664-679.

Hagnaeur, R.; *Chemotaxonomic der Pflanzen*, Vol. 2, Birkhauser Verlag, Basel, 1963.

Ianchu, T.C.; Shiloh H.; Dembo L. (1986). Hepatomegaly following short term high dose steroid therapy. Gastroenterol *J. Pediatr. Nutr.* 5(1), 41-6.

Inno, Onwueme (1999). Taro Cultivation in Asia and the Pacific. Food and Agriculture Oganisation of the United Nations (FAO). Regional Office for Asia and the Pacific. Bangkok, Thailand. RAP publication: 1999/16.

Keefe, Emmet B.; Friedman, Lawrence M., (2004). Handbook of liver diseases. Edinburge: Churchill Livingstone. 104-123. ISBN 0-443-06633-7.

Lee, Seong Wei; Najiah, Musa; Chuah, Tse Sengm; Wendy, Wee; Noor Azhar Mohd Shazili (2008). Antimicrobial properties of tropical plants against 12 pathogenic bacteriaisolated from aquatic organisms *African Journal of Biotechnology* 7(13), 2275-2278.

Lee W.; No date Taro (*Colocasia esculenta*). Ethnobotanical leaflets. http://www.siu.edu/-ebl/leaflets/taro.htm.

Leslie A., Sunell and Patrick L., Healey. (1979). Distribution of Calcium Oxalate Crystal Idioblasts in Corms of Taro (*Colocasia esculenta*) *American Journal of Botany* 66(9), 1029-1032.

Lynch T., Price A. (2007) The effect of cytochrome P450 metabolism on drug response, interaction and adverse effects. *American Family Physician* 76 (3), 391-6.

Maheshwari J.K.; Singh K.K.; Saha S. (1986). Ethnobotany of tribals of Mirzapur District, Uttar Pradesh Economic Botany Information Service, NBRI, Lucknow.

Manov, I.; Motanis, H.; Frumin, I.; Ianchu, T.C. (2006), Hepatotoxicity of anti-inflammatory and analgesic drugs: ultrastructural aspects *Acta Pharmacol. Sin.* 27(3), 259-72.

Masui, H.; Kondo, T.; Kojima, M. (1989). An antifungal compound 9,12,13-trihydroxy-10(E)-octadecenoic acid isolated from *Colocasia antiquorum* inoculated with *Ceratocystis fimbriata Phytochemistry*, 1989, 28, 2613-2615.

McNally, Peter F. (2006). GI/Liver Secrets: with STUDENT CONSULT Acess Saint Louis: C.V. Mosby. ISBN 1-56053-618-7.

Michalets, E.L. (1998). Update clinically significant cytochrome P-450 drug interactions *Pharmacotherapy*, 18 (1), 84-112.

Mumoli N.; Cei M.; Cosimi A. (2006). Drug related hepatotoxicity *J. Med.* 354 (20), 2191-3.

Muriel, P.; Rivera-Espinoza, Y. (2008). Beneficial drugs for liver diseases *J. Appl. Toxicol.* 28(2) 93-103.

Nair R.; Kalarya, T.; Chanda, Sumitra (2005). Antibacterial activity of some selected Indian Medicinal Flora *Turk J. Biol.* 29, 41-47.

N. Shah Biren *et al.* (2007). The anti inflammatry activity of the leaves of Colocasia esculenta. *Saudi Pharmaceutical Journal* 15 No. 3-4.

Ostapowicz, G.; Fontana, R.J.; Schiodt, F.V. *et al.* (2002). Results of a prospective study of acute liver failure at 17 tertiary care centres in the United States Ann. *Intern. Med.* 137 (12), 947-54.

Patil, M.; Tuse, T.; Harie, U.; Tende, S.; Rajgure, D. (2008). Hepatoprotective activity of *Colocasia antiquorum* against carbon tetrachloride and paracetamol induced liver injury in rats *Indian J. Pharmacol.* 40 supplement 2.

Pir Mohammed, M.; Breckenridge, A.M.; Kitteringham, N.R.; Park, B.K.; (1998). Adverse drug reactions *BMJ* 316 (7140), 1295-8.

Rai, M.K. (1989). Ethnomedicinal studies of Chhindwara district (M.P.). I. Plants used in stomach disorders *Indian Medicine.* 1, 1-5.

Reddy, P.S.; Jamil, K.; Madhusudhan, P. *et al,* (2000). Antibacterial activity of isolates from Piper Longum and Taxus baccata *Pharmaceutical Biol,* 39, 236-238.

Reuben, A. (2004). Hy's law *Hepatology* 39 (2), 574-8.

Sakano, Yuichi; Mutsuga, Motoh; Tanaka, Rie; Suganuma, Hiroyuki; Inakuma, Takahiro; Toyoda, Masatake; Goda, Yuihiro; Shibuya, Masaaki; Ebizula, Yutaka (2005). Inhibition of human lanosterol synthase by the constituents of *Colocasia esculenta Biological and Pharmaceutical bulletin* 28(2), 299-304.

Skett, Paul; Gibson, G. Gordon (2001). Introduction to drug metabolism. Cheltenham, UK: Nelson Thornes Publishers. ISBN 0-7487-6011-3.

Stuffness M. and Douros J. (1982). Current status of the NCI plant and animal product program *J. Nat. Prod.* 45, 1-14.

Suhaila, Mohamed; Suzana, Saka; Saleh, H.; El-Sharkawy; Abdul, Manaf Ali; Sepiah, Muid (1996), Antimycotic screening of 58 Malaysian plants against plant pathogens *Pestic. Sci.* 47, 259-264.

Surh, Y.J.; Chun, K.S.; Han, S.S.; Keum, Y.S.; Park, K.K.; Lee, S.S. (2001). Molecular mechanisms underlying chemopreventive activities of anti-inflammatory phytochemicals: down regulation of COX-2 and iNOS through suppression of NF-kappa B activation *Mutat Res* 480-481, 243-68.

Taylor, R.S.L.; Manandhar, N.P.; Hudson, J.B. *et al.* (1996). Antiviral activities of Nepalese medicinal plants *J. Ethnophamacol* 52, 157-263.

Tom, Agbor-Egbe; June, E. Rickard (2006). Identification of phenolic compound in edible aroids *Journal of the Science of Food & Agriculture* 51(2) 215-216.

Vlietinck, A.J.; Van Hoof L.; Tott, J.; *et al.* (1995). Screening of hundred Rwandese medicinal plants for antimicrobial and antiviral properties *J. Ethnopharmacol* 46, 31-47.

Yau, Sang Chan; Jack HO Wong; Tzi Bun Ng (2009). A cytokine inducing Hemagglutinin from small taros *Protein Pept Lett* 19807671 (PSGEB).

Zimmerman, H.J. (1978). Drug induced liver disease *Drugs* 16 (1), 25-45.

20

Performance of Certain Upgraded Poultry Variety in Agro-Climatic Condition of West Tripura

N. Islam, P. Dutta, S. Malik and *A.K. Singha*

Introduction

West district of Tripura is situated between Latitude 23°16′ North to 24°14′ North and Longitude between 91°09′ East to 91°47′ East. Farm inputs are not available adequately and are very costly. Hot and humid climate prevailing in Tripura is conducive for incidence of diseases in poultry. Due to excessive selection pressure, the indigenous germplasm of poultry birds is getting extinct day by day thus having a necessity of bio-diversity conservation. To maintain the bio-diversity, the productivity of local germplasm should be explored and modified to meet the production demand. The present study is carried out to know the performance of some high yielding poultry varieties similar to local birds aesthetically, carrying local germplasm.

Poultry farming in West Tripura district is mainly done by unorganized sectors in a very small flock size and through backyard rearing for household micro income generating operations. Broiler bird and local nondescript ducks are reared in small flocks. Improved poultry bird like Kuroiler, Swarnadhara, Gramapriya are reared to some extent but due to low supply of chicks it is difficult to adopt in a larger scale. Khaki Campbel ducks are also reared in backyard system along with local ducks. Commercial livestock farms are negligible in number while

Government farms are not in sufficient number and production level to supply the optimum requirement of the district. As per the livestock census 2003, the district has 2,858,043 numbers of poultry birds.

Per capita availability of meat and egg in this district are 4.058 kg/year and 37.99 numbers per year respectively (Anonymous, 2009). As per the recommendations by Nutritional Advisory Committee of ICMR, the requirement of meat and egg for an adult person is 18 kg/year and 183 numbers per year respectively. When India ranks 4th in egg production and 5th in broiler production in the world, growth rate of poultry in broiler sector is 10-12 per cent and in layer sector is 5-7 per cent (Sharma and Chatterjee, 2006) than in West Tripura district, there is a huge gap between the requirement and availability of the livestock and poultry originated foods. As per the estimation of 2006-07, yearly requirement of meat and eggs in this district are 25230.0 MT and 5550 lakh numbers respectively while productivity is 14097.89 MT and 615 lakh numbers respectively. So, there is a large gap between requirement and production of meat and eggs by 11044 MT and 4935 lakh numbers per year respectively. To reduce this gap and to bring out revolutionary change in this sector, optimum numbers of technical manpower, infrastructure, proper utilization of finance and technologies, market organization and regulation, co-ordination of related Government and private organization, formation and efficient running of farmer's interest groups, co-operatives, livestock insurance and sufficient credit delivery by the financial institutes are in urgent need. Keeping this trend, present study was carried out to know the performances of the three varieties of poultry bird, viz., Kuroiler, Swarnadhara and Gramapriya reared in both Intensive and backyard system.

Materials and Methods

The present study was carried out within January 2008 to June 2009 at several locations, viz., State Poultry Farm, Gandhigram, Agartala, West Tripura, ICAR Research Centre for NEH Region, Tripura centre, Lembuchera, Agartala, West Tripura, Divyodaya KVK-West Tripura (DKVK), Chebri and Gandhigram farm, Bishalgarh, Kamal Nagar, North Chebri and Jambura village of West Tripura district.

Performance of Kuroiler bird in Intensive system of management was recorded at State poultry farm, Gandhigram, Agartala, of Gramapriya at ICAR Research Centre for NEH Region, Tripura Centre and of Swarnadhara at DKVK. While, birds of these three varieties were distributed to the farmers through Frontline Demonstration (FLD) and On Farm Testing (OFT) programme of the KVK to rear in backyard system at Bishalghar, Kamalnagar, North Chebri and South Jambura village of the district. Hundred birds from each group were taken for observation of different economic traits in terms of intensive and backyard system. Egg collected from the demonstrated bird was selected and hatched in ICAR Research Cente for NEH Region, Tripura Centre.

For comparison of performances of the varieties in Intensive and Backyard system following parameters/traits were taken:

1. Fertility in percentage
2. Hatchability—(a) TES, (b) FES in Percentage
3. Body Weight at- 4th, 6th, 8th, 12th, 20th and 40th week of age separately for male and female.
4. Age at 1st lay in days.
5. Egg upto 40 weeks of age (no.)
6. Egg Per Year Per Hen (no.)

Feeding and watering were done twice in a day in intensive system. The birds were reared in deep litter providing optimum brooding, light and temperature. Crude protein percentage of starter, grower and layer ration were 20 per cent, 16 per cent and 15 per cent respectively. Crude Fibre percentage of starter, grower and layer ration were 7 per cent, 8 per cent and 10 per cent respectively.

While, in backyard system the birds were reared in scavenging system providing household materials like rice polish, kitchen wastage, etc. Optimum brooding, lighting and temperature were not possible to maintain.

Results and Discussions

Performances of the three varieties of poultry birds in Intensive and Backyard system were recorded individually and the same was compared in respect of different traits as follows:

Performances of three varieties of poultry birds reared in both Intensive and backyard system and data on their comparative study presented in Table 20.1, showed that fertility percentage of Kuroiler, Gramapriya and Swarnadhara birds in Intensive system were 80.35 per cent, 81.25 per cent and 75.00 per cent respectively while the same was 76.00 per cent, 73.00 and 71.00 per cent in Kuroiler, Gramapriya and Swarnadhara birds respectively in backyard system. So it was clear that fertility percentage of egg in Intensive system was highest among all the 3 varieties than backyard system. Fertility percentage in Gramapriya bird (81.25%) was highest among the three varieties reared in intensive system, while the same was highest in Kuroiler bird (76.00%) among the three varieties reared in backyard system.

Hatchability percentage in Kuroiler, Gramapriya and Swarnadhara in terms of Total Egg Set (TES) was 62.65 per cent, 64.71 per cent and 61.33 per cent respectively in Intensive system, while the same was 60.65 per cent, 61.25 per cent and 59.45 per cent in Kuroiler, Gramapriya and Swarnadhara respectively in backyard system (Table 20.1). So, it was evident that, hatchability percentage in terms of Total Egg Set is highest in Gramapriya bird among the three varieties reared in both Intensive system and backyard system.

Hatchability percentage in terms of Fertile Egg Set (FES) in Kuroiler, Gramapriya and Swarnadhara was 76.35 per cent, 79.97 per cent and 70.45 per cent respectively in Intensive system of rearing while, the same was 74.45 per cent, 70.71 per cent and 68.35 per cent respectively in Kuroiler, Gramapriya and Swarnadhara bird reared in backyard system. Therefore, it was evident that Fertile Egg Set percentage was also highest in case of Gramapriya bird (79.97%) among these varieties in Intensive system, while the same is highest in Kuroiler birds (74.45%) in backyard system in comparison to other two varieties.

Body weight gain at 4th week of age of male bird was highest in case of Kuroiler bird (362.00 gm) in comparison to Gramapriya and Swarnadhara reared in intensive system, while in backyard system it was highest in case of Swarnadhara (270 gm) birds . In case of female birds highest body weight gain at this age was found in Swarnadhara variety in both intensive (300.00 gm) and Backyard system (244.00 gm) (Table 20.1)

At sixth week of age highest body weight of male bird was

Table 20.1 : Performance of Different Traits of Kuroiler, Gramapriya and Swarnadhara Bird in Intensive and Backyard System.

Trait		*Intensive System*			*Backyard System*		
		Kuroiler	*Gramapriya*	*Swarnadhara*	*Kuroiler*	*Gramapriya*	*Swarnadhara*
Fertility%		80.35	81.25	75.00	76.00	73.00	71.00
Hatchability%	1.TES	62.65	64.71	61.33	60.65	61.25	59.45
	2.FES	76.35	79.97	70.45	74.45	70.71	68.35
Body Weight							
(1) 4th week	Male	362.00	312.73	351.00	250.00	243.00	270.00
	Female	297.00	285.62	300.00	230.00	224.00	244.00
(2) 6th week	Male	462.00	469.87	473.00	313.00	306.00	361.00
	Female	391.00	395.23	402.00	295.00	282.00	302.00
(3) 8th week	Male	752.00	751.47	782.00	603.00	597.00	698.00
	Female	613.00	625.02	634.00	570.00	512.00	603.00
(4) 12th week	Male	1363.00	1358.79	1384.00	1123.00	1084.22	1154.00
	Female	1178.00	1164.36	1189.00	1012.00	928.15	997.00
(5) 20th week	Male	2122.00	2107.65	2214.00	1722.00	1699.36	1787.00
	Female	1712.00	1613.05	1745.00	1489.00	1413.21	1497.00
(6) 40th week	Male	3243.00	3213.82	3307.00	3055.00	3034.22	3214.00
	Female	2752.00	2331.78	2789.00	2214.00	2192.67	2298.00
Age at 1st lay		165.00	127.00	165.00	190.00	193.62	195.00
Egg upto 40 weeks of age (no.)		59.00	62.13	48.00	32.00	34.62	25.00
Egg per hen per year (no.)		147.00	147.00	123.00	39.00	44.22	29.00

gained in Swarnadhara bird in both Intensive (473.00 gm) and Backyard system (361.00 gm). In case of female birds also highest body weight was gained in Swarnadhara birds reared in Intensive (402.00 gm) and Backyard system (302.00 gm) in comparison to other two varieties.

Body weight gain of male birds of Swarnadhara was highest in both Intensive (782.00 gm) and Backyard system (698.00 gm) in comparison to other two varieties at 8th weeks of age. While in case of female birds also highest body weight gain was obtained in Swarnadhara birds in both Intensive (634.00 gm) and Backyard (603.00 gm) system.

At the age of 12th weeks, body weight gain of Swarnadhara male bird was highest in both Intensive (1384.00 gm) and Backyard (1154.00 gm) rearing in comparison to its counterpart in Gramapriya and Kuroiler. While in case of female bird highest body weight gain was obtained in Swarnadhara bird (1189.00 gm) in Intensive system of rearing, but in Backyard system body weight gain of female birds at this age was highest in Kuroiler birds (1012.00 gm).

Highest Body weight gain was obtained in Swarnadhara male bird at 20th weeks of age in both Intensive (2214.00 gm) and Backyard system (1787.00 gm) in comparison to its counterpart in Kuroiler and Gramapriya bird. In case of female birds also body weight gain in Swarnadhara bird was highest in both Intensive (1745.00 gm) and Backyard (1497.00 gm) system in comparison to Gramapriya and Kuroiler female birds at this age.

Highest Body weight gain was obtained in Swarnadhara male bird at 40th weeks of age in both Intensive (3307.00 gm) and Backyard system (3214.00 gm) in comparison to its counterpart in Kuroiler and Gramapriya bird. In case of female birds also body weight gain in Swarnadhara bird was highest in both Intensive (2789.00 gm) and Backyard (2298.00 gm) system in comparison to Gramapriya and Kuroiler female birds at this age.

Table 20.1 also revealed that Gramapriya bird required less number of days (127.00 days) to come in laying in Intensive system, while the same age is less (190 days) in case of Kuroiler bird in Backyard system in comparison to other two varieties.

Egg numbers upto 40 weeks of age is highest in case of Gramapriya bird in both Intensive (62.13 nos.) and backyard system (34.62 nos.) in comparison to Kuroiler and Swarnadhara birds.

Egg number per hen per year is highest in case of Kuroiler and Gramapriya bird in Intensive (147.00 nos.) system while in Backyard system it is highest in Gramapriya bird (44.22 nos.).

The variability of the economic traits found in this study may be due to the intrinsic transmissibility of the trait by the varieties in same system of rearing. On the basis of the study, we can select Swarnadhara as best meat production variety in both Intensive and Backyard system of rearing, while Kuroiler and Gramapriya can be best suited for Egg production in Intensive system and Gramapriya alone for egg production in Backyard system.

Conclusion

Even though, the above mentioned three varieties are reared in the district, we need to explore the local germ plasm and to conserve the biodiversity by keeping the trend of rearing local non descript birds. We may cross these birds with the previously mentioned three varieties for more productivity and sustainable income to the farming community.

REFERENCES

17th Livestock Census. (2003). Department of Animal Husbandry and Dairying. Ministry of Agriculture, Government of India, New Delhi.

Dutta, P.; Chakraborty, S.; Datta, A.; Islam, N.; Nath, D. and Rahman, B. (2008), *Decision Support System for West Tripura* Volume-I, Publ. by SRSK, Kolkata.

Sharma, R.P. and Chatterjee (2006). Research priorities in Poultry Genetics and Breeding to 2020. In *Poultry Research Priorities to 2020.* CARI Izatnagar-243122 (U.P.) India.

Statistics of State/UT Animal Husbandry Departments (2003-04), Govt.of India Publication.

21
Diversity of Flowers in North-East India

L.C. De and *R.P. Medhi*

Introduction

"Biological diversity" or biodiversity is that part of nature which includes the differences in genes among the individuals of a species, the variety and richness of all the plant and animal species at different scales in space, locally, in a region, in the country and the world, and various types of ecosystems, both terrestrial and aquatic within a defined area. There are three levels of biodiversity found in a region, genetic diversity, species diversity and habitat diversity. Genetic diversity indicates diversity within the species and forms the gene pool from which our crops and domestic animals have been developed. The number of species of plants and animals present in a region constitutes its species diversity. This diversity is available both in natural ecosystems and in agricultural ecosystems. Habitat diversity refers to the many kinds of microclimates in existence today. For example, there are tropical rainforests, deserts, plains, alpine regions, and many more. The non-living and living things affect each other. If one species becomes extinct, other living things may suffer. Maintaining a wide diversity of species in each ecosystem is necessary to preserve the web of life that sustains all living things.

The world now realizes that the loss of biodiversity contributes to global climatic changes. Forests are the main mechanism for the conversion of carbon dioxide into carbon and oxygen. The loss of forest cover, coupled with the increasing release of carbon dioxide and other gases through industrialization results into the

"Greenhouse effect". Global warming is melting ice caps, resulting in a rise in the sea level which will submerge the low lying areas in the world. Biological diversity is also essential for preserving ecological processes, such as fixing and recycling of nutrients, soil formation, circulation and cleansing of air and water, global life support (plants absorb CO_2, give out O_2), maintaining the water balance within ecosystems, watershed protection, maintaining stream and river flows throughout the year, erosion control and local flood reduction. Food, clothing, housing, energy, medicines, are all resources that are directly or indirectly linked to the biological variety present in the biosphere.

It has become obvious that the preservation of biological resources is essential for the well-being and the long-term survival of mankind. In 1973, an international treaty known as CITES (the Convention on International Trade in Endangered Species of Wild Fauna and Flora) was enacted. Its aim is to ensure that international trade in specimens of wild animals and plants does not threaten their survival.

Among the biologically rich nations, India stands among the top 10 or 15 countries for its great variety of plants and animals, many of which are not found elsewhere. India has 350 different mammals (rated eight highest in the world), 1,200 species of birds (eighth in the world), 453 species of reptiles (fifth in the world) and 45,000 plant species, of which most are angiosperms, (fifteenth in the world). These include especially high species diversity of ferns (1,022 species) and orchids (1,330 species). It is estimated that 18 per cent of Indian plants are **endemic** to the country and found nowhere else in the world.

North-East India, a mega-biodiversity centre and a hotspot, comprises eight States, viz., Arunachal Pradesh, Assam, Manipur, Meghalaya, Mizoram, Nagaland, Sikkim and Tripura. It occupies 7.7 per cent of India's total geographical area supporting 50 per cent of the flora (ca. 8,000 species), of which 31.58 per cent (ca. 2,526 species) is endemic. It is a transitional zone between the Indian, Indo-Burman–Malaysian and Indo-Chinese regions. It is also a part of the Vavilovian centre of biodiversity and origin of many important cultivated plant species and some domesticated animals. The region supports a rich biodiversity spanning from tropical rainforests to alpine scrubs. Takhtajan describes the region as the "cradle of flowering plants" because of its diversified angiosperms. This rich biodiversity has a significant role in the maintenance of the ecosystem. Besides, the biodiversity of the region is used ethnologically by locals for various socio-economic and developmental purposes. The region is rich in orchids, ferns, oaks (*Quercus* spp.), bamboos, rhododendrons (*Rhododendron* spp.), magnolias (*Magnolia* spp.), etc. The region is rich in medicinal plants and many other rare and endangered taxa.

The following Figures highlight the biodiversity significance of the region :

1. 51 Forest types are found in the region broadly classified into six major forest types, viz., tropical moist deciduous forests, tropical semi-evergreen forests, tropical wet evergreen forests, subtropical forests, temperate forests and alpine forests.
2. Out of the 9 important vegetation types of India, 6 are found in the North-Eastern region.
3. These forests harbour 8,000 out of 15,000 species of flowering plants. These include:
   - 40 out of 54 species of gymnosperms.
   - 500 out of 1,012 species of Pteridophytes.
   - 825 out of 1,145 species of orchids.
   - 80 out of 90 species of rhododendrons.
   - 60 out of 110 species of bamboo.
   - 25 out of 56 species of canes.

In terms of floral species richness the highest diversity is reported from the States of Arunachal Pradesh and Sikkim amongst the North-Eastern States as shown below :

State Species richness (flowering plants)

Arunachal Pradesh 5000
Sikkim ± 4500
Meghalaya ± 3500
Assam ± 3010
Manipur ± 2500
Nagaland ± 2250
Mizoram ± 2200
Tripura ± 1600.

These species belong to about 200 plant families out of 315 recorded from North-East India. Some of the families such as Nepanthaceae, Illiciaceae and Clethraceae are unique in the world. These families are reported from the South-East Asian countries and are represented by a limited number of species like *Clethra* sp.

Fig. 21.1 : Lilium mackliniae and Nepenthes Khasiana

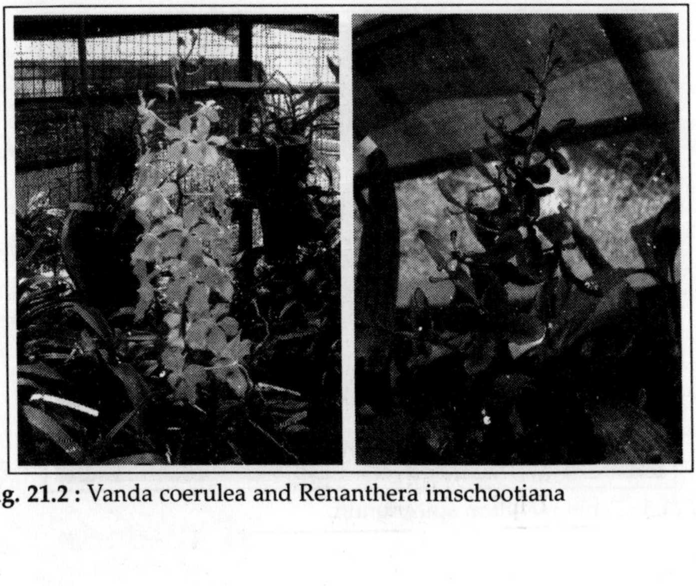

Fig. 21.2 : Vanda coerulea and Renanthera imschootiana

and *Nepenthus khasiana* in North-East India. Siroy Lily (*Lilium mackliniae*), a ground lily that produces beautiful flowers, is a narrow endemic found in the eastern border area of Manipur.

There are very interesting areas in the region that are termed as "Isolation belts" that have led to the isolation of certain species. *Meconopsis bella, Cathcartia lyrata, Senecio chola, Sausrea laneana, Geranium spp., Primula elwesiana, P. wattii* and *Swertia burkilliana* serve such examples in the Sikkim Himalaya.

Orchids

Orchids, believed to have evolved in this region, form a very noticeable feature of the vegetation here. Of about 1,330 species of orchids, belonging to 186 genera reported from India, North-East India sustains the highest concentration with about 856 species. As many as 34 species of orchids from North-East India are listed among the threatened plants of India. The following are some ornamental orchids of the region: *Paphiopedilum fairieanum, P. insigne, P. villosum, P. spicerianum, P. hirsutissimum, P. venestum, Anoectochilus sikkimensis, Vanda coerulea, Vanda teres, Renanthera imschootiana, Pleione maculata, Cymbidium eburneum, Dendrobium hookerianum, D. densiflorum, D. devonianum, D. thyrsiflorum* and *Thunia marshalliana.*

Fig. 21.3 : Paphiopedilum spicerianum

Table 21.1: Orchid Distribution under Forest Cover in North-East

State	Area	Dense Forest	% Forest Cover	Orchid	
	000 km^2			Genera	Species
Arunachal Pradesh	83,743	54,542	65.13	130	600
Assam	78,438	15,842	20.19	74	182
Manipur	22, 327	5,309	23.77	67	207
Meghalaya	22,429	3,305	14.73	98	352
Mizoram	21,081	4,279	20.29	74	249
Nagaland	16,579	3,531	21.29	64	241
Sikkim	7,096	2,403	38.86	132	540
Tripura	10,488	1,825	17.40	37	66

Biodiversity of orchids in Arunachal Pradesh: There are 600 species of orchids in Arunachal Pradesh alone—the highest number in any State (of these, 377 are epiphytes, 160 are autophytic terrestrials, and about 20 are saprophytes). Major epiphytic genera include *Aerides. Arachnis, Bulbophyllum, Coelogyne, Dendrobium, Cymbidium, Eria, Cleisostoma, Rhynchostylist, Vanda,* etc. Most of the epiphytic orchids are ornamentals. In the tropical valleys of Arunachal Pradesh, one can find cascades of colourful flower-spikes of *Rhynchostylis retusa, Aerides odorata, A. williamsii, A. rosea, Cymbidium pendulum, C. aloifolium, Dendrobium aphylla, D. nobile, D . moschatum, D. fimbriatum,* etc., loaded on tree trunks during spring time which add beauty to the surrounding wood. In sub-tropical hill forests, bunches of "pineapple orchids" the *Dendrobium densiflorum, D. giganteum, D. grandiflorum, D, eburnium, D. mastersii, Vanda coerulea, Renanthera imschootiana* (red Vanda), *Coelogyne,* etc., greet the onlookers. The pink flowers of *Anthogonium gracile* found on the cut ends of rocks and edges carpet the exposed areas adding beauty to the landscape.

Among terrestrials, *Acanthephippium, Arundina, Anoectochilus, Calanthe, Phaius, Paphiopedilum* are common. Amongst them, *Arundina graminifolia,* the "bamboo orchid" is normally seen grown in the open sunny areas amongst grassy patches in the foothills. In the thick forests, *Anoectochilus* and *Geodorum,* popularly referred to as the "Jewel orchids" group having beautifully designed velvety leaves. Arunachal is the home State of rare and endangered Lady's Slipper orchids, Paphiopedilum species, viz. (1) *P. fairrieanum* (2) *P. venustum* and (3) *P. spicerianum*. Saprophytic genera like *Epipogium, Stereosandra, Gastrodia, Eulophia* and *Galeola* that grow on decaying organic matter on the forest floor thrill the onlooker.

Biodiversity of Orchids in Assam: In Assam, as many as 182 species of orchids are reported. Tropical wet evergreen forests of Lakhimpur district and its adjoining foothills of Arunachal Pradesh is very much rich and more than hundreds of eye-catching and colourful wild orchids are seen to bloom throughout the year. Mostly they are epiphytes. *Goodyera procera* and *Spiranthis sinesis* are adapted to aquatic habitant whereas *Vanilla pilifera* and *Galeola altissima* are climbers. Orchids grow best in the Evergreen and Semi-Evergreen forest and to some extent in Moist Deciduous forests. Species belonging to genera *Acanthephippium, Anoectochilus, Apostasia, Agrostophyllum, Coelogyne, Cymbidium, Dendrobium, Eria, Oberonia,, Calanthe, Eulophia, Geodorum, Habenaria, Malaxis, Nephelaphyllum, Vanilla, Zeuxine, Didymoplexis, Galeola, Bulbophyllum, Camarotis* are the commonly found orchids. Assam has as many as 26 species threatened orchids. Amongst endemic orchids, *Bulbophyllum obrienianum, Calanthe odora, D. parciflorum, D. spatella, Eria pumila, Eulophia candida, Liparis plantaginea, Luisia macrotis, Phalaenopsis mastersii, Tainia barbata* are reported from the State.

Biodiversity of Orchids in Manipur: Many epiphytic and terrestrial orchids of immense horticultural value are grown in wild. About 207 species belonging to 67 genera of the family *Orchidaceae* have been reported from this State. *Venda coerulea* (Blue Vanda) and *Rananthera imschootiana* (Red Vanda) are included in Schedule VI (plants) of the Indian Wildlife (Protection) Act 1972 (Amended 1991). Due to overexploitation most of the orchids have already been depleted considerably and several are seen only in orchidaria. Some of the *Taxa* facing threat of survival are *Anoectochilus tetraplerus, Aldrovenda vasiculosa, Ascocentrum ampullaceum, Ascocentrum miniatum, Dendrobium bensoniae, Dendrobium draconis, Dendrobium heterocarpum* and *Dendrobium wardianum.*

Biodiversity of Orchids in Meghalaya: The Khasi, Jaintia and Garo hills around Shillong in the State of Meghalaya boast of more than 300 species of orchids. Here epiphytic orchids can be seen on the stunted trees of Rhodendron arboreum, Quercus and Castonopsis species. Ground orchids like ***Anoectachilus brevilabris,*** the jewel orchid and ***Liparis pulchella*** can be seen.

Other orchid species available in the State are *Paphiopedilum insigne, P. venustum, Rynchostylis retusa, Coelogyne corymbosa, Dendrobium devonianum, Cymbidium elegans* and *Vanda coerulea.*

Biodiversity of Orchids in Mizoram: Mizoram is the natural home of *Vanda coerulea* (Blue Vanda) and *Renanthera imschootiana* (Red Vanda) among North-Eastern State. Mizoram is also natural home of *Paphiopedilum hirsutissimum* and *P. villosum.* Apart from these, there are many orchid species which are having ethnobotanical values are *Arundina graminifolia, Eria spicata, Eulophia nuda, Geodorum densiflorum, Malaxis acuminate, Phaius tankervilleae, Pholidota imbricata, Rhyncostylis retusa* and *vandal testacea.* Other tuberous orchids having medicinal importance are *Eulophia* and *Habenaria.*

Biodiversity of Orchids in Nagaland: Nagaland has about 241 species out of 1,330 species of orchids found in India. Most of the Orchids here are epiphytes or lithophytes. A few terrestrial orchids are also found in the State. Major genera are *Acampe, Acanthephippium, Aerides, Anoectochilus, Anthogonium, Aphyllorchis, Arachis, Ascocentrum, Bulbophyllum, Calanthe, Ceratostylis, Cleisostoma, Coelogyne, Cryptochilus, Cymbidium, Dendrobium, Diplomeria, Eria, Eulophia, Flickingeria, Galeola, Gastrochilus, Goodyera, Habennaria, Kingidium, Liparis, Luisia, Malaxis, Micropera, Oberonia, Otochilus, Paphiopedilum, Paplionanthe, Perisrtylus, Phaius, Pholidota, Pleione, Renanthera, Rhyncostylis, Spathoglottis, Thunia, Vanda* and *Zeuxine.*

Biodiversity of Orchids in Sikkim: The entire peculiar geographical feature helps Sikkim to become a biodiversity hot spot and it harbours around 540 species which are distributed in humid sub-tropical, temperate and alpine forest up to an elevation 5000 m above mean sea level. The most beautiful and very rare plants of the Alpine zone are *Cypripedium tibeticum, C. himalicum* and *C. elegance.* Some endemic species of orchids reported are *Oberonia micranthus, Malaxis saprophyllum, Liparis dongchenii, Calanthe trulliformis, C. alpina, C. whiteana, C. chloroleuca, C. anganii, C. keshabii, C. yuksomensis, Risleya atro purpurea, Dediciea cunninghamii, Cymbidium whiteae, Taeniophyllum retro-apiculatum, T. crepidiforme, Thrixpermum pygmaeum, Uncifera lancifolia, Biermannia bimaculata, Gastrochillus affinis, Vanda pumila.*

Biodiversity of Orchids in Tripura: There are 66 species of orchids of which *Dendrobium* has the highest species diversity (14 species). Endangered orchids like Blue vanda (*Vanda coerulea*) and Red vanda (*Renunthera imschootiana*) are found in the State.

Table 21.2 : Distribution of major orchids in North-East States

State	Orchid species
Arunachal Pradesh	*Cymbidium ensifolium, C. grandiflorum, Dendrobium aphylla, D. chrysanthum, D. gibsonii, D. nobile, Paphiopedilum fairrieanum, P. venustum, P. spicerianum, Calanthe masuca, Rhyncostylis retusa.*
Assam	*Arundina graminifolia, Eulophia mannii, Goodyera procera, Calanthe angusta, Rhyncostylis retusa, Aerides multiflora, Aerides odorata, Acampe papillosa, Cymbidium aloifolium, Dendrobium aphyllum, D. acinaciforme.*
Manipur	*Ascocentrum ampullaceum, Paphiopedilum spicerianum, Vanda amsiana, Vanda stangeana, Vanda coerulea.*
Meghalaya	*Paphiopedilum insigne, P. venustum, R. retusa, Coelogyne corymbosa, Phaius tankervilliae, Dendrobium devonianum, Cymbidium elegans, Vanda coerulea.*
Mizoram	*Vanda coerulea, Renanthera imschootiana, Paphiopedilum hirsutissimum, P. Villosum.*
Nagaland	*Goodyera viridiflora, Liparis caespitosa, Luisia trichorrhiza, Malaxis latifolia, Oberonia pyrulifera , Spiranthes sinensis.*
Sikkim	Alpine zone (2500-3000 m): *Orchis, Habenaria, Tipularia, Satyrium, Cypripedium.*
	Temperate and Sub-temperate zone (1850-3500 m): *Goodyera, Calanthe, Pleione humilis, Cymbidium hookeranum, C. devonianum, C. longifolium, Coelogyne cristata, Dendribium hookeranum.*
	Subtropical zone (850-1250 m): *Anoectichilus, Calanthe, Phaius, Eulophia, Paphiopedilum fairrieanum, P. venustum, Dendrobium, Bulbophyllum, Coelogyne, Arachnis.*
	Tropical Zone (250-850 m): *Phalaenopsis, Dendrobium, Aerides, Vanda, Arundina graminifolia.*
Tripura	*Dendrobium (14 spp.), Vanda teres, V. coerulea, Renanthera imschootiana.*

Rhododendrons

Rhododendrons are known for their showy flowers and foliage. Out of 82 species of rhododendrons recorded from Himalaya, 70 species are confined to eastern Himalaya. Hooker's expedition to Sikkim in 1848 revealed 45 new species, which included the yellow flowered *Rhododendron campylocarpum* and *R. weighti*; the red-flowered *R. thomsoni,* the small tree *R. falconeri* and the large *R. griffithianum* with massive white flowers. However, unfortunately, nearly half of the Rhododendron species have

Fig. 21.4 : Rhododendron thomsoni and Rhododendron campylocarpum

become rare and threatened and some of the very ornamental species are now facing extinction e.g., *Rhododendron nuttalli, R. falconeri, R. edgeworthii, R. elliotii, R. hookeri, R. macabeanum* and *R. watti.*

Hedychiums of the family Zingiberaceae make excellent ornamental plants and the following are rare and threatened ornamental species of this group: *Hedychium luteum, H. aureum, H. radiatum, H. robustum, H. dekianum.*

North-East India also has a high diversity of non-flowering plants. Of about 1,000 species of ferns found in India, nearly half are represented in North-Eastern India. *Dipteris wallichii, Asplenium nidus, Osmunda cinnamomea, O. claytoniana, O. regalis, Helminthostachys zeylanica, Botrychium lanuginosum, Angiopteris evecta, Cyathea gigantea, C. spinulosa, Psilotum nudum, Phagopteres auriculata, etc.*, are some of the rare and interesting non-flowering vascular plants. Of these, *Platycerium wallichii* (Staghorn Fern) from Manipur appears to be the first report of its occurrence within India. This epiphytic fern grows in the moist deciduous forests in the Indo-Myanmar border areas in great profusion. Fern-allies such as *Lycopodium* and *Selaginella* are also diverse in this region.

Causes of Biodiversity Loss

Rapid biodiversity loss worldwide could be attributed to the following reasons:

Habitat loss, Deterioration and Fragmentation

A number of species have lost their habitat (place where a species lives) because of increased human interference like construction of dams, roads, railway tracts or bridges across natural ecosystems, mining activity or industries. Habitat fragmentation due to deforestation or any other biotic stress has caused much harm to precious biodiversity. Deforestation rate is increasing due to burgeoning population and this has destroyed the natural homes of species. In fresh water ecosystems, construction of dams has destroyed large habitat of hundreds of aquatic flora and fauna. Likewise, in marine ecosystems, the coastal development has affected the communities, particularly species rich ecosystems like coral reefs.

Exotic Species

Exotic species are those which have been introduced either purposely or entered accidentally in some environmentally distinct zone from the other geographically different areas. These have caused much harm to native plant communities than expected and enhanced the extinction (loss of species) rate. The phenomenon is more common on the islands or isolated ecosystems. A number of example exist world over when an introduced species has become a serious pest or problem. For example, *Lantana camara* introduced as an ornamental hedge in India has now become a serious invader of forests. The example of accidental entry is the Congress grass (*Parthenium hysterophorus*) that is now a major problematic weed in India, Australia and other parts of the world. A number of reasons such as fast growth, rapid colonization, better and efficient resource utilization, wider adaptability and the absence of natural enemies in the invaded areas.

Over Exploitation

Some of the species have become threatened and even gone extinct due to their over exploitation by the humans for their food, feed or some other beneficial purpose. In fact, a number of ecosystems have got damaged both in terms of number and variety of species that these are beyond repair in the near future.

Environmental Pollution

Air, water, and soil pollution is one of the major reasons for biodiversity loss in the modern era. Modernization, urbanization, increasing population, and changing life style are some of the prime reasons for the increased levels of pollution in the natural environment. It has not only affected the number of existing species but has also caused the loss of a variety of species that could not tolerate the increased pollutant levels in the atmosphere and have gone extinct. Excessive use of synthetic chemicals as herbicides, pesticides and insecticides has polluted the soil and water environment and greatly threatens the diversity and richness of the species. Due to increased industrialization, the intensity of the acid rain has increased and greatly affected the natural vegetation and the forests in different regions of the world.

Global Warming

Climate change due to global warming is another reason for the depletion of natural biodiversity in the recent times. The increase in the earth's temperature has already shown its impact in terms of depletion of forest resources in many parts of the world. For example, temperate or the Taiga forests are reducing in size whereas tropical/sub-tropical forests are slightly increasing. Additionally, the temperature rise also alters the tolerance limit of the species and greatly changes the structure and ecosystem function. The increased global temperature would result in melting of ice caps and rising of sea levels. It would result in submerging of many islands and inundation of coastal areas thereby greatly affecting the biodiversity of such regions.

Commercialization of Agriculture and Forestry

During the last century there has been a great change in the agricultural practices and the forest operation. Of late, agriculture has shifted from low-input traditional systems involving crop rotations into highly commercialized monocultural practices that utilize high yielding varieties, monocultural operations and use of harmful synthetic chemicals and fertilizers. It has resulted in the depletion of the biodiversity base not only of the plant species in such intensive ecosystems but also affected the animals and other species dependent upon them. Likewise, to meet the increased demand of the timber natural forest has been cut. In order to maintain the forest cover, a number of fast growing tree species have been promoted but in monocultural or pure strands. It has resulted in formation of large areas of plantations/forests that have only one type of species and resulted in loss of other useful species that naturally occurred in the natural forests or exist in the mix-culture type of forests.

Other reasons for losses of biodiversity in the region are:

- *Jhum* cultivation,
- Tea plantations,
- Timber Felling,
- Forest Fires,
- Unscientific method of harvesting,
- Hunting,
- Soil Erosion,
- Encroachment Problem,
- Construction of reservoirs and dams,
- Charcoal making,
- Grazing.

How to Check the Loss of Biodiversity?

India has strengthened its hold on biodiversity conservation by implementing the Indian Forest Act 1927; the Wildlife (Protection) Act 1972; the Forest (Conservation) Act 1980; the Environment (Protection) Act 1986; the Biodiversity Act 2002; the Biodiversity Rule 2004, etc. India became a party to Convention on International Trade in Endangered Species (CITES) since 1976. India is also a signatory of the Convention on Biological Diversity (CBD) since 1992. A network of protected areas – biosphere reserves, sanctuaries, national parks, arborata, botanical gardens, etc., have been established throughout the country, of which this region had its share. The region has four biosphere reserves, 48 sanctuaries, 14 national parks, and two world heritage sites. But lack of awareness at the grassroots level hampers the process of biodiversity conservation. Awareness programmes such as seminars and workshops should be held in schools, and colleges and even for the local folks. Public displays in the form of billboards and handing out pamphlets showing about the importance of biodiversity and the need of its conservation are needed. It is time for concerned authorities to take up the necessary actions to conserve this rich biodiversity, before it is too late. Biodiversity is vital for our existence. Its depletion at a faster rate is a cause of concern for everyone. It is thus very important to conserve it and in this direction steps have been taken at the local, regional, national and even at the international levels. The conservation of biodiversity can be *in situ* (in which species are conserved within their natural range) or can be *ex situ* (where the conservation is done outside the natural range of species).

Ex situ Conservation

Ex situ conservation means "off-site" conservation. In this practice the species of plants and animals to be protected are removed from the natural habitats and are placed in the safer areas under the control of man. Botanical gardens, zoos and the arboreta are the traditional methods of *ex situ* conservation. Here species of plants and animals are conserved by providing the congenial conditions. ***Germplasm banks or Seed banks*** (also ***Gene banks***) are some other methods of *ex situ* conservation. Storing the germplasm in the seed banks helps in conserving rare and endangered species in order to restore genetic diversity. Seeds have a natural tendency to undergo dormancy and hence can be preserved for a longer time. **Orthodox seeds** that can be dried at low humidity or temperature can be stored for a longer time whereas **Recalcitrant seeds** that cannot be dried at low humidity and temperature are, however, difficult to be stored for a longer time. The plants whose seeds can not be conserved in seed banks their vegetative propagating parts such as corms, cuttings, bulbs, tubers and plants or propagules raised through *in vitro* conditions are stored in the gene banks using cryogenic conditions. Likewise, the important animal germplasm like eggs, sperms or embryos can be preserved in the gene banks.

Several international organizations like CGIAR (Consultative Group on International Agricultural Research), IBPGR (International Board for Plant Genetic Resource), IPGRI (International Plant Genetic Resources Institute), and CIFOR (Centre for International Forestry Research) are linked with the *ex situ* conservation through establishment of gene banks and gene libraries.

In situ Conservation

In situ conservation means "on-site" conservation, i.e., protection of species within the natural habitat of the species of animals and plants. It includes protection in the wildlife sanctuaries, national parks and biosphere reserves, etc., that have been formed to protect threatened and even rare species. These methods help to conserve biodiversity without affecting their natural environment. All activities like hunting and poaching are prohibited in the protected areas.

In India we have 608 protected areas. These include:

- National Parks: 95
- Biosphere Reserves: 13
- Wildlife Sanctuaries: 500

Biosphere Reserves

These are the areas of terrestrial and coastal ecosystems that conserve biodiversity in a sustainable way. These are also known as living laboratories for demonstrating integrated management of land, water and biodiversity. The objectives of the biosphere reserves are to conserve biodiversity, to facilitate human and economic development and to provide logistic support to the people to undertake research and education activities and information exchange at international level. These are recognized internationally but are nominated by national Government and remain under sovereign jurisdiction of the country where they are located. The Biosphere Reserves are organized into three inter-related zones namely Core Zone, Buffer Zone and Transition Zone. It is the core area which requires legal protection while some constructive activity may occur in buffer and transition zone.

The origin of concept of Biosphere Reserve goes back to Biosphere Conference—the first inter-governmental conference organized by UNESCO in 1968. The aim of this was to establish terrestrial and coastal ecosystem on earth in which all genetic resources would be protected. Later in 1970, Man and Biosphere (MAB) was officially launched by UNESCO and one of the MAB's projects was to establish world network of new protected areas which were designated as Biosphere Reserves. At present, there are now 499 Biosphere reserves recognized in 110 countries world over.

In India, there are four internationally recognized Biosphere Reserves: ***Nilgiri,*** recognized in 2000, ***Gulf of Mannar*** in 2001, ***Sunderbans*** in 2001 and ***Nanda Devi*** in 2004 by MAB (Man and Biosphere Programme of UNESCO). Besides, Sunderbans is also a National Park and a World Heritage Site. In addition, Ministry of Environment and Forests (MoEF), Government of India has also identified 13 biosphere reserves (Nilgiri, Nanda Devi, Nokrek, Great Nicobar Islands, Gulf of Mannar, Manas, Sunderbans, Simlipal, Dibru-Saikhowa, Dehang-Debang, Panchmarhi, Khangchendzonga and Agasthyamalai) at the national level including the four biosphere reserves recognized by MAB.

Biodiversity Hotspot Zones

In order to identify the areas having rich biodiversity and endemic species (those found only in a particular area and not anywhere else), British ecologist Norman Myers gave the concept of "**biodiversity hotspots**" in 1988 and identified 10 such regions in the tropical forests. Later, the concept of hotspots was adopted by Conservation International (CI) and at present this concept has been extended to **34 such areas present worldwide**. For an area to be qualified as Hotspot region, it should have at least 1,500 species of endemic vascular plants and should have lost about 70 per cent of its original habitat. In India, three hotspot regions have been recognized. These are: **the Himalayas, Western Ghats (extending up to Sri Lanka) and Indo-Burma region.**

The Himalayan Hotspot has over 10,000 plant species of which 31.65 per cent are endemic. These include pines, firs, spruces, rhododendrons and variety of orchids, mosses and ferns. Besides, a number of birds and mammals including vultures, tigers, elephants, rhinos and wild water buffaloes exist in the Himalayas.

Western Ghats and Sri Lanka is one of the richest biodiversity areas with a high rate (52%) of endemism of plants species. A number of unique and rare plants and ferns are present in this hotspot. However, the forests in this region are under tremendous logging pressure. Besides, the region is also home to some of the rare animals like endangered Asian elephant. Unfortunately, there has been excessive human interference in this region resulting in great loss of habitat and biodiversity.

Indo-Burma hotspot region extends from North-East India to

Burma and has a rich treasure of biological resources. The region has a remarkable diversity of fresh water turtles and bird species (over 1,300 species). A number of dipterocarps, orchids and ginger 11 species are present in this region. However, due to various political and social reasons, the knowledge about the plant diversity of this region is incomplete.

Biodiversity Act of India (2002)

In order to protect precious biodiversity of the country, the Government of India approved biodiversity bill (which seeks to deal with the problem of biodiversity loss and biopiracy by giving tough punishment to the offenders) in December 2002 which became an act known as **Biological Diversity Act of 2002.** Later, **Biological Diversity Rules 2004** were formulated as a step towards conservation of biodiversity. According to this Act anyone who destroys biodiversity in anyway or takes it away for commercial utilization for any other purpose without approval of authorities is liable to be imprisoned for up-to five years or to pay a fine of Rs.10 lakh. The offences under this Act are cognizable and non-bailable. For implementing the provision of the Act, National Biodiversity Authority, State Biodiversity Boards and Biodiversity Management Committees at the local level are constituted. The Act also lays down procedures for the use of nation's biodiversity by the people. For this one is required to get prior clearance from the National Biodiversity.

Using Satellite Remote Sensing and Geographic Information System by the Indian Institute of Remote Sensing and Department of Space (IIRS), Government of India.

Priority Sites Identified by IIRS

Arunachal Pradesh: Highlighting the fact that Tropical forests are acclaimed world over for their biodiversity richness and uniqueness, NESAC deduced that rich forests occur in Namdapha National Park and border areas of West Kameng, East Siang and Lohit districts. Alpine pastures and temperate conifer area also indicate high richness.

Assam: Assam has two famous valleys Assam and B arak river valleys supporting famous vegetation association like

Dipterocarpus macrocarpus—*Shorea assamica*—Msua ferrea in the Assam valley and Mesua ferrea—*Dipterocarpus turbinatus* – Palaquium polyanthum in the Barak valley.

Manipur: Highest biological richness in Manipur is reported in Chingpi in Churachandrapur, Dzuku and Maram in Senapati, Tegnopaul area in Chandel and northern inaccessible hills of Tamenglong district.

Meghalaya: Important Biorich sites in Meghalaya are the Nokrek amd Balpakram National Park.

Mizoram: Areas under high biological richness regime have been mapped in the report but not categorically spelt out.

Nagaland: The Biological richness map is provided in the report indicated high biodiversity in high altitude inaccessible hills Tuensang, Phek, Mon and Kohima.

Sikkim: Highest biological richness spot on the inaccessible mountains, transition zone of broad leaved hill forest and east Himalayan wet temperate forest and along difficult river courses in all the four districts of Sikkim. Some of the location names showing higher biological richnenss were:

- East Sikkim: Pangthang, Rumtek, Rongli, Nathula.
- North Sikkim: Namprikdang mountains nearby Mangan.
- South Sikkim: Rabangla area.
- West Sikkim: Barsey, Dentam and Barsey.

It is pertinent to mention here that the States of North-Eastern region have their respective remote sensing centres. It will be useful to compile and collate information available through these centres.

Information generated through GIS techniques by the institutes and organizations outside the State like the Salim Ali Centre for Ornithology and Natural and Wildlife Institute of India.

Essential Elements of the State Biodiversity Strategy and Action Plans

India is a signatory to the convention of Biological Diversity and has a commitment to prepare for herself a National Biodiversity Action Plan. Each of the States in India has prepared an action plan that feeds into the NBSAP. Although many of the States have officially launched their respective SBSAP's, the official endorsement by the Ministry of Environment and Forests is yet to come, nevertheless the respective State Biodiversity Conservation Action Plans was an opportunity to compile the existing information and highlight the biodiversity status of the States. Unlike the Biodiversity Conservation Prioritisation Project (BCPP) which attempted identification of biodiversity rich sites under different ecosystems like forests, rangelands and grasslands, the State Biodiversity Strategy Action plans were developed individually for the states.

REFERENCES

Abraham, A. and Vatsala, P. 1981. *Introduction to orchids with illustrations and descriptions of 150 South Indian Orchids*. Tropical Botanic Garden and Research Institute, Thiruvananthapuram, Kerala (India), pp. 533.

Chowdhery, H.J. 2009. Orchid diversity in North-Eastern States of India. *J. Orchid Soc. India,* 23 (1-2): 19-42.

Hegde, S.N. 2000. Conservation of North East Flora. *Arunachal Forest News*. Vol. 18 (1 & 2).

Medhi, R.P. and Chakrabarti Shyamali. 2009. Traditional Knowledge of NE people on Conservation of Wild Orchids. *Indian Journal of Traditional Knowledge,* 8(1): 11-16

Mercy, S.T. and Dale, B. 1997. Orchids. St. Josephs Press, Thiruvananthapuram, Kerala (India), p. 132.

Singh, F. 1984. *Cymbidium munronianum*. The Fragrant Cymbidium. Orchid Reviews, 92: 231.

Singh, F. 1990. Indian orchids. *Indian Horticulture,* 35(1): 14-15.

Tandon, P. Abrol, Y.P. and Kumaria, Suman. 2007. In: *Biodiversity and its Significance,* published by I.K. International Pvt. Ltd., pp. 370.

Tripathi, R.S. and Barik, S.K. 2003. National Biodiversity Strategy and Action Plan Report for North-East India. Ministry of Environment and Forests, New Delhi.

Yumnam, J.Y. 2008. Rich biodiversity of North-East India needs conservation. *Current Science,* 95 (3): 3, 10.

22

One Decade Study Report on Diversity Status of Turtle Fauna and their Conservation Initiative in Northeast India

Kulendra C. Das

Introduction

Inventories of species in particular regions are essential data sets for conservation and resource management and the acquisition of baseline data on the distribution and status of even common species is important. Furthermore, knowledge of local species diversity is fundamental to understanding community and ecosystem dynamics. Biodiversity is the current research area in biological sciences throughout the world (Raven and Wilson, 1992; Discarti and Yones, 1994). India is home to a very large and diverse assemblage of chelonians and has one of the most diverse chelonian faunas in the world. It ranks among the top five Asian countries in terms of its importance for turtle conservation (Stuart and Thorbjarnarson, 2003). Twenty eight species of freshwater turtles and tortoises occur in India and three of these, *Indotestudo travancorica, Nilssonia leithii* and *Geochelone silvatica* are endemic to India (Das, 1985; 1995a, b; 2002; Das and Andrews, 1997).

Of the diverse turtle fauna of India, five species of marine turtles are available in the Indian waters viz., *Caretta caretta, Chelonia mydas, Eretmochelys imbricata, Lapidochelys olivacea* belonging to Chelonidae family and *Dermochelys coriacea* belonging to Dermochelyidae family. This is followed by another group of 28 species of non-marine turtles and tortoises belonging to 3 families.

The Geoemydidae family consists of 7 genus and 16 species, viz., *Batagur baska, Cuora amboinensis, Cyclemys oldhami (Cyclemys dentata), Geoclemys hamiltonii, Geoemyda silvatica (Heoseys silvatica), Hardella thurjii, Kachuga dhongoka, Kachuga kachuga, Pangshura smithii (Kachuga smithii), Pangshura sylhetensis (Kachuga sylhetensis), Pangshura tecta (Kachuga tecta), Pangshura tentoria (3 subspecies of Kachuga tentoria), Melanochelys tricarinata, Melanochelys trijuga (4 subspecies), Morenia petersi* and *Pyxidea mouhotii (Cyclemys mouhotii).* These are semi aquatic in nature, inhabiting in hill stream, riparian vegetation, upstream river and marshy low lying areas.

Another important group of Testudinidae family consists of 4 species viz., *Geochelone elegans, Indotestudo elongata (Geochelone elongata), Indotestudo travancorica (Geochelone travancorica)* and *Manouria emys (2 subspecies of Geochelone emys).* These are predominantly terrestrial in nature, inhabiting deep forest, sal forest and teak forest. The most interesting freshwater softshell turtles belongs to Trionychidae family consists of 8 species viz., *Amyda cartilaginea, Nilssonia gangetica (Trionyx gangeticus), Nilssonia hurum, Nilssonia leithii, Nilssonia nigricans, Chitra indica, Lissemys punctata (2 subspecies) and Pelochelys cantorii (Pelochelys bibroni).* These are mostly aquatic in nature, inhabiting water bodies such as river, lake, ox-bows, pond etc.

The Indo-gangetic plain and the Terai region also have a diverse chelonian fauna with the occurrence of 20 species (Das, 2002; Rao, 1990). Northeast India has the largest species diversity with 24 species or 25 taxa, of which, *Geochelone elegans, Pelochelys cantorii* and *Kachuga dhongoka* need confirmation (Choudhury, 1995a,b,c; 1998). Around one decade later the 'Turtle Hotspot' of Northeast India is reported the home to 21 out of 29 species of freshwater turtles and tortoises found in India (Ahmed *et al.*, 2009). The distribution of chelonian species richness and diversity in India is not only nationally significant but also globally. The species found in Northeast India share their ranges with South East Asia or Burma-Chinese region, other making then Indian political non-endemics. Besides, heavy precipitation and large tract of tropical evergreen forests, providing maximum number of microhabitats, have made the Western Ghats and Northeastern India the hotspots of chelonian biodiversity (Myers *et al.*, 2000).

The literature survey on chelonians reveal that relatively little attention has been paid to the study of chelonian fauna and their conservation in this region. Among the important works are those of Anderson (1871); Smith (1931); Das (1990, 1991, 1995a,b); Bhupathy *et al.*, (1992); Frazier and Das (1994); Choudhury (1995a); Sengupta *et al.*, (1998a,b); Pawar and Choudhury (2000); Gupta (2002); and Das and Gupta (2004, 2011, 2013); Das (2008); Das *et al.*, (2012). However, from the survey of literature it appears that a through intensive survey of the Northeast would result in more new records of species (Kundu *et al.*, 2013; Singh *et al.*, 2013), especially similar to the types found in the Southeast Asian region. Hence, the present paper aims at preparing a report on existing diversity status of turtle fauna and their conservation initiative during study period from 2002 to 2012 in Northeast India.

At the same time environmental education and public awareness are important tools in any long-term conservation strategy. Tortoises and turtles in India play a very important role as religious symbols, in folklore and culture (Das, 1995). Ecologically they play an important role in aquatic and terrestrial ecosystems. The freshwater turtles are known to be water purifiers (Tripathi and Mishra, 2005), while they are also used as biological control agents (Premkishore and Chandan, 1995). The freshwater turtles and tortoises belonging to the Reptilian Order Chelonia comprise a morphologically and ecologically unique group of animals that are increasingly becoming endangered due to various anthropogenic activities. As a part of the objectives of the present study, an attempt has also been made to introduce an approach to people's participation in community based conservation of turtles and generate awareness among the common people and the urgent need to ensure their protection and conservation.

Materials and Methods

Study Area

India in her Northeastern region (Latitude 21°58′ and 24°35′ N, Longitude 92°15′ and 93°29′ E) consists of eight States, *viz.*, Arunachal Pradesh, Assam, Meghalaya, Manipur, Mizoram, Nagaland, Tripura and Sikkim. This part of India is mainly a mountainous terrain, largely of tertiary origin and has remarkably luxuriant vegetation. The region has three distinct physical features: The Brahmaputra Valley, The Surma or the Barak Valley and a series of mountain and hilly ranges—with the Himalayas in the North, Khasi, Garo and Jaintia Hills in the South; the Patkoi and Naga hills and the Manipur Plateau in the east and the Lushai or Mizo hills extending from south of Manipur to Burma as the Arakan Yoma. Bhutan, West Bengal and Bangladesh lie to the west of Northeast India. Northeast India has two major river systems, Brahmaputra and Barak with many tributaries which are largely sandy and suitable for nesting of diverse turtle population. Highly humid tropical climate prevails with a long monsoon period stretching from April to September.

Survey of Chelonian

Sporadically abundance of diverge population of turtles is found throughout Northeast India. A random survey is conducted (2002 to 2012) last ten years in different parts of Northeast India inclusive of different markets, villages and informed places of turtle population. Live specimens found in the field were released immediately after making thorough examination and measurement and taking photographs. The turtle species are identified on the basis of morphological characteristics (Das, 1991, 2002).

Community Based Conservation and Awareness Programme

Rescued turtles from markets and turtle hunters were released during 2002-2007 in different temple tanks and in privately owned ponds of willing citizens. All the measurements including weight were recorded (Table 22.2). Environmental awareness and capacity building programs were also conducted in different places to educate the people about the value of turtles for future conservation. Environment awareness campaigns and meetings among target groups like turtle hunters and trappers, fishermen, school children, teachers and students, government officials, politicians and policy-makers, NGO activists, media persons, local community and the common people about the value of turtles, need for conservation of turtles and to abstain from consuming turtle and tortoise meat and eggs were conducted. The media was urged and encouraged to cover confiscations and publicize stories on turtle and tortoise trade as described by CFH/MCBT (2006). A total of 156 awareness campaigns in different schools, government offices, NGOs, public places, urban crowd, press media and religious places were conducted. Awareness materials in the form of about 3000 leaflets and 300 posters in both English and Bengali highlighting the importance of turtles and the need for their conservation were distributed during the campaign programmes in schools and other places (Plate 22.1). The various programmes includes postering (P), Leaflet Distribution (LD), rescued turtle released to protected community or Temple tank (RT), writing article and/or news clips on turtle conservation (W), turtle rescued from market (T), discussion (D) with the target groups, special lectures in public gathering (L), memorandum submission (M) to law enforcement agencies, participation in exhibitions (E), arrangement of car rallies and processions in the public places, urban centers, etc. Popular articles on the importance of turtles and the threats faced by them were published in leading local dailies {Dainik Jugasankha, Dainik Sonar Cachar, Dainik Samayik Prasanga, Dainik Statesmen (Bengali daily paper), Shibaji (Bengali biweekly paper), Prottoy (Bengali weekly paper), Barak Bangla (Bengali weekly paper), Dainik Purboday (Hindi daily paper), Prerona Bharati (Hindi weekly paper), The Frontier Sun (English daily paper). The Impression (biannual English student news paper)} and magazines (Evergreen, Assam University Newsletter, Prachi Prangan, The Sentinel: melange). Programmes on turtle conservation and its importance were telecast in electronic media such as the Doordarshan and private TV channels both at national as well as regional levels. Participation and presentation in various seminars, conferences, publication of research articles in professional journals were the other activities undertaken.

RESULTS

Inventorying of Turtles and Tortoises Species in North East India

A total of 18 species belonging to three families are recorded from the four States i.e., Assam, Tripura, Arunachal Pradesh and Mizoram States of Northeast India (Tables 22.1). Indirect evidence in the form of shells (carapace) records is observed for ten species. Table 22.1 focus that 14 species are globally threatened according to IUCN Red List (IUCN, 2011). Five species comes

Table 22.1. Inventorying of turtle and tortoise species in North-East India during July, 2002 to June, 2012.

Sl. No.	*Taxa*		*Place of*	*Nature of*	*Status of*		
	Common Name	*Scientific Name*	*Record*	*Record*	*CITES*	*IWPA*	*IUCN*
	Family: Trionychidae						
1.	Indian Softshell Turtle	*Nilssonia gangetica*	AS, AP, TR	L, J, A, C	Appendix I	Sch-I	VU
2.	Black Softshell Turtle	*Nilssonia nigricans*	AS, AP	L, A	Appendix I	None	CR
3.	Indian Peacock Turtle	*Nilssonia hurum*	AS, TR	L, J, A, C	Appendix I	Sch-I	VU
4.	Narrow-headed Softshell Turtle	*Chita indica*	AS, AP	L, A, C	Appendix II	Sch-IV	EN
5.	Indian Flapshell Turtle	*Lissemys punctata Andersonii*	AS, TR	L, J, A, C	Appendix II	Sch-I	SNA
6.	Malayan Softshell Turtle	*Amyda cartilaginea*	AS, MZ	L	Appendix II	None	VU
	Family: Geoemydidae						
7.	Malayan Box Turtle	*Cuora amboinensis*	AS, AP	L, J, C	Appendix II	None	VU
8.	Indian Black Turtle	*Melanochelys trijuga*	AS, MZ	L, A, C	None	None	NT
9.	Keeled Box Turtle	*Cuora mouhotii*	AS, AP, MZ	L, A, C	Appendix II	None	EN
10.	Indian Eyed Turtle	*Morenia petersi*	TR	L, A	None	None	VU
11.	Indian Roofed Turtle	*Pangshura tecta*	TR	L, A	Appendix I	Sch-I	LC
12.	Assam Roofed Turtle	*Pangshura sylhetensis*	AS, AP, MZ	L, J, C	Appendix II	Sch-I	EN
13.	Indian Tent Turtle	*Pangshura tentoria*	AS, MZ	L, J	Appendix II	None	LC
14.	Spotted Pond Turtle	*Geoclemys hamiltonii*	AS	L, J	Appendix I	Sch-I	VU
15.	Indian Leaf Turtle	*Cyclemys gemeli*	AS, MZ	L, J		None	
16.	Brown Roofed Turtle	*Pangshura smithii*	AS	L, J	Appendix II	None	NT
	Family: Testudinidae						
17.	Asian Brown Tortoise	*Manouria emys*	AS, MZ	L, A, C	Appendix II	Sch-IV	EN
18.	Elongated Tortoise	*Indotestudo elongata*	AS, MZ	L, A, C	Appendix II	Sch-IV	EN

CR = Critically Endangered, EN = Endangered, VU = Vulnerable, NT = Near Threatened, LC = Least Concern, SNA = Status not assessed, L = Live specimen, C = Carapace, A = Adult, J = Juvenile, IWPA = Indian Wildlife Protection Act, 1972, IUCN = International Union for Conservation of Nature and Natural Resources, CITES = Convention on International Trade in Endangered Species of Wild Fauna and Flora, AS = Assam. TR = Tripura, AP = Arunachal Pradesh, MZ = Mizoram, Sch=Schedule, Appendix I = Most threatened species (No trade allowed), Appendix II = Species likely to be threatened due to unregulated trade (Trade is allowed through licensing).

under CITES-Appendix I and ten species under CITES-Appendix II. According to Indian Wildlife Protection Act (IWPA), 1972, six species are included in Schedule I and other four species belongs to Schedule IV, while the rest six species are not under legal protection in India. As shown in the Table 22.1, in terms of occurrence of number of individual, *Lissemys punctata andersonii* is recorded most frequently, followed by *Pangshura tentoria, Nilssonia gangetica, Nilssonia nigricans* and *Geoclemys hamiltonii,* while the other species are recorded relatively infrequently: *Nilssonia hurum, Indotestudo elongata, Manouria emys, Chitra indica, Pangshura sylhetensis, Melanochelys trijuga, Cuora mouhotii, Cuora amboinensis, Cyclemys gemeli, Morenia petersi* and *Pangshura tecta* respectively. These species are recorded both market as well as fields.

Awareness Programme for Community Based Conservation

A total of 43 turtles and tortoises, *viz.*, twelve *Nilssonia gangetica* (range of wt. 0.4-2.0 kg), nineteen *N. hurum* (0.1-1.5 kg), one *Chitra indica* (1.6 kg), eight *L. p. andersonii* (0.75-2.1 kg), two *Pangshura sylhetensis* (0.35-0.9 kg) and one *Indotestudo elongata* (2.5 kg), which were rescued from markets and turtle hunters were released during the study period in different temple tanks, community tanks and Tea garden ponds in Barak Valley, Assam (Table 22.2). Turtles have historically received community-sanctioned religious protection in many temple tanks, in this region. Examples include softshell turtles protected in the Nagshankar temple at Sonitpur district, Kamakhya temple at Guwahati, Hazo temple near Guwahati, Assam and *Nilssonia gangetica* in the Tripureshwari temple at Udaipur, Tripura. More recently, the Shiva temple at Tinsukia, Kachakanti temple in Udarbond, Shamananda Ashram temple, Kathiababa Ashram temple and Gopal Akhra temple in Silchar at Cachar, Assam has started offering turtles sanctuary (Plate 2). Thus *ex situ* conservation of turtle in community and temple tanks as well as in public gardens could also constitute a useful mechanism for conservation (Das *et al.*, 2012).

Awareness materials in the form of about 3000 leaflets and 300 posters in both English and Bengali highlighting the importance of turtles and the need for their conservation were distributed during the campaign programs in schools and other

Table 22.2: Lists of rescued turtles tagged and released for community based conservation in the Barak Valley, Assam (CL: Carapace length; CW: Carapace width; T.E: Tea estate; N; Nilssonia; P: Pangshura; L.p: Lissemys punctata)

Sl. No.	*Species Name*	*Weight (Kg)*	*Size (cm) CL × CW*	*Date of release*	*Enclosure size (m)*	*Nature of enclosure*	*Site of release*
1.	*N. hurum*	1.1	21x19	28.9.02	20x10x3	Lake	Barham Baba Temple, Silcoorie
2.	*N. gangetica*	0.8	21x19	03.04.03	14x5x2	-do-	Srikona Park, Silchar
3.	*N. hurum*	1.5	23x21	10.10.02	-do-	-do-	-do-
4.	-do-	1.3	22x19	12.12.02	55x36x3	-do-	Rosekandi T. E., Cachar
5.	-do-	1.1	22x20	-do-	-do-	-do-	-do-
6.	-do-	1.4	23x20	8.11.02	20x14x3	-do-	West Jalinga T. E., Cachar
7.	-do-	1.2	20x17	07.06.03	80x50x3	-do-	Dwarbond T. E., Cachar
8.	-do-	0.15	12x10	04.11.03	-do-	-do-	-do-
9.	-do-	0.18	11.5x10	-do-	-do-	-do-	-do-
10.	-do-	0.10	8.5x7.5	-do-	-do-	-do-	-do-
11.	*L. p. andersonii*	1.0	20x19	03.10.04	20x12x3	Pond	Private pond, Karimganj
12.	-do-	0.75	19x18	-do-	-do-	-do-	-do-
13.	-do-	1.0	21x19	31.05.04	-do-	-do-	-do-
14.	-do-	0.75	20x17	-do-	-do-	-do-	-do-
15.	-do-	0.8	19x18	29.03.04	10x7x2	-do-	Private Pond, Silchar Town
16.	-do-	1.1	21x17	-do-	-do-	-do-	-do-
17.	*N. hurum*	1.15	21x17	-do-	-do-	-do-	-do-
18.	-do-	1.2	22x20	-do-	-do-	-do-	-do-
19.	-do-	0.45	18x17	05.09.04	-do-	-do-	-do-
20.	-do-	0.30	16x15	-do-	-do-	-do-	-do-
21.	-do-	0.45	18x17	-do-	-do-	-do-	-do-
22.	-do-	1.2	23x22	13.06.05	-do-	-do-	-do-
23.	-do-	1.5	25x22	31.01.04	15x10x3	Pond	Radhamadhab Temple, Silchar
24.	*N. gangetica*	1.3	24x21	31.01.04	16x10x3	-do-	Shyamananda Ashram, Silchar
25.	-do-	1.2	23x22	19.06.04	-do-	-do-	-do-
26.	-do-	0.8	20x18	5.09.04	12x8x4	Pond	Gopal Akra Temple, Silchar
27.	-do-	0.7	19x17	-do-	-do-	-do-	-do-
28.	-do-	0.45	10x17	-do-	-do-	-do-	-do-
29.	-do-	0.4	10x7	-do-	-do-	-do-	-do-
30.	-do-	0.4	15x14	16.03.05	15x10x3	Pond	Radhamadhab Temple, Silchar
31.	-do-	2.0	27x25	15.05.05	18x12x3	Pond	Kachakanti Temple, Udarbond.
32.	-do-	0.7	20x18	-do-	-do-	-do-	-do-
33.	*N. hurum*	1.3	21x18	05.06.05	14x5x2	Lake	Srikona Park, Silchar, Cachar
34.	*N. gangetica*	0.45	18x17	05.06.05	-do-	-do-	-do-
35.	-do-	0.755	21x19	05.06.05	-do-	-do-	-do-
36.	*P. sylhetensis*	0.350	17x16	05.06.05	-do-	-do-	-do-
37.	-do-	0.9	21x20	-do-	-do-	-do-	-do-
38.	*I. elongata*	2.5	31x28	04.05.04	10x 6x 3	Terrestrial	-do-
39.	*Chitra indica*	1.6	27x25	07.06.05	-do-	-do-	-do-
40.	*L. p. andersonii*	2.1	28x27	03.08.05	29x16x3	Pond	Ramkrishna Mission, Silchar
41.	-do-	1.7	27x26	-do-	-do-	-do-	-do-
42.	*N. hurum*	1.3	21x18	19.06.04	-do-	-do-	-do-
43.	-do-	0.4	15x14	-do-	-do-	-do-	-do-

places. A total of 156 awareness campaigns in different schools, government offices, NGOs, public places, urban crowd, press media and religious places were covered in which (25%) Academic institutions, (28%) government offices, (17%) Non-Governmental Organizations (NGOs), (8%) public places, (12%) media, (4%) religious places, and (6%) tea gardens of this region (Fig. 22.1). The other activities included publication of research articles, paper presentations in international, national and regional seminars and conferences, popular articles in magazines and newspapers, popular talk and interaction in radio, TV programmes, etc. continued till date which focuses the importance of turtles and their endangered status as well as threats (Table 22.3).

Fig. 22.1: Percentage of awareness programme covered during study period in Barak Valley, Assam.

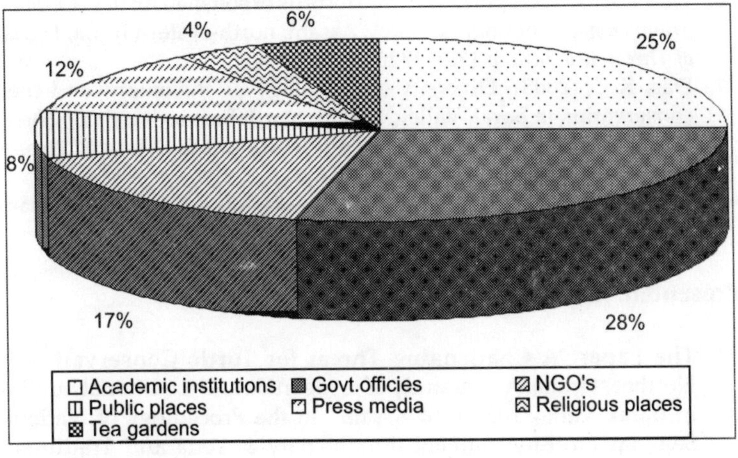

Table 22.3: Activities done for capacity building on turtle research and conservation in Northeast India

Publications: Manuscripts

1. **Das, K.C.** & A. Gupta (2013). Preliminary Breeding Behavioral Observation of Captive *Lissemys punctata andersonii* with Some Ecological Notes, pp 196-199. In edited book '*Bioresources and Traditional Knowledge of Northeast India*, ISBN 98781-92432137 MIPOGRASS & PUC, Mizoram, India.

2. Kundu, S., **K.C. Das** & S.K. Ghosh (2013). Taxonomic rank of Indian tortoise: revisit with DNA barcoding perspective, *DNA Barcodes*, In press.
3. Kundu, S., **K.C. Das**, H.T. Lalremsanga, A. Gupta & S.K Ghosh (2013). A New Report for All Representatives of Asian Forest Tortoise has Their Footmarks in Northeast India, Pp 241-245. In edited book *'Bioresources and Traditional Knowledge of Northeast India*, ISBN 98781-92432137 MIPOGRASS & PUC, Mizoram, India.
4. Singh, K.K, **K.C. Das** & H. Lalruatsanga (2013). *Bioresources and Traditional Knowledge of Northeast India*, 424Pp, ISBN 98781-92432137 MIPOGRASS & PUC, Mizoram, India.
5. **Das, K.C.**, S. Kundu, S. K. Ghosh & A. Gupta (2012). Traditional Knowledge on Zootherapeutic Uses of Turtle is an Issue for International Conservation.Pp 81-89. (Edited by K.B. Singh and K. Lalchhandama) *Proceedings of the National Seminar on Recent Advances in Natural Products Research*, ISBN 9878192432120 MIPOGRASS & PUC, Mizoram, India.
6. **Das, K.C.** & A. Gupta (2011). Site records of softshell turtles (*Chelonia: Trionychidae*) from Barak Valley, Assam, north-eastern India, *Journal of Threatened Taxa* 3: 1722-1726.
7. **Das, K.C.** (2008). Diversity and Ecology of chelonians and their conservation in Barak Valley, Assam, North East India. *Ph.D. Thesis*. Department of Ecology and Environmental Science, Assam University, Silchar, 213 pp.
8. **Das, K. C.** & A. Gupta (2004). Turtle market survey in Silchar, Assam. Northeast India. *Turtle and Tortoise Newsletter* 8: 16-17.

Presented: (Abstracts Published)

9. The Paper "A Challenging Threat for Turtle Conservation in Northeast India: A case study of turtle trade and traditional hunting in Barak Valley region of Assam" in the Procedings of National Seminar on 'Environment, Biodiversity & Veda and Traditional Systems' 10-12th April, 2012. Mizoram University, Aizawl
10. "Molecular Identification and Phylogenetic Relationship of Endangered Soft shell Turtles of Northeast India" in the Procedings of "22 Pacific Science Congress sessions on Barcoding Pacific Invasive and Pest Species" 14-17th June, 2011. Kuala Lampur, Malaysia.
11. "DNA Barcoding of Endangered Softshell Turtles in Northeast India" in the Procedings of Section of Agriculture and Forestry, in 98th Indian Science Congress, organized by SRM University, Chennai, January 3-7, 2011
12. "The Phylogenetic Analysis and Evolutionary Ecology of the Freshwater Turtles in Northeast India " in the Procedings of Section of Animal,

Veterinary and Fishery Sciences, in 98th Indian Science Congress, organized by SRM University, Chennai, January 3-7, 2011. pp 75.

13. "Studies on DNA Barcode of Turtle Genetic Diversity of Northeast India" in the Procedings of Section of Animal, Veterinary and Fishery Sciences, in 97th Indian Science Congress, organized by University of Kerala, Thiruvanthapuram, January 3-7, 2010. pp 212
14. "DNA Barcode of Life: the Species-specific DNA Sequences from East and Northeast Indian Biodiversity" in the Procedings of Section of New Biology, in 97th Indian Science Congress, organized by University of Kerala, Thiruvanthapuram, January 3-7, 2010. Pp 100
15. "Mitochondrial Genome: The Biomaker for Indian Biodiversity" in the Procedings of 3rd International Barcode of Life, Maxico City, 7-13 November, 2009.
16. "Awareness Program on Turtle and Tortoises Conservation in Barak Valley, Assam, Northeast India" in the proceedings of National Seminar on Biodiversity Spectrum of North-East India", organized by Dept. of Zoology, A.V. College, Guwahati, Assam, September 18-19, 2009. pp.32
17. "Site records of Soft-shell turtles (Chelonia: Trionychidae) from Barak Valley, Assam, North East India" in the proceedings of a National Seminar on Current Research in Herpetology, organized by P.G. Department of Zoology, North Orissa University, Orissa, March 29-31, 2009. pp 55
18. "An Approach on Community Based Conservation of Turtle and Tortoise in Barak Valley, Assam, Northeast India" in the 96th Indian Science Congress, organized by North Eastern Hill University, Shillong, Meghalaya, January 3-7, 2009.
19. "Environmental Quality Assessment of Freshwater Turtle Habitats of Barak Valley, Assam, NE India" in the proceedings of an International Conference on Water Resource Management: Challenges and Opportunities in 21st Century, organized by Dept. Of Ecology & Environmental Science, Assam University Silchar, April 23-25, 2007. pp. 72
20. "Diversity Status and Conservation of Turtles and Tortoises in Barak Valley, Assam, North East India" in the proceedings of a National Seminar on Biodiversity Conservation, The Post Rio Scenario in India, organized by Dept. of Ecology & Environmental Science, Assam University Silchar April 19-21, 2006. Pp 15
21. "Socio-Ecological Aspects of Patni Community in Barak Valley, Assam, Northeast India" in a National Seminar on Globalization and North-East India: Problems and Possibilities, organized by Dept. of Sociology, Assam University Silchar, April 26-28, 2006.
22. "Trade of Turtles and Tortoises in Barak Valley, Assam, Northeast India" in the 93rd Indian Science Congress, organized by Acharya N.G. Ranga Agricultural University, Hyderabad, January 3-7, 2006.

23. "A Survey of Chelonians in Barak Valley, Assam, Northeast India" in the proceedings of a National Seminar on Biodiversity Conservation and Future Concern organized by Northeast Biotechnological Association (NEBA) & Dept. of Biotechnology, Gauhati University, Guwahati, June 17-18, 2005. Pp 48.
24. "Diversity and Distribution of Chelonians in Barak Valley, Assam, North East India" in the 92nd Indian Science Congress, organized by Nirma University of Science and Technology, Ahamedabad, January 3-7, 2005.
25. "Anthropogenic Impact on the Water Quality and Capture Fisheries of River Barak, Assam, India" in the Proceedings of an International Conference on Tropical aquatic ecosystems: Health, Management and Conservation organized by National Institute of Ecology, Nainital (India), October 25-30, 1999.

Popular Talks/Articles In Periodicals/Dailies/ Magazines

26. "Conserve Wildlife: Turtles and Tortoises are in Danger!" An article published in Evergreen: IPPES Fourth Annual Magazine, 5th June, 2005 pp29-30.
27. "Appetite knows no Bound; Turtles take a Tumble in Barak Valley "an article published in THE IMPRESSION First Complete Student Newspaper in India, Dept. of Mass Communication, Assam University Silchar. vol, x (2).April 2, 2005.
28. "Save threatened turtles and tortoises in Barak Valley, Assam" an article published in PRACHI PRANGAN, Assam University Magazine, 2006 pp. 7-8.
29. "Save Turtles, Save Environment" on The Sentinel: mélange, October 9, 2005.
30. Several news and popular articles on Turtles and Tortoises conservation are published in the Indian and regional newspapers
31. Several news on release of turtles in community ponds were telecasted on local cable channel, Doordarshan (DD1) as well as All India Radio, Silchar
32. Documentary on turtle research and conservation telecasted on DD1 Northeast program
33. Popular talk on interview based programme in Doordarshan Silchar regarding conservation of Turtles in Barak Valley on 11th June, 2005.

Participation in Conferences /Workshops and Training / Exhibitions/Rally

34. Ten days national workshop of hands on Training Course "Basic Tools in Molecular Biology and Genomics" organized by Prof. (Dr.)

Sankar K. Ghosh, Head & Course Director, Department of Biotechnology, Assam University, Silchar, Assam, 7th to 16th December, 2010.

35. Fifteen days Workshop on "PCR Based Advanced DNA Fingerprinting" organized by Prof. (Dr.) Sankar K. Ghosh, Head & Course Director, Department of Biotechnology, Assam University, Silchar, Assam, 21st April to 5th May, 2010.
36. One day Workshop on "Current Trends of Wildlife Researches in N.E. India" organized by Dept. of Ecology and Environmental Science, Assam University, Silchar, September 4, 2009.
37. One day National Workshop on "DNA BARCODE OF LIFE" organized by Department of Biotechnology, Assam University Silchar, Assam, April 7, 2009.
38. Three days workshop on "Traditional Knowledge, Culture, and communication: Common Grounds in India and Canada" organized by Assam University Silchar, in collaboration with Shastri Indo-Canadian Institute, New Delhi, February12-14, 2007.
39. Four days workshop training on Indian Freshwater Turtle Conservation and Management organised by Madras Crocodile Bank Trust, Chennai, October 26-29, 2006.
40. Twelve Days workshop on" Forest, Wildlife and Livelihood, issues for NE India" – An adventure mountaineer trakking at Nandadevi, organized by Center for Science and Environment, New Delhi, March 20-31, 2006
41. Four days workshop on "Canadian Studies of Culture, Society and Environment" organized by Assam University Silchar, March, 7-10, 2005.
42. Participated in Exhibition on three days International Conference on "Current Trends in Algal Bioresource Utilization" organized by Dept. of Ecology & Environmental Science, Assam University Silchar, December 4-6, 2006.
43. Participated in Science Exhibition on Save Turtles & Tortoises at Assam University Conference Hall in the National Science Day, 28th February 2005.
44. Road march conducted on Conservation of Turtle in Silchar from Link Road via National Highway Fish Market and Sanjay Fish Market to Fatak Bazar Fish Market on 15th May, 2005.
45. Conducted a rally and postering on Save Turtles in 15 Schools of Silchar on 5th June, World Environment Day.
46. Four days car rally for distribution of leaflets on turtles conservation to the common people of the Cachar, Karimganj and Hailakandi district.
47. Participated in one day Science & Arts Exhibition with school students on Save Turtles & Tortoises conducted by Holy Cross School, Silchar, 12th August, 2005.1

Discussion

Since tortoises and turtles in India play a very important role as religious symbols, in folklore and culture. The turtle supported the cosmic vessel where gods and demons first mixed the portion from which the world was created and the turtle supported this creation on its back. The turtle was also chosen as one of the ten incarnations, in the form of Kurma, of the Hindu god Vishnu, who helped in creating the nectar of immortality and in the victory of good over evil. In this point of thought, turtles and tortoises reared in temple ponds, tanks and enclosures where devotees feed them since long past. These can be seen in Tamil Nadu, Andhra Pradesh, Orissa, Gujarat, Uttar Pradesh, Madhya Pradesh, and West Bengal and in some north eastern states. Turtles are also depicted on temple walls and pillars. Turtles are kept in village ponds and tanks and are protected by villagers and tample authority. The Bharuch Muslim communities in Gujarat rescue turtles during drought years and keep them in ponds and tanks, and feed them. In Tamil Nadu, Kerala and Bihar people keep land tortoises in their houses with vermillion on them, and these are venerated. A clan of the Kamar tribe in India show great reverence for the turtle and it is their totem (Das, 1995a; CFH/MCBT, 2006).

In last ten years a growing number of turtle hobbyists have expressed interest in participating in turtle conservation through captive breeding and rearing efforts. Several organizations that promote this idea have sprung up in the U.S. and Europe. In India, Madras Crocodile Bank Trust, Kukrail Breeding Centre in Lucknow, Wildlife Institute of India, Bombay Natural History Society, Madhya Pradesh Forest Department, Andhra Pradesh Forest Department, Rajasthan Forest Department, Salim Ali Centre for Ornithology and Natural History, Wildlife Preservation Society of India, Wildlife Trust of India, Zoo Outreach Organization, World Wide Fund for Nature, Society for Conservation of Nature, Aaranyak Nature Club, Nature's Beckon, Jiwaji University, Gauhati University, Assam University, Mizoram University, Aizawl Zoological Park, Environmental Society of South Assam, Uttar Pradesh Forest Department, West Bengal Forest Department, Durrell Wildlife Conservation Trust and Researchers have taken keen interest regarding the turtle research and conservation. In

North East India, many indigenous communities do not kill turtles as it a taboo for them. The 'peers' of Barak Valley, Assam, who are sufi saints, also conserve plants in protected groves and fish species and turtles in the ponds of their Mokams (place of worship). Besides trying to ensure conservation of turtles in their natural habitats, attempts have also to be made to take steps for *ex-situ* conservation in water bodies outside their natural habitats. Since, it is a time-honoured tradition in India to release turtles in temple tanks. In North East India, the Kamakhya Temple at Guwahati, Hoigreeb Madhab Tample at Hazo in Assam, and the Tripureshwari Temple at Udaypur in Tripura, harbour a large number of turtles belonging to the species *Nilssonia gangetica, Nilssonia nigricans,* and other semi softshell turtles. Besides, a Hanuman Temple at Tinsukia and in many Satras (Namghar), Bishnu Mandhir (temple) in Assam was also found to have turtles in its tank without scientific management of captive species.

Conclusion

The impact of the awareness programmes and other activities during the present study for a period of around ten years is now slowly being felt. Several local NGOs and individual activists and groups are now actively preventing turtle sales and helping the enforcement authorities. Several turtles in the recent days have been rescued from the markets and released into natural habitat by the activists and forest officials. It appears that both frequency and number of turtles appearing in markets for sale has to some extent declined. The forest officials at the field level as well as the police have also become more aware of the threatened status of turtles. Temple authorities, tea garden management and people in general are also coming forward to introduce turtles into natural habitats. It is felt that there is very urgent need for proper management of captive turtles in very old ponds of different temple. As the Northeast India is a 'Turtle Hotspot' and a home to 21 out of 29 species of freshwater turtles and tortoises found in India, it is the right time to establish the turtle and tortoise Sanctuary in Northeast India wnich will harbours turtle diversity as an attraction of wildlife photographers, tourists, researchers, scientists etc.

Plate 1: Different Types of Turtle Conservation Awareness Programmes and Education

Plate 1A: Exhibition on Science Day in Assam University

Plate 1B:Awareness education in village school at Baskandi, Cachar

Plate 1C: Exhibition in Holly Cross School, Silchar

Plate 1D: Road march in Silchar Town

Plate 1E: Meeting with forest officials

Plate 1F: Car rally conducted in Barak Valley, Assam

Plate 2: Turtle Research Activities and Community based Conservation Initiatives for Rescued Turtle

Plate 2A: Case for rescued soft shell turtle behaviour study

Plate 2B: Behaviour observation of rescused *Indoltestudo elongata*

Plate 2C: Case for softshell turtle behaviour study in community pond

Plate 2D: Morphometric study of pet *Manouria emys* species in Mizoram

Plate 2E: Egg of *Lissemys punctata andersonii*

Plate 2F: Turtle eggs laid in captivity at Silchar

Plate 2G: Natural enclosure of softshell turtle at Silchar

Plate 2H: Release of rescued turtle in Kachakanti temple pond at Udharbond, Cachar district

Acknowledgements

I am grateful to the G.B. Pant Institute of Himalayan Environment and Development, Almora, Uttaranchal for granting a research project (July, 2002 to March, 2005) entitled *"In–situ & Ex-situ* Conservation of Freshwater Turtles in Barak Valley, Assam, Northeastern India." I also grateful to University Grants Commission, New Delhi, for awarding RGNJRF & RGNSRF (April, 2005 to June, 2009) under Rajiv Gandhi National Fellowship Scheme of GOI on a research topic "Diversity and Ecology of Chelonian and Their Conservation in Barak Valley, Assam, Northeast India". and the Department of Biotechnology, Govt. of India for awarding DBT-Post Doctoral Associateship (July, 2009 to June, 2011) in the scheme of DBT Post-Doctoral Fellowship Programme, Ministry of Science and Technology, Government of India on a research topic "Molecular Population marker as DNA barcode of Turtle Genetic Resources from Northeast India". I am grateful to Department of Ecology & Environmental Science as well as Department of Biotechnology, Assam University, Silchar, for providing me the facilities. I specially acknowledge my Ph D Supervisor Prof. Abhik Gupta and Post Doc Mentor Prof. Sankar K. Ghosh for their continuous support and guidance. I sincerely acknowledge the support lent by the Department of Forests, Govt. of Assam as well as Govt. of Mizoram and other States of Northeast India. I thank to Shantanu Kundu, Dr. Abhijit Das, Dr. H.T. Lalremsanga, Rakesh Saoud, Joynal Abedin, Gunodhar Kunwar and other fellows for their assistance to do this work in time to time.

REFERENCES

1. Ahmed, M. F., A. Das & S. K. Dutta (2009). *Amphibians and Reptiles of Northeast India - A Photographic Guide*. Aaranyak, Guwahati, India. i-xiv and 1-168pp.
2. Anderson, J. (1871). A list of the reptilian accession to the Indian Museum, Calcutta from 1865 to 1870, with a description of some new species. *Journal of the Asiatic Society of Bengal* 40 (Part 2): 12-39
3. Bhupathy, S., B.C. Choudhury & M.O. Moll (1992). Conservation and Management of Fresh Water Turtles and Land Tortoises of India, Technical Report, May 1991 – July 1992. Wildlife Institute of India, Dehradun.

4. Choudhury, A. (1995a). Turtles recorded in Dibru-Saikhowa Wildlife Sanctuary, Assam. *J. Ecol. Soc* 8: 33-39
5. Choudhury, A. (1995b). The Assam roofed turtle *Kachuga sylhetensis* in Sadiya– a new locality record. *J. Bombay Nat. Hist. Soc* 92(3): 426
6. Choudhury, A. (1995c). Some freshwater turtles from Lakhimpur District, Assam. *Cheetal* 34(3-4): 18-24.
7. Choudhury, A. (1998). *Pyxidea mouhotii* (Gray) in southern Assam and Mizoram. *J. Bombay Nat. Hist. Soc* 95(3): 511-512
8. CFH/MCBT. (2006). Conservation Action Plan for Endangered Freshwater Turtles and Tortoises of India. Madras Crocodile Bank Trust, Post Bag 4, Mamallapuram 603104, Tamil Nadu, South India
9. Das, I. (1985). *Indian Turtles: A Field Guide*. World Wildlife Fund—India, Calcutta
10. Das, I. (1990). Distributional records for the chelonians from North Eastern India, *Journal of the Bombay Natural History Society* 87: 91 – 97
11. Das, I. (1991). *Colour guide to the turtles and tortoises of the Indian Subcontinent*. R. and A. Publishing Limited, Portishead, U. K. 133pp.
12. Das, I. (1995a). *Turtles and Tortoises of India*. WWF India and Oxford University Press, Bombay, Delhi, Calcutta and Madras, xi +174pp
13. Das, I. (1995b). An illustrated key to the turtles of insular South-east Asia. *Hamadryad* 20: 27-32. Same title reprinted In: Proc. International Congress of Chelonian Conservation. SOPTOM (Ed.), Editions Soptom, Gonfaron, France, 77-80pp.
14. Das, I. (1996). *Biogeography of the Reptiles of South Asia*. Krieger Publishing Company, Malabar, Florida. 87pp.
15. Das, I. (2002). *A photographic guide to snakes and other reptiles of India*. New Holland Publishers (UK) Ltd. Garfield House, Edgware Road, London W2 2EA, UK. 144pp.
16. Das, I. and H.V. Andrews (1997). Checklist of Indian reptiles. Pp. 1-11- In: B. C. P. P. C A M P., India. Reptiles. 19-23 May 1997. Zoo Outreach Organization, 79 Bharati Colony, Peelamadu, Coimbatore-641004, India.
17. Das, K.C. (2008). *Diversity and Ecology of chelonians and their conservation in Barak Valley, Assam, North East India. Ph.D. Thesis*. Department of Ecology and Environmental Science, Assam University, Silchar, 213 pp.
18. Das, K. C. & A. Gupta (2004). Turtle market survey in Silchar, Assam. Northeast India. *Turtle and Tortoise Newsletter* 8: 16-17.
19. Das, K.C. & A. Gupta (2011). Site records of softshell turtles (*Chelonia: Trionychidae*) from Barak Valley, Assam, North-eastern India, *Journal of Threatened Taxa* 3: 1722-1726.
20. Das, K.C. & A. Gupta (2013). Preliminary Breeding Behavioural Observation of Captive *Lissemys punctata andersonii* with Some Ecological Notes, Pp 196-199. In edited book *'Bioresources and*

Traditional Knowledge of Northeast India, ISBN 98781-92432137 MIPOGRASS & PUC, Mizoram, India.

21. Das, K.C., S. Kundu, S. K. Ghosh & A. Gupta (2012). Traditional Knowledge on Zootherapeutic Uses of Turtle is an Issue for International Conservation.Pp 81-89. (Edited by K.B. Singh and K. Lalchhandama) *Proceedings of the National Seminar on Recent Advances in Natural Products Research,* ISBN 9878192432120 MIPOGRASS & PUC, Mizoram, India
22. Discarti, F. & T. Younes (1994). Diversitas: yesterday, today and path towards the future.- *Biol. Internal.*29: 3-23.
23. Frazier, J.G. & I. Das (1994). Some notable records of testudines from the Indian and Burmese Subregions, *Hamadryad* 19: 47- 66
24. Gupta, A. (2002). The beleagured chelonians of northeast India. *Turtle and Tortoise Newsletter* 6: 16-17.
25. IUCN (2011). *IUCN Red List of Threatened Species.* Version 2011.2. www.iucnredlist.org.
26. Kundu, S., K.C. Das & S.K. Ghosh (2013). Taxonomic rank of Indian tortoise: revisit with DNA barcoding perspective, *DNA Barcodes,* In press.
27. Kundu, S., K.C. Das, H.T. Lalremsanga, A. Gupta & S.K Ghosh (2013). A New Report for All Representatives of Asian Forest Tortoise has Their Footmarks in Northeast India, Pp 241-245. In edited book *'Bioresources and Traditional Knowledge of Northeast India,* ISBN 98781-92432137 MIPOGRASS & PUC, Mizoram, India
28. Myers, N., R.A. Mittermeier, C.G. Mittermeier, G.A.B. da Fonseca & J. Kent (2000). Biodiversity hotspots for conservation priorities. *Nature* 403: 853-858.
29. Pawar, S.S. & B.C. Choudhury (2000). An inventory of Chelonians from Mizoram, North-East India: new records and some observations of threats. *Hamadryad* 25 (2): 144-158.
30. Premkishore, G. & M.R. Chandran (1995). Use of turtles as biological control agents. *Zoos Print* 10(7): 55-56.
31. Rao, R. J. (1990). Ecological relationships among freshwater turtles in the National Chambal Sanctuary. Study Report. Wildlife Institute of India. New Forest. Dehra Dun. India. 212pp.
32. Raven, P. H. & E. Wilson (1992). A fifty year plan for biodiversity surveys. Science 258: 1099-1100.
33. Singh, K.K, K.C. Das & H. Lalruatsanga (2013). *Bioresources and Traditional Knowledge of Northeast India,* 424Pp, ISBN 98781-92432137 MIPOGRASS & PUC, Mizoram, India
34. Sengupta, S., M. Baruah, & N. K. Choudhury (1998a). Report on turtles of Pabitora Wildlife Sanctuary. *J. Nat. Conv.*10 (2): 209-210.

35. Sengupta, S., N. K. Choudhury, M. Baruah, S. Saikia & B. Hussain (1998b). Diversity and distribution of Turtles fauna in Kamrup District of Assam. *Tropical Zoology* 2:
36. Smith, M. A. (1931). *The Fauna of British India, Ceylon and Burma: Amphibia and Reptilia. Vol. I-Loricata, Testudines,* Taylor and Francis Ltd., London, 185pp.
37. Stuart, B. L. & J. Thorbjarnarson (2003). Biological prioritization of Asian countries for turtle conservation. *Chelonian Conservation and Biology*. 4: 642-647.
38. Tripathi, A. & S. N. Mishra (2005). Fresh water turtles as water purifiers, their conservation and management. Pp.4. In: proc: of the ninety second session of the Indian Science Congress. Section of Animal, Veterinary and Fishery Sciences. Part III (Advance Abstracts). Ahmedabad, 2005.

Part 5
Socio-Economic Issues and Biodiversity

23

Impact of Economic Crisis on Tribal Society, Degeneration of Traditional Institutions, Pattern of Social Change in Tribal Society

Jitendra Chaudhury

It is true that the scheduled areas are a repository of rich natural resources and they hold most of the nation's wealth, whether physical, social, ecological, environmental, economic or aesthetic. The resources have been sustained over the centuries and maintained with little destruction more due to the social and cultural practices of the forest dwelling tribal communities whose systems of livelihood ensure minimum harm to the ecology. State perceptions of utilisation of resources are diametrically opposed to the Tribal worldview of resource exploitation and this divide has only widened further with the intrusion of globalization's market oriented philosophy of development. The experience of indigenous communities in other developing and underdeveloped countries outside India wherever globalization had descended has proved that indigenous knowledge systems, livelihoods, lands and forests have been brutally overridden by these forces. Experiences of all these communities have been gruesomely similar—that State transferred control over resources from communities and even from itself to industries and private institutions, that resources were exploited not because there was an urgent and immediate need for their utilisation, that there was no long term or planned perspective to the utilisation of these resources, commercialization and commoditization of resources became the primary concern and not ensuring that the resources were available and sustained for optimal usage and for majority benefit. Their experiences have further proved that resources conserved for millions of years were depleted beyond repair within a short period of globalised economies and that it has led to aggravated poverty of communities living in the areas of these resources while the industries and private institutions prospered enormously. This aggressive nature of resource exploitation has led to civil wars, strife, famines, political disturbances and violence in otherwise peaceful communities before globalization took away their resources. Some of the Fifth Schedule areas in India have been witnessing to such destruction mainly where mining projects and dams were built.

Globalisation and privatization are the key focal areas of our new economic policy. This policy is being aggressively introduced in the tribal areas which are rich in natural resources in order to cater to the global corporate and private interests. As the tribal areas are safeguarded by Constitutional protections like the Fifth Schedule, there is a determined attempt to amend or violate the laws by the State itself in order to pursue its privatization policies. Hence, there is an imminent threat lurking to the lands and natural resources of the tribal people as well as to their customary practices and traditional rights. Food security, potable water and sanitation will be a serious crisis in the health and survival of tribal children as these resources will become less accessible to tribal communities due to their commercialization.

Tribal children are forced to compete with a highly imbalanced and exploitative external society. Therefore, protection of the Constitutional laws is the first savior of *adivasi* children's rights to land and resources as global greed exploits their natural resources will strangulate their lives in future. Primary education and awareness of legal and traditional rights is the most important vehicle of creating tribal assertion among the next generations of tribal. Assertion of tribal self rule, right to ownership and decision-making over natural resources and right to information are, therefore, crucial. Present global financial crisis shows how these problems are compounded when the centre is itself under economic stress.

Meeting the Challenges

To take advantage of globalization the tribal economy will require: (a) improved human capital, (b) more access to physical infrastructure like roads and (c) better political governance and constitutional safeguards, and (d) cultural adjustments.

A view of human capital situation in the tribal societies in the North-East India can be found from the Table 23.1.

Table 23.1 : Literacy Rate of STs in States and India

Sl. No.	*States*	*1961*	*1971*	*1981*	*1991*	*2001 Total*	*2001 Female*
1.	Assam	23.58	26.02	—	49.16	62.5	52.4
2.	Manipur	27.25	28.71	39.74	36.79	65.9	58.4
3.	Meghalaya	—	29.49	31.55	53.63	61.3	59.2
4.	Nagaland	14.76	24.01	40.32	46.71	65.9	61.317
5.	Sikkim	—	—	33.30	19.44	67.1	60.2
6.	Tripura	10.01	15.03	23.07	27.89	56.5	44.0
7.	Arunachal Pradesh	—	5.20	14.04	56.62	49.6	40.6
8.	Mizoram	—	53.49	59.63	82.71	89.3	86.9
9.	**India**	**8.54**	**11.29**	**16.35**	**29.60**	**47.1**	**34.8**

Source: *Yojana*, Vol. 54, p. 30, June 2010.

Table 23.1 shows that in terms of literacy rate of Schedule Tribes, the STs in North-East India are better placed than the all India level. Therefore, in terms of human capital they have a better status than the rest of the country. Therefore, one can expect that STs of North-East India will be more capable in meeting the challenge of globalization in due course of time.

The Way Forward : North-East India Perspective

The North-Eastern region of India is rich in natural resources like bamboo, rubber, tea, horticulture, orchids, medicinal plants, flora and fauna and cultural diversities. In fact, out of the ten bio-diversity hotspots, one is North-East of India, other two being Eastern Ghat and Western Ghat. The human resource is also considerable. North-East of India is corridor to South-East Asian countries. It is a route to China also. In spite of such resources North-East of India in general and tribals in particular is economically one of the most backward regions of the country.

This massive poverty in the midst of natural and human wealth is a great puzzle. Development of human capital and physical infrastructure, better governance and cultural flexibility and openness can lead to a more prosperous North-East.

Commonalities between the 1930s and Present Global Economic Melt Down

The sub-prime crisis in US and Europe developed into a global financial crisis by the end of the year 2008 and further deteriorated in the year 2009. There are symptoms of the crisis blowing into a full-fledged economic crisis. There are various questions regarding the causes of the crisis, transmission process of the crisis and impact of the crisis for developing countries like India and China. There are also implications for regional or sub-national economic units like North-Eastern Region of India.

Trade cycles are important features of industrialized economies. The trade cycles have not only a recurrent character but also seem to be unpredictable. The "Great Depression" of 1929-33 led to the birth of an important branch of Economics, namely, macroeconomics with the publication of "The General Theory of Employment, Interest and Money" in 1936 by J.M. Keynes. Often the global financial crisis of 2008 is suspected to be similar in its impact on output and employment to the "Great Depression".

In early 1930, credit was ample and available at low rates, but people were reluctant to add new debt by borrowing. By May 1930, auto sales had declined to below the levels of 1928. Prices in general began to decline, but wages held steady in 1930, then began to drop in 1931. Conditions were worse in farming areas, where commodity prices plunged, economic inequality and jobless growth restricts aggregate demand which in turn leads to financial and economic crisis. The financial crisis occurs because consumers are encouraged to purchase goods and assets through bank loans because they do not have sufficient purchasing power. As the quality of debt recovery is put into risk the banks ultimately face the problem of insolvency. As bank finances dry up, the industries find it difficult to carry on their business. They restrict output and employment. This has a ripple effect on other industries through fall in demand. This process ultimately ends up in an economic crisis. In such a situation encouraging employment generation programmes, investment in infrastructure, encouraging small and minor industries, rural development and expenditures on primary education and primary health care by the government rather than bailing out banks and financial institutions are likely to be supported by the Marxist point of view.

The prevailing global financial crisis came to its peak in October 2008. Economists differ regarding the span of this crisis. However, it cannot be denied that the roots of the crisis had implanted themselves earlier when loans were being given to the customers without verifying their repayment capacity and these loans were financed through securities which did not clearly indicate the quality of the role and risk involved. The phase of the financial crisis when the results became visible may have a span of one or two years. But the foundations were laid prior to that.

The second aspect to be recognised about this financial crisis is that it began from the United States but ultimately touched the financial system through the sale of securities of the mortgaged loans of the whole world. In India the nationalised commercial banks were not touched by these securities but certain private banks were contaminated through exposure to these questionable types of securities.

Other Aspects of Globalization

Globalization as such is not a current phenomenon. In a sense, it is as old as human history. It is a global process where billions of people of the world are involved. The process of globalization can, therefore, is supra-national in its strength and vigour. Therefore, each nation and community has to create proper strategies for meeting the opportunity and challenges emanating from globalization.

Globalization cannot be and should be understood as a purely economic phenomenon. Apart from the economic aspect there are social, political and cultural dimensions of the process of globalization.

In the purely economic sense, globalization is free trade of a country with the rest of the world. It also implies free flow of physical capital and finance capital. Of course, today the general meaning of globalization is capitalizing on the economic aspects only, besides the political structure. But while analyzing the impact of globalization on the economy of indigenous society, the tribes of North-East India, these four aspects of globalization have to be given their due importance.

In the social sense, globalization implies the capacity to adjust with other societies which have their own social structure. In the political sense, globalization may implies the dominance of hegemony over the so called less developed countries.

In the cultural aspect globalization may implies uniformisation of cultures in terms of food habits, dress codes, marriage practices, age old value systems and their traditional form of art and culture.

Major Features of Tribal Economy and Life in India

The country has 85 million tribal population living in the Fifth Schedule areas of eight States of Andhra Pradesh, Chattisgarh, Jharkhand, Himachal Pradesh, Gujarat, Madhya Pradesh, Orissa, Rajasthan and Maharashtra and in the eight North-Eastern States. Their percentage to the total population of India is 8.1 with a sex ratio of 972 while that of the total population is 927. As per 1991 Census, 87.19 per cent of ST population depended on agriculture, either as settled and shifting cultivators of agricultural labourers or as collectors of forest produce. These Figures corroborate the close association with land and forests as a means of survival, livelihood and a social way of life for the tribal people. (K. Bhanumathi Samata, 2010).

A very significant and alarming trend that is visibly upsetting is the depreciation in the percentage of ST cultivators from 68.18 per cent as per 1961 Census to 54.50 per cent in 1991 Census and an increase of agricultural labourers from 19.71 per cent to 32.69 per cent. This clearly indicates the alienation of tribal lands for various purposes like construction of dams, mining projects, setting up of forest based and other industries, notification of wildlife sanctuaries, construction of government infrastructure and encroachments by non-tribals. The official Figures for land alienation in the Planning Commission report of January 2000, the area alienated from tribals in all the States is 9,17,590 acres and those displaced between 1951-90 are 21.2 lakh (39.4%). Almost 80 per cent of the forest and mineral resources of the country are found in the scheduled areas the exploitation of which have been the primary causes of land alienation among the *adivasis*. These areas, particularly the Eastern and Western Ghats are the catchments to a number of rivers which form the life systems for the large "development" projects built during the 1960s and 1970s. The diversity of natural resources available in these forests brought in two major stakeholders from the outside during this period—the non-tribals who wanted to occupy the rich lands of the tribals and the State which launched its apparently public/national interest projects which were large scale, capital intensive and causing millions of people, mainly *dalits* and *adivasis* to be uprooted from their lands. They were based on the Nehruvian philosophy of development where the voiceless millions living in the midst of these resources have to forfeit their livelihoods for the progress of the nation. Thus the setting up of energy and hydro electric projects, public sector industries like mining, development of a network of roadways and railways in these scheduled and forest regions for the transportation needs of the industries and the expansion of government infrastructure were the important vehicles of economic growth undertaken by the State. By the nineties, the public sector has been heaped with the choicest of abuses and accusations for having failed to deliver any progress to the nation. The resources available in the scheduled areas were considered as having vast potential for exploitation and the new economic policy reflected a clear shift in the State's reverence for the private sector. The protective and welfare role so far played by the State suddenly began to shrink from the 1990s once the State decided to make accessible these natural resources to global and private powers. The subsequent changes in policies and laws or wherever possible, contravention of laws by the State in the scheduled areas has been the immediate consequence thereby exposing the remote tribal in an unknown hamlet to the fangs of globalization.

Dependence on Indigenous Form of Cultivation

The shifting cultivation method is not of course restricted to the tribal folk of North-East India only. Estimates of the actual number of shifting cultivators vary from 250 million to 300 million globally (V.T. Darlong, 2010). Taking the world population to be around 6 billion, the number of shifting cultivators is 3 to 5 per cent of the world population. Therefore, in terms of population share, the number of shifting cultivators may not be very significant. But if one looks at the geographical spread of shifting cultivators then one finds that 45 per cent of tropical agriculture area is under shifting cultivation. One-third of agriculture in South-East Asia is under shifting cultivation. Moreover, 60 per cent of Africas food is produced through shifting cultivation.

Table 23.2 : The Forest Area affected by Shifting Cultivation in North-East India

State	*Forest Area Affected (sq. km.)*	*Percentage of actual forest area*
Arunachal Pradesh	8,521	12.4
Assam	7276	27.9
Manipur	13846	77.4
Mizoram	12442	68.5
Nagaland	10641	74.1
Tripura	3315	62.3

Source: Shifting Cultivation in Search of Alternatives (2010).

Table 23.2 shows that the percentage of actual forest area affected by shifting cultivation is highest in Manipur (77.4%) and lowest in Arunachal Pradesh (12.4%). Nagaland, Mizoram, Tripura are in the next ranks and Assam has the fifth rank. Food cultivation is not only economically unviable today but also a major contributed to deforestation and a threat to bio-diversity. Therefore, most of the experts on tribal economy are of the opinion that the shifting cultivators have to be shifted to types of occupations where there is better economic returns and lowest negative environmental consequences. If one assumes that a typical tribal household has three adult equivalents and also an adult requires five hundred grams of rice per day then the daily requirement cf rice per household is 1.5 kg. and monthly requirement is 45 kg. Yearly Requirement is 540 kg. A typical household can cultivate one hectare of land. Due to shortening of *jhum* cycle one hectare of land can provide 6.25×80 kg = 500 kg of rice per year. Which was 800-900 kg in 1961-1970 periods (Tawnenga, Uma Shankar and R S Tripathi, 1996). Therefore, at present a *jhumia* family cannot meet the requirement of rice from *jhum* cultivation alone. This indicates economic non-viability of shifting cultivation in many parts of North-East India at present.

The tribal economy of North-East India is mainly based on shifting cultivation. In shifting cultivation a particular plot is selected from the forest by the cultivators. Then the forest trees and shrubs are cut down. Then it is allowed to get dry for a few days. This activity is carried out in the months of December and January. From mid-February fire is set on the dried up branches and timbers. Then shifting cultivators wait for the rain. Planting of seeds consisting of various crops is done from mid-March to early-April. Some seeds are broadcasted also. From May to September weeding is done and also a lot of time is spent in guarding the crop from different types of forest animals. Harvesting of the crops in different phases are carried out from the month of September. There is also thrashing work in this period especially for the women folk. Harvested crops are also stayed in this period.

Environment and Shifting Cultivation

Shifting cultivation affects environment mainly through deforestation and soil erosion (M. Datta and N.P. Singh, 2010) show that shifting cultivation is one of the causes of soil erosion in Tripura. This is showing in Table 23.3:

Table 23.3 : Loss of Soil through Erosion under Different Uses in Practice

Land Use	*Soil loss (t/ha/yr)*
Shifting Cultivation (7 ha area)	5.1-83.3
Tuber crops on raised beds (bun)	40.0-50.0
Pineapple cultivation along the slope (first two years)	24.0-62.6
Homestead area	16.8
Mixed crop of maize and rice	19.7-21.0
Rice on slope	32.9-45.0
Bare fallow	83.8
Cropping systems	51.0-83.8
Planting grass cover	10.83
Natural bamboo forest	0.04-0.52

Source: Shifting Cultivation in Search of Alternatives (2010).

Table 23.3 shows that a seven hectare area under shifting cultivation causes soil loss of 5.1-83.3 tonne per hectare per year. In sharp contrast a natural bamboo forest causes 0.04-0.52 tonne per hectare per year soil loss. This soil loss causes a decline in net productivity of the following order as shown by Datta and Singh.

The Negative Impact of Global Financial Crisis on the Tribal Economy

If one studies the relation between global financial crisis and the tribal economy in a superficial manner then one may find a weak linkage between the global situation and the North-Eastern economy of the tribals. This is due to the fact that a very insignificant amount of commodities are sold to the formal market mechanism. But the issue has to be studied in terms of the linkage between access to natural resources, production of commodity using the natural resources and marketing of products. In this manner if one links the different stages of value addition from collection of the natural resources to processing of natural resources and then finally marketing of this product then one can find out, however, global financial crisis impacts the tribal economy in the first stage of value addition process. Unfortunately much of these collections either of timbers or non-timber forest produces operate through informal grey markets. As a result data availability is very limited.

There is another aspect of globalization also as the present global economic crisis has reduced the growth rate of GDP of the Indian economy by 2 to 3 per cent according to experts. As a result, revenue collection of the government is likely to suffer. The public sector expenditures to improvement in human capital, creation of physical infrastructure and social amenities like providing safe drinking water, health centres and primary schools are likely to experience a slow down. This also creates a negative impact on the tribal economy of North-East India. However, some time must elapse before a proper assessment of the consequence of the present financial crisis can be made.

Cultural Dimensions of the Tribal Economy

The cultural activities are deeply rooted in shifting cultivation of the tribes. There are *pujas* to make the elements happy and bountiful. Selection of the *jhum* sites and beginning of shifting cultivation also lead to various religious and cultural functions.

There are song and poetry for the nights spent in guarding the crop land. Sometimes they are love song. Similarly, harvesting, thrashing and storing are also woven with songs and poetry providing a cultural dimension to the fundamental economic activities of tribal societies. Therefore, one can imagine of taking away shifting cultivation from tribal society without taking away tribal culture and even in a sense the basis of tribal identity. In other words the challenge of transformation of tribal society can not be understood without looking at the cultural, social and political aspects of tribal life.

24
Biodiversity, Demography and Economy : An Exploration of Linkages

Amitabha Sinha

Introduction

Wikipedia observes that the current textbook definition of "biodiversity" is "variation of life at all levels of biological organisation", that is, genes, species and habitations existing on land, water and air. According to the HIPPO hypothesis of Edward O. Wilson (1988), the threat factors for biodiversity are: Habitat destruction (H), Invasive species (I), Pollution (P), Human overpopulation (P) and Overharvesting (O). One of the aspects of habitat destruction. Availability of flora and fauna, on the other hand, can be related to availability of forest area. This can be measured in terms of total geographical area of the country as percentage of forest area in total geographical area, It can be also looked upon from the context of total population. Dividing the forest area by total population, per capita forest area can be calculated, since Per capita GDP is a measure of economic productivity of a country. In economics, production is value addition or prevention of value loss. Here, not only exchange value but also use value and non-use value have to be considered. Similarly, per capita forest is a measure of biodiversity productivity of a country (Bhattacharya, R. N., 2001). Taking this approach, one can employ production function and efficiency frontier method naturally. This is elaborated in the next section.

The Model

The model proposed in the present study has two layers. Habitat is captured by the proxy variable per capita forests of a country. Economic development is measured by per capita GDP. In the traditional analysis of the relationship between biodiversity and economic development, it is implicitly assumed that each country operates at the margin of technologically determined production possibility frontier. This assumption is replaced by the possibility that the country may operate inside the production possibility frontier. Michael Farrell (1957) introduced a methodology to measure economic, technical (TE), and input and output allocative efficiency (AE). According to Farrell, TE is associated with the ability to produce on the frontier isoquant, while AE refers to the ability to produce at a given level of output using the cost-minimizing input ratios. Alternatively, technical inefficiency is related to deviations from the frontier iso-quant, and allocative inefficiency refers to deviations from the minimum cost input ratios. Thus, EE is defined as the capacity to produce a predetermined quantity of output at minimum cost for a given level of technology (Farrell and Michael, 1957; Dewatt and Billie R. 1979). Therefore, the production function is *not* written as follows:

$$Y_i = \beta_0 + \beta_1 X_i + V_i \qquad ...(1)$$

Here *i* represents the country and V_i is white noise. We write the production function as:

$$Y_i = \beta_0 + \beta_1 X_i + V_i - U_i \qquad ...(2)$$

Here U_i represents the gap between the actual production possibility frontier and the efficient production possibility frontier. Obviously, U_i is a negative term. Only when $U_i = 0$, the country operates at efficient level. We assume that V_i is a stochastic variable which has a half normal distribution because U_i cannot have positive values. The maximum value it can have is zero. Obviously, U_i is a measure of technical efficiency. In the first layer of analysis, we estimate the technical efficiency of rich and poor countries. Then we introduce the demographic factor in the second layer.

Population density represents the demographic dimension of population. Here two types of questions are addressed. Firstly, what is the impact of population density on the technical efficiency of the countries? Secondly, is there any difference in this impact between the rich and the poor countries? For testing this hypothesis, we construct the following econometric model.

$$Y_i = \beta_0 + \beta_1 X_i + \beta_2 d_1 + \beta_3 d_2 + V_i \quad ...(3)$$

Here Y represents technical efficiency, X represents population density, d_1 is a dummy variable which takes the value of 0 for poor countries and 1 for high income countries. Similarly, d_2 is 1 for middle income countries. Here, V_i is the white noise. The interpretation of the coefficients in the case of dummy variable model can be briefly discussed here. Let us take the case when d = 0. Then, we have

$$Y_i = \beta_0 + \beta_1 X_i + V_i \quad ...(4)$$

However, if $d_2 = 1$ and $d_1 = 0$, which is the middle income country case, we shall have

$$Yi = (\beta_0 + \beta_3) + \beta_1 X_i + V_i \quad ...(5)$$

Therefore, β_3 measures the difference in technical efficiency of middle income and poor countries caused by population density. We expect that β_3 is positive and statistically significant. Similarly, for β_2. We expect that β_1 is negative and statistically significant.

Data

We obtained data from http://www.mongabay.com/deforestation_pcover.htm. These data, based on FAO for forests, have been criticised for their uneven quality across nations and inconsistencies in dentitions. But despite this, they remain important source of cross-national information on forests and the total amount of forest cover. Per-capita GDP is in US $ for the year 1997. Forest data are for the year 2000. Population densities data refer to 1999. Based on availability of data, 112 countries are selected for analysis. The countries have average per capita forests less than or equal to 2 hectares. Major three categories of World

Bank, namely, High, Middle and Poor income classification is adopted (World Bank, 2003) in classifying the countries.

Results

It is argued in this chapter that the capacity of the high income countries to protect their forest resources can be analysed assuming that these economies are technically at the efficiency frontier. If this possibility is not taken for granted, then one may try to relate per capita GDP in terms of TE to maintain average per capita forest area of a country. This can be done using Stochastic Frontier Model. The results are summarised in Table 24.1.

The sign of the income coefficient is negative. This implies that per capita forest is lower in those countries which have higher per capita GDP on the average. However, the statistical significance of the estimate is very low as shown by the Z value which is –0.41. For the estimated log likelihood value we obtain average per capita forest of 1.09 hectare. Among log likelihood ratio test, the lagrangian multiplier test and the Wald test, the Wald statistic is considered to be more applicable. The *p* value for the Wald statistic is 0.68. This means that the goodness of fit of the model is not very high. These limitations of the data have to be kept in mind while studying Table 24.2. Ten countries (including highest and lowest ranking in terms of per capita income, population density and technical efficiency) as major countries among 112 selected countries are reported in Table 24.2. These 10 countries are classified in terms of World Bank classification by income as high, low and low (medium), per capita income ranking, population density ranking and technical efficiency ranking. If the countries are ranked according to technical efficiency and classified as: high technical efficiency (rank 1 to 37), medium technical efficiency (rank 38 to 74) and low technical efficiency (rank 75 to 112), but considers World Bank categories of high, medium and low income countries, then one finds that only 4 countries out of the 37 countries of high technical efficiency belong to high income group. However, if the countries are ranked according to the per capita GDP and one considers the countries with rank 1 to 37 as high income countries then one finds that 10 countries out of the high income countries belong to high technical efficiency group. In other words, the general impression that high income countries

Table 24.1 : Efficiency Analysis

Per Capita Forests (Dependent)	*Coefficient*	*Std. Error*	*Z*	*P > Z*	*[95% Conf. Interval]*	
Per Capita GDP	−0.0000021	0.0000052	−0.41	0.681	−0.000012	0.0000080
Constant	0.5446	0.2482	2.19	0.028	0.0582	1.031
/lnsig2V	−1.3151	0.1337	−9.84	0	−1.5771	−1.0531
/lnsig2Uu	−10.5422	117.9498	−0.09	0.929	−241.72	220.6352
sigma_V	0.5181	0.0346	—	—	0.4545	0.5907
sigma_U	0.0051	0.303	—	—	3.25E-53	8.13E+47
$sigma^2$	0.2685	0.0359	—	—	0.1981	0.3389
Lambda	0.0099	0.3061	—	—	−0.5899	0.6098

Stochastic Frontier Normal/half-normal Model
Log likelihood = −85.277955
Number of observations = 112
Wald $chi^2(1)$ = 0.17
Prob>chi^2 = 0.6811

Data Source: http:/mongabay.com/deforestation_pcover.htm.

are always better in managing their environment in biodiversity is not supported by the present set of data. Table 24.2 focuses on 10 countries which includes apart from India, China and U.S.A. the countries which have the highest and lowest rank in per capita GDP, population density and technical efficiency. It may be noted that the country with the highest per capita income has rank 1 and the country with the lowest per capita income has rank 112. Similarly, the country with the highest technical efficiency has rank 1 and the lowest has the rank 112. In the case of population density, the country with the highest population density has the rank 1 and the lowest 112. India and China are low in per capita income rank and very low in technical efficiency rank. U.S.A. fares better in technical efficiency with a rank of 27 as shown in Table 24.2.

Table 24.2 : A Few Major Countries' Location Pattern

Name of the Country	*World Bank Classification*	*Per Capita Income Rank*	*Population Density Rank*	*Technical Efficiency Rank*
1. Switzerland	High	1	15	64
2. **USA**	High	7	92	27
3. **India**	Low	87	3	106
4. China	Low	76	22	102
5. Japan	High	2	2	65
6. Germany	High	5	13	84
7. Ethiopia	Low	112	64	112
8. New Zealand	High	12	102	1
9. Republic of Korea	High	16	1	86
10. Mauritania	Low	84	112	105

Data Source : http://www.mongabay.com/deforestation_pcover.htm

Note: Rank according to descending order.

At the second layer of analysis, we ask two questions: (a) how does population density impact on technical efficiency of the countries; and (b) is there any difference between the impacts among the rich and the poor countries. Table 24.3 shows that the coefficient of population density is negative and statistically significant. However, the coefficient of the dummy variable is positive in the case of high income and negative in the case of medium income countries. However, the coefficients are not statistically significant. The positive sign of dummy of high income countries implies that given population density

Table 24.3 : Regression Results

Source	SS	df	MS	
Model	0.000000080	3	0.000000027	Number of observations = 112
Residual	0.00000022	108	0.0000000020	F(3, 108) = 13.26
Total	0.00000030	111	0.0000000027	Prob > F = 0
				R-squared = 0.2691
				Adj R-squared = 0.2488
				Root MSE = 0.000045

Efficiency	Coefficient	Standard Error	t	P>t	[95% conf.	Interval]
Population Density	–0.00000032	0.000000053	–6.03	0	-0.00000042	-0.00000021
Dummy High	0.0000145	0.000014	1.06	0.292	–0.0000127	0.0000417
Dummy Medium	–0.0000086	0.0000094	–0.92	0.361	–0.0000273	0.00001
Constant	0.9966236	0.0000080	—	0	0.9966077	0.9966394

technical efficiency is higher in high income countries compared to the low income countries which can be thought of as the control group. But the dummy has a negative sign for medium income countries implying a poorer performance in efficiency compared to the poor income countries. However, these results are not statistically significant. This means that no significant difference is found in technical efficiency given population density among high, medium and poor countries.

Discussion

The results obtained in the present study do not support the proposition that an economically advanced country manages its environment and biodiversity more efficiently. In spite of the limitations of data this major finding seems to be a reasonable finding, the vast literature which has emerged in environmental economy (Bhattacharya, 2001) show that environmental goods exhibit the properties of non-rivalry and non-excludability. In the case of such goods there is market failure. This means that market driven solutions are not *pareto efficient*. Pareto efficiency is the sum total of technical efficiency and allocative efficiency. The relationship between public good, property rights and technical efficiency is not analysed in the literature as thoroughly as the relationship between *pareto efficiency* and public good. But the essential economic logic may not be so difficult to understand. Due to unclear ownership pattern of natural resources like forest their economic value which may be considered to be the sum total of used value and non-used value may not be properly recognised by the producers. This may lead to over exploitation of natural resources—often called "Tragedy of the Commons" (Hanley, Nick, Jason F. Shogren and Ben White, 1997). Therefore, technical efficiency may not be exhibited by countries which are mainly market driven economies.

Conclusions

Economic development has led to industrialisation, greater use of fossil fuel, population explosion and a high degree of regional inequality. A deeper analysis will show that it is not economic development as such but market led economic development and market failures which are at the root of the environmental crisis of the present world. Interventions by government and national and international level have thus become important. The United Nations Environmental Agency has been organising conferences to create a common platform of nations from 1972 onwards. The Copenhagen Summit held in the period (7 to 18) December, 2009 on climate change fail to bring about a comprehensive global commitment indicating the fact that national policies of advanced countries often serve the interest of big business. The profit interests obstruct the corporate decision making process from adopting initiatives which are perceived to have negative implications for profitability. The long term point of view may sometimes be sacrificed at the altar of immediate gains. The civil society throughout the world must adopt a more clear stance to countervail the short-run perspective for a more sustainable human development process not only at regional and national level but also at global level. This conclusion emanates from the premise that the macro always dominates the micro in the socio-economic spheres.

REFERENCES

Bhattacharya, Rabindra N. (2001). *Environmental Economics : An Indian Perspective*, Oxford University Press.

Chakravarty, Satya R.; Dipankar Coondoo; Robin Mukherjee (1998). *Quantitative Economics: Theory and Practice*, Allied Publishers Limited, New Delhi.

Dewatt, Billie R. (1979). *Modernization in a Mexican Ejido: A Study in Economic Adaptation*, New York, Cambridge University Press.

Farrell, Michael (1957). *"The Measurement of Productivity Efficiency"*, Journal of the Royal Statistics Society, Series A, 120, Part 3: 253-90.

FAO, (2003). *The State of the World's Forests 2003*, http://www.mongabay.com/deforestation_pcover.htm.

Hanley, Nick; Jason F. Shogren and Ben White (1997). *Environmental Economics*: In *Theory and Practice*, Macmillan Press Limited, Delhi.

Wilson, Edward O. (ed.) Frances M. Peter (Associate editor) (1988). *Biodiversity*, National Academy Press, online edition.

World Bank (2003). *World Development Report 2004: Making Services Work for Poor People*, The World Bank, USA.

25

Biodiversity of Medicinal Plants in Tripura and their Problems and Need for Conservation

Sukhen Chandra Das and *A.K. Deb*

Introduction

Tripura have a large number of valuable naturally growing medicinal plants that are predominantly shared by rural poor and tribal communities. The agro-climatic conditions of Tripura favour the cultivation of different medicinal plants and the State is considered to be the hot-spot of medicinal plants. State has in abundance, a diverse range of herbs, shrubs, trees and vines that have significant medicinal value whose healing properties are known to the local healers and traditional doctors. Rural people suffering from common ailments like cold and cough, diarrhoea, bronchitis, routine skin and eye irritations, veterinary healers, etc. Tripura being one of richest centre of biodiversity, more than 270 species of medicinal plants have been identified for their medicinal value (Das *et al.*, 2009; Das *et al.*, 2010; Chandra Das, Sukhen and Deb, A.K, 2011). Out of 270 medicinal plants 245 medicinal plants have been listed in Table 25.1. In Tripura, medicinal plants are mostly found in hilly parts of Tripura and also found in homestead garden, road side, fallow land, waste land, forest land, agricultural fields and horticulture orchards without desired care and management. The demand of the medicinal plants are increasing day by day even in the home markets due to side effects of several allopathic drugs and development of resistance to currently used drugs for infectious diseases have led to increased emphasis on the use of plant materials as a source of medicines for a wide variety of human ailments. The parts used are seed, root, leaf, bark, fruit, flower, flower buds, stem, rhizome, bulb, tuber, wood or even whole plant. The major health problems among the peoples inhabiting interior areas of Tripura are malnutrition and the common diseases are diarrhoea, malaria, gastroenteritis, leprosy, tuberculosis, eye diseases and various kinds of skin diseases. Ulcerous, wound, perforation of stomach and colic pains are commonly found among the tribals who are habituated of excessive country liquor, children often suffer from protein and vitamin deficiencies. Use of medicinal plants by the tribals for common health problems revealed that maximum number of plants, either alone or in combination were used against eye diseases, diarrhoea, dysentery, loss of hair, bone fracture and female diseases, etc.

Materials and Methods

The State of Tripura with an area of 10,491 sq. km and four districts (North, South, Dhalai and West district) of Tripura. It lies between 22° 56′ N to 24° 32′ N latitude and 90° 09′ E to 92° 20′ E longitude is the study area for this study. Intensve survey work was conducted in all the districts namely, North, South, Dhalai and West district including forest area. Efforts have been made to collect the medicinal plants which were in flowering and fruiting conditions and were identified with the help of local people and practitioner. The uses of plants particularly for medicinal use were confirmed by many cross checking as possible in different localities. Under the above conditions the information recorded are botanical name, common name, family and part used for medicinal values.

Results

In the present study diversity of medicinal plant species with scientific name, common name, family, part used for medicinal values have been recorded which are being potentially exploited by the peoples of Tripura in curing different human- health related problems as shown in Table 25.1. The different families include Acanthaceae, Rutaceae, Moraceae, Asclepiadaceae, Euphorbiaceae,

Rutaceae, Verbenaceae, Zingiberaceae, Combretaceae, Salanaceae, Lamiaceae and other families. Among the different medicinal plant species recorded are trees, shrubs, herbs and climbers as shown in the Table 25.1. For the preparation of the traditional medicine, these tribal and local practitioner used different parts of the plant species in different concentration of gum, root, fruit, seed, latex, root, bark, whole plant and flower, etc.

Discussion

In the present investigation diversity of medicinal plant species have been recorded and used by the different local peoples and practitioner of Tripura for different ailments. Different ailments/ diseases are being treated by these plant species (Table 25.1). The wide range of remedies for asthma, body pains, bone fractures, cold, cough, cuts and wounds, dysentery, diarrhoea, eczema, gastric ulcers, night blindness, skin troubles, stomach ache, syphilis and other problems these medicinal plants singly as well as in combination of two or three herbs are being used. In this studies total two hundred and forty five beneficial medicinal plants have been recorded with scientific names, common names, family and part used for medicine.

Conservation of Medicinal Plants

Conservation is the protection, preservation, management, or restoration of natural resources and survival of many medicinal plant species and habitats which are threatened due to human activities, deforestation, *jhum* cultivation, illegal collection of medicinal plants etc. Conservation can broadly be divided into two types: *in situ* and *ex situ*.

***In situ*:** Conservation of habitats, species and ecosystems where they naturally occur. *In situ* approach can protect specific varieties and the habitat, it involves establishments of protected areas in carefully selected localities in the form of reserves, sanctuaries and national parks, also establishment of herbal gardens or "vanaspati vans" and replantation of most important medicinal plants in degraded forest areas (*in situ* conservation).

***Ex situ*:** The conservation of elements of biodiversity out of the context of their natural habitats is referred to as *ex situ* conservation.

Table 25.1 : Diversity of Medicinal Plants in Tripura and Parts used for Medicinal Value (Das *et al.*, 2009; Das *et al.*, 2010; Chandra Das, Sukhen and Deb, A.K., 2011)

Sl. No.	*Botanical name/ Local name/Family*	*Parts used*	*Utilization of Medicinal plants*
1.	*Abroma angusta* (Olat Kambal) Sterculiaceae	Root and Bark	Uterine tonics, itches, arthritis, rheumatism, gout, dropsy, swelling.
2.	*Abrus precatorius* (Gunchi/ Shon Kainch) Fabaceae	Roots, Seeds and leaves	Purgative, aphrodisiac, nervous, disorders, leucoderma, skin disease, emetic.
3.	*Abutilon indicum* (Country mallow) Malvaceae	Barks, leaves, seeds, roots	Diuretic, leucoderma, piles, arthelmintic.
4.	*Adatoda zeylanica* (Basak) Acanthaceae	Leaves, Roots	Antiasthimatic, Cold, cough, fever, jaundice, anthelmintic
5.	*Acacia caesia* (Aila) Mimosaceae	Bark and flowers	Skin problem and menstrual disorders
6.	*Abrus precatories* (Sonkaich) Fabaceae	Root, seeds leaves,	Purgative, emetic, aphrodisiac, nervous disorders, Cough, fever, Inflammation.
7.	*Achyranthus aspera* (Apang) Amaranthaceae	Whole plant and Root	Anti-inflammatory, cough, stomachache, skin eruptions, piles, snakebites, ophthalmia, dysentery.
8.	*Acorus calamus* (Boch) Araceae	Rhizome	Carminative, stomachic, flavouring, Appetiser, aids, brain development, kidney stones, memory loss and as a laxative.
9.	*Adenanthera pavonina* (Rakthakanchan) Fabaceae	Bark, leaves, seeds ,wood	Arthritis, vata, pitta, gout, burning sensation, vomiting, fever, hemorrhoids and diarrhoea.
10.	*Aegle marmelos* (Bael) Rutaceae	Root, leaves, Bark, fruit	*Leaf:* peptic ulcers. Fruits-cooling, laxative, bleeding, diarrhoea, *Root*-Ear problems.
11.	*Ageratum conizoides* (Uchunti) Asteraceae	Whole herbs	Constipation, hepatitis, antidysentric, cold, staemorrhoides, wounds, sores, renal, epilepsy, diarrhoea, fever, pneumonia and vesical calculi.

(Contd.)

Table 25.1 : *(Contd.)*

Sl. No.	Botanical name/ Local name/Family	Parts used	Utilization of Medicinal plants
12.	*Albizia lebbeck* (Siris tree)	Bark, flower, seeds	Asthma, Skin disease, leucoderma, ulcers, night blindness
13.	*Allamanda cathartica* (Harkakra)Apocynaceae	Leave and bark	Cathartic, colic, wound healing and Abdominal pain
14.	*Alocasia indica* (Mankach), Araceae	Root and tubers	Pain, rheumatism and oedema
15.	*Aloe barbadensis* (Ghritakumari) Liliaceae	Leaves	Carminative, purgative, liver disorders, chronic ulcer, cold, Haritonic, skin care, laxative, rashes, purgative, vermifuge, Sunburns, anti-cancerous
16.	*Alpinia calcarata* (Kalanja) Zingiberaceae	Rhizome	Aromatic, Stimulant, expectorant, arthritis, rheumatism, dropsy, swelling, oedema, gout, naso-pharyngeal infections.
17.	*Alpiinia galangal* (Greater galangal, mahabali bach)	Rhizome	Asthama, bronchitis, hiccups, dyspepsia, obesity, diabetics, rheumatoid arthritis, insecticide, stomach disorders, headache, sore throat, stimulant
18.	*Alstonia scholaris* (Chatim) Apocynaceae	Bark	Febrifuge, antidysentic, diarrhoea, skin disease, blood pressure, ulcer, paralysis.
19.	*Amaranthus spinosus* (knata note) Amaranthaceae	Leaves, root, seeds	Diarrhoea, gonorrhoea, leucorrhoea, Laxative, Emollient.
20.	*Amorphophallus paveonifolius* (Ool) Araceae	Tuber	Dysentery, piles, stomachic, laxative and rheumatism
21.	*Anacardium occidentale* (Kaju badam) Anacardiaceae	Bark, root and kernal	Leprosy, urinary troubles, tooth problems, hypertension, astringent, anti-diarrhoeal, anti helminthic

(Contd.)

Table 25.1 : *(Contd.)*

Sl. No.	Botanical name/ Local name/Family	Parts used	Utilization of Medicinal plants
22.	*Ananas comosus* (Anaras) Bromeliaceae	Leaves, fruit	Leaves: antithelmintic and purgative Fruit: anticorbutic, digestion of protein-rich foods, Anti-inflammatory and disperse blood clots
23.	*Andrographis paniculata* (Kalomegh) Acanthaceae	Whole plant	Febrifuge, antidysentric, Antiperiodic, general debility, anthelminitic, dyspepsia, Anti malaria and hypotension
24.	*Annona reticulate* (Ramphal) Annonaceae	Leaf, fruits, seeds and bark	Anti-diarrhoeal, blood dysentery, antihelminthic, ulcers and skin disease.
25.	*Annona squamosa* (Seetaphala/Swarupa) Annonaceae	Stem, Fruit and root	Anti-diarrhoeal, insecticidal, antihelminthic, ulcers and skin disease.
26.	*Anthocephalus cadamba* (Kadam) Rubiaceae	Bark	Tonic, febrifuge, fever, rheumatism, jaundice and cholera and anti fertility agent
27.	*Argemone mexicana* (Shial knata/mexican poppy) Papaveraceae	Whole plant	Diuretic, Purgative, Stomach disorders, disease of nervous system, worm infestation, leprosy and poisoning.
28.	*Asteracnatha longifolia,* Acanthaceae	Leaves, Root	Anaemia Tonic, Inflammation of hand and foot.
29.	*Asparagus racemosus* (Shatamuli) Liliaceae	Tuber	Improve memory, Tonic, aphrodisiac, diuretic, Anti dysenteric and galactagogue
30.	*Azadiracta indica* (Neem) Meliaceae	Bark, fruit, leaves	Anti diabetic, Antiseptic, Antifungal, blood purifier, skin diseases and cosmetics.
31.	*Aquilaria agallocha* (Agar) Thymeleaceae	Heart wood and Oil	Cardio tonics anti-inflammatory antileprotic, rejuvenating, rheumatoid arthritis, asthma pneumonia, bronchitis, leprosy and ulcers.
32.	*Artocarpus chaplasha* (Chamal) Moraceae	Bark, leaves and fruits	Skin problems, swellings of lymph glands and appetite.
33.	*Artocarpus lakoocha* (Dhaewa) Moraceae	Fruits and seeds	Laxative, cure boils, skin problems and anti cancerous properties.

(Contd.)

Table 25.1 : *(Contd.)*

Sl. No.	Botanical name/ Local name/Family	Parts used	Utilization of Medicinal plants
34.	*Averrhoa carambola* (Kamranga) Oxalidaceae	Fruit	Bleeding piles, jaundice, chicken pox, ringworms, scabies haemorrhages and Antipyretic
35.	*Basella alba* (Puisag) Basellaceae	Leaves, stem and root	Astringent, cooling, aphrodisiac, demulcent, laxative, antidote, diuretic and alleviate labour pain
36.	*Bacopa monnieri* (Brahmi) Scrophulariaceae	Whole plant	Nerve and brain, tonic, improve memory, epilepsy and potent diuretic, cardiotonic
37.	*Bauhinia racemosa* (Shweta kanchan) Fabaceae	Bark, leaves, seeds, and heartwood	Bark astringent, dysentery (Give with onions) diarrhoea and anthelmintic.
38.	*Bauhinia variegata* (Rakta kanchan) Fabaceae	Bark and flower	Laxative, anthelmintic, diarrhoea, vermifuge, antiulcerative, carminative, dyspepsia flatulence and tonic
39.	*Bixa orellana* (Annatto/ Lipstick tree) Rangumaale	Seeds, leaf, flower	Cardiac problems natural dye, anti-periodic and antipyretic
40.	*Blumea lacera* (Kurkur Shuka) Compositae	Leaves	Swelling of the legs and diuretic.
41.	*Borassus flabellifer* (Tal) Araceae/ Palmae	Root and fruit	Intestinal worms leprosy, skin disease, and gonorrhoea
42.	*Brayphlium calycinum* (Pathar Kuchi) Crassulceae	Leaves	Bladder stones, Diuretic, constipation, spleen and stomach pain, indigestion, bruises, dropsy, piles.
43.	*Boerhaavia diffusa* (Punarnava) Nyetaginaceae	Leaves	Anaemia, Jaundice, cardiac, stimulant, framation of body, diuretic, cough, asthma, fever, against dropsy.
44.	*Bombax ceiba* (Semul) Bombaceae	Root, flower, fruit and latex	Against dysentery, influenza, ulceration of ladder and kidney and wounds healing.
45.	*Butea monosperma* (Palash) Fabaceae	Bark, leaves, flowers, seeds gum	Flatulent, colic, cough constipation, arthritis, skin diseases, astringent aphrodisiac, night blindness and tonic

(Contd.)

Table 25.1 : *(Contd.)*

Sl. No.	Botanical name/ Local name/Family	Parts used	Utilization of Medicinal plants
46.	*Cajanus cajan* (Arhar) Fabaceae	Leaf and seed	Leaf prevents osteoporosis, improves immunological functions, anti-inflammatory, against fracture and heart diseases.
47.	*Cardiospermum helicacabum* (Tejovat/ Kapal futki/ Sibjhul) Sapindaceae	Leaf and root	Sedative, diaphoretic, diuretic, laxative and anti inflammatory, rheumatism, nervous disorders, homoeopathy.
48.	*Careya arborea* (Kumbhira) Lecythidaceae	Stem, bark and root	Tumours, antihelminthic, bronchitis, antipyretic.
49.	*Carica papaya* (Papaya) Caricaceae	Fruit and seed	Anti-inflammatory, antifungal, antihelminhic, digestive, appetizer, Latex is digestive and tonic
50.	*Calotropis gigantia* (Akanda) Asclepiadaceae	Root, bark and leaf	Diruretic, purgative, intermittent fevers, colds, cough, asthma, and indigestion, ear-ache, paralysis.
51.	*Calotropis procera* (Akanda) Asclepiadaceae	Leaves, roots and bark	Leprosy, good tonic expectorant anti helminthic, expectorant , laxative coughs.
52.	*Cantharanthus roseus* (Nayantara) Apocynaceae	Root, stem, leaf	Diabetic, blood cancer, hypertensive, anticancer, leukaemia, hodkins disease, low blood pressure, insect bite.
53.	*Carissa carandas* (Benbal current / karamcha)	Roots, leaves fruits	Stomachic, anthelmintic, curing anemia and fever.
54.	*Cascabela thevetia* (Yellow olender) Apocynaceae	Stem	General debility, sleepness, hyper acidity, burning of eyes and palms, body resistance to disease, graying of hairs, antidysenteric
55.	*Cassia alata* (Dad mardan) Caesalpiniaceae	Leaf, seed, bark	Astringent, purgative, laxative, antifungal and antibacterial properties.

(Contd.)

Table 25.1 : *(Contd.)*

Sl. No.	*Botanical name/ Local name/Family*	*Parts used*	*Utilization of Medicinal plants*
56.	*Cassia fistula (*Kakke gida/ Sonal/ Bandar lati) Caesalpiniaceae	Root, bark, leaf flower, fruit pulp.	Astringent, purgative, antipyretic. Against leprosy, rheumatism, ulcer, heart diseases and abdominal pains
57.	*Cassia Sophera (*Kalkasunda/ Chotto eski) Fabaceae	Seeds, leaves	Purgative, skin Disease, laxative
58.	*Cassia occidentalis* (Haittenga/ Eski) Caesalpiniaceae	Whole plant	Digestive, anti-inflammatory, diabetics, epilepsy, elephantiasis, leprosy, wounds, ulcers, bronchitis, fever, constipation and dyspepsia.
59.	*Cassia tora (*Chakunda goleski / Chavuka) Caesalpiniaceae	Leaves, seeds, pods	Laxative, ring worm and itching purgative, scabies and respiratory problems
60.	*Ceiba pentandra* (Cotton) Bombacaceae	Root, bark, leaf, flower, seed	Anuresis, constipation, diarrhoea
61.	*Centalla asiatic* (Thankuni) Umbellifera	Whole plant	Improving memory, Nerve tonic, leprosy, Dysentery, Anti Cancerous.
62.	(Pyrethrins) *Chrysanthemum cinerariifolium,* Asteraceae	Flower, roots	Insecticide, livestock sprays, fever, indigestion, anthelmentic, mosquito coils.
63.	*Cinnamum tamala* (Tajpata) Lauraceae	Leaf	Carminative, colic, diarrhoea, rheumatism, decrease blood sugar level
64.	*Cinnamomum zeylanicum* (Dalchini) Lauraceae	Bark, leaves and oil	Indigestion, Tooth problems, carminative.
65.	*Cissus quadrangularis* (Harvanga) Vitaceae	Stem	Bone fracture, Inflammation to Injury, scurvy, bleeding dysentery.
66.	*Cleome viscose* (Wild mustard /Hurhura) Capparaceae	Leaf and seed	Stimulant, vermifuge, digestive, wounds, ulcers, ear pain, anthelminthic, cardiac stimulant, fever and diarrhoea
67.	*Clerodendeon fragrens* (Gandharaj) Verbenaceae	Roots	Antibacterial, anti-inflammatory, menstrual disorders, osteodynia, hypertension, disinfectant

(Contd.)

Table 25.1 : *(Contd.)*

Sl. No.	Botanical name/ Local name/Family	Parts used	Utilization of Medicinal plants
68.	*Clerodendeon ineme* (Smooth volkameria) Verbenaceae	Roots	Glanlular swellings, eczema, scabies, snake poison.
69.	*Clerodendrum viscosum* (Byte phul) Verbenaceae	Root and leaf	Antiseptic, anti inflammatory, tumours, leprosy, skin disease, asthama, cough, vermifuge, laxative.
70.	*Clitoria ternatea* (Aparajitha) Fabaceae	Root, leaf, flower	Eyesight, dropsy, bronchitis, constipation, cathartic
71.	*Coccinia grandis* (Telakucha/ Kandhoori) Cucurbitaceae	Whole plants	Anti diabetic, skin disease, laxative, coolant anthelminthic, asthma, fever, anaemia, diabetics, aphrodisiac, and bronchitis.
72.	*Coleus aromaticus* (Patherchur) Lamiaceae	Whole plant	Against urinary disease, dyspepsia, cholera, bronchitis, asthma, scorpion bite.
73.	*Colocasia esculanta* (Kochu) Araceae	Rhizome, leaf	Inter haemorrhages, stimulant, laxative, demulcent.
74.	*Commelia bengalensis* (Kanshira) Commelinaceae	Whole plant	Leprosy, nervous system problems
75.	*Commelia paludosa* (Kanshira) Commelinaceae	Root, leaf	Antidote, snake poison, vertigo, fever.
76.	*Costus specious* (Keo/ Kaew) Zingiberaceae	Rhizome	Cold, Skin disease, astringent, worms, purgative, snake bite, cough, asthma, dyspepsia, diuretic, antispasmatic and cardiotonic.
77.	*Couroupita guianensis* (Anathasajja) Lecythridaceae	Fruit pulp, bark, flowers, leaves	Headache, antimicrobial and fungal, cure skin disease, malaria and toothache.
78.	*Crataeva nurvala* (Barun) Capparidaceae	Bark, leaf, root and fruit	Urinary tract infection, kidney stones, anti-inflammatory, osteomyelitis, stomach, purgative.

(Contd.)

Table 25.1 : *(Contd.)*

Sl. No.	*Botanical name/ Local name/Family*	*Parts used*	*Utilization of Medicinal plants*
79.	*Crinum asiaticum* (Spider lilly/Nagdam) Amaryllidaceae	Leaf and bulb	An emetic, convulsions sprains, fractures, Haemorrhoids.
80.	*Croton bonplandianum* (Ban tulsi) Euphorbiaceae	Leaves	Skin disease and wounds
81.	*Crescentia cujete* (Calabash tree) Bignoniaceae	Fruit, leaf, wood	Diarrhoea, stomach ache, cold, bronchitis, Cough, asthma, urethriris, hypertension.
82.	*Curculigo orchioides* (Chotto Tal muli) Amaryllidaceae	Root	Aphrodisiac, alternative, appetizer, joint pains, biliousness, fatigue, blood related disorders, carminative, tonic, antipyretic, bronchitis, piles, diarrhoea, ophthalmia, indigestion, vomiting, gonorrhea, hydrophobia,.
83.	*Curcuma longa* (Halud) Zingiberaceae	Rhizome	Antiseptic and anti-cancerous
84.	*Cynnodon dactylon* (Durba) Poaceae	Leaves	Blood dysentery, epilepsy, strengthens nerves, external bleeding, tonic
85.	*Cuseuta reflexa* (Swarnalata) Cuscutaceae	Whole plants	Liver enlargement, purgative, fever, paralysis, bronchitis and jaundice.
86.	*Cymbopogon nardus* (L.) Rendle (Citronella) Gramineae	Leaves	Stomachic, digestive, stimulant, carminative, antispasmodic, diaphoretic and rubefacient.
87.	*Cyperus rotundus* (Mutha) Cyperaceae	Rhizome	Menstruation, diarrhoea, fever, purifies mother milk and increase urine.
88.	*Datura metel* (Dhutura-white flower) Solanaceae	Seeds, whole plant	Rabies, snake bite, anti-septic, narcotic sedative, digestive and anti-asthmatic
89.	*Datura stramonium* (Dhutura/ Indian thorn apple)Solanaceae	Leaf, fruits	Antispasmodic, anodyne, motion sickness, pre-anaesthetic, childbirth, ophthalmology, asthma.
90.	*Desmodium gyrans* (Indian telegraphic plant) Fabaceae	Whole plant	Remedy for diabetics mellitus.

(Contd.)

Table 25.1 : *(Contd.)*

Sl. No.	Botanical name/ Local name/Family	Parts used	Utilization of Medicinal plants
91.	*Desmodium trifolium* (Kudaliya lata) Fabaceae	Whole plant	Expectorant, bronchitis, wounds, dysentery, burning sensation, abscess and sores.
92.	*Dillenia indica* (Chalta/ Elephant apple) Dilleniaceae	Fruit, bark, leaf	Laxative, astringent, abdominal pains, fever, cough.
93.	*Dillenia pentagyna* (Hargaza) Dilleniaceae	Fruit, bark, leaf	Against arthritis, cough, wounds, diabetics, neuritis, pleurisy, pneumonia and burning.
94.	*Dioscorea alata* (Chupri alu/ khamalu/ Yam) Dioscoreaceae	Tubers	Carticosteroids and hoeomones, birth control, leprosy, piles and gonorrhoea.
95.	*Dioscorea bulbifera* (Ban alu/ gaicha alu) Dioscoreaceae	Tubers	Ulcers, piles, dysentery, syphilis, burns, boils and sores
96.	*Dioscorea floribunda* (Oushodhi kham Alu) Dioscoreaceae	Tubers	Anthelimintic, leprosy, piles, cortico-steroids hormones, and sex hormones, birth control
97.	*Dioscorea esculenta* (Suthnialu) Dioscoreaceae	Tubers	Birth control
98.	*Dioscorea pentaphylla* (Kukur alu) Dioscoreaceae	Tubers	Treat piles, disperse swelling and as tonic
99.	*Dipterocarpus turbinatus* (Garjan) Dipterocarpaceae	Barks	Treat leprosy, gonorrhoea, skin disorders and chronic bronchitis.
100.	*Drynaria quercifolia* (Garur/ Gundia) Polypodiaceae	Rhizome	Anti bacterial, laxative, anti-inflammatory, typhoid, cough and diarrhoea.
101.	*Eclipta prostrates* (Keshuth) Asteraceae	Whole plant	Liver and spleen disorders, eye disease, uterine haemorrhages, greying of hairs, hair Tonic,
102.	*Elaeocarpus ganitrus* (Rudraksha) Elaeocarpaceae	Fruit	Bark: Haemetemesis, bilousness and indigestion, Nuts: rheumatism, typhoid and epilepsy. Seed: convulsions, insomnia, hypertension, bronchitis.

(Contd.)

Table 25.1 : *(Contd.)*

Sl. No.	*Botanical name/ Local name/Family*	*Parts used*	*Utilization of Medicinal plants*
103.	Elaeocarpus *floribundes* (Jalpai) Eleocarpaceae	Bark and leaf	Haemetemesis, rheumatism, ulcer, etc. An antidote for poison. Flowers and fruits are used against sores and ulcers.
104.	*Emblica officinalis* (Amlaki) Euphorbiaceae	Fruits, roots and bark	Carminative, cardiac disease, constipation, cough, chronic fever, haemorrhage and eye disease, hair growth, diabetics, asthma, bronchitics, cholic, etc.
105.	*Eleutherine subaphylla* (Gagner) Iridaceae	Bulb	Antibacterial, demulcent, haemostatic, diabetics, sorethroat, jaundice, boils, pertussis.
106.	*Emilia sonchifolia* (Sudhimudhi) Asteraceae	Whole plant	Febrifuge, infantile tympanitis, diarrahoea, soar ears and night blindness.
107.	*Enhydra fluctuans* (Helencha) Asteraceae	Whole plant	Diuretic, skin disease, liver ailments and insomnia.
108.	*Eryngium foetidum* (Bilaiti dhania) Apiaceae	Whole plant	Stomachic flavouring agent, digestive, kidney stone and diuretic
109.	*Euphorbia hirta* (Dudhi) Euphorbiaceae	Whole plant	Bronchitis, asthma, cough, vomiting, gonorrhoea and increase lactation.
110.	*Euphorbia nerifolia* (Manasa) Euphorbiaceae	Latex, root, and fruit	Heals wounds. Laxative, purgative, leprosy, skin diseases, gastritis, rheumatism, jaundice.
111.	*Euphorbia thymifolia* (Choti dudhiya) Euphorbiaceae	Latex, root, and fruit	Aphrodisiac, expectorant, antibacterial, dermatitis and wounds.
112.	*Euryale ferox* (Paniphal) Nymphaeceae	Seed	Weakness, retrovirus and antioxidant.
113.	*Feronia limonia* (Kaith bel, Wood apple) Rutaceae	Leaf, fruits	Carminative, astringent tonic, antiscorbutic.
114.	*Ficus bengalensis* (Bat) Moreceae	Bark, bud, flower, fruit	Root: vomiting, osteomalacia, leucorrhoea. Bark: burning, diabetics, skin diseases, ulcers, leprosy, allergy. Bud: diarrhoea, dysentery.

(Contd.)

Table 25.1 : *(Contd.)*

Sl. No.	*Botanical name/ Local name/Family*	*Parts used*	*Utilization of Medicinal plants*
115.	*Ficus benjamina* (Bat) Moreceae	Bark, bud, flower, fruit	*Root*:vomiting, osteomalacia, leucorrhoea. *Bark:* burning, diabetics, skin diseases, ulcers, leprosy, allergy. *Bud:* diarrhoea, dysentery.
116.	*Ficus carica* (Anjir) Moreceae	Fruit and latex	Anti-bacterial, inflammation swelling and burns, digestive, tumours , gum abscisses, expectorant, bronchitis.
117.	*Ficus religiosa* (Aswattha/ Pipal) Moreceae	Bark, bud, flower, fruit	Blood purification, diabetics, skin diseases and uterine diseases.
118.	*FIcus glomerata* (Joyjadamur) Moreceae	Bark	Female disease
119.	*Gardenia jasminoides* (Gandharaj) Rubiaceae	Leaf and fruits	Fever, jaundice, dysuria, conjunctivitis wounds.
120.	*Gmelina arborea* (Gamar) Verbenaceae.	Root, leaf and fruit	Hallucinations, fever, dyspepsia, bleeding, headache, relaxes nerves.
121.	*Garcinia pendulat* (Baikal, Amelvet) Gutiferae	Fruits, seeds	Rheumatism, obesity, purgative, astringent.
122.	*Hedychium coronarium* (Dulal champa) Zingiberaceae	Flowers and rhizomes	Carminative, stimulant, bruises, sprains.
123.	*Heliotrapium indicum* (Hatisur) Boranginaceae	Whole plant	Eye disease, skin disease, fever, rheumatism, ringworm, bronchitis, insect bites, bronchitis, wounds, gonorrhoea, stomachic.
124.	*Hemidesmus indicus* (Anatamul) Peripocaceae	Root, leaf and stem	Skin disease, leucoderma, urinary problems, scorpion bites, epileptic fits, syphilis, jaundice disorder of blood, wounds, gout.
125.	*Hibiscus rosa-sinensis* (Jaba) Malvaceae	Roots, leaf and flower	Itches, scabies and also used as hair shampoo.
126.	*Hibiscus sabdariffa* (Mastha/ Roselle) Malvaceae	Leaf, calyx, seeds	Soft drink, cough, fever, cold, blood pressure, antispasmodic and source of iron.

(Contd.)

Table 25.1 : *(Contd)*

Sl. No.	*Botanical name/ Local name/Family*	*Parts used*	*Utilization of Medicinal plants*
127.	*Holarrhena antidysenterica* (Kurchi) Apocynaceae	Bark, seed	*Bark:* amoebic dysentery, anthementic. *Seed:* astringent, febrifuge, antidysentery, anti anthementic, respiratory problems, wounds.
128.	*Homalonema aromatica* (Sugandhamantri/ Gandhaki) Araceae	Rhizome	Rheumatism, dyspepsia, anti-inflammatory, anodyne, stomachic, arthralgia, osteodynia and skin disease.
129.	*Hydnocarpus kurzii* (Chalmoogra) Flacourtiaceae	Fruit and oil	Leprosy, injury and skin disease.
130.	*Hygrophila auriculata* (Kulekhara) Acanthaceae	Roots, leaf and seeds	Diuretic, anti-inflammatory, aphrodisiac, eye disease, jaundice, dropsy, rheumatism.
131.	*Hyptis suaveolens* (Tokma/ Bilati tulsi) Lamiaceae	Leaf, flowers, seeds	Stimulant, carminative, skin disease, indigestion, insect bites, uterine and boils.
132.	*Jatropha curcas* (Shada Keran) Euphorbiaceae	Stem, latex	Blood dysentery, pyorrhoea as tooth brush, oedema. Latex cures scanies, eczema and laxative.
133.	*Jatropha gossypifolia* (Lal Keran) Euphorbiaceae	Seeds, latex	Purgative, leprosy, haemostatic agent.
134.	*Justicia gendarussa* (Jagatmadan) Acanthaceae	Roots leafs	Chronic rheumatism, fever, paralysis, bronchitis, diarrhoea, haemorrhages, ascites, cephalangia, etc.
135.	*Kaempferia galanga* (Ekangi) Zingiberaceae	Rhizome	Respiratory problems, vomiting nasal problems.
136.	*Kyllinga brevifolia* (Mutha) Cyperaceae	Whole plant	Liver diseases
137.	*Lagerstroemia speciosa* (Jarool) Lythraceae	Bark, leaves, root	Purgative, diuretic, diarrhoea, stimulant, hypoglycaemic activity.
138.	*Lannea coromandelica* (Badi) Anacardiaceae	Bark, leafs	Wounds, sprain, skin disease, vomiting, toothache, boils, filariasis, astringent, stomachic, anodyne, diarrhoea, dysentery.

(Contd.)

Table 25.1 : *(Contd.)*

Sl. No.	*Botanical name/ Local name/Family*	*Parts used*	*Utilization of Medicinal plants*
139.	*Lawsonia inermis* (Mehendhi) Lythraceae	Leaves, flowers, seeds	Dysentery, liver disorders, skin disease, hair dye Jaundice, brain disorders.
140.	*Leucas aspera* (Danda Kalash) Lamiaceae	Whole plant	Febrifuge, skin disease, against worms, wound healing, poison bites, fever, eye disease, cold, nasal problem, leucorrhoea, disinfectant.
141.	*Litsea glutinosa* (Kukur chitta) Lauraceae	Bark, leaves, Flower buds	Antispasmodic, bruises and wounds.
142.	*Lygodium scandens* (Fern) Schizaeaceae	Whole plant	Eye problems, conjunctivitis and dysentery.
143.	*Mallotus philippinensis* (Kamela/ Sindhoor) Euphorbiaceae	Leaf, flower, seed, oil, fruit	Glandular hairs from fruits yield a powder called 'kamala' powder, anthelmintic, abdominal disorders, worm infestation, constipation, skin disease.
144.	*Marsilea quadrifolia* (Sushnisag) Marsileaceae	Whole plant	Ophthalmic problems, diuretic, expectorant, psychopathy, bronchitis, leprosy, fever, insomnia.
145.	*Melastoma malabathricum* (Ban padam) Melastomaceae	Bark, leaf, flowers	Diarrhoea, leucorrhoea, skin disease, wound healing,
146.	*Mentha aruensis* (Pudina) Lamiaceae	Leaves	Carminative, stomachic, diuretic, cold and fever.
147.	*Mentha spicata* (Podena) Lamiaceae	Whole herb.	Tooth paste, mouthwash, pain balms, flavouring food, Perfumes, cosmetics.
148.	*Mesua ferrea* (Nageshwar) Guttiferae	Flower, seed oil, stamens	Cough, asthma, leprosy, scabies, vomiting, impotency, cardiac debility, fever, arthritis, skin
149.	*Meyna spinosa* (Mon kata) Rubiaceae	Leaves	Boils, skin disease, wounds
150.	*Michelia champaca* (Champa) Magnoliaceae	Flower, root, bark, bud	Scorpion stings, dyspepsia, nausea, fever, diuretic, gonnorhoea, gastric and rheumatism, cephalagia, stimulant and febrifuge.

(Contd.)

Table 25.1 : *(Contd.)*

Sl. No.	*Botanical name/ Local name/Family*	*Parts used*	*Utilization of Medicinal plants*
151.	*Mimosa pudica* (Larjwabati) Mimosaoeae	Leaves, root	Piles, fistula, urinary complaints, sinus, sores, whooping cough, haemorrhoids, asthma, diabetic
152.	*Mimusops elengi* (Bakul) Sapotaceae	Bark, flowers, fruit	Diarrhoea, epilepsy, fever, headache, brain tonic. Bark used in gargling
153.	*Mirabilis jalapa* (Nandadual) Nyctaginaceae	Roots, seeds, tubers, leafs	Purgative, wounds, bruises, urticaria, aphrodisiac, inflammations.
154.	*Momordica charantia* (Karela/ Bitter gourd) Cucurbitaceae	Leafs, fruits	Leprosy, malignant ulcers, stomach worm, fever, hypertension, diabetes, dysentery, skin problems, piles, gout, spleen, leprosy.
155.	*Monochoria hastate* (Kachuri) Pontederiaceae	Flower, leaf, stem	Curring burning sensation, gastriopathy, hepatopathy, cough, burns, epilepsy.
156.	*Morinda citeifolia* (Noni) Rubiaceae	Roots, leaves, Fruits	Cathartic and febrifuge. Gout, spongy gums, throat complaints, dysentery, leucorrhoea.
157.	*Moringa oleifera* (Sajna) Moringaceae	Bark, flower root, fruit and leaves	*Root:* anorexia, diarrhoea, paralysis, fever, epilepsy. *Bark:* Ring worm. *Seeds:* Antipyretic, neuralgia, intermittent fevers, ophthalmopathy. Oedema, arthritis, hypertension, pneumonia, hernia, urinary disorders.
158.	*Mucuna pruirens* (Cowhage/ Bandarhola/alkushi) Fabaceae	Seeds, roots.	Menstrual disorders, spermatorrhoea, nervine tonic, anti-parkinson disease, dropsy, fever, deliria, arthritis, kidney disorders, elephantiasis.
159.	*Mukia maderaspatana* (Bilari) Cucurbitaceae	Tender shoot and root	Tooth ache, vertiligo and biliousness.
160.	*Murraya koenigii* (Curry pata) Rutaceae	Leaf, bark, root	Hyperdipsia, burning sensation, skin diseases, anorexia, digestion, poison bites, allergy, etc.

(Contd.)

Table 25.1 : *(Contd.)*

Sl. No.	*Botanical name/ Local name/Family*	*Parts used*	*Utilization of Medicinal plants*
161.	*Murraya panniculata* (Kamini) Rutaceae	Bark, flower, leaf	Stomachic, refrigerant, digestive, fever, cough, giddiness, hysteria and burning of skin.
162.	*Mussaenda roxburghii* (Wild mussanda)	Bark, root and leaves	Bone fracture, ulcer, rheumatic pain, sore throat, Hernia, liver trouble.
163.	*Myristica fragrans* (Nutmeg) Myristicaceae	Fruit, nutmeg and mace	Digestive disorders, insomnia, depression, dehydration, eczema, rheumatism, stimulant.
164.	*Nelumbo nucifera* (Indian lotus) Nymphaeaceae	Rhizome, stem, flowers	Cuttings, rhizomatous stem/runners, diarrhoea, dysentery, demulcent and nutritive.
165.	*Nerium oleander* (Indian oleander) Apocynaceae	Bark, leaves, stem	Resolvent, skin disease, leprosy.
166.	*Nyctanthes arbour-tristis* (Night jasmine) Oleaceae	Leaves, bark, seed	Expectorant, rheuma
167.	*Nymphaea stellata* (Water lilly/shapla) Nymphaeaceae	Rhizome, stem, flowers	Cardiac pain and rhizomes cure dysentery and diarrhoea.
168.	*Neptunia oleraceae* (Horai/ Panilajuk) Mimosaceae	Whole plant	Otalgia, cephalgia, syphilis, burning sensation, diarrhoea, helminthiasis.
169.	*Ocimum basilicum* (Sweet basil) Lamiaceae	Whole plant	Rheumatism, nervous disorders, arthritis, anorexia and malaria, etc.
170.	*Ocimum canum.* Syn.*Ocimum americanum* (Holy Basil) Lamiaceae	Leaves, Flower	Stomachic, cough, cold, antiseptic, diaphoretic, antiperiodic, stimulating.
171.	*Ocimum gratissum (*Ram Tulshi) Lamiaceae	Leaves, Flower	Stomachic, cough, cold, antiseptic, diaphoretic, antiperiodic, stimulating
172.	*Ocimum tenuiflorum* (*Syn.Ocimum Sanctum*) (Tulsi or Sacred Basil) Lamiaceae	Leaves, Flower	Stomachic, cough, cold, antiseptic, diaphoretic, antiperiodic, stimulating, anti-pyretic and improving memory.
173.	*Oldenlandia corymbosa* (Khet para) Rubiaceae	Whole plant	Fever, jaundice, liver troubles, itches and scabies.
174.	*Oroxylum indicum* (Kanai dinga/ Thana) Bignoniaceae	Root, bark, fruit	Arthritis, chest pain, dysentery, diaphoretic, ulcers, rheumatism, purgative, stomachic, diarrhoea

(Contd.)

Table 25.1 : *(Contd.)*

Sl. No.	*Botanical name/ Local name/Family*	*Parts used*	*Utilization of Medicinal plants*
175.	*Oxalis corniculata (*Amrul sak) Oxaliadaceae	Leaves, stem	Scurvy, convulsions, healing fractured bones, stomachic, dysentery, purify blood, anaemia, piles, fever, tympanitis.
176.	*Peaderia foetida* (Gandha bhadali/skunk vine) Rubiaceae	Leaves	Diarrhoea, indigestion, urinary bladder problems, rheumatism, flatulence, fever.
177.	*Parkia javanica* (Puikka tetoi) Mimosaceae	Flowers and Fruits	Diarrhoea, dysentery, indigestion, gastritis and Anti cancerous.
178.	*Peuraria thomsonii (*Kudzu bean) Fabaceae	Tuberous roots	Fever, influenza, headache, snake bite.
179.	*Passiflora edulis* (Passion fruit) Passifloraceae	Fruit pulp	Natural colour, flavour, Vit C, aphrodisac, cardiac problems.
180.	*Phoenix humilis (*Khajoor) Palmae (Arecaceae)	Fruit, seed, sap	Laxative, fever, respiratory disease, cephalgia, inflammations and wounds. Sap (toddy) is digestive, tonic and bronchitis.
181.	*Phyllanthus acidus* (Horboroi) Euphorbiaceae	Fruit, root, seed	Liver tonic bronchitis, vomiting, piles, anaemia, constipation. Root and seeds: cathartic, diabetes, influenza, rheumatism, diuretic, anthelminthic
182.	*Piper betel (*Pan) Piperoceae	Leaves	Carminative, stimulant, digestive, aromatic. Catarrhal and pulmonary infections, respiratory illness and diphtheria.
183.	*Piper longum (*Pipul) Piperoceae	Spike, stem, root	Bronchitis, aphrodisiac, bronchitis, jaundice, anti rheumatic, cough, asthma, pneumonia, fever, diarrhoea, viral hepatitis, gastritis, piles.
184.	*Piper nigrum (*Kalimirch) Piperoceae	Fruit and root	Fever, cough, cold, arthritis, jaundice, abdominal disorder, malarial fever, vomiting, earache.
185.	*Peperomia pellucida* (Luchipata) Piperaceae	Whole plant	Cuts and wounds. Stomach problems.

(Contd.)

Table 25.1 : *(Contd.)*

Sl. No.	*Botanical name/ Local name/Family*	*Parts used*	*Utilization of Medicinal plants*
186.	*Phyllanthus amarus* (Bhuamlaki) Euphorbiaceae	Whole plants	Liver disorders like Hepatitis-B and jaundice, intestinal infection, diabetes, bronchitis, leprosy, asthma, eye disease, anaemia, hiccough.
187.	*Psidium guineense* (Ban peyara/Ban gayam) Myrtaceae	Leaves, fruits, bark, twig	Laxative, diarrhoea, gum pain, cough, dysentery, painful menstruation, premature labour in women
188.	*Prerocarpus acerifolium* (Kanak chamap) Sterculiaceae	Bark, leaves, flower	*Flower*: Inflammations, ulcers and tumours. *Leaf:* stop bleeding. *Bark:* glandular swelling. Anti diabetic and anti bacterial.
189.	*Pongamia pinnatga* (Indian beech) Fabaceae	Bark, leaf, seed, flowers	Diabetes, gonorrhoea, leprosy, skin disease, rheumatism, green manure.
190.	*Punica granatum* (Dalim) Punicaceae	Fruit, bark, root, flowers	Anti dysenteric, diarrhoea, piles, bleeding from nose, bronchitis, tape worm infection, syphilis.
191.	*Psoralea corylifolia* (Babchi) Fabaceae	Seeds	Against leucoderma, leprosy and skin diseases.
192.	*Quisqualis indica* (Rangoon creeper/ Rongon)	Fruit and seed	Ascariasis, malnutrition, diarrhoea, fever, skin problems.
193.	*Rauvolfia serpentina* (Sarpagandha) Apocynaceae	Root	Anti-hypertension, anti spasmodic, skin disease, sedative, mental illness, snake bite, eye disease.
194.	*Ricinus communis* (Verenda) Euphorbiaceae	Seeds, leaves	Purgative, diuretic, bronchitis, ascites, leprosy, arthritis, laxative, cooling, jaundice, rheumatic swellings, breast tumour, boils, purgative, skin.
195.	*Samanea saman* (Rain tree, Vilaiyiti siris) Fabaceae	Leaf, bark, root	Antipyretic, antimalarial, cold, fever, influenza and snake bites.

(Contd.)

Table 25.1 : *(Contd.)*

Sl. No.	*Botanical name/ Local name/Family*	*Parts used*	*Utilization of Medicinal plants*
196.	*Santalum album* (Chandan) Santalaceae	Wood, root	Skin disease, disinfectant, cardiotonic, hyper acidity, diuretic, diaphoretic, expectorant, cooling agent.
197.	*Saraca asoca* (Asoka) Caesalpiniaceae	Bark, root, flower	Uterine tonic, menstrual bleeding, piles, internal haemorrhage, dysentery and scorpion bite, diabetes.
198.	*Schima wallichii* (Kanak) Theaceae	Bark, flower	Cuts and wounds, cure flatulence, powdered bark is fed to cattle to kill intestinal worms.
199.	*Schefflera venulosa,* Araliaceae	Roots	Dropsy
200.	*Scoparia dulcis* (Jangali jeera) Scrophulariaceae	Whole plant	Anti-inflammatory, diuretic, sore throat, measles, boils and dry cough.
201.	*Sesamum indicum* (Til) Pedaliaceae	Seeds and leaves	Piles, cough, emollient, lactogogue, diuretic, digestive, anthelminthic, skin disease.
202.	*Sesbania grandiflora* (Bak phul) Fabaceae	Barks, leaves, flowers, fruits	Anthelminthic, body pain, fever, worm infestation, haemorrhage, night blindness, epilepsy, memory. Cures itches and scabies. Pox, headache, cold, cough.
203.	*Sida cordifolia*(Bala/ Hethuthi/ Berala/ Balikari) Malvaceae	Roots, leaves	Cool, pain, nervous, cardiac disease, dysentery, piles, jaundice, demulcent, fever, aphrodisiac, opthalmia, diabetes, uterine disorders, skin disease
204.	*Sida rhombifolia* (Jangli methi) Malvaceae	Roots, leaves	Aphrodisiac, rheumatism, colic, diarrhoea.
205.	*Smilax zeylanica* (Kumarika) Smilacaceae	Roots	Muscular spasms and cramps, increase sex drive in females, supplement food for AIDS patients.
206.	*Solanum indicum* (Titbegun) Solanaceae	Fruit, Roots	Diarrhoea, stomachic, cough, fever, asthma, bronchitis, skin disease, diabetes, hypertension, respiratory disease, epilepsy and constipation.

(Contd.)

Table 25.1 : *(Contd.)*

Sl. No.	Botanical name/ Local name/Family	Parts used	Utilization of Medicinal plants
207.	*Solanum nigrum* (Black night shade/Ban begun) Solanaceae	Whole plants	Swellings, cough, asthma, bronchitis, wounds, ulcers, hiccough, vomiting, skin disease and cardiopathy, eye disease, fever, rat bite, hepatitis.
208.	*Solanum turvum* (Big titbegun) Solanaceae	Fruits	Liver and spleen enlargement, cough, sedative, diuretic.
209.	*Solanum viarum* syn. *S. Khasianum* (Sodom apple) Solanaceae	Fruits	Antifertility, cortisones, sex hormones, birth control, anorexia, anabolic and anti-inflammatory
210.	*Solanum xanthocarpum* (Kantakari) Salanaceae	Root	Cold, cough, fever, asthma, bronchitis, epilepsy, skin disease, hypertension, constipation, dyspepsia, cardiac disease and leprosy.
211.	*Spilanthes paniculata* (Tooth ache plant) Asteraceae	Flower, leaves, seeds	Gum pain, sore throat, paralysis, tongue, inflammation, scabies, psoriasis, stammering.
212.	*Stachytarpheta indica* (Brazilian tree) Verbenaceae	Whole plant	Bruises, dysentery, gonorrhoea, sprain and anti-inflammatory
213.	*Stemona tuberose,* Stemonaceae	Tuberous roots	Bacteriostatic, cough, scabies, respiratory illness, Insecticidal property.
214.	*Stevia rebaudiana* (Stevia) Asteraceae	Leaves, stem	Blood sugar levels, digestion, skin disease, mouth sores.
215.	*Streptocaulon juventas* Asclepiadaceae	Tubers	Snake bites, anaemia, renal, ostealgia, hepatic hypofunction, dispepesia, insomnia,chronic malaria, rheumatism, menstrual disorders.
216.	*Spondias pinnata* (Amra) Anacardiaceae	Bark, root, fruit	Menstrual problems, diarrhoea, muscular rheumatism, otalgia.
217.	*Stephania japonica* (Nimukhya) Menispermaceae	Tuberous roots and leaf	Jaoundice, anemia, abdominal disorders and cardiotonic
218.	*Sterculia villosa* (Udal) Sterculiaceae	Bark and Petiole	Skin disease, cephalgia, ulcer, helminthiasis, leprosy, neuropathy, seminal weakness.
219.	*Streblus asper* (Shaora) Moraceae	Bark, latex and root	Dental problems, pyorrhoea, fever, abdominal pain, wounds antiseptic.
220.	*Suregada multiflora* (Suregada) Euphorbiaceae	Bark and root	Skin disease, antiviral.

(Contd.)

Table 25.1 : *(Contd.)*

Sl. No.	*Botanical name/ Local name/Family*	*Parts used*	*Utilization of Medicinal plants*
221.	*Syzygium cumini* (Jam/Black berry) Myrtaceae	Roots, fruits leaf, bark	Diabetes, diarrhoea, eczema, antidote for strychnine poisoining.
222.	*Syzygium jambos* (Rose apple /Golap jam) Myrtaceae	Leaf, fruits and bark	Diabetes, leprosy, syphilis ulcers and helminthiasis.
223.	*Tagetes erecta* (Gada/ marigold) Asteraceae	Leaves and flowers	Rheumatism, cold, bronchitis, laxative, renal dysfunction, muscular pains, boils.
224.	*Tamarindus indica* (Tetul) Caesalpiniaceae	Bark, flower and fruits	Hyperacidity, leucorrhoea, ulcers, anaemia, epilepsy, wounds, dysentery, diarrhoea.
225.	*Tectona grandis* (Teak) Verbenaceae	Wood, bark, seed, flower	Eczema, scabies, Flower bronchitis, and urinary discharges, bark-astringent.
226.	*Terminalia arjuna* (Arjuna) Combretaceae	Barks, leaf, fruits	Heart disease,, cough, skin disease, bleeding, Ear-ache, fractures, febrifuge.
227.	*Terminalia bellerica* (Bahera) Combretaceae	Fruit	Digestive, astringent, throat, tonic, laxative, hair tonic and chest infections.
228.	*Terminalia catappa* (Marking nut) Combretaceae	Barks, kernel, fruits	Scabies, cutaneous infections, diuretic, cardio-tonic and dysentery
229.	*Terminalia chebula* (Harataki) Combretaceae	Fruit	Laxative, stomachic, tonic, alternative, asthma, Constituent of triphala.
230.	*Thespesia populnea* (Palashpipul) Malvaceae	Leaf, bark, fruit	Cough, influenza, headache, dysentery, diabetic, gonorrhoea, ulcer, worms, breast cancer, urinary.
231.	*Thevetia peruviana* (Karabi) Apocynaceae	Seed and root	Cardio tonic, tumours, Tincture of the bark is emetic.
232.	*Thunbergia grandiflora* (Gundi lata) Acanthaceae	Climbing stem	Nervous disorder, skin disease.

(Contd.)

Table 25.1 : *(Contd.)*

Sl. No.	Botanical name/ Local name/Family	Parts used	Utilization of Medicinal plants
233.	*Tinospora cordifolia* (Gulancha) Menispermaceae	Stem	Anti rheumatic, seminal weakness, urinary infections, fever, jaundice, liver disease, general debility, skin diseases.
234.	*Toona ciliata* (Puma/ Toon) Meliaceae	Bark, gum, oil, flower, leaf.	Astringent, carminative, diarrhoea, flatulence.
235.	*Tridax procumbens* (Bhengra) Asteraceae	Whole plant	Dashapushpas, reduce blood pressure, bleeding, anti diabetic, haemorrhage, dysentery, diarrhoea.
236.	*Typhonium trilobatum* (Kharkon) Araceae	Whole plant	Rheumatism, piles, urinary troubles and gut disorders.
237.	*Urena lobata* (Banokra) Malvaceae	Bark, root and leaves	Jaundice, labour pain, cough and cold.
238.	*Vernonia cinerea* (Shialmutra) Asteraceae	Whole plant	Diarrhoea, skin diseases, inflammations, chronic, ringworms, conjunctivitis, fever, anti cancerous, indigestion, fever, urinary troubles.
239.	*Vanda teselata* (Rasna) Orchidaceae	Leaves,roots	Anti-rheumatic, fever Inflammation of limbs, cough.
240.	*Vitax negundo* (Nishinda) Verbenaceae	Leaves	Headache, anthelminthic, expectorant, epilepsy, anti rheumatic, throat infection, sores in mouth, joint pain, malaria, fever, etc.
241.	*Wedelia chinensis* (Wingaraaj) *Asteraceae*	Whole plants	Jaundice, cough, menorrhagia, tonic, skin disease
242.	*Withania somnifera* (Ashwagandha) Solanaceae	Roots and leaves	Diuretic, arthritis, insomnia, nervous breakdown, aphrodisiac, skin disease, fever, cough, adaptogen, general tonic, impotency, febriguge.
243.	*Zanthoxylum limonella* (Bajna/ Bojrang)	Fruit, bark, seeds	Antiseptic, digestive, carminative, liver tonic, asthma, bronchitis, hearing problems, indigestion, toothache, rheumatism, cholera.

(Contd.)

Table 25.1 : *(Contd.)*

Sl. No.	*Botanical name/ Local name/Family*	*Parts used*	*Utilization of Medicinal plants*
244.	*Zingiber officinale* (Ada) Zingiberaceae	Rhizome	Carminative, stimulant, cardiac disease, piles, colic, indigestion, nausea, filariasis,
245.	*Zingiber serumbi* (Aam ada) Zingiberaceae	Rhizome	Carminative, stimulant

Ex situ approach demands removal of species and varieties; breeding, storage, cloning or rescue are tools to ensure such approach. Botanical garden, Arboretum, zoological parks, Aquaria and Seed banks serve the purpose of *ex situ* conservation. Microbial culture collection also provide another method of *ex situ* conservation. Over the years many medicinal plant species have become extinct and the extinction rate is on the increase due to the influence of human activity. Presently, conservation status in the State is very poor but their is urgent need to conserve the threatened or endangered medicinal plant species of Tripura, which are most important like *Abroma angusta, Adatoda zeylanica, Alpiinia galangal, Ageratum conizoides, Andrographis paniculata, Bacopa monnieri, Boerhaavia diffusa, Centalla asiatic, Emblica officinalis, Eryngium foetidum, Homalonema aromatica, Hygrophila auriculata, Mucuna pruirens, Ocimum gratissum, Parkia javanica, Phyllanthus amarus, Piper longum, Saraca asoca, Sida acutifolia, Sida cordifolia, Sida rhomblifolia, Solanum indicum, Spilanthes paniculata, Terminalia arjuna, Terminalia bellerica, Terminalia chebula, Tinospora cordifolia, Vitax negundo, Rauvolfia serpentina, Wedelia chinensis, Withania somnifera,* etc.

Problems for Development of Medicinal Plants are:

(1) Indiscriminate collection wild medicinal plants and burning of forest areas due to shifting cultivation that finally cause huge loss of valuable wild and traditional medicinal plants.

(2) Lack of systemic collection and conservation of wild and traditional medicinal plants.

(3) Lack of knowledge for identification of valuable wild and traditional medicinal plants.

(4) Inadequate supply of quality planting materials to the tergeted farming community.

(5) Poor knowledge on scientific cultivation of quality medicinal plants.
(6) Limited and inadequate marketing supports and infrastructure facilities for transportation, storage and processing.
(7) Unorganized trade and lack of support price for medicinal plant.
(8) Lack of awareness among the peoples and farming community regarding conservation and medicinal value of medicinal plants.
(9) Lack of systematic researches for standardization of different agro-technology.
(10) Limited application of advance on-farm agrotechniques.
(11) Lack of application of innovative and novel technologies such as biotechnology, organic cultivation for enhancement of productivity.
12) Improper institutional arrangements and limited role played for setting up of industrial and medicinal plant based industrial units.
13) Lack of knowledge regarding chemical ingredient or chemical compound or alkaloids present in the valuable medicinal plants.

Conclusion

The above mentioned medicinal plants are used by the interior and rural peoples for their health security, nutritional security, poverty elevation and used for common ailments. Tripura is blessed with huge plant genetic resources especially medicinal plants. Systematic cultivation of medicinal plants is very less as compared to other crops available in the State. These plants are playing a vital role in providing food, nutritional and economic status to poor masses in the State. There is tremendous scope to popularize these in non-traditional areas and these crops may earn lot of foreign currency in the State in near future. Further, the huge genetic diversity in various medicinal plants has vast scope for collection and conservation (both *in situ* and *ex situ*) of medicinal plants in the State. The increase in area and production of these medicinal plants will not only provide health security and save money and boost the State economy in near future.

REFERENCES

Chakraborty, N.K. (2007). *Medicinal Plants of Tripira.* Jnan Bichitra Prakshani, Tripura.

Chandra Das; Sukhen; and Deb, A.K. (2011). Studies of bio-diversity of medicinal plants and their prospects and problems in Tripura. *Ann. Pharm. & Pharm. Sci.*, 2 (1 and 2) : 62-71.

Das, S.C.; Jai Prakash.; R.C. Samui and T. Bishwas. (2010). Traditional Medicinal plants used by Hilly Tripura. In Proceeding: International Conference on Horticulture (ICH-2009), Horticulture for Livelihood Security and Economic Growth, Bangalore, India. pp. 1240-1246.

Das, S.C.; Jai Prakash; A. K. Deb and T. Bishwas. (2009). Medicinal Value of Underutilized Fruits in Hilly Tripura. Abstract published in 2nd International Symposium on Medicinal and Nutraceutical plants, conducted by International Society for Horticultural Sciences (ISHS), Levuen, Belgium, November, 25-27.2009. AIIMS, New Delhi, India, p.108.

Das, S.C.; Jai Prakash; A.K. Deb and T. Bishwas. (2009). Studies of Indegenious and Tribals Medicinal Plants in Hilly Tripura. Abstract published in 2nd International Symposium on Medicinal and Nutraceutical plants, conducted International Society for Horticultural Sciences, (ISHS), Levuen, Belgium, November, 25-27.2009. AIIMS, New Delhi, India, p. 109.

Farooqi, A.A.; Vasundhara, M. and Agarwal, A. (2001). Production Technology of Medicinal and Aromatic Crops. Trust for Medicinal Plant Research and Development, Bangalore-560 100.

Kishore, D.B. (1994). Tribal folk medicine of Tripura. Tribal Research Institute, Tripura.

Mehrotra, S. and Mehrotra, B.N. (2005). Role of traditional and folk lore herbals in the development of new drugs. *Ethnobot.* 17: 104-111.

Shanley, P. and Luz, L. (2003). The impacts of forest degradation on medicinal plant use and implication for health care in Eastern Amazonia. *Bioscience*, 53 (6): 573-584.

Toledo, V.M. (1995). New paradigms for a new ethnobotany; reflections on the case of Mexico. In: Schultes, R.E. and Von Reis, S. (eds.) Ethnobotany: Evolution of a Discipline. Chapman and Hall, London, pp. 75-88.

26
Biodiversity : The Indian Scenario and its Value to Our Society

P. Biswas

Introduction

Biological diversity or the biodiversity as we call it may be defined as the element of nature which encompasses all life forms or variations in genes of all life forms. The variation amongst the individuals of a species is the diversity of that species. The variety and richness of all plant and animal species taken together at different spatial scales—locally, regionally or in a country is what we call the biodiversity resource of that region or the country. So, the biodiversity is the presence of vast array of the ecosystems, both terrestrial and aquatic within a defined area. Biodiversity deals with the degree of nature's variety in the biosphere. This variety can be observed at three levels—the genetic variability within a species, the variety of species within a community and organization of species in an area with distinct plant and animal communities.

The great variety of life forms on Earth has been meeting the needs of the human beings over thousands of years. This diversity of living creatures forms a support system which has been used by each civilization for their sustenance, growth and development. Those that used this bounty of nature carefully and sustainably survived and flourished, while those that overused or misused it, got destroyed, disintegrated and were lost in oblivion.

India—A Mega Diversity Nation

Our country is recognized as one of the Mega biodiversity regions of the world. And there exists a definite reason why has it been declared so. If we analyze the studies made on Plate tectonics and formation of the continents, we find that the landmass of our country—the Indian Sub-continent—had evolved as a result of split in the single giant continent around 70 million years ago, which led to the formation of Northern and Southern Continents, with India as part of Gondwanaland—the southern landmass, together with Africa, Australia and the Antarctica. Later tectonic movements had pushed the Indian subcontinent northward across the equator to join the Northern Eurasian landmass (continent). As the intervening shallow *Tethys* Sea had dried up, the great Himalayan mountain system slowly emerged because of friction. Interestingly, this mighty mountain system has been protecting our landmass since then from the harsh, chill gush of wind of the Arctic region.

There was, therefore, a steady movement and migration, succession and climax of the plants and animals into our sub-continent that had evolved both in Europe and in the Far East Asia because of conducive, favourable climatic condition for survival, growth and above all the protection from the Himalayan mountain system. A final influx came from African continent with Ethiopian species in particular which were adept in the Savannas and semi-arid regions.

The geographical location of our country is unique. Its one extreme touches the Indian Ocean while the other merges into the highest mountain system of the world with a large number of snow covered peaks. It has the largest deltaic region of the world with unique mangrove forest eco-system (Sunderbans). The Great Indian Desert is located in the western extreme whereas the eastern extreme receives the highest rainfall of the world. The country also enjoys the monsoon climate which is yet another unique climatic feature not found elsewhere (except the Gulf of Mexico). The country is truly diverse. Therefore, it is but natural that the landmass has to be the repository of the mega biological diversity resources of the world. Thus, India's special geographical position or "niche" between three distinctive centres of biological evolution and radiation of species has contributed towards its rich and varied biodiversity.

India stands among the top 10 bio-resource diverse countries of the world for its great variety of plants and animals, many of which are not found elsewhere. India has 350 different mammals (rated the eighth highest in the world) and 45,000 plants species, of which most are Angiosperms, (fifteenth in the world). These include especially high species diversity of Ferns (1,022 species) and Orchids (1,082 species). India has 50,000 known species but the Naturalists claim that it could be several times higher. It is estimated that 18 per cent of Indian plants are endemic to the country and are found nowhere else in the world. Among the plant species, the flowering plants have a much higher degree of endemism, a third of these are not found elsewhere. Among Amphibians found in India, 62 per cent are unique to this country. Among Lizards, of the 153 species recorded, 50 per cent are endemic. High endemism has also been recorded in various groups of insects, Marine worms, Centipedes, Mayflies and Freshwater sponges.

India's World Ranking	Number of species in India
Mammals 8th	350
Birds 8th	1200
Reptiles 5th	453
Amphibians 15th	182
Angiosperms 15th-20th	14,500

Apart from the high biodiversity in Indian wild plants and animals, there is also a great diversity in the cultivated crops and breeds of domestic livestock. This is a result of several thousands years of amalgamations during which civilizations have grown, flourished in the Indian subcontinent. The traditional cultivars included 30,000 to 50,000 varieties of rice and a number of cereals, vegetables and fruit. The highest diversity of cultivars is concentrated in the high-rainfall areas of the Western Ghats, Eastern Ghats, Northern Himalayas and the North-Eastern hills. It is interesting to note that the Gene-banks are collected over 34,000 cereals and 22,000 pulses grown in India. India has 27 indigenous breeds of cattle, 40 breeds of sheep, 22 breeds of goats and 8 breeds of buffaloes. Many of these varieties today have died out or are dying out due to our misguided adoption of all "phoren" things—Jerseys and Holsteins have largely replaced the Indian cattle like the Brahma bull, high-yielding cultivars have eaten away into century old landraces of crops. The cash crops have replaced food crops, Eucalyptus and Wattle plantations have replaced the mixed indigenous forests. We know of many fresh water fishes which were in plenty during our childhood have become rare now. One of the reasons of depletion is attributed to large scale use of the chemical fertilizer and pesticides in the contiguous farmland.

We are aware of the fact that Vulture, the foremost scavenging bird of our country is on the path of extinction for some time now. Perhaps no other bird species in the world has seen a more rapid decline than those of Gyps vultures in recent times. The International Union for Conservation of Nature (IUCN) in its resolution, at the third session in Bangkok in November 2004 on the Gyps species of vultures, pointed out that the Long-billed (*Gyps indicus*) and White-rumped (*Gyps bengalensis*) vultures and Red headed or King Vulture (*Sarcogyps calvus*), endemic to South-East Asia, have declined by more than 97 per cent during the last 10 years. In Tripura we have not seen a vulture after 1994. The Indian landscape is slowly but surely beginning to lose its individuality, diverse mosaic and has started resembling other landmasses of the world.

Therefore, it is my submission that the concept of biodiversity is, though relatively new and we have started appreciating its role very recently, but by now we have already gauged its importance and potential. We can realize how blessed are we even today when we realize the treasure that has been inherited by us. It is yet another tool with which we can Fight the poverty and malnutrition of our teeming population especially in the days of Intellectual Property Rights and Clean Development Mechanism, just by way of value addition and selective use. It is in this context that we must realize the fact that our forefathers who had trodden in this land were really visionaries. They regarded all life forms with veneration. And so we find umpteen stories in our literatures where the animals and plants are all characters that could talk, had emotions like humans and were actually the part of our everyday life! It is through this characterization that they wanted to send the message to protect the unique biodiversity resources. The accomplishment of our forefathers in understanding plants and properties of their roots, stems, leaves, flowers and fruits is simply a result of long and intimate association with the flora and their dependence on them since their knowledge is based on experimentation on human beings. Advances in science, notably during the last two centuries, better understanding of human body and its physiology has led to isolation of many of the active ingredients of the plants found in our country in pure form, with or without herbal extracts.

The treatise of our highly advanced *ayurvedic* medicines are based on the studies of nature carried out by our forefathers over a very long period of time, usage of various medicines and the results made them come to a conclusion about the use of drugs prepared from various herbs/shrubs in treating the diseases. So, we may say that it is the strength of the biodiversity of the natural resources that has been made use of in ancient times. The World Health Organization (WHO) has recognized the role of traditional systems of medicine and considers it to be a strategy to provide health care to the masses. Written records of the use of plants for curing human ailments can be traced back to earliest scriptures of the people of our land. Thus the science of well-being and treatment of diseases or the whole gamut of happy, long human life involving physical, meta physical and the spiritual aspect of life was also developed in our land in the days of yore because of the biodiversity. The very illustrative and monumental works of *Charak Samhita* and *Shusrut Samhita*, the two epic treatises, came to be in use during that time, which are being followed by people of our country even today. It is thus that our people had attempted to classify and categorize the variability in nature for over a century. This has led to an understanding of its organization into communities of plants and animals. This information has helped in utilizing the Earth's biological wealth for the benefit of humanity and has been integral to the process of "development". This includes better health care, better crops and the use of these life-forms as raw material for industrial growth, which has led to a higher standard of living. It was only during the alien British rule, the social and economic conditions of our country had undergone change, the process of urbanization had begun and the growth of forests was neglected. It was during this time that the people lost their root with the forests. It is also a fact that the compilation and dependence on our own resources were discouraged and there was a systematic policy of discouraging the native (!) products and branding them to be of inferior origin, crude and poisonous. But, the diversity of life on our land is so great that despite all these insinuations from various quarters the biodiversity resources continued to exist and if we use it sustainably we can go on developing new products from this wealth for many generations. This can only happen if we manage our treasure as a precious resource and prevent the extinction of species.

Biodiversity at Global, National and Local Levels

There are at present 1.8 million species known and documented by scientists in the world over. And at the same time, however, the scientists have estimated that the number of species of plants and animals on Earth could vary from 1.5 to 20 billion.

Most of the world's bio-rich nations are in the south; in other words, they are the "Developing" nations. In contrast, the majority of the countries capable of exploiting biodiversity are the Northern nations, in the economically "Developed" world. These nations, however, have lower levels of biodiversity. Thus, after centuries of exploitation, the "developed" world has come to realize the fact that biodiversity must be considered to be a "Global resource". However, if biodiversity should form a "Common Property Resources" to be shared by all nations, there is no reason to exclude petroleum, natural gas or uranium, or even intellectual and technological expertise from the list of the global assets. Therefore, we can surely conclude that India's sovereignty over its biological diversity resources cannot be compromised without a revolutionary change in thinking about sharing of all types of natural resources of the world.

Some of the countries which stand in the same pedestal in terms of higher biodiversities with India are located in South-East Asia and South America, especially Brazil. The species found in these countries, however, are different from our own. This makes it imperative to preserve our own biodiversity as a major economic resource. It is quite disturbing to know that some of the "Mega-biodiversity nations" have started recklessly exploiting their resources for the development, the biotechnology and bio-engineering and this fact has made us more conscious. We must spread and enlighten our people on the richness of our biodiversity and their judicious usage for our betterment.

International agreements, treatise, like that of World Heritage Convention, Rio Summit, Kyoto Protocol, Ramsar Convention are all aimed at protection of such areas and sites. India is a signatory to the conventions and it has taken steps to include the areas for protection as World Heritage Sites. Some of these include Manas and Kaziranga in Assam, Bharatpur in Rajasthan, Nandadevi in the Himalayas, and the Sunderbans in the Gangetic delta of Bengal. Kaibul Lamjao national Park nestling in Loktak Lake in Manipur is another such area. We also approached to declare the unique Bas relief of Unokoti in Tripura (Kailashahar Division) to be declared so. India has also signed the Convention in the Trade of Endangered Species (CITES), which is intended to reduce the utilization of endangered plants and animals by controlling trade in their products and in the pet trade.

Values of Biodiversity

The biodiversity provides us a variety of environmental services from the species and ecosystems that are essential at the global, regional and local levels. The production of oxygen, reduction of carbon dioxide, maintenance of the hydrological cycle, protection of soil from erosion is just some of the important services rendered. The world now acknowledges the fact that the loss of biodiversity contributes to global warming and climatic changes. Forest ecosystem is the main mechanism for reversing the trend and mitigating the ill effects of the carbon dioxide. The resultant effect of the loss of forest cover, coupled with the "Greenhouse gas effect" is the Global warming. The melting ice caps, flow of excess water resulting in rise in the sea-level submergence of the low-lying areas are the fears that the Naturalists apprehend because of the loss of biodiversity. The predicament is major atmospheric change leading to increase in surface temperatures, serious droughts and unexpected floods. People shall face miseries and distress. The catastrophes are also not ruled out.

Therefore biological diversity is essential for preserving ecological processes and saving the civilization from the brink of disaster. By way of the biodiversity conservation, we may fix and recycle the nutrients, soil formation, and circulation and cleansing of air and water, global life support by way of carbon sequestration, maintaining the water balance within ecosystems, watershed protection, maintaining streams and river flows throughout the year, erosion control and local flood reduction.

Food, clothing, housing, energy, medicines are all resources that are directly linked to the biological diversity, gathering of resources from the forest, harvesting fish in marine or freshwater ecosystem are all linked to the same. Urban communities generally use the greatest amount of goods and services, which have spiralling effect on natural ecosystems. It has become obvious that preservation of biological resources is essential for well-being and the long-term survival of mankind. This diversity of living organisms, which is present in the wilderness as well as in our crops and livestock, plays a major role in the process of "Development". The preservation of "Biodiversity" is, therefore, the core issue and an integral part of any strategy that aims at improving the quality of human life. And the Government (which?) has now realized that the conservation of Biodiversity resources has taken the centre stage of all forestry activities of the country. It is the core issue, if we can conserve the biodiversity it shall take care of conservation of the entire ecosystem.

Consumptive Use Value

A straightforward example of it is the direct utilization of timber, food and fodder by the people who live in and around the forest. The biodiversity contained in the ecosystem provides forest dwellers all their daily requirements, viz., food, shelter, building material, energy, fodder, medicines and a variety of other goods and services which they barter or trade. Fisherman is completely dependent on harvesting fish and knows precisely where and how to catch fish and other edible aquatic animals and plants. The biodiversity of a region influences every aspect of the life of people who inhabit it. Their livelihood depends on the type of ecosystem that they sustain. Even people living in urban areas are dependent on the ecological services provided by the wilderness. But we do not realize the push and pull force that the urban demand exerts on nature as it is not necessarily overt. The vanishing wildlife resource and the remnants of once thriving species (Tiger, Rhino) have the telltale effect. The quality of water we drink and use, the air we breathe, the ecosystem with which we are linked are all because of the biodiversity. It is also obvious that fungi, small soil invertebrates and even microbes are essential for the plants to grow and, therefore, our life and its development depends entirely on the life of the ecosystem.

The truth that a natural forest ecosystem acts as the reservoir of water that flows in the river and the flow is directly proportional to the quality of the ecosystem or the fact that the absence of ants would destroy life on Earth, are to be appreciated in order to understand how we are completely dependent on the living "Web of life" on Earth. The wilderness is an outcome of a long evolutionary process that has created an unimaginably large diversity of living species and the various ecosystems on Earth in which all living creatures live. This includes mankind as well. And so we cannot but want to protect our Earth's unique biodiversity.

Productive Use Value

The Biotechnologist uses bio-rich areas to "Prospect" and search for potential genetic properties in plants or animals that can be used to develop better varieties of crops for use in farming and plantation programmes or to develop better livestock for our prosperity and wellbeing. To the Pharmacist, biological diversity is the raw material from which new drugs can be identified. To the industrialists, biodiversity is a rich storehouse from which he could develop new products. For the Agricultural Scientist, the biodiversity means assessment of strength and quality of the wild relatives of crops for developing better crops for human use and consumption.

Genetic diversity enables scientists and farmers to selectively develop better crops and livestock through careful breeding programmes. Earlier, this was done by selecting or pollinating crops artificially to get a more productive or disease-resistant strain. Today, it is increasingly being done by Genetic Engineering-selecting genes from one plant and introducing them into another. New crop varieties (cultivars) are being developed using the genetic material found in wild relatives of crops through biotechnology.

New species of plants and animals are being constantly discovered in the wild. The wild species are the building blocks for the betterment of human life and their loss is a great economic loss to mankind. Among the known species, only a tiny fraction has been investigated for their value in terms of food, or medicinal or industrial potential. The preservation of biodiversity has now become essential for industrial growth and economic development. A variety of industries, like pharmaceuticals, are highly dependent on identifying compounds of great economic value from the wild species of plants located in undisturbed natural forests. This is called "Biological Prospecting".

Commonly-used modern drugs derived from plant sources :

DRUG	PLANT SOURCE
ropine	Belladonna
Bromelain	Pineapple
Caffeine	Tea, coffee
Camphor	Camphor tree
Cocaine	Cocoa
Codeine	Opium poppy
Morphine	Opium poppy
Colchicine	Autumn crocus
Digitoxin	Common foxglove
Diosgenin	Wild
L-Dopa	Velvet bean (Mucona pruriens)
Erotamine	Smut-of-Rye or Ergot
Glaziovine	Ocotea glaziovii
Gossypol	Cotton
Indicine N-oxide	Heliotropium Indicum
Menthol	Mint
Monocrotaline	Cotolaria sessiliflora
Papain	Papaya
Penicillin	Penicillium fungi
Quinine	Yellow cinchona
Reserpine	Indian snakeroot (Rauvolfia)
Scopolamine	Thorn apple
Taxol	Pacific yew (Texas baccata)
Vinblastine,	Rosy periwinkle
Vincristine	Vinca rosea (*Sadabahar/Nayantara*)

Social Value

While traditional societies that had a smaller population and required less resources had preserved their biodiversity as a life-supporting resource, the modern man has rapidly depleted it up to the extent of leading to the irrecoverable loss due to extinction of several species. So, apart from the local use or sale of products of biodiversity, there is also the social aspect in which more and more resources are used by affluent societies. Our biodiversity has, to a great extent, been preserved by traditional societies that valued it as a resource and appreciated that its depletion would be a great loss to their society. Therein lies a lesson which we would be wise to learn from. The consumptive and productive value of biodiversity is closely linked to social concerns in traditional communities. "Ecosystem people" value biodiversity as a part of their livelihood, as well as through cultural and religious sentiments. A great variety of crops have been cultivated in traditional agricultural system and this permitted a wide range of produce to be grown and marketed throughout the year and act as an insurance against the failure of one crop (today's monoculture). In recent years, farmers have begun to receive economic incentives to grow cash crops for national or international markets, rather than to supply local needs. This has resulted in local food shortages, unemployment (cash crops are usually mechanized), landlessness, growing of slums in the cities, and increased vulnerability to drought, floods and famine.

Ethical and Moral Values

Ethical values related to biodiversity conservation are based on the importance of protecting all forms of life. Most religious and secular creeds believe that all forms of life have the right to exist on Earth. Man is only a small part of the Earth's great family of species. Plants and animals have equal right to live. We do not know if life as we know it exists anywhere else in the universe. Apart from the economic importance of conserving biodiversity, there are several cultural, moral and ethical values, which are associated with the sanctity of all forms of life. Indian civilization has, over several generations, preserved nature through local traditions. This has been an important part of the ancient philosophy of many of our cultures. We have already discussed about it. In our country a large number of sacred groves exist which are preserved by people. and these around ancient sacred sites and temples act as gene banks of life forms.

Aesthetic Value

The appreciation of the presence of biodiversity for its inherent value and beauty, as well as for the contribution it makes to our knowledge—our aesthetics, imagination and creativity—are other reasons to preserve it. Quite apart from killing wildlife for food, it is important as a tourist attraction. Biodiversity is a beautiful and wonderful aspect of nature. It gives a great joy to quietly sit in a forest and listen to the chirping of birds or to watch a spider weave its complex web or to observe a fish feeding. It is magnificent and fascinating apart from the fact that it enriches our knowledge of the intricacies of the nature. Our history and culture is replete with plant and animal imagery. The sage Valmiki begins his epic story with a couplet on the unfortunate killing of a crane by a hunter. The sacred Basil or *"Tulsi"* which is being grown in the courtyards of each household of our country for centuries only points to the awareness of our ancient people towards this aspect of the nature.

Option Value

Keeping future possibilities open for their use is called the option value. It is impossible to predict which of our species or traditional varieties of crops and domestic animals will be of greatest use in the future. To continue to improve cultivars and domestic livestock, we need to return to wild relatives of crops, plants and animals. Thus, the preservation of biodiversity must also include traditionally-used strains already in existence in crops, domestic animals and in our aquatic life forms.

Finally, my submission is that the biological diversity resources are our strength and it has to be conserved and used rationally so that there is no more depletion.

The Threats

The threats that we encounter in conservation and development of the biological diversity resources of the country are because of the following :

1. Shifting cultivation (*Jhum/Podu*).
2. Propagation of monoculture species in large areas.
3. Encroachment into the forest land leading to decimation and degradation.
4. Incendiary fire.
5. Unsustainable/destructive extraction.
6. Poaching of the wildlife leading to imbalance in the nature.
7. Invasion of aliens/exotics.
8. Weeds.
9. Unplanned expansion/urbanization.
10. Proliferation of the illegal trade of wildlife and wildlife trophies.

The list is only indicative but not exhaustive and there could be many more reasons why we are facing threats on this count. The shifting cultivation and associated fire is one of the prime causes of the destruction of the biodiversity resources of our country. It not only kills all the life forms in the forest floor and higher canopies but pulverizes and chars the viable rootstock of the entire micro flora and fauna present in the environment. Quite frequently the shifting cultivation fire engulfs the nearby areas and in the process a vast area gets devastated. The loss is thus enormous. The people are yet to realize impact of devastation and so NE part of the country despite being the most important component of the Mega biodiversity zone reels under the continuous threat. Monoculture of a species over a large area poses yet another threat which does not need further elaboration. The damage due to large scale creation of Eucalyptus tereticornis, Tectona grandis, Poplar deltoides and their resultant effects, controversies are known to each one of us. Incendiary fire constitutes another threat which is different from the shifting cultivation fire but its effect is same. We have experienced the ill effects of the unsustainable and destructive extraction of the resources and it is a major threat in the conservation efforts of the medicinal plants and wildlife because such trade can be carried out clandestinely without being detected because of ignorance, laxity in enforcement mechanism, wrong notions amongst the people on usage of wildlife products. Poaching for the body parts of the animals is another serious threat to the biodiversity resources and its magnitude is so much so that many species have dwindled or are totally wiped out from the nature.

We have introduced many alien species in our country without assessing the havoc they could play towards our environment and to biodiversity. We are quite aware of the menace of the *Parthenium* spp. especially in the southern States and how have they invaded the farm lands. There is a school of thought that it reached India in the sixties with the sack full of wheat sent under the PL 480 programme. All attempts to wipe out the weed resulted into failure. Urban agglomeration is another serious threat not only to the biodiversity as such but it has tended to change the lifestyle of our people in very large number posing a health hazard and ultimate blow to the biodiversity. It is because of our consumerist attitude and greed that made us rob the wildlife resources from its natural habitat and is a reason why the biodiversity is facing a challenge. Our development needs without sacrificing the values of biodiversity which is the life insurance of life itself.

27
Organisations and Environment

Bijit Debbarma

The dictionary meaning of environment is "the surrounding or conditions in which a person, animal or plant lives or operates". Meaning of organization is a group of people working together towards attaining a common goal. Organizations can be divided into business, government and non-profit, etc. Organizations operate in the environment and obtain resources from the environment; hence, it is the responsibility of the organizations to protect the environment or the nature.

The chapter discusses about the role different organizations play in protecting and their efforts in restoring the nature. Numerous reports informs about the destructions this world is facing and the active role played by different organizations.

Earlier different organizations have been accused of polluting environment, cutting down trees, spilling oil and dumping waste to river and sea (bringing harm to aqua-marine life), etc. But thanks to the growing concern of different activists and government initiatives which leads to imposition of strict regulations and then some business organizations role, which has created a strong mindset of being responsible to environment in a positive manner.

Another serious issue that this world currently is facing is from a serious problem: Global warming. And some of the important reasons, which contributes, to this is cutting down trees mercilessly, increase in carbon emission by factories and different modes of transportation, usage of modern gadgets like air coolers, etc. Though government has come up with strict norms to cut carbon emission and reduce pollution and introduction of different concepts about planting trees, more awareness is required from individual level too.

The focus of this chapter is to find out the activities of different organizations-business, government and non-government, by taking different initiatives through research and development, through efficient waste management, through involvement in different projects meant to protect the nature and promoting non-destruction.

A brief detail of some responsible organizations-government and businesses that are in the process of making this world beautiful place to live in are mentioned below:

AFORESTATION

Government Initiatives

Concept of Vanomahotsava

Vanamahotsava Day (week) is celebrated some time in the month of July when new saplings are planted. This is a reminder of the *Chipco movement* to spare the trees.

The concept Vanomahotsava (meaning of *Van* is Forest and *Maho Utsav* is festival) was first initiated by (Late) K.M. Munshi, the then Union Minister for Food & Agriculture in the year 1950, a great festival for the nature lovers. However, it was only in the 1970s that greater impetus was given to the conservation of India's forests and wildlife. It was the vision and wisdom of the great leader (Late) K.M. Munshi, that the issue of environmental degradation, unless timely action is taken to prevent and restore, it may go beyond human control and threaten the survival of any living organisms on this earth planet. While survival and development of human being is important, it is also equally important to preserve the nature which is the only source of oxygen and other essentials required for our living.

People celebrate Vanamahotsava by planting trees in schools, offices, colleges, homes, etc. Awareness programmes are also held at different levels. And novel programmes like free distribution of trees are also taken up. This is a part of Government of India "Go Green" initiative.

THE MINISTRY OF ENVIRONMENT AND FORESTS, GOVERNMENT OF INDIA

The Ministry of Environment and Forests (MoEF) is the nodal agency in the administrative structure of the Central Government for the planning, promotion, co-ordination and overseeing the implementation of India's environmental and forestry policies and programmes.

The primary concerns of the Ministry are implementation of policies and programmes relating to conservation of the country's natural resources including its lakes and rivers, its biodiversity, forests and wildlife, ensuring the welfare of animals, and the prevention and abatement of pollution. While implementing these policies and programmes, the Ministry is guided by the principle of sustainable development and enhancement of human well-being.

The Ministry also serves as the nodal agency in the country for the United Nations Environment Programme (UNEP), South Asia Co-operative Environment Programme (SACEP), International Centre for Integrated Mountain Development (ICIMOD) and for the follow-up of the United Nations Conference on Environment and Development (UNCED). The Ministry is also entrusted with issues relating to multilateral bodies such as the Commission on Sustainable Development (CSD), Global Environment Facility (GEF) and of regional bodies like Economic and Social Council for Asia and Pacific (ESCAP) and South Asian Association for Regional Co-operation (SAARC) on matters pertaining to the environment.

The broad objectives of the Ministry are:

- Conservation and survey of flora, fauna, forests and wildlife;
- Prevention and control of pollution;
- Afforestation and regeneration of degraded areas;
- Protection of the environment; and
- Ensuring the welfare of animals.

These objectives are well supported by a set of legislative and regulatory measures, aimed at the preservation, conservation and protection of the environment. Besides the legislative measures, the National Conservation Strategy and Policy Statement on Environment and Development 1992; National Forest Policy 1988; Policy Statement on Abatement of Pollution 1992; and the National Environment Policy 2006 also guide the Ministry's work.

INITIATIVES OF BUSINESS ORGANISATIONS

Indian Oil Corporation

Indian Oil Corporation a Navratna and Fortune 500 listed company in its effort towards environmental protection has taken the following steps :

- Extensive tree plantation has been undertaken in different refineries and townships to develop green cover.
- Mathura Refinery has planted about 115,000 trees in the Taj Reserve Forest near Taj Mahal under the 10-Point Initiative of the Ministry of Petroleum & Natural Gas for improvement of environment in the Taj Trapezium.
- Mathura Refinery has developed a sprawling area of 18,000 sq.m around its polishing ponds into an ecological park. A large number of migratory birds have made the ecological park as their habitat. Similar parks have also been developed at Barauni and Gujarat refineries.
- The existence of rich flora and fauna in these parks is a clear testimony of the clean and eco-friendly environment in and around the refineries. The other refineries are in the process of developing such ecological parks.

ITC Ltd.

Indian Tobacco Company one of India's foremost private sector companies with turnover of over US $ 5 billion with varied business interest has contributed immensely towards environmental causes. Some of their activities are:

Afforestation : The social and farm forestry programme started in 1998 has been taken up in 65,000 hectares. This has helped to sequester over 2,000 kilo tonnes of carbon dioxide, as a firm commitment to combating climate change. It has planned to develop 100,000 hectares with planting of 600 million saplings.

Rashtriya Ispat Nigam Ltd. (RINL)

Rashtriya Ispat Nigam Limited, Visakhapatnam Steel Plant is planting saplings for environmental conservation. Also supported awareness about water conservation and adoption of technology for recycling and eliminating wastage.

SAIL

Steel Authority of India Limited another Navratna company has taken up conservation of water to drought prone districts in Madhya Pradesh. SAIL has a policy to create positive impact on the environment and promote good environmental practices.

NALCO

National Aluminum Company Limited has contributed towards environmental care and plantation. NALCO has taken adequate steps for pollution control and effective environment management.

AIRCEL "SAVE OUR TIGER INITIATIVE"

One of India's mobile service providers Aircel has involved into India's Royal Bengal tiger population from extinction. Aircel has initiated a "Save Our Tigers" project in partnership with Dentsu Communications (an advertising firm) and WWF India to create an awareness among public about the protection of the country's national animal. As per the current Figures the tiger population has dropped to a current total of 1,411 in comparison to 40,000 tigers a hundred years ago. The campaign calls for immediate action as the specie pushes nearer to extinction.

Aircel in its initiative is encouraging people to not only make donations but join the movement and spread the information about saving tigers. A television campaign has been created which portrays the world as its seen through the eyes of a six-months old tiger cub named *Stripey* by Dentsu Communications. The cub is shown waiting for his mother that will never return. In reality tigers are more vulnerable and confused than their portrayal as majestic and dangerous animals seen on most documentaries.

The campaign has called on the support of prominent Indian

athletes Mahendra Singh Dhoni and Baichung Bhutia and actors Suriya, Kabir Bedi and Shernaz Patel. All efforts are supported through the website www.saveourtigers.com as well as executions on popular networking websites like Facebook, Twitter and YouTube.

Turtle Limited

Turtle Limited is an internationally well-known Indian company operating as a Manufacturer, Supplier and Exporter of all types of Men's Wear and Accessories is committed to the protection of Olive Ridley Turtles. Turtle Limited take keen initiative to protect Olive Ridley, the green, the fresh water and the leather back turtles in Orissa and Gujarat. Presently, the company work in collaboration with WWF and Local NGO's to save the species from extinction. Fvery time a Turtle product purchased, Turtle limited contribute to WWF and Wildlife Society of Orissa.

CONSERVATION OF ENERGY

IGATE Corporation

IGATE Corporate an Indian IT firm, under the leadership of its CEO, Phaneesh Murthy, has used light emitting diodes (LED) to light the office space thus conserving energy. Murthy took the novel decision and invested Rs. 37 lakh to light 57,000 sq. ft. of office space at IGATE's new development centre inside the DLF SEZ at Manapakkam, Chennai. The benefit: reduction in carbon emission by 78 tonnes annually !

Though LED has been used to backlight flat televisions, digital advertising hoardings, street/passage lightings and in basement car parks, but before IGATE no one else has considered for office lighting on such a large scale. Says Murthy. "After all, we complain so much about lack of power, but we lack the determination to do our bit to bring down power consumption".

Apart from the lighting project other projects which IGATE has implemented is connecting air-conditioners with employees' entry cards. The cards activate the air-conditioners only in the sector they work and only after they walk in. LED usage will help optimize this as the light is "cool" and dissipates lesser heat. These efforts have made the AC requirements down by 11 to 12 per cent and the load will come down further because of LED by 4-5 per cent.

Mahindra and Mahindra Ltd.

Indian automobile major Mahindra & Mahindra Ltd., in its response to the environmental issue, has taken several measures. In their manufacturing plant in Chakan, Maharashtra Mahindra & Mahindra has taken several like eco friendly initiatives environment which not only mitigate environmental degradation but also reduce waste. **Solar energy** and waste heat from the oven exhaust are used to reduce the consumption of LPG and electricity in the paint shop, leading to reduction of 3,500 tonnes of Carbon Dioxide/annum at full volume. A cluster of 70 solar dishes heat water which is used to cool the paint used for ED on the vehicle bodies, *via* a vapour absorption machine.

Apart from this, recycling of waste water through reverse osmosis and multiple effect evaporation ensures that the plant is a zero discharge plant. Reverse Osmosis rejects the dissolved salts in the water and the residual water is equivalent to the raw water supplied by the MIDC to the Plant. Other conscious efforts by the plant management were to increase the green cover in the vicinity by aiming to plant approximately 7,000 trees across the entire plant area.

RECYCLING

Reliance Industries Limited

Reliance Industries Limited in its support towards environment has taken several measures. In the Financial Year 2008-09, RIL undertook an exercise to establish world class corporate environmental standards like discharge of gases to atmosphere, emissions from stationary sources, waste management, ground water protection, environment performance evaluation and reporting, covering all major environmental aspects, etc. To ensure effective implementation of the environment standards, an exercise to make independent audit protocol and site-related standard operating procedures was initiated.

Installation of a state-of-the-art water treatment plant of 18,000 m^3/day capacity for the domestic water supply to township and refinery at Jamnagar has been seen. A trial for the re-utilisation of Polyethylene Terephthalate (PET) waste into Polyester Fibre Fill (PFF) recycling plant was successfully carried out at Hoshiarpur Manufacturing Division. Vermi-compost of waste is being carried out at manufacturing divisions located at Vadodara, Hazira and Naroda. A significant improvement in re-use of energy content of waste by eco-friendly fuel briquette and biogas resulted in about 19.18 per cent increase in direct renewable energy generation compared to previous year. To reduce water dependence from natural sources, rainwater harvesting is being practiced at most manufacturing divisions.

Infosys

Infosys, one of the best Information Technology firm of India has acted towards development against the deterioration of the environment. Infosys believes in reducing carbon footprint even as they expand their global presence.

Infosys looks into matters like:

- Conservation of resources; and
- Prevention of pollution.

The Health, Safety and Environmental Management System (HSEMS) at Infosys is called the "Ozone Initiative". Infosys's "Project Ozone" campaign spreads environmental awareness and implements eco-friendly practices across development centres worldwide. Further, this vision is supported by voluntary groups of employees organized into eco-clubs.

Infosys' vision is to become "carbon and water neutral". Other initiatives to neutralize environmental impact as :

- *Water Management*

Harvesting rainwater and consistently reduce the use of fresh water. In addition, recycling of waste water to be reused for primary and secondary purposes.

- ***Energy Conservation***

Infosys uses energy responsibly by measuring utilization of energy through energy audits. The data collected is used to achieve increasing levels of energy conservation.

- ***Waste Management***

Waste is recycled scientifically.

ITC Ltd.

Indian Tobacco Company one of India's foremost private sector companies with turnover of over US $ 5 billion with varied business interest has contributed immensely towards environmental causes. Some of their activities are:

Environmental Conservation: The company is striving to achieve a "zero solid waste" discharge status; have recycled over 90 per cent of solid waste produced.

Organizations Tripura : Their Contributions

ONGC

ONGC as a part of its main exploration and exploitation of hydrocarbon activity, care for the environment. ONGC is engaged into plantation of around 300 plants every year on World Environment Day. While ONGC are in drilling wells, they are in protecting the soil from pollution by keeping impervious sheets in the mud pits. ONGC are certified under OSHAS 18001. ONGC are also doing ground water recharging through abandoned water wells. ONGC also restores the drill sites after completion of our drilling operations.

NEEPCO

NEEPCO Tripura unit has planted around 30,000 saplings in its premises and is in the process of planting more. It is concerned about environment and responds accordingly.

National Social Service

NSS has 258 units across the State of Tripura in different schools and colleges and every year every unit plants 15 saplings. Apart from this different NSS units participate in rally and conducts seminar and cultural programmes related to environment awareness campaign.

BSNL

BSNL is concerned about the environment and has responded by creating green islands in the city area, i.e., doing beautification in different areas of the city by creating islands. Apart from it BSNL has started pilot project on solar energy, where 115 sites in remote areas has been identified and will be supported by solar power.

Conclusion

This is heartening that people now are coming forward and doing their part to perform their responsibility towards the environment. As it is time to realize that we cannot Fight against nature, as if we want to destroy the wealth of nature, nature has its own way of punishing us. And it is already felt and realized by people across different countries what havoc nature could play. Hence, we should become responsible by becoming more serious and involving ourselves into different activities which would support the environmental causes. Business organizations on their part will act accordingly either through development of new technology through investment into R&D which will help in developing machines consuming fewer fuels or using alternative fuels and pollute less. Planting trees and recycling of water and wastes are other measures that could be taken. Government and its organizations too on their part are doing every bit to respond to the environment causes. We also as a responsible citizen support the different causes. As per information from different thinkers and activists, planting good number of trees every year and keeping our surrounding clean would make the world a better place to leave in.

REFERENCES

Business Today October 18, 2009 (Led'ing the Way; Igate has shown the World That LED Lighting Can Be Used to Illuminate Office Space. Others Are Beginning to Follow Suit.

Interaction with company and government officials.

Websites of Different Companies.

Index